Teach Me Dreams

FIGURE 1. Mandala of "The Self" by A. B. in *The Columbian Magazine*, February 1789.

Teach Me Dreams

The Search for Self in the Revolutionary Era

MECHAL SOBEL

Princeton University Press

Princeton and Oxford

Library of Congress Cataloging-in-Publication Data
Sobel, Mechal.
Teach me dreams : transforming the self in the revolutionary era / Mechal
Sobel.
p. cm.
Includes bibliographical references and index.
ISBN 0-691-04949-1 (alk. paper)
1. United States—History—Revolution, 1775–1783—Social aspects—
Sources. 2. United States—History—Revolution, 1775–1783—Influence—
Sources. 3. United States—Social conditions—To 1865—Sources. 4.
Dreams—Social aspects—United States—History—18th century—Sources.
5. Dreams—Social aspects—United States—History—19th century—
Sources. 6. Emotions—Social aspects—United States—History—Sources. 7.
Self-perception—United States—History—Sources. 8. Social interaction—
United States—History—Sources. 9. American prose literature—1783–
1850—History and criticism. I. Title.
E209 .S68 2000
973—dc21   00–021230

This book has been composed in Trump

Epigraph source: Francis LaFlesche as cited in John Dunn Hunter, *Memoirs
of a Captivity Among the Indians of North America*, edited by Richard Drinnon, New York, [1824] 1973, ix.

For Zvi
with love

And in memory of

Bernard Steinberg and Brian Stonehill

for their dreams and for their lives,
which ended too soon

Stand Asleep or Vigil Song

I make myself sleep. I make myself sleep.
I bring myself to dream. I bring myself to dream.
Come here dreams. Come here dreams.
Teach me dreams. Teach me dreams.

Osage Tribe, "The Rite of Vigil"

Contents

Illustrations

Acknowledgments

I HAVE BEEN working for over a decade on this project; during that time I found that it took hard (figurative) bangs on the head to get me to see what was in my hands in a new way. Much like the people I was writing about, I, too, could not move out of a fixed view without a powerful emotional experience and a new commitment. The critiques of Betty Adelson, Greg Dening, Michael Fellman, Bill Freedman, Lorry Greenburg, Grey Gundaker, Linda Kerber, Kenneth Lockridge, Donna Merwick, Fredrika Teute, Al Young, and David Waldstreicher played important roles for me in this process. I found many of their comments crucial as I rethought the issues involved. Nevertheless, some of the important questions they raised remain unanswered. For example, Betty Adelson asked, and I have not fully answered, "Where are the mothers?" So little was said of them in life narratives.

I also want to thank those who shared dream reports they found while doing their own research: Maya Talmon Chveiser, Elaine Crane, Douglas Deal, Haggai Doron, Robert Gross, Sharon Halevi, Graham Hodges, Dick Newman, Anthony Shafton, Manfred Wasserman, and most especially Jon Butler, who sent me a number of dreams he had assembled in the course of his work on Colonial New England. Jenna Loosemore and Cathy Grosfils have my special thanks for graciously facilitating the acquisition of a large number of the illustrations.

Many others have given me support, among them Montague Ullman, Ron Hoffman, Loretta Valtz Mannucci, and Mark Mancall, who long ago said "do it," and Brigitta van Rheinberg, who as sponsoring editor at Princeton University Press played an important role. I also want to thank my children, Mindy Ivry, Daniel Sobel, and Noam Sobel, and their families, Adam, Asa, Avigael, Danny, Elya, Era, Hadas, Hillel, Ilanah, Nahum, and Nira, who have given me so much, and most especially my husband, Zvi Sobel, who accepted with grace my spending "endless" days and nights with dreamers long dead.

Teach Me Dreams

Introduction

"In the process of writing or thinking
about yourself, you actually become
someone else."
Paul Auster[1]

ODAY the acceptance of an inner consciousness of self is so
widely taken for granted that it is hard to realize how modern
this development is. At the outset of the eighteenth century
most people seemed to regard themselves as having porous boundaries and as part of a wider or "we-self."[2] It was in the hundred-year
period between 1740 and 1840, the greater Revolutionary period, that
many people in America first came to accept that they had an inner
self that controlled their emotions and actions and to believe that
they themselves might alter this self.[3] In this period, and as part of
this process of change, the churches and then the new state encouraged the written reevaluation of life experiences in journals and in
autobiographies. Writing a self-narrative became virtually a ritual act,
and as a result myriad life narratives were written by "ordinary" people, black and white, male and female. Well diggers, wall plasterers,
mechanics, farmers, robbers, poor rapists and murderers sentenced to
death, cross-dressers, madmen, wanderers, and spiritual seekers
wrote narratives of their lives. A great many of these narratives were
published, often by the writers themselves. By writing themselves on
to the public stage they were making a public claim to newly recognized rights, and leaving evidence of their changing selves.[4]

When the writing of self-narratives became ritualized, it was also,
in part, because transforming images, often first taken note of in visions and dreams, could be preserved in these documents. A very
large number of the autobiographical narratives from the early modern period—over half of the more than two hundred autobiographies
considered for this study—contain such dream and vision reports.
When written, these dramatic envisionings of dreams were much like
plays, which may well have helped the writers see themselves as
actors in a drama.[5] The narratives, the dream reports, and the dream
interpretations by the narrators provide vivid evidence of the change
in self-perception in ideal and functioning selves. They also provide

3

powerful evidence that American culture was a dream-infused culture and that work with dreams provided an important bridge into the modern period, helping people change their self-view and their selves.[6]

Studies of self-fashioning in other places and/or other periods have suggested that such change is brought about by opposition to an enemy other and through commitment to a legitimating authority.[7] These life narratives, although often opaque and difficult for a modern reader, contain evidence that enemy others and outside authorities were also crucial for self-fashioning Americans in the Revolutionary era. All through this hundred-year period new religious groups, focusing on adherents to the old religions as their enemies, were the most important outside authorities for Americans. The Revolution, however, provided a society-wide issue of self-commitment and a focus on enemies for most every person then in the colonies. While it is often recognized that becoming a revolutionary brought about a change in self, evidence in the narratives suggests that many of those who chose to oppose the Revolution also significantly changed their selves in the process.[8]

At the opening of this period, life narratives retold what had happened to a person: Events were recounted by narrators who viewed themselves as observers of happenings and emotions that had taken them over. Over the course of this period, as narrators moved from a sense of a "we-self" to a far more individuated "I," they began to attest to changes they believed they were initiating both in their outer and inner lives, and a radical change began to take place in their narratives. It was as these narrators began to document their acts of commitment to outside authorities and to recognize or create enemy others that they began, as well, to see their lives as patterned dramas in which they had to make fateful choices. Increasingly, individuals began to see themselves as dramatic actors, and some went further and came to see themselves as self-creators.

In creating these new narratives of their lives these individuals found coherence and purpose and gave new structure to the self. The narratives these people wrote not only record these changes occurring in the self; they were also agents of change in and of themselves. In the early modern era writing a life narrative aided in the reframing of the past, expanded the consciousness of self, and prepared the individual (as well as many of those who read the narrative) for a new future.[9]

By the close of this period, the ideal white male was individuated, self-concerned, and determined to succeed in a rapacious market economy. The subtext of this ideal was the expectation that white women and all blacks would remain enmeshed in a communality and serve the needs of increasingly individuated white males. Women, white and black, and black males had to respond to this situation as best they could. Some tried to adopt the same goal of individuation that white males were adopting; others reacted against it and actively sought to strengthen communality; most (including most white males) were limited by both social and economic circumstances to continuing their more communally embedded self-orientation.

Although in Europe class antagonism and class "others" played the central role in the development of individuality during this period, in America, in good part because the Revolutionary elite felt compelled to forge working bonds with the middling and poorer sort, gender and race (often in combination) became the central focuses of alterity and identity.[10] White males increasingly defined themselves as not-black and not-female, while women increasingly recognized the male as the alien other. Blacks recognized whites as their enemy other, although this was in part complicated by an historic African appreciation of the color white seen as betokening purity and good fortune, but more tellingly by African Americans' need to protect themselves from the whites who had virtually unlimited power over them. The open expression of aggression by blacks and women was always dangerous. Most blacks and most women had to deal with their own rage at their alien others at the same time that they had to cope with the increasing otherness projected onto themselves.[11]

Both Africans and Europeans began developing in opposition to each other—those whom they would "not be"—however, this process actually made them dependent on their oppositional others. In addition, insofar as not-me or alien other figures were often projections of rejected aspects of the self, they were potentially reclaimable through a process of introjection whereby hated attributes of the other became cherished attributes of the self. The narratives are rich in evidence of this process of introjection, and it clearly played a significant role in the development of individuality in America. For many whites this development can be seen as a peaceful borrowing from blacks, which sometimes occurred without either party consciously recognizing what was happening. In other cases whites took by force, generally through psychological manipulation, that which had belonged to blacks. Evidence provided by the life narratives suggests that a range of adaptive and extractive processes was underway: that whites indeed often stole mental content and affective processes from blacks and that whites were undergoing change in part as a result of Africans' values and emotions. While whites' borrowings often resulted from their jealousy of what seemed to be blacks' freer libidinal enjoyment, at the same time whites were frightened of "them" and of what might happen to themselves should they be like "them."[12]

Blacks widely hated whites but often needed and/or wanted to share in the dominant culture, which meant that they too were following the other's ways. The fact that they were often also compelled to do so led African Americans to fear the loss of their sense of African selfhood and increased their anger at the white other and their ambivalence about the attraction that the dominant culture held for them.

Native Americans also played a significant role as alien others for whites and blacks as whites and blacks did for native Americans. An early text indicating Indian awareness of this is that of Samson Occum, a Mohegan Christian missionary teacher, who wrote a "Short Narrative" of his life in 1768, perhaps the first recorded Native American autobiography. Occum bitterly lamented his mistreatment at the hands of white people and concluded: ". . . I *Must Say*, 'I believe it is because I am a poor Indian.' I Can't help that God has made me So; I did not make my self so.-" These words suggest that Occum felt being Indian was a cross he had to bear. Occum became a severe critic of white society and turned away from participating in it, although he continued to accept Christianity. Notwithstanding Occum's testimony and other narrative evidence of the white othering of the Indian and the Indian othering of the white, this study focuses on black-white interaction inasmuch as this relationship was *the* defining self-other relationship for most of the narrators in this study and has remained central in American culture since that time.[13]

The changes in commitments and alterity were stimulated by many crucial and interrelated social shifts and economic upheavals: a shift in religious affiliation began with the First Great Awakening of the 1740s and continued in waves of revivals and new church growth that followed during which a great many Americans moved from Congregational and Anglican affiliations to become Baptists and later Methodists.[14] These new churches welcomed individual conversions made in opposition to the family, which was often regarded as the enemy. As a result individual choice and commitment came to play a far more significant role than they had previously.

A shift in racial makeup was brought about by the importation of enslaved Africans who, by the time of the Revolution, came to equal some 20 percent of the total population. Significant areas of the South were over 50 percent African, and overall 42 percent of the southern population was African or African American. As a result of the demographic change and of the shift in population during the vast turmoil of the Revolution, myriad whites and blacks came into daily contact with "alien" others, which led them to alter their selves.[15]

The economy shifted from one based in good part on exchange to widespread market production, which brought in its wake a cyclic pattern of expansions (1750s, 1795–1807, 1827–1837) and downturns, with particularly hard times for most between 1776 and 1790, and with depressions following political or economic crises in 1807, 1819, and 1837. The rapid growth of slavery in the eighteenth century, the addition of the newly freed in the North to the ranks of the free poor during and after the war, and the growing concentration of wealth made for an alteration in the class structure. Nevertheless, many individuals buffeted by the economic "tidal waves" felt personally responsible for their own failures or successes.[16]

These economic changes affected a shift in gender roles as more men began to work outside households while most women remained within them. This shift placed men in a double bind as they increasingly idealized independence in a world where economic dependence was growing; it also led to a new modal view of women (ideally protected in the home from the rapacious market) as more virtuous than men. This seemingly positive change for women was, however, utilized in males' increasing bid for control of women.[17]

The changes in religious affiliation, racial makeup, class structure, gender roles, and the economy were all related to the positing and creation of a kingless democratic society by means of a revolutionary war, which led the elite males to an alliance with and reliance on many of those white males who until that point they had regarded as outcasts, such as Baptists in Virginia, and the lower classes more generally (many of whom served in the Revolutionary army). The same Baptists, as well as Methodists, blacks, the poor, and downtrodden females (overlapping groups) engaged in "fantasies of freedom" as well as acts intended to change both their selves and their social situations; many of them opted for personal wars of independence by opposing the national war of independence.[18] Radical changes in self-perception were thus taking place along with the social, economic, and political changes.

The Revolutionary period was clearly a time of social upheaval and the loosening of many bonds. The enslaved widely took their own freedom, and many in other repressed groups sought to change their lives. When the war was over those in control were determined to reestablish limits on the expression of the formerly repressed desires

7

of the lower sort and the nonconforming. In the nineteenth century the expansion of both slavery and the limitations imposed on African Americans in the areas outside the slave South reestablished and extended the pre-war repression of most African Americans; the economic upheavals of the post-war period and the instabilities of capitalist expansion that culminated in the depressions of 1819 and 1837 led to an increase in the economic oppression of many whites as well. A new, more standardized life course built around the extension of education was fostered in part to control the white population, as were the new "purer" ideals for women, which were limits they were expected to internalize.[19] White females were increasingly expected to be controlled by what was now seen as their superior moral sensitivity, while white males were pressed to share in the Revolutionary ideal of independence at the same time that more white men were becoming part of the dependent working class.

Although at the outset of this hundred-year period people did not generally own their own emotions, over the era emotional awareness grew.[20] Both intentionally and through indirection, the personal narratives reveal the emotional toll that most paid as a result of these economic and social changes: many narrators wrote of their outer "Sufferings" (a term that appears in the title of many of the narratives) while their dream reports reveal painful aspects of their interior lives.

It is well known that American Indians and the whites they adopted into their societies were taught to attend to their dream life and that dream or vision quests were central to Native American spiritual development.[21] One of the earliest recorded Indian dream reports is from the Sauk chief Na-nà-ma-kee, or Thunder. Dating from the early 1600s, it was preserved in the life narrative of his great-grandson, Ma-Ka-Tai-Me-She-Kia-Kiak or Black Hawk (born in 1767), whose father had told him of the dream. When Thunder was a young man he had dreamed that "at the end of four years he should see a *white man*, who would be to him a father." Many subsequent dreams reaffirmed this promise, and Thunder reportedly shared them with his community. At the appointed time Thunder took his two brothers on the journey he had dreamed of and led them to their first meeting with a white man. This white man told them that he too had been directed by his dreams to come to this meeting, and that while the King of France had laughed at this idea he had approved of his journey. The white man chose Thunder over his older brother to serve as the supreme chief who would lead his people into war and presented him with European arms, clothes, and a medal signifying the role he had bestowed upon him. Black Hawk reports that Thunder's father accepted this change as "directed" by the "great Spirit" and handed over his powers to his younger son. This dream report of a search for a "white father" (which may record Samuel De Champlain's arrival in North America in 1603) can be seen to open an Indian narrative of white settlement in North America that places racial interchange, power redistribution, and dreams at its center.[22]

Anthropological studies suggest that many Africans held views of the positive value of dream teachings similar to those of Native Americans.[23] Africans brought these traditions to America, where they flourished. It has not been widely recognized, however, that in this period European Americans also often turned to dreams for wisdom and that a great many came to important new understandings of themselves and/or acted in radically new ways on the basis of their dreams, many influenced by African American approaches.[24] While in all three traditions, the Indian, African and Anglo-American, dreams were widely assumed to foretell a preordained future, many of the dreamers in this study began to regard their dreams as relevant to difficult choices they had to make. Dreams were used to legitimate participation in as well as opposition to the Revolution. Dream interpretations were directly involved in slaveholders' decisions to free their slaves, as well as in the decisions of the enslaved to revolt against enslavement. Dreams widely legitimated changes in behavior by people who were on the margins of society—most women, blacks, and the poor whites—and often helped these people to act in ways that those in power opposed. Deborah Samson dreamed of "girding her loins" before she fought in the Revolution as a man; Nat Turner dreamed of a battle between black and white spirits before he initiated his 1831 rebellion. Interior landscapes and dream actions were often directly connected to social reality and future realization, and particularly to the changing perception of the nature of individuality and self-development.[25]

In the period following the Revolution, as reason was more widely seen as replacing emotion and faith and as those in power sought to limit or control the "fantasies of freedom" of the downtrodden, there was a widespread reversal in the evaluation of dreams from portentous and likely to be God-sent to useless or dangerous—something that only blacks and women relied on.[26] The growing disrepute in which dreams were regarded, as well as the white male rejection of the communally connected or "we-self," which was increasingly seen as feminine, led to a serious loss for both individuals and society and to a dangerous growth in distance from interiorized desires and emotions that played a role in the growth of racial and other violence in the nineteenth century.[27]

The dreams and narratives that were often tools of change can now be used to analyze the nature of the change in self that was undergone, particularly the commitment to an outside authority and the creation of an alien other as well as the process of introjection of values from the alien other. This is a central part of this study, in which I am primarily concerned with the dreamers' own understanding and use of their dreams at the same time as I accept that these dreams also reflect the social changes underway in the society, or, in Montague Ullman's term, a "social unconscious."[28]

I have been deeply impressed by the study of dream reports collected in Nazi Germany between 1933 and 1939 by Charlotte Beradt. In a key passage, Beradt records a dream that a sixty-year-old factory owner, a Social Democrat, who afterward unsuccessfully attempted to conform to Nazi demands, told her he had dreamed three days after Hitler took power:

> Goebbels was visiting my factory. He had all the workers line up in two rows facing each other. I had to stand in the middle and raise my arm in the Nazi salute. It took me half an hour to get my arm up, inch by inch. Goebbels showed neither approval nor disapproval as he watched my struggle, as if it were a play. When I finally managed to get my arm up, he just said five words— "I don't want your salute"—then turned and went to the door. There I stood in my own factory, arm raised, pilloried right in the midst of my own people. I was only able to keep from collapsing by staring at his clubfoot as he limped out. And so I stood until I woke up.

Beradt concludes that this man and most of the dreamers in her cohort had begun to conform to Nazi demands in their dreams long before they did in life, and that those who eventually resisted had resisted in their earlier dreams. Moreover, some of the early dreams envisioned death camps and other horrors that were first imposed years later. Beradt's work demonstrates that dream reports can indicate the internalized impact of social and political life long before the individual is aware of this impact and that dreams can also attest to the preparation of the inner self for later reactions to outward political change.[29]

Heinz Kohut's approach to dreams and the self also grew out of his analysis of dream reports from the Nazi period. Kohut came to see the dream of Franz Jägerstätter, an Austrian peasant, who became a martyr-hero resister to the Nazi regime, "as a triumph of the nuclear self."[30] Jägerstätter, who chose to die rather than serve the Nazi regime in any capacity, tied his decision to the following dream, which he had in the summer of 1938:

> I was shown a beautiful railroad train which circled around a mountain. Not only the grownups but even the children streamed toward this train and it was almost impossible to hold them back. I hate to tell you how very few of the grownups there were who resisted being carried along by this occasion. But then I heard a voice which spoke to me and said: "This train is going to Hell."[31]

This dream moved Jägerstätter deeply and, for the first time led him to acknowledge that he and his friends and neighbors were moving toward a moral disaster. He decided that whatever the cost he would have to stand in opposition to the mass euphoria surrounding him. Although he had not been politically active, he chose to voice his opposition even as he recognized that such an act might (and did) lead to his death. Kohut found this a type-setting example for his important theoretical concept of "self-state dreams"—those in which the manifest dream indicates a meaningful reaction to a real threat to the self.[32]

While Kohut regarded only some dreams as self-state dreams, many of Kohut's followers as well as those in other schools of interpretation now view virtually all "dreaming [as] organized around the development, maintenance, and restoration of the self."[33] In contradistinction to Freud, who was convinced that the manifest dream deceives, these analysts believe that the manifest dream often presents knowledge about the dreamer and the dreamer's existential situation that he or she is not consciously aware of.[34] In this study dreams and narratives are explored in relation to their role in "the development, maintenance and restoration of the self." Both work with dreams and the writing of narratives are regarded, in Michel Foucault's terms, as technologies of the self.[35]

Ernst Lawrence Rossi is among those who hold that every dream can be shown to reflect the status of the dreamers' self-perception. Rossi has developed a scale with which to judge a dreamer's level of self-reflection, the lowest being those dreams in which there are no people, the medium levels those in which the dreamer is present, and the highest those in which there are multiple states of being and multiple levels of awareness which are seen as "characteristic of the process of psychological growth and change." Rossi's scale for evaluating psychological growth through dreams has been applied to key dreams in this study.[36]

These understandings are reinforced by Christopher Bollas's view of dreams as the place for playing with the possibilities of self, other, and reality, and as a crucial part of imagining and making a future.[37] Bollas also pays particular attention to the process termed "extractive introjection," which occurs when in the course of development a person borrows or steals ideas or emotions from another.[38] Taken together these ideas suggest an understanding of an internalized interplay between self and other, both in dreams and in waking life, that involves giving and taking, both by force and through play, a process which is always ultimately serious.

These views have deeply influenced my interpretation of Revolutionary-era dreams, which are seen as indicating that threats to the self were coped with in dreams and then in the narrated lives. Change in the self was often worked out on the dream-screen, and this change was then played out in the narrative report of the waking life. In crucial dreams in the narratives written by people in the eighteenth and early nineteenth centuries, an alien other was targeted and a dream-screen commitment was made. Many people awoke determined to act on this recognition and commitment. As introjection occurred in these dreams as well, dreams both targeted enemy others and helped to bring about a more inclusive reconstruction of the self.

In this study I have taken the narrators at their word: It is their words that are the significant data. These are the views they arrived at, or the views they wanted others to have of their lives. This makes them "true," or the basic data for a study of changing self-perception and self-representation. This is not to deny that narrators knowingly and unknowingly sought to affect their readers' views through omission or commission: John Leland (born in 1754) and William Watters (born in 1751), both leaders in what became an important movement to alter the popular consciousness, barely mention their significant antislavery roles. Eleazer Sherman (born in 1795), a workingman who preached to the poor at new mills and factories, who defended women's right to preach and who sought out contact with Africans, wrote three triumphant autobiographies in which he was proud of these acts and of himself, before he was charged with and convicted of sodomy. He wrote a promised continuation afterward but chose not to note the nature of the charges made against him nor the fact that he had confessed to them: He wrote that he had been vilified, and his every action taken out of context and exposed.[39] Other narrative writers also put an ironic spin on their past, while some no doubt constructed fictive parts or the whole of their narratives, knowingly or unknowingly. Nevertheless, it still holds true that these narratives are the views they wanted us to have of their lives, views that many hoped would have influence.

There is evidence that many of the accounts published between 1740 and 1840 did influence the lives of readers. One way in which an individual prepares for a new role is "through 'anticipatory socialization.'" Traditionally, young people watched others play roles and followed their patterns. But as small community life was changing, and so many people were breaking with family, friends, and mentors, and as more knew how to read, reading began to be a more common source of new knowledge and published life narratives began to play a significant role for identification through imagination.[40] A number of the narrators attest to the power other written narratives had over them. The enslaved African James Albert Ukawsaw Gronniosaw (born about 1714) took the dramatized life of Bunyan (and his dreams) to heart: Bunyan's sins repelled him but the narrative made him much more anxious for conversion. George Peck (born in 1797), who became a preacher, informs us that when he was a boy his family sat together in the evenings and listened to books being read aloud: "What a glorious time we had reading the Life of Benjamin Abbott!" Peck was referring to *The Experience and Gospel Labours of the Rev. Benjamin Abbott* (1805), filled with dreams of hell and heaven, as well as the narrative of Abbott's rebirth and dedicated life. Ebenezer Thomas (born in 1775) records that while Bunyan was most important to him at a young age, by the time he was twenty he set out with "Franklin's life in my pocket" and tried to follow in Franklin's footsteps. Many narrators reported that their conversions were facilitated by conversions they read of, while others emulated key nonreligious activities they had learned of in narratives. This pattern was incorporated into fictional autobiographies of the period: Lucy Brewer, alias Eliza Webb (allegedly born in 1790), "wrote" that she modeled her 1812 break to freedom from a life of prostitution on Deborah Samson's act of taking on the role of a male soldier in the Revolutionary War, as told of in Samson's narrative.[41] Inasmuch as many of these narratives describe the acceptance of a new, more regulated, life, they helped prepare others to do so as well, so that while the books were often freely chosen by readers and came to mark a break with their pasts, they were in fact exerting influence in the direction of conformity to new patterns.

For the writers, presenting oneself for evaluation in a narrative was a form of "public confessional," a new disciplinary form, a new way to reframe the past, and at the same time a way to get income. It was a selling of the self, in both material and psychological terms.[42] Above all, it was a venue for dreaming of and creating a new self.

This book focuses on four elements that were of key significance in the self-fashioning of the greater Revolutionary period (1740–1840). These are:

1. The dream, as an authoritative forum for representing the self; in Foucault's terms, a technology of the self.[43] The dream was both a witness to the self and a catalyst for change in self, in that key commitments were made in dreams and alien others were often targeted for attack there.

2. Alien others, against which the new self differentiated itself. As noted, this study focuses on black-white and female-male interaction. While alien others were oppositional forces that the individual sought to destroy, it is crucial to recognize that narrators often built their sense of self through both externalizing *and introjecting the other.* Blacks and whites and men and women were doing this with and to one another; attacking each other *and* taking crucial parts of themselves from one another.[44]

3. Authorities, who enabled and legitimated the change in self. The need for an authoritarian power outside the self seems antithetical to the goal of a self-fashioning individual, but many theories of change recognize this seemingly contradictory need. These theories maintain that in order to change, an individual must reframe the past. However, a person with a fixed self-view and a fixed worldview is highly unlikely to be able to do this inasmuch as "a rule for the change of . . . rules . . . must be introduced from the outside." Such a new evaluation can come about as a result of a traumatic emotional experience, or through submission to an outside authority.[45] Sects and churches provided the key authorities that individuals submitted to down to the revolutionary period, when the revolutionary movement and then the new state became jealous institutions that played a similar role for many people.[46]

4. Life narratives. The mapping of the new territories that the self was occupying in this period demanded a new cartography: the writing of self-narratives was quickly ritualized into an almost sacred method for this map work.[47] Narratives increasingly reflected the newer view that a life should be seen as a patterned drama rather than as a series of acts. Analysis of these very documents allows us to begin to reimagine the inner lives of these people.

Narratives published in the greater Revolutionary era are the basic primary data for this study, which focuses on the personae that individuals wanted others to perceive. I have read as wide a range of published narratives as I could, both those with and those without dream reports, written by people who came of age between 1740 and 1840 and who lived in America for a significant period of time. I found dream reports in narratives written by Quakers, Baptists, and Methodists, as I expected, but also in those written by Congregationalists, Presbyterians, Lutherans, and unchurched African and European Americans.[48]

While this work is concerned with the period in which many came to believe in a bounded inner self, in the contemporary or postmodern period many of those opposed to white male domination are embracing the richness of possibilities in "fluid, multiple subjectivities."[49] Both the variety of selves in different cultures and the radical changes in self-perception that can occur over time in any one culture (as they have in the West) clearly indicate that there is no one natural or proper sense of self and that the sense of self is deeply influenced by society.[50] The evidence of the malleability of the self does not, however, support the conclusion that the lack of a sense of a unified self is socially viable or desirable. On the contrary, a sense of the self as unified seems to be a crucial component of "ontological security." If the self as a unified entity is an illusion (as many postmodernists suggest), I believe it is, as Christopher Bollas holds, "an illusion essential to our way of life."[51]

Inasmuch as we are faced with a serious division over the direction self-fashioning should take, an analysis of early modern self-fashioning may help clarify some possibilities and dangers. Moreover, in and of itself I have found it fascinating to observe this self change, which is documented both in these narratives and in the dream reports they contain, and which I believe should be taken into account as a causal factor in the history of this period.

This book opens with a consideration of the interrelationship of self-fashioning, dream interpretation, and life narratives in the greater Revolutionary period. In the chapters that follow narrators are considered in (overlapping) categories, and each group of narrators is analyzed when focusing on a key enemy other. Whites focusing on blacks as their alien other are the subject of chapter 2, while blacks focusing on whites as their enemy is the concern in chapter 3. Men attacking women are considered in chapter 4, and women opposing men in chapter 5. Most of these narrators both hated and loved, attacked and "borrowed" from their enemy others. While relationships to the other were thus highly ambivalent, commitment to an authority facilitated behavior that was generally predicated only on the negative response to the other. As a result, all these individuals, and society as a whole, suffered. The concluding chapter considers some of the implications of this ironic process, in which as a result of the growing need to develop an individuated self, irrational hatreds came to further dominate our lives.

The Jewish liturgy for the New Year includes an ancient prayer for the "repair" of dreams, asking God to strengthen those dreams that are "for good" and "cure" or "heal" those that are not. By the post-biblical period, Jewish commentators seemed to emphasize the efficacy of human action, suggesting that alternative dream interpretations can alter reality.[52] While the primary intention in this study is to assess the extent to which there was a significant change in self-perception and self-presentation over the greater Revolutionary period and to consider the dynamics and effects of this change, I also hope that these dreams and narratives can be reinterpreted or "repaired" so as "to give dignity to the commonplace, to let sad and frightened voices speak, to sing 'close to the magic of what happens,' to set free."[53]

Chapter One

"Teach Me Dreams": Learning to Use Dreams to Refashion the Self

I was forced to consult Mr Locke over
and over, to see wherein personal Identity
consisted, and if I was the very same Selfe.
Eliza Lucas [Pinckney], 1741

W ITH THIS half-joking comment, Eliza Lucas [Pinckney] provides important evidence of what was a new and spreading
concern with the self.[1] What gave rise to her comment was
the fact that when she returned from an entertaining visit to the city
of Charleston she found that her previous pleasure in her Carolina
plantation home had changed to gloom. Her own emotional volatil-
ity gave her cause to worry jokingly, but worry nevertheless, that her
self was not a "true self"—a stable self that would (or should) remain
fixed or constant through life. To have such a true self was a new
and important Western ideal, held by a small but growing group in
the American colonies in the 1740s.[2]

In her statement, Eliza Lucas [Pinckney] was probably referring to
John Locke's "An Essay Concerning Human Understanding" (1694),
in which he equated self with consciousness and memory, an idea
that actually came to undermine the belief in a true self.[3] Eliza Lucas
[Pinckney], who read very widely, was no doubt influenced by ideas
of the true self found in far more popular literature, such as Daniel
Defoe's *Robinson Crusoe* and Samuel Richardson's *Pamela*. She criticized *Pamela* for taking "that disgusting liberty of praising herself"
but not for maneuvering to get her rapacious (but wealthy) pursuer
to propose marriage.[4] It is not unrelated that Eliza Lucas soon after
married a wealthy man of her own choosing.[5] Pinckney had come to
believe that she had to consciously decide to act, that her acts could
affect change in her life, and that her life should have pattern and
shape. In her personal resolves of 1745 she "resolved to believe in
God" (suggesting she had doubts but would no longer tolerate them),
and she "resolved" to control all her actions as well as her beliefs. In
effect, she resolved to become perfect:

I am resolved . . . to govern my passions, to endeavor constantly to
subdue every vice and improve in every virtue, and in order to this
I will not give way to any the least notions of pride, haughtiness,

ambition, ostentation, or contempt of others. I will not give way to Envy, Ill will, Evil speaking, ingratitude, or uncharitableness in word, in thought, or in deed, or to passion or peavishness, nor to Sloath or Idleness, but to endeavour after all the contrary Virtues, humility, charity, etc, etc, and to be always usefully or innocently imploy'd.[6]

Few others set themselves such totally encompassing goals or accomplished as much as Eliza Lucas Pinckney did. Pinckney successfully managed four plantations; introduced indigo production into the Carolinas; taught basic reading skills to her siblings and to black children; and educated her own children according to Locke's and Revolutionary ideals. Many others, however, did come to share her determination to change their selves.

This chapter analyzes the change from a permeable or collective sense of self to a far more individual and interior one, a change that was accompanied by the revision of the understanding of life from a random string of events to a dramatic pattern. The extraordinary boom in the writing of life narratives in the eighteenth and early nineteenth centuries was both a result and a sign of the new concerns with self and a most important means for myriad people to reframe their pasts and envision new futures. In this process they re-created their selves. This chapter assesses the means used to bring about these changes, particularly the commitment to authority and the creation of enemy others, both in dreams and in life narratives. Dreams are evaluated as cultural productions in which the popular images and values of the societies of origin (African as well as European) were put to use in the colonies. Several cases are presented and analyzed in which, in order to change the self, significant use was made of a number of dreams over a long period of time. To close the chapter, evidence is presented that in the Revolutionary era dreams also served a very important role in bringing collective wishes to consciousness. This personal and communal evidence indicates that both individuals and society as a whole made creative use of dreams, visions, enemy others, and commitment to bring about change.

Porous Observers

Most eighteenth-century Americans, both men and women, black and white, apparently perceived themselves as having porous boundaries open to outside influence, making for what might be termed a

18

type of communal or "we-self." In diaries people sometimes used the plural pronoun "we" in place of "I," as in: "We are cleaning the house," or "Wee are much hurred drying apples."[7] While they acted as part of a communal "we" most "expected God to tell them everything they ought to do," as Methodist minister Jacob Young noted uncritically about the people in his church in 1803.[8] They did not own their emotions but felt attacked by them, and they saw life as a series of unconnected events over which they had little control. When they wrote of their lives, they enumerated the events that had "happened" to them.[9]

Although it is generally assumed that before the modern era Western men were somewhat more individuated than were Western women, apparently both shared this communal sense of self. In a careful study of developments in England, John R. Gillis concludes that "throughout the seventeenth and eighteenth centuries, men experienced a sense of connectedness very similar to that of women. Their sense of self was no less porous; and they thought of themselves not as autonomous individuals but as part of an interdependent whole."[10] David Warren Sabean finds that much the same was true in Germany. It seems likely that until the mid-eighteenth century, as suggested, most Western men and women had "as yet no notion of the person as a single, integrated center of awareness."[11]

The narratives written by people who had a porous sense of self were generally repetitive tales of events the narrators passively endured. They did not see themselves as having fashioned their lives or as being responsible for their selves. This view of life as a series of events that happened to the narrator was an ancient one.[12] The narratives of these early Americans are apparently much like those Georg Misch found in classic Egyptian, Greek, and Roman sources or those H. David Brumble believes were characteristic of the oral narratives of Native Americans before Western contact.[13] These were lives seen as the sum total "of deeds done, of hardships endured, of marvels witnessed, of crops harvested, of . . . [animals] killed, of ceremonies accomplished."[14]

In 1760, African American Britton Hammon wrote a litany of the "hardships" he had "endured," while on a thirteen-year journey (1747–1760) during which he was in several shipwrecks, taken by cannibals, and jailed for over four years. Clearly, he had negotiated his way through these extraordinary trials, but he described himself as having endured "uncommon sufferings" at the end of which he underwent a "surprising deliverance."[15] In her life narrative, Olive Cleaveland Clarke (born in 1785) emphasized "marvels witnessed": the endless pealing of bells at the death of Washington, the

FIGURE 2. A marvel witnessed. From the broadside "Canada Subjected." Boston, 1755.

extraordinarily deep snowstorms of 1802 and 1806, and the total eclipse of the sun at eleven o'clock on a June day in 1806, when "stars were to be seen."[16] Although she noted that she had been a schoolteacher and had met the man she later chose for her husband while mountain climbing, nevertheless she seemed to see her life controlled from without.

This view of life as a series of events that happened to the self dominated the early narratives and continued to be held by many throughout the greater Revolutionary period. The narrative of John Robert Shaw, born in England in 1761, can be seen as emblematic of this normative reading of the communal self and the endured life. In the account of his life that he published in 1807, he recorded that he ran away from home at age sixteen and soon after enlisted in the British army. Shaw witnessed and perhaps participated in "carnage" during the Revolutionary War, and he changed sides, serving with the American army after he decided to stay in America. After the war he became a fortune-teller, a well digger, and an alcoholic. As he reviewed the "incidents, vicissitudes and errors of my life," Shaw recalled a series of repetitive dreams from the spring of 1793, when he was earning money as a well digger, spending all he earned on drink and often injuring himself with the explosives he used for digging:

> It was about this time that I dreamed a singular dream, which was that I heard a voice calling to me saying: "Shaw! Shaw! repent or you will be damned. . . ."

FIGURE 3. "'The deplorable situation of JOHN R. SHAW. . .surrounded by his Friends and distressed Family--23d August, 1806."

A few weeks later he had another dream, in which he heard the same voice say:

"Shaw! Shaw! repent and you shall be saved."

Shaw reported that he was very upset and discussed these dreams with friends, who indeed advised him to alter his behavior radically, but that he continued on what he termed "my mad career." He recorded that soon after, when very drunk, he fell asleep in the woods, and that at

> midnight, when being awoke by a noise which I could not account for, I jumped up rather amazed, and within nine or ten feet of me saw a ball of fire, apparently as large as a bushel, and at the same time heard a voice over my head, crying "Shaw! Shaw! will not you speak to me?"

Shaw resolved to become "a better man." A few nights later he again had this vision, seeing the ball of fire and hearing the voice, but this time he also saw the figure of a "venerable old man" who may well have symbolized a savior. Shaw, however, continued drinking, and in a succeeding vision he saw the ball of fire accompanied by the devil. He now felt himself lost.[17]

Shaw did not envision himself in his own dreams, a condition that the analyst Ernst Lawrence Rossi suggests indicates a very low level of self-individuation. Rossi's scale to categorize and judge this process in dreams begins at minimal individuation when:

    1. No people or personal associations [are] in the dream.

He maintains that if individuation develops, dreams change and move through the following stages:

    2. People and personal associations are present in the dream but the dreamer is not.
    3. The dreamer is completely caught up in the drama of the dream.
    4. The dreamer is present as an observer in the dream, but takes no active part in its drama.
    5. Soliloquy and dialogue [are] in the dream. [The dreamer thinks over an idea or has definite communication with someone.]
    6. Multiples states of being [are] in the dream. [Transformations of body, role, emotion, age, ...]
    7. Multiple levels of awareness [are] in the dream. [The dreamer (experiences) . . . simultaneous participating and observing; a dream within a dream; noticing oddities while dreaming.][18]

Rossi holds that if there is change from one level to another within a single dream, this signals that self fashioning is underway, and if there is progression along this scale in a series of dreams this indicates that a more individuated self has developed.

All of Shaw's dreams can be categorized as being at level two: Shaw was not an actor in his dreams, nor, ostensibly, in his life, and this did not change over time. He was called by name, but he did not appear. A ball of fire did, however, much like the explosions that actually took off part of his leg and several fingers. When both "a venerable old man" and the devil appeared, Shaw, not being "there," could not engage them in any way.

There had been no venerable old men in Shaw's life. In fact, he indicates that he venerated no one. He left his home after his father beat him, and he refused to be redeemed from the army when his father found him and sought to get him to return. He felt betrayed by the British army officers who tricked him onto the boat to America and forced him to witness and perhaps participate in atrocities. He was left with memories of "the shrieks and screams of the hapless victims." Captured by the Americans, he remembered being dreadfully ill treated and physically abused. Nevertheless, when he ran away, he joined the Revolutionary army, where he was tricked out of pay; when he did get money, he drank it up. Although he married twice, he seems to have regarded women as objects to be used. At the end of the war he abandoned a woman, commenting, "I left my bed-fellow at home, hoping that she would not suffer, as one soldier is always ready to help another in time of need."[19]

The devil was a far more constant companion. Shaw reported that as a youth he was drawn "into vicious company" and started his life pattern of drinking to excess; that he was "rolled by doxies" and was often vermin-ridden and homeless. In his own dreams he could not envision himself, nor could he envision any change for the good. The venerable old man was replaced by the devil, and the ball of fire drew closer to him.[20]

Shaw never seemed to believe that he faced choices. As a young man, leaving home, he went to a magician to find out what his fate was, and later in life he himself became a fortune-teller and then a "water-witch," using a magical forked rod to find the place to dig. He claimed that while others believed in his magic, he did not. He saw his life as a series of unrelated, unpatterned, and mostly dreadful incidents, and he believed that all his acts were determined from outside his self by others and by fate. In fact, it is unlikely that he thought of himself as having an inner self. He summarized his accomplishments in his narrative by totaling up the feet he had dug in all his wells: "The whole amounting to 177 wells, and 2,608 feet."[21]

Many of the narrators who presented their lives as scenes they had passed through added up their deeds. William Lee was an Englishman who saw himself as having suffered for what "others" had done to the Indians, and who also blamed others for the fact that he had abandoned his wife and newborn child near Savannah, Georgia, on August 7, 1781, "for there was no safety in the country, as both loyalists and rebels went about plundering and killing all who joined the opposite parties." He indicated no remorse for this action, and seemed proud of the thirty-five hundred miles he calculated he had traveled in thirteen years. Levi Redfield (born 1745), whose narrative was an "account of some memorable events and occurrences" he had witnessed when he was a soldier in both the Seven Years War and the Revolution, and of his peacetime activity as a music teacher, enumerated the battles he had participated in and also advertised the fact that he had taught 3,785 students to sing. Preachers totaled their meetings: Joseph Thomas, born in 1791, counted up the three hundred meetings he had preached at and noted that in 1809, during his first year's work as an itinerant "suckling boy" preacher with the Church of God in Virginia, seventy-three people had converted. Robbers enumerated their crimes: Johnson Green, born in 1757 to an African American father and an Irish mother, catalogued in detail the many acts of robbery he had engaged in, as well as the fact that "I have had correspondence with many women, exclusive of my wife, among whom were several abandoned Whites, and a large number of Blacks; four of the whites were married women, three of the Blacks have laid children to me besides my wife, who has been much distressed by my behaviour." Shortly after he wrote his narrative in 1786, Green was executed for his last listed theft from Justice Belknap's home.[22] All these people were accounting for their own significance, which they saw as based on an accumulation of acts. Quantity was paramount.

These narratives were also, in part, records of material possessions. As such, they included powers gained in governing or through knowledge of magic or medicine, which were tantamount to possessions, and indeed could often be inherited or purchased.[23] The dreams recorded in these narratives were also seen as potentially valuable: dreams often disclosed the location of hidden treasures, which the dreamer later searched for and sometimes found, or revealed potential evils, helping the dreamer avoid life-threatening harm.[24]

These writers indicated no sense of paths not taken, nor any awareness of character development. They did not seem to view their lives as having alterable patterns, nor did they suggest stages or turning points.[25] Levi Hathaway, together with Seth Coleman, John McCorkle, and many others, waited for signs from God before they would act.[26] While Hathaway, Coleman and McCorkle were by and large upright people, most of the criminals also claimed that they had been fated to be what they became, and could not make other choices in life. They believed they had exhibited their evil nature since childhood.[27]

The early narrative writers generally wrote very little about childhood, and many did not mention marriage or name a spouse. Children were often referred to only at their death. It was not considered proper to record personal happenings or much emotion. In fact, the great majority of American life narratives of the eighteenth and early nineteenth centuries were written by individuals who apparently sought to limit or eliminate their personal concern with self. A large number of narratives might be better titled "Accounts of Pain Endured in the Process of Trying to Endure Without Concern for Self."[28]

Dramatic Actors

In the second half of the eighteenth century the "territories of the self" began to undergo a radical transition. Not only elite white males, but many of those of the middling sort and the poor (including both black and white women and men), began to desire to be bounded and separate individuals. Protestant sects played an important but ambivalent role in fostering this change. These church groups required members to analyze their selves closely, although at the same time the churches condemned self-concern. They emphasized daily documentation of the acts of the self and periodic evaluation of the life of the self in order to limit the self. Their congregants were caught in a bind, as these methods and concerns often contributed to an opposite end: enlargement of self. No scrutinized behavior remains the same, and someone constantly observed, stimulated, and pressed in a particular direction often alters, grows, and goes in unpredicted (but perhaps covertly sought) ways. In the very course of the prescribed analyses, individuals emerged more individuated and certainly with more self-concern than these groups wanted or thought they were leading toward. Many people began to envision themselves as having a separate inner self.[29]

What should be viewed as a vast self-change project, one in which new territories were being mapped and colonized, was underway.[30] Thousands of individuals, most of them of the middling sort or poor, including many at the margins, were enjoined or volunteered to write narratives of their lives, most to be saved for posterity.[31] Some were published, often by the writers themselves, who sometimes marketed them as well. It is now fairly widely believed that this type of writing served the interests of middle-class holders of private property.[32] What has not been recognized is how early and how significantly the poor and disadvantaged participated in writing their selves. These were new and even revolutionary acts: the writing and selling of selves by those without power or pretense to high culture. By writing themselves onto the public stage, they too were making a public claim to newly recognized rights.

This extensive body of self-narratives from the early modern period provides graphic and detailed evidence of the changing conception of the self. Although alternative conceptions of the self were always in existence (even in small and isolated communities), there were dominant views that changed over time.[33] In light of this, the writing of selves by the marginal, which *was* revolutionary, was at the same time also a move to participate in the creation of the emerging view of the self and involved the acceptance of new limits on self.[34]

This self-change project extended and reified "a split along gender lines between the ideal of a separate, autonomous, objective male self and a relational, connected, and empathic female self."[35] The autonomous male self came to be seen not as an ideal but as a fixed reality: males were generally expected to have a basic true self that would be constant through life.[36] During the same period in which Shaw saw himself as having no control over his own life, many others began to see themselves as dramatic actors on a public stage. This view became widespread among white males in the late eighteenth century and came to be held by a minority of blacks and white women as well. How did this change come about?

As in earlier periods, individuality often developed through opposition to acceptable selfhood. In his seminal study of Renaissance self-fashioning, Stephen Greenblatt maintained that to achieve a new identity an individual had to discover or invent an "alien, strange or hostile" other that had to be "attacked and destroyed." In order to carry this act out, submission "to an absolute power or authority" in part outside the self, was necessary.[37] Very much the same can seen to have been true for those coming of age in the greater Revolutionary period in America. The issues of the creation of an alien other, conflict with the other, as well as introjection of aspects of the character and values of the other, and submission to an authority, were central both in the dreams and the lives described by dramatic narrators and self-fashioners. The communal self became associated with blacks and women, who were the central alien others for large numbers of white males (including both Garrettson and Rush, discussed later in this chapter), who both loved and hated them; whites were the central alien others of blacks, while each gender focused its alterity on the other.

At any given time during their lives narrators can be viewed (and sometimes viewed themselves) as at a particular point along a theoretical continuum from we-self-witness to I-self-fashioner, sometimes having moved forward, as it were, and sometimes backward. Some individuals developed alien others but could not commit themselves to an outside authority; some came to commitment and could not focus on an alien other. Some created aliens that consumed them, others entered into a moratorium, and some became permanently immobilized.[38]

The recognition of otherness was, of course, not new to the early modern period. The recognition of sexual and out-group otherness was no doubt one of the basic ways in which human beings always defined themselves.[39] All individuals begin with a potential for a range of expression of their sexual, emotional, intellectual, spiritual, and artistic characteristics and learn to reject aspects of their own potential while creating their selves. These rejected aspects of the self "are consolidated into an *anti-Me*," which is projected onto the enemy/other.[40] Throughout history the opposite sex and the foreign other have been of significance as the focus for an oppositional identity or negative role model.[41] However, when identities were widely shared within traditional cultures, males and females were other in fairly stable categories, as were other peoples who were communally

26

alienated. Both men and women, sharing common enemy others, grew up and into shared senses of self, coming to maturity with the familial or we-selves referred to previously. When in the early modern period white males felt a new pressure to develop an I-self through heightened personal concern with what they would not be, white males aggressively separated themselves from the collective self they had in part shared with women, and they did so by characterizing that self as feminine.

It is generally assumed that Europeans in early America naturally came to view Indians and then enslaved Africans as their most dangerous and threatening enemies. Although both groups were objective threats to European settlers, the dangers posed by both native Americans and enslaved Africans were significantly inflated and the opponents demonized so that they could be used by white Americans for important self-work.[42] These alien others were made to play the role of the "not-me" for individual white males seeking both to refashion themselves and to justify genocide and the renewed and vastly expanding institution of enslavement. In England, in contrast, class otherness maintained its traditional primary place and took preference over race.[43]

Insofar as the character of the enemy other was created of rejected inner characteristics, it remained an important part of the self as well, an inner alien that could be reaffirmed. Insofar as the alien other was from another culture, foreign patterns and values could be introjected and made one's own, in some cases by means of theft.[44] Christopher Bollas, in his cogent analysis of such "extractive introjection," notes that it "occurs when one person steals for a certain period of time (from a few seconds or minutes, to a lifetime) an element of another individual's psychic life."[45] Bollas maintains that both "mental content" and "affective process" can be taken over by another in such a way that the originator loses his or her sense that they ever owned these ideas or emotions.

Submission to an ideology, a movement, or a leader enabled an individual to reframe reality, reorient values, target the new enemy other, and project a new life for a changed self. The need for an authoritarian power, in part outside the self, seems antithetical to the growth of a self-fashioning individual, but many theories of growth recognize this seemingly contradictory need. These theories maintain that in order to change an individual must reframe the past, but that a person with a fixed self-view and a fixed worldview is highly unlikely to be able to do this. Accepting new values and reevaluating the past can come about only as a result of a traumatic experience or through submission to an outside authority.[46] In this historic period, the new churches were the formal authorities most often submitted to, although the Revolution and the new nation came to play a significant role as reframing authorities as well.[47] Both the new churches and the Revolution legitimated projecting hated parts of the self on an other and helped the individual reframe the past and begin a new path in life.

The new church institutions asked for total commitment or for individuals to give up their old lives and make new ones. Sins were recounted publicly, and since all of an individual's earlier life was reviewed, life histories were necessary. These histories were often told to ministers or to the community. Since old lives were to be given up as a whole, they needed to be encapsulated, and with the great expansion of literacy the oral testimonies gave way to written narratives. The recountings of past evil were followed by those of saintly lives in the new order. These narratives were often edited and completed after the death of the subject. This project was a vastly expanded version of the lives of the saints, new in its encompassing a massive cohort. An extraordinary example can be found in the vast number of autobiographies collected by the Moravians: thousands of German, American, and African converts wrote or dictated their lives, which were stored in archives for posterity. The Moravians, like most of the sects, saw these collections of lives as virtual pattern books for future generations to emulate.[48]

Like the Puritans and the Quakers, who, over time, came to promote the keeping of journals and the writing of autobiographies, the Moravians called for control over the self, limits to be put upon the self, and self-abnegation. The first enemy that many became aware of was their own self, and they did indeed set out to destroy it. Seventeenth-century Puritans had been adjured to "Hate our selves."[49] By the eighteenth century this call had been internalized by many American Protestants. Congregational minister Samuel Hopkins (born 1721) revealed: "I . . .have generally reflected on myself, character and conduct, . . .with a *painful shame* and self condemnation. . . . I am truly ashamed of myself." The Quaker Anthony Benezet (born 1713), who is remembered for his extraordinary work to end slavery, maintained in his last illness that " 'he wished to live only for the sake of improving his time better than he had done,— and bringing down *self*.' "[50] The Presbyterian minister John McCorkle (born 1750) asked God to choose all his life "changes" for him so that he would not use his own self will, while Ann Byrd (born 1797), a Quaker who followed Benezet's example by working with and for poor children and by practicing severe self-denial, castigated herself for "the unlawful indulgence of *self*."[51] Seth Coleman, a Congregationalist (born in 1740), also castigated himself, but this did not stop Coleman from marrying himself to Jesus. Coleman took Christ as his *husband*, envisioning that he himself would play the role of subservient wife and renounce his own will. In 1761 he wrote this contract into his journal and signed it:

> I do hereby solemnly join myself in a marriage covenant in [Christ]. . . . O blessed Jesus! I come to thee, [a] wretched loathsome creature: a guilty, condemned malefactor, unworthy to wash the feet of the servants of my Lord; much more to be solemnly married to the King of Glory. But since such is thine unparalleled love and condescension I do here with all my heart accept and take thee for my head and husband, to love, serve, honour and obey thee before all others; and this to death. . . . I renounce my own wisdom, and do take thee for mine only guide. I renounce my own will, and take thy will for my law.
>
> *Seth Coleman*[52]

Both Sarah Osborn (born 1714), a Congregationalist, and her close friend and colleague, Susanna Anthony (born 1726), experienced self as an enemy alien, and, as leaders of a women's' group, became important role models of painfully successful self-attackers.[53] Anthony particularly hated her own "carnality and self confidence" and sought to destroy it, praying, "Lord, empty me of self." She was so tortured by what she suspected was inside her that she came to "fear [she was] offering strange fire" to God. A climax to her crisis was brought about by a dream that promised her immortality: "And my mind was much more calm." This dream acceptance enabled her to finally leave her hated parents' faith (the Society of Friends) and join a Congregational church.[54] Anthony's dream life did not end her self attacks, but it did enable her to live a life of devotion and spiritual development and to play a very significant role in her community of believers. Directed by their new church authority, Anthony, Osborn, Hopkins, Coleman, and so many others attacked a part of themselves as if it were alien. They were thereby prepared to recognize these hated characteristics in the "others" who became their enemies. This development was a crucial part of the process of commitment, a task that focused their energies and brought about self change and led them to participate in societal change.

As in Anthony's case, the act of joining a new sect or church was generally a mixed one. It meant the submission to a new authority at the same time that it involved the rejection of old authorities. It enabled sons and daughters as well as wives and husbands to distance themselves or break away entirely from mothers and fathers, husbands and wives. Many grew thereby in self-possession, at the outset deciding who would be their authority figures and their (fictive) families.[55] Radical self-change followed, often stimulated by deep self-hate. Further change generally focused on an enemy alien as the symbol of all the good person should not be.

Thousands joined these sects, and thousands more became Baptists and Methodists. These groups too demanded a personal decision to submit to authority, which in the early period often meant a harsh break with the family of origin and an ongoing self-analysis. Again, the act of joining such a new group and breaking with parents or spouse was often legitimated in a dream or vision reported in a self-critical autobiographical narrative. The new fictive families generally criticized the new member's self as well, as in the Baptist business meetings and in Methodist classes. The business of life was the business of everybody in the group. Although charismatic sectarian leaders played a special role, by and large the self was shared with the new communities, and the dyadic relationship of priest and communicant was opened to more democratic forces that made for a new conformity to group norms and expressed a new common will. The changing self was thus enmeshed in a process that demanded change in a commonly dictated direction.

Often individuals made their first and crucial submissions in their dreams and afterward regarded these actions as committing them to new behaviors in their waking life. Unlike those who continued to regard themselves as observers of their own lives, the dramatic narrators and the self-fashioners did not simply see their dreams as foretelling the future; they came to believe that they had to find ways to achieve goals posited in dreams in order to change themselves and their lives.

The narrative of Freeborn Garrettson, who chose to become a Methodist, can be seen as emblematic of the changing self-view developed by creating an enemy other and through conscious personal commitment to an outside authority. Garrettson, born in Maryland in 1752, was the son of an Anglican plantation and slave owner. At the outset of the Revolution, when he was planning to join the Revolutionary forces, he became increasingly troubled. He found himself deeply attracted to the Methodists, a faith that violated many of his father's most deeply held values, as well as the values of his friends and neighbors. In June of 1775, in the midst of his crisis over his future, he reported the following dream:

In the night I went to bed as usual; and slept till day break—Just as I awoke, I was alarmed by an awful voice, "Awake, sinner, for you are not prepared to die." This was strongly impressed on my mind, as if it had been a human voice as loud as thunder.

That very day Garrettson was to have gone to a review of Revolutionary troops, ostensibly to enlist. Instead he went to hear a Methodist sermon. Returning from this meeting, he stopped for solitary prayer in the woods where "I sensibly felt the presence of two spirits, one on each hand." One was a "good spirit" while the second was the "devil." The good spirit said that Garrettson could not delay a decision, that he had no time, but Garrettson, apparently impressed by the devil's advice, replied "I will take my own time." He moved on toward home, but after he had gone but a short distance he heard the Lord speaking directly to him:

"I have come once more to offer you life and salvation, and it is the last time: chuse or refuse."

Garrettson cried out "Lord, I submit," and felt immediate "faith and love."[56]

Garrettson, much like Shaw, heard an unembodied voice call him in his first dream. Garrettson could not act as, much like Shaw, he was not present in this dream. It is clear that he did not yet envision himself as an independent actor in his life. In a later dream the devil appeared to Garrettson again as he had to Shaw, but by then Garrettson was very much an actor in his own dreams, and a "good spirit" (which could well have been that of a venerable old man) was advising him. Garrettson, unlike Shaw, had respected his father, and although he had been attracted to the Methodists while his father was alive, it was only after his father's death that he could make a choice that violated his father's will. While he leaned toward the devil's advice, his visions gave him another chance: God appeared to him, and asked Garrettson to "chuse or refuse."

Garrettson came to see himself as at a crucial crossroads and believed that the choice he had to make would affect the rest of his life. He chose to join the Methodists, which led to a range of other decisions, including his refusal to participate in the war. Thereafter he believed he could and should affect change in his own life. He came to view himself as a dramatic actor on a stage of ultimate importance. He had committed himself, first in his dreams and visions and then in his life, and he had to oppose an enemy alien. The enemy that he chose to oppose was the very self that was being appropriated by other southern white males. He now set out to become just the opposite of what he had been brought up to be. From this time forward he would not use violence to prove his manhood, nor would he fight in a war of rebellion. And as we shall see later, he would not own slaves nor would he choose, at this point or for many years after, to marry and govern a family. In all of these ways he violated accepted norms but followed the norms of his new faith.

Growth in self-awareness is reflected in Garrettson's narrative as well as in many others. (Judged by Rossi's scale, Garrettson's dreams move from level two to the very highest levels—six or seven.) He and a large number of the other writers began to present parts of their accounts as dramas in which they acted. To varying degrees, these dramatic narrators began to picture themselves as characters who changed over the course of time, whose lives did have turning points, suggesting they might have decided to go different ways. Dreams were often experienced at these turning points and seen as indicating the direction the dreamer should go. These dreams challenged narrators, demanding commitments, and clarified what was to be abjured.

Narration of "self," seeing oneself as part of a dramatic story that begins at birth or before, with beginning, climax, and end in mind—which we have come to regard as the normal or natural way to see the self—was expanded significantly in these narratives and was as well at the core of the fictive autobiographies written as novels in this period.[57] This idea of the self was transmitted by this literature as well as by mothers, fathers, and others who talked to young children about the stories of their lives. As the work of Fredrika Teute has shown, Margaret Bayard Smith (born 1778) openly used her own family experiences in the literature she wrote for didactic purposes. Writing about her own children and their black servant, Matty, she scripted their interdependent selves (describing how Matty often instructed the children both in morals and in factual matters) while she drew "proper" and very different futures for the white children (as benevolent mistresses) and their black companion (as submissive servant/slave). She no doubt read these stories to them, preparing them to accept and fulfill these projected roles, much as she hoped that other mothers would do.[58]

BOUNDED SELF-FASHIONERS

A small number of these narrators came to view themselves as self-fashioners who were fully responsible for the direction their lives were taking.[59] Among this group, too, dreams were often used to further work on the self, but many began to fear that concern with dreams was a throwback to an earlier worldview, and as a result self-fashioners began to report fewer dreams. At the same time, emotions, earlier viewed as virtually possessing the individual, were increasingly "owned" as a product of the self; values were identified as legitimating action; and personal acts were seen as part of a story or drama.[60] Some of this small number, however, perhaps frightened by the hubris of believing themselves self-fashioners, seemed to retreat from this radical new view, apparently wanting to return to a belief that forces outside themselves were responsible for their life's path.

Benjamin Rush (born 1746) can be seen as emblematic of this third group. His father had died when Rush was five and a half, and Benjamin early sought to pattern himself after one of his fictive fathers, his teacher Rev. Samuel Davies at the College of New Jersey, who was, according to Rush a "self-made man." It was, however, during the two years that he spent studying medicine at Edinburgh, away from all his old mentors and moorings, that he was able to consciously change his worldview. There he came to question "the sun in the solar system"—that is, he began to question the hereditary powers of the king and found that as a result he was ready to question all inherited knowledge. Rush returned to America psychologically prepared to be a revolutionary, not only politically but also in regard to medical theory, religious beliefs, and much else. However, while he no longer thought that tradition controlled him, he was convinced that he, with his new wisdom, should control others.

Rush entered the arena of changing others' views with his attack on slave keeping in 1773 and then became a leading agitator for independence. He clearly recognized the need for a rallying call to the people, and he both encouraged Thomas Paine to write *Common Sense* and edited it. Rush served in the Continental Congress, and as a physician in the army. In virtually every arena he entered he developed plans for significant reform, and in every case he met with much opposition.

After the Revolution Rush wanted to "to prepare the principles, morals, and manners of our citizens, for . . . [the new] forms of government," much as he had earlier wanted to prepare his beloved wife to be his proper companion by providing her with a library of the proper reading. His desire to control others may well have been tied to his need for self-control, as he continued to rapidly alter his evaluations of many individuals and ideas, including religious ideas, and over the course of his life often became embroiled in conflict. He instituted a new approach to control yellow fever and other illnesses through massive bloodletting, and developed plans for controlled education for the citizens of the new state as well as far stricter controls to be instituted in the penal resocialization of "criminals" who had violated its laws.

In the midst of his political activities a dream brought Rush up short and led him to the realization that he had better take another turn.

About the year 1790 I imagined I was going up Second Street in our city and was much struck by observing a great number of people assembled near Christ Church gazing at a man who was seated on the ball just below the vane of the steeple of the Church. I asked what was the matter. One of my fellow citizens came up to me and said, the man whom you see yonder has discovered a method of regulating the weather, and that he could produce rain and sunshine and cause the wind to blow from any quarter he pleased. I now joined the crowd in gazing at him. He had a trident in his hand which he waved in the air, and called at the same time to the wind, which then blew from the northeast, to blow from the northwest. I observed the vane of the steeple while he was speaking, but perceived no motion in it. He then called for rain, but the clouds passed over the city without dropping a particle of water. He now became agitated and dejected, and complained of the refractory elements in the most affecting terms. Struck with the issue of his conduct, I said to my friend who stood near me, "The man is certainly mad." Instantly a figure dressed like a flying Mercury descended rapidly from him, with a streamer in his hand, and holding it before my eyes bid me read the inscription on it. It was: "De te fabula narratur." ["The story is told of you yourself."] The impression of these words was so forcible upon my mind that I instantly awoke, and from that time I determined never again to attempt to influence the opinions and passions of my fellow citizens upon political subjects.

This is a dream that in Rossi's terms indicates "multiple levels of awareness" both in the dream and in Rush's personality. In the dream Rush was both "participating and observing," as well as "noticing oddities" and recognizing meanings for his waking life. As Carl Binger has noted, the message was "to stop deceiving himself and to become aware of his own limitations." Rush had seen himself in an elevated position and recognized his own (failed) desire for total control, both in the dream and in his life.

Benjamin Rush developed a medical approach to dreams, ascribing them to physiological causes, including sexual urges. He ostensibly held that the content of dreams was "nothing but incoherent ideas" which derange the imagination, memory, and judgment. Nevertheless, he knew that his own dreams had deeply influenced his views of poverty, of social responsibility, and of himself. He recorded prescriptive dreams of others and kept a record of many of his own dreams, using several of them in his correspondence to make telling points to others. (A dream that he reported to John Adams brought Adams back into contact with Thomas Jefferson after years of silent anger on both their parts.) His personal use of dreams for self-change in this case (and others that are discussed in following chapters) was far more complex than his own theory allowed for, and he himself knew they often played a very significant role. They had helped him to become a bounded self-fashioner.[61]

DREAMS AS CULTURAL PRODUCTIONS

Both the content of dream reports and the "signifying universe"—the range of meanings "potentially available" to each person in the society—are culture bound.[62] In addition, the range of symbolically significant items varies for those of different backgrounds within the same society. When, for example, Ezra Stiles had his portrait painted in 1771, he insisted on the inclusion of a circle and a "trajectory around a solar point," symbols that he saw as representing Newton's concept of the solar system; the Tetragrammaton, which stood for God; and white and black spots, which he saw as representing innocence and evil in the world. Stiles held that "These Emblems are more descriptive of my Mind, than the Effigies of my Face."[63] The first two of these symbols were certainly not in use by all Americans in this period, but the third was widely shared and can be found in dream reports. Other dream symbols and themes were also widely shared.

The dream most often reported in a particular culture, which has been termed a culture pattern dream, differs from culture to culture.[64] The most frequently reported dream in the European Christian tradition was that of a journey to the other world that involved meetings with the dead, a postbiblical dream pattern brought into the tradition by European converts. In the early modern period Paul Bunyan (born 1628) used this dream of the journey to the other world for a revolutionary purpose: consciously planned change in self. Bunyan believed he had been a sinning youth and reported that he had suffered "fearful dreams and dreadful visions" as punishment for his immoral behavior. His spiritual development was marked by grim nightmares of the underworld, which led him to change his conduct, and he was then rewarded with glorious visions of a journey to

FIGURE 4. "These Emblems are more descriptive of my Mind, than the Effigies of my Face." Ezra Stiles, portrait by Samuel King, 1771.

heaven. He first wrote a personal narrative of these happenings in his life in 1666 in *Grace Abounding,* and then, in *The Pilgrim's Progress* of 1678, he reworked them into an archetypal version of spiritual death and rebirth to provide a model for others to follow consciously. This second volume was extraordinarily successful, providing a pattern for proper Christian dream and vision experiences as well as for the narrative construction of an ideal self; it was widely read in America and reached the poor and the enslaved.[65]

The culture pattern dream of travel to the other world, at the center of Bunyan's works, was also the dream reported by more American narrators than any other dream.[66] A particularly moving set of images was recorded by John Barr, born in Pennsylvania in 1749. Barr reported that when he was between three and four years old he dreamt of Christ coming to judge the dead, and he saw

> the dead rising in every direction. Some had got on their feet—others appeared in a sitting position—whilst only the heads of some were to be seen above ground.

Over sixty years later, Barr was still terrorized by what he had dreamt,

> . . . which I suppose I shall never forget, so long as I am capable of remembering any thing. A separation took place in this vast assembly—one part seemed to mount as on eagles' wings toward heaven. I followed them with a wishful eye till out of sight, but remained with those left upon the ground. It was not long however till the multitude on the ground was put in motion by legions of frightful beings which, I had no doubt were devils.

Pushed by these frightful beings down a steep incline to the threshold of hell, Barr hoped to keep himself from falling into the "dismal place" by saying the only prayer he knew, the Lord's Prayer, but he awoke, weeping, before the outcome was resolved. This dream remained with him all his life, and praying that he might be saved from hell remained one of his central concerns.[67]

Barr's dream shows the influence of what might be termed the living Bible, both an oral and a written tradition tied to the pre-Christian past. With the proliferation of printed material in the early modern period, people had increasing access to pictures of heaven and hell in illustrated Bibles, as well as to published dream manuals, both in twenty-four-page chapbooks and in lengthier versions.[68] Dream manuals were printed in voluminous numbers, and peddled in every country: it is likely that a large number were imported into the colonies.[69] In 1767 a dream dictionary entitled *The New Book of Knowledge* was published in America; although it was called "new" it was directly copied from earlier English publications. Moreover, most remarkably, this American publication, like the English works, was largely based on the work of Artemidorus, a second-century A.D. interpreter whose dream books, although much simplified, had been passed down through the generations. This ancient dream lore had an extraordinarily long life and broad appeal: it was the basis for a large body of shared images and meanings across cultures and over the centuries.

In this extraordinarily influential five-volume work on dream explication, Artemidorus held that all dreamed events that violate nature or acceptable behavior signify "trouble," and he therefore advised dream interpreters to "learn local customs and the peculiarities of every place." Artemidorus also recognized the complicated nature of the normative and generally suggested interpretations that differentiated outcomes according to the class, family position, and gender of the dreamer. While he did assign fixed meanings to certain dreamed of actions (for example, he generally explained sexual acts as betokening the future economic condition of the dreamer), in actual practice, however, much like Freud, he did not interpret dreams by any one simple system and went far beyond the denotated. He often built his interpretations around puns, anagrams, and homonyms, as well as accepted emblems and symbols. Artemidorus's commentaries formed the basis for a popular, widely shared approach to dreams throughout the Western world, a tradition that was extraordinarily stable, although influenced by the various cultures that adopted it, but which became simplified and attenuated over the generations.[70]

On January 11, 1863, twenty-year-old Lucy Breckinridge of Virginia reported to Dolly, her enslaved servant, that she had dreamt of peaches.[71] Dolly responded, "To dream of fruit out of season is trouble without reason." Her words were a direct echo of Artemidorus's, written some sixteen hundred years earlier. (Artemidorus had written that "all things [dreamed of], with few exceptions, that are out of season, are bad.")[72] But they also fit Dolly's African American culture, with its orientation to the natural, and indicate as well Dolly's sensitive response to Lucy Breckinridge's life problems. Breckinridge had earlier reported that after she visited the grave of her beloved brother, which was near a peach tree, she had dreamt that her brother asked her to join him in the grave. Dolly clearly recognized the symbolic significance of the peaches in the second dream, and the danger they represented.[73]

The significant changes in perceptions, ideas, and metaphors of the early modern period were reflected in changes in the visual imagination, although these changes only slowly made their way into dream manuals. Evidence of such a change in the visual imagination can be found in the fact that Masonic imagery was filtering into popular usage: the Masonic compass, which stood for the "circumscribing of desires" and the "all-seeing eye," which represented the "Supreme Being's" ability to see inside the individual heart, were becoming common images, both suggesting a new conception of inner-directedness, and of the need for inner control.[74]

Other common images were changing as well. In this period the devil was moving from a perverse collection of attributes (clawed or cloven feet, hairy body with batlike wings and animal ears, some-

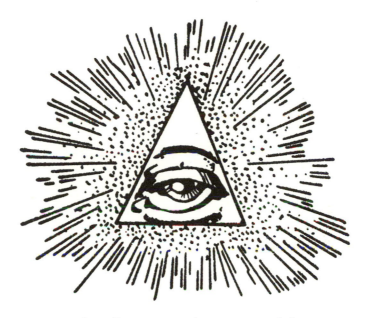

FIGURE 5. The "All Seeing Eye." This Masonic symbol, suggesting that what is within human beings can be seen, was widely used in the Revolutionary period. It can be found on the Great Seal of the United States and on the one-dollar bill.

times part female with exposed breasts, and often with dark skin) to a figure recognizable as a black male. Charles Deas's powerful painting *The Devil and Tom Walker* (1838) illustrated a story by Washington Irving of the same title. Irving wrote that this devil was "neither negro nor Indian" and that "his face was neither black nor copper-color, but swarthy and dingy, and begrimed with soot." Throughout the story, however, Irving referred to the devil as "a black man," and Deas clearly painted him as an African American.[75]

Some of the other symbols that were coming into common usage were also color coded. The Masons introduced checkerboard blocks of black and white pavement, which stood for evil and good, supposedly as in Solomon's Temple. This color symbolism was, of course, not new. Cosmologies and world views both in the West and in Africa were often based on a binary construction in which white was correlated with both the good and the masculine while black was correlated with evil and the feminine.[76] Thus, it is not surprising that the pre-Revolutionary diary or "Monitor" of young Mary Osgood Sumner had a "Black Leaf" for wrongdoings and a "White Leaf" for duties performed, or that in 1767 six-year-old Ephraim Stinchfield dreamt that all the righteous approaching God were white while all those who were evil were black.[77] A number of Africans shared in this use of black and white to symbolize evil and good. Among the Temne, for example, black clothing and other black things seen in a dream were associated with illness and death, while white objects and white people betokened something good.[78]

Color coding can be found in a popular early American dream manual, *The Universal Dream-Dictionary*, of 1795, another volume that was based on English texts.[79] The dictionary noted that dreamed-of faces with white or pale skin were "a sign of trouble, poverty and death," while "a black face denotes long life." The color of flesh was considered separately, as if not connected to the same body as the face: "If any one dreams his flesh is grown spotted, or black, like a moor, it signifies he will deceive those he trades with by lying and craft. If a woman dreams thus, she will be taken in adultery, and put away or repudiated by her husband." The color of garments held out a similar promise for the future of the dreamer: White clothing signified joy, whereas black clothing betokened the temptation to sin.[80] Bodies and clothing were thus in conflict with faces or heads: a black face was a positive sign of long life, whereas a black body or a black robed body betokened evil or sexual license.

From the ancient period to the early modern, dream manuals recorded the significance of separate body parts paralleling a segmented view of life. *The Universal Dream-Dictionary* of 1795 stated, "To dream a man's back is broken, hurt, or scabby, shews his enemies will get the better of him." "To dream of bleeding at the nose, signifies loss of goods, and decay of riches." "To dream you have hairy breasts, and the paps covered with hair, denotes gain and profit to men, but to a women loss of her husband."[81]

Such damaged and separate body parts were conspicuous in self narratives of the early modern era. In analyzing Samuel Sewall's diary, Mary Hilmer has noted "the absence of whole bodies" and the presence of myriad damaged body parts: a "bruis'd Nose,' a "foot hung in the Stirrup," a thigh where "the bones pierce through the skin," a broken "knee-pan" from which "Much blood issued out," and numerous malformed body parts.[82] Images of the body damaged and in parts can also be found in the journal of African American Lewis Clarke (born 1812), who reported that "The slaves often say, when cut in the hand or foot, 'Plague on the old foot,' or 'the old hand; it is master's—let him take care of it.'" Some whites in the same period were imagining a reunion of body parts: a white female follower of the Universal Friend, Jemima Wilkinson, reported that Wilkinson "dreamed that there was a great women head brought to the Friend and it talked with the Friend and sed that it was agoen to have its body again."[83]

The Universal Dream-Dictionary of 1795, following Artemidorus, still explicated many dreams by simple congruence ("carrion signifies sadness") and by opposites ("gladness and joy denote trouble"), and made specific prognostications according to class and gender: The poor profit from dreams of dung, while for all others "it is heaviness and hurt." If a woman dreams of a "monstrous or unnatural birth," it signifies "success and comfort" will follow, while for a man it "betokens no good to the dreamer."[84]

While so much was still in the ancient tradition, early American dream dictionaries were far less explicit about sexual matters than Artimedorus had been.[85] Of the 105 entries in Chloe Russell's dream book of 1800, only one was overtly related to a sexual theme: "If you shew your naked back [in a dream], you will be engaged in some scene of lewdness."[86] *The Universal Dream-Dictionary* did consider birds' nests and cages womblike, and held that an empty nest or cage signified that a woman's "maidenhead is gone," and that "to dream that you take hold of one's nose, signifies fornication." Most often, following Artemidorus, "the private parts" of the body were understood to symbolize economic or physical trouble or success: breasts "full of milk" signified profits to be realized, while envisioning the groin indicated friendships were strong and the economic position of the dreamer was secure. Reversing the symbolism, dreams of losing money were believed to predict women's "loss of modesty, honesty or their maidenheads."[87]

The signifying universe of early European settlers was enriched by the dream interpretations of Africans and Native Americans, who widely took dreams very seriously. American Indians and the whites they adopted into their societies were acculturated to attend to their dream life, and dream or vision quests were central to Native American spiritual development.[88] In the seventeenth century missionaries to the Indians believed that the intensity of Native American dream beliefs severely hampered Christian missionizing. The missionary Father Ragueneau described an overarching belief in the need to fulfill dreams in 1649:

[T]he Hurons believe that our souls have . . . desires, which are, as it were, inborn and concealed. These, they say come from the depths of the soul. . . .

Now they believe that our soul makes these natural desires known by means of dreams, which is its language. Accordingly, when these desires are accomplished, it is satisfied; but on the contrary, if it be not granted what it desires, it becomes angry, and not only does not give its body the good and the happiness that it wished to procure for it, but often it also revolts against the body, causing various diseases, and even death. . . .

In consequence of these erroneous ideas, most of the Hurons are very careful to note their dreams, and to provide the soul with what it has pictured to them during their sleep. . . . And they call this *Ondinnonk*—a secret desire of the soul manifested by a dream.[89]

Although at the outset missionaries fought Native Americans' belief in dreams, by the eighteenth century, missionaries were, in fact, making use of the Native Americans' reliance on dreams as a bridge to bring them to Christianity.[90] In doing this they may well have unwittingly been opening themselves up to the influence of Indian beliefs.[91]

While African cultures had a range of approaches to dreams, most took dreams very seriously. Most importantly, dream reports and dream explication were interwoven with the life cycle and the daily pattern of most African people. Dreams were widely regarded as valuable in relation to foretelling most negative and positive events, including births and deaths; illnesses and cures; failures or successes in love, economic pursuits, and warfare; they were understood to bestow both spiritual and social power upon individuals. Dreams were widely believed to be "the wishes of the spirits."[92]

Zulu elders said: "Dreams are our eyes in the work" and held that "without dreams, true and uninterrupted living is not possible." The Temne of the Guinea Coast region, who believed in multiple worlds, regarded dreams as one of the "means of mediation" between these worlds. The Temne also held that

the vision and knowledge of diviners are largely . . . [due] to accomplishments in dreaming, through which they become experts on the dreams of their clients. Not only, then, do their dreams have power; they have power over other people's dreams.[93]

The reliance on diviners to interpret dreams was (and is) very widespread in West Africa.[94] The Igbo (and many others) relied upon dreams in choosing candidates for religious office, as well as at other significant junctures. The Yunsi of Zaire were one of the groups that practiced dream explication at funerals: members of a deceased's household were adjured to tell their dreams, which were then analyzed to determine *who had caused the death*, as the Yunsi believed that virtually all deaths were caused by the evil intentions of another person. These dreams too had to be, as they put it, "turned the right way up," "opened up," and "picked over" by an interpreter.[95]

Among the Ashanti, dreams were believed to describe the actions of the dreamer's soul, for which the dreamer was held responsible. It is widely reported that the Ashanti hold that

> If you dream that you have had sexual intercourse with another man's wife and any one hears of it, and tells her husband, then you will be fined the usual adultery fees, for your soul and hers have had sexual intercourse.

While this may be an explanation that was given by an Ashanti, the reality may have been a bit more complicated. The telling of such a dream might also have been viewed as an insult to the husband, necessitating a fee to set social relations aright.[96]

Given the widespread and wide-ranging concern with dreams among African traditionalists, which was shared by African Muslims (who had a rich tradition of written dream manuals), it is not surprising that dreams were significant in African and African American conversions to Christianity, and were cited in narratives and testimonies.[97] Myriad black dream visions that were recounted in biracial church love feasts, at baptisms and at funerals, revealed to whites that many blacks possessed extraordinary means of understanding dreams. The publication of a dream book attributed to black Chloe Russell in 1800 suggests that there was a market for black interpretations of dreams among whites as well as blacks. While the text appears to be a copy of an English chapbook, the cover page pleads the bona fides of the author with a drawing of "A woman of Colour of the State of Massachusetts, commonly termed the Old Witch or Black Interpreter, who certainly possesses extraordinary means of foretelling remarkable events."[98] Against the African background it is not surprising that the narrative richest in dreams in this entire cohort was that of a black woman, Rebecca Cox Jackson, who became a Shaker eldress and a remarkable visionary.[99]

African Americans widely fostered and even institutionalized dream incubation and dream interpretation. One of the traditions we know a good deal about comes from the antebellum Sea Island black communities, where many African folkways (as well as language patterns and vocabulary) were a significant part of the culture. On these islands there were recognized spiritual guides, both women and men, who helped individual "seekers" work with their dreams.[100] A central feature of the method used by these analysts was to seek a central image in each dream that they would then use as

FIGURE 6. Chloe Russell, black dream interpreter. Frontispiece to *The Complete Fortune Teller and Dream Book*, Boston, 1800.

a key to unlock the dream's meaning. Much as among the Temne, recognition of the image that would suit the particular individual's problems was supposed to come to the guide in a dream as well. No doubt there were well-established traditions of dream interpretation and a specific repertoire of key elements, but there was an individualized aspect as well, based on the personal assessment of the seeker by the guide. The guide sent the seeker back to pray, fast, and dream "until the seeker reports a vision which, because of the whiteness of the object envisaged, the activity of the one seen, the meaningful message spoken, or some other clue, seems to the spiritual teacher to compare favorably with or fit into his own dream or vision concerning this particular seeker."[101] This key image marked what was regarded as the climax dream of the seeking process, signifying that the seeker had "come through," or been accepted by the spirit, and was vouchsafed salvation. Although detailed evidence of this type of work has only been recorded in the Sea Islands, it is likely that dream advisers once functioned over a wider area or that the black religious leadership on plantations in other locations, both prior to Christian conversions and after, played a similar role, as dream reports were central in African American spiritual life in all locations.[102]

Spirit travels also played an important role in African American dream reports, but these journeys, rather than down to hell and then up to heaven, as in the white reports, were often through the air, as if the dreamer were a bird—the ubiquitous African spirit figure that came to North America. As Harriet Tubman noted, when she "used to dream of flying over fields and towns, and rivers and mountains," she felt that she was "looking down upon them 'like a bird," and African Americans Elizabeth, Rebecca Cox Jackson, and Moses Grandy, among many others, reported that they too traveled through the air and looked down on the earth below.[103]

When the enslaved did begin to experience spirit travels down to a Christian hell and then up to heaven, their visions differed from European American spirit travels in several very significant respects, both paralleling African patterns. First, African Americans often saw multiple spirits within themselves—a "little me" in a "big me," and secondly, a little white guide took many on their journeys; whiteness dominated their descriptions of spirit and heaven as well.[104] Myriad African American visionaries recounted that when God "struck them dead" and they began their spiritual travels toward rebirth, they saw themselves as twofold, "a being in a being." "I saw myself in two parts," one said. Similar phrases appear in most black conversion narratives: "He showed me myself in two parts of me," or "I saw myself in two bodies"; "There is . . . a man in a man"; and "Little

FigURE 7. An African, perhaps drawn by an African American, with what appears to be a "little me" spirit figure. From a Charleston broadside, 1769.

Mary came out of old Mary."[105] This understanding was a very traditional African one. In a study of *West African Religion* published in 1949 Geoffrey Parrinder maintained that West Africans believe that in each person is the "thing in itself" or "the essential being," which is spirit, and that "real life is spent in touch with the supreme spirit." Parrinder noted, *"The African might say that . . . 'in every man there is a little man.' "*[106] This understanding remained of great importance for Africans in America: This "little me" did not die in the transition to America or in the slave period but was largely hidden, and then renewed in the African Christian faith. In America, this African interior "me" might seem to have been like the new Western idea of an inner self, but it was part of a very different world view, one in which the little me was believed to have existed before it was embodied, and would continue to exist after the death of the person.

The African American concern with whiteness has often been taken note of but has been largely misunderstood, in that it is widely seen as an expression of self-hatred based on whites' values. What has not been taken into account is the strong African tradition correlating whiteness with purity and goodness. As noted previously, among the Temne black clothing and other black things seen in a dream were associated with illness and death, while white objects and white people betokened something good. Black skin, however, simply signified *"an ordinary human being."*[107] The color values held by the Meru of Kenya were very similar to those of the Temne and to those of Aristotle: the Meru viewed *white* (and right as well as male) as superior to *black* (left and female). The Meru divided

46

themselves into what they regarded as superior and inferior clans and termed the superior clans the *"white clans"* and the inferior black, indicating again that these colors were symbolic of ascribed value, and not of skin color.[108]

Concern with whiteness, and the assumption that white stands for purity and holiness, can be widely found in African American dreams and visions from the period of slavery. The dreams of thirteen-year-old African American Frederic W. Swan, recorded in 1822, were almost all about key white objects, as in this, his first recorded dream:

> I dreamt I set out to go to my mother in a thunder storm—I thought I saw the devil coming toward me—I thought I had no way to shun him but to go back, and as I turned, I saw one all in white, and he said unto me, 'You should not fear him, but fear me;' and I awoke, and was terrified.[109]

In following dreams Swan envisioned a white temple; a white house that he felt betokened peace; two white men, probably prophets; enormous white sails on a ship, apparently traveling toward salvation; a white man with a holy book; a white ladder—a Jacob's ladder to heaven; and a large white bird, which became a white angel who gave Frederic Swan a cup and bade him drink. This he believed brought him assurance that he would be converted. Swan died soon after this vision, apparently having experienced conversion and the surety of acceptance.[110]

Both dreams and dream interpretations were widely shared by whites and blacks, enriching and changing both traditions. James Ireland (1748–1806), although born in Scotland, had grown up in Virginia and was likely to have heard African women and men discuss dreams. He also, no doubt, had heard white preachers talk of biblical dreams and particularly of Joseph, whom he was also likely to have read about in a popular chapbook. Ireland came to believe that he himself had "got to be a Joseph, a great dreamer." Ireland, who became a powerful Baptist preacher, was baptized together with blacks and was beaten for preaching to blacks. It is not surprising that while thinking of himself as a biblical figure, he regarded his dreams much as an African might have and learned from them who his enemies were and how they were planning his downfall: "It pleased God graciously to condescend to give me information in the visions of the night, pointing out the persons and the way they were pursuing, by which I was prepared before hand."[111] His use of this power frightened his opponents.

This sharing of dreams was not an isolated aspect of interracial exchange. Sharing dream life was an addition to a complicated counteridentification that was taking place. While black alien figures were attacked by whites, as were white enemies by blacks, the dreamscape also provided a protected space for negotiations with the other, and a reacceptance of part of the abjured self. When dreams opened inner worlds to penetration by the white or black other, they prepared the black or white self for change in the outer world.[112]

A parallel process can be discerned in male and female interrelationships, as males attacked female enemy figures and also adopted much from them, and women did much the same with their male others. Rebecca Cox Jackson's absorption of a white male dream figure into her heart (discussed in chapter 3) is the clearest example of this process, and her use of this figure to expand her actual abilities (in reading, comprehension, and leadership) is an indication of its importance.[113]

DREAMS AS A TOOL FOR THE GROWTH OF SELF AND SOCIETY

A few American thinkers consciously recognized that dreams could be used to expand and change self consciousness. Jonathan Edwards, the Congregationalist minister who played a significant role in the First Great Awakening, wrote in his private diary on May 2, 1723: "I think it a very good way to examine dreams every morning when I awake; what are the nature, circumstances, principle, and ends of my imaginary actions and passions in them, to discern what are my chief inclinations."[114] Edwards assumed that dreams revealed his own tendencies and passions rather than God's plans. Many others used dreams to expand their understanding of themselves without acknowledging any such theory.

Many people at the margins were refashioning themselves, often by means of writing their life narratives, and/or working with their dreams, thus becoming far more individuated than those in power desired. Much of the rest of this study is devoted to women and men, black and white, who did this; an exemplar of such dream work and life change can be found in the narrative of Jacob Ritter (born in 1757), a very poor Lutheran youth. Dreams were important in Ritter's life from his adolescence, when he felt great anger at his "high spirited," father a poor German immigrant, who had put Jacob "to hard work as soon as I was able." Ritter's language suggests that his father was quick to anger, and that he probably treated Jacob harshly, as he contrasted his father with his mother, who "was always kind and tender to me." When, just before his sixteenth birthday, he dreamt that two angels in "pure white" took him to heaven, it was his mother who heard his report and interpreted it.

[T]wo men came to me clothed in white; one of them laid his hands upon my breast, and the other placed his behind my shoulders. I then perceived that they were angels, for they stretched out their wings over me, and lifted me up, telling me they would shew me the gates of heaven.—When we came to the place, I beheld our Saviour with outstretched arms, and was told I must enter in by Christ who was the door.—When I had passed into the glorious city, I beheld that everything was clear and pure, and that there was no light of the sun or moon, but Christ was the light thereof. The two angels who had brought me thither, set me upon an elevated seat, and I saw an innumerable company round me, all shining and bright, and they sang the song of Moses and the Lamb.

When this heavenly harmony had ceased there was a great silence, and then the shining host all passed in quietude away, except my two conductors, who came and told me I must not stay there then, but must go back again. When I came to myself, heavenly love covered my mind, and I got up in the morning in much quietness of spirit. My mother took notice of it, and asked me the cause, but I feared to show her the vision, until at length she pressed me so hard to tell her, that I did so, and she replied: "Jacob, my son, this is certainly a foresight of some great work thou wilt have to do; mind now be a good boy and fear God."

Under pressure from his church, Jacob Ritter joined the Revolutionary army in 1777, but he experienced a vision of "the horrors of war" and refused to fight. He was soon taken prisoner by (or perhaps surrendered to) the Hessians, who brutally "abused" him as "he could not defend himself." After the war he married and moved to Philadelphia, where, although both he and his wife worked, they and their children were starving. At this low point in his narrative he reported a second dream, one in which he moved from the passivity of his first vision, in which he had appeared but was acted upon, to one in which he realized he was being encouraged to act when he was given forewarning that a minister in a church belfry was to be consumed by fire. Ritter awoke with the feeling that a great revelation had been given to him, most likely about the sinful nature of his minister. He soon joined the Society of Friends. Not long after he became a Quaker, his wife followed him, against the strong admonitions of her mother. When his wife died soon after, Ritter's guilt feelings brought him to think of his anger at the Englishmen and Hessians "who had so cruelly beaten and abused me." In this mood he finally had a dream in which he took responsibility for himself and acted in the face of a dangerous threat.[115] Ritter reexperienced the demeaning period when he was a prisoner in this crucial dream, in which he successfully escaped from imprisonment, risking his life by braving his way through enemy fire. He had probably been a *deserter*, or at the least he felt like one; now, in his dream, he chose to follow a bright light through a *desert* to safety. He had put desertion behind him. Awake, he reframed the suffering he had undergone during the war as a trial set by God, who in his dream had led him to see his inner light and his inner strength. As a result of this dream, which was the first he reported in which he was active in his own defense, he was suddenly able to forgive the men who had tormented him, thereby preparing himself to become a proper Quaker. By reframing his past he was enabled to change both his present emotions and his future.[116]

Evidence of such crucial reframing also occurred within the dreams reported by William Glendinning, which spanned the greater Revolutionary period. Glendinning, born in Scotland in 1747, was apprenticed as a tailor after his father's death when he was "about 13." This was clearly a traumatic period for him, during which, while "reading *John Bunyan's* Holy War I was alarmed, and brought to a sense of the dangerous state of my soul." In 1767, he, much like Shaw, experienced a recurring vision of a fire, but in Glendinning's vision the fire engulfed the whole world. Soon after Glendinning finished his apprenticeship his mother died, and the money she left him enabled him to journey to America, but this move did not make him more secure. In Baltimore his vision of the world in flames recurred, stimulating a spiritual quest that led him to become a Methodist and to serve as an itinerant preacher in the South during the war. While preaching in Brunswick, Virginia, in 1784, Glendinning, in an obvious state of depression and confusion, spoke of his worries about "what had been before God was" and asked "if angels were governed by law" and "could saints fall in heaven." He related that he had experienced "dismal dreams, of going over dreary mountains, and falling into bottomless abysses." He felt hatred for God and for himself, and he tried to take his own life. Fellow Methodists restrained him and took him to various physicians for treatment, but when he did not improve, they brought him to the plantation of a Methodist supporter where he was housed in a cabin like that of slaves, and cared for by the enslaved. He reported that Lucifer, whom he described as having a face "black as any coal," began to visit him two or three times a week. For over five years he continued to be tormented both during the day and in his sleep, visited by devils in both states.[117]

After five years of dreaming of devils, Glendinning's dreams alerted him to a change in his condition:

> I now began to dream of being with human creatures, frequently of being in churches or houses, standing up and speaking for the Lord, to great numbers of people.

In 1786 a dream brought him the message that God would not allow Lucifer "to carry me off." Given this assurance, the next time he saw the devil, he assertively protected himself in his dream and

> commanded him to depart. At which he shrunk back, and went toward the other fallen angels—in a little time, they all departed, and I saw him no more.[118]

Glendinning's dream life presaged a radical change in his behavior, which began to appear more normal. Glendinning soon returned to preaching but found himself troubled by the changes that had taken place while he had been out of contact with the world—the comparative worldliness in the Methodist Church, and the increasing justification of slaveholding. Methodist Church leaders found him difficult to accept as well, especially as he insisted on talking of visions of hell and eternity and the figures that he had "known" in his dreams.[119]

Glendinning's last reported dreams can be seen as "self-state dreams," in which, as Heinz Kohut suggests, consideration of "the manifest content will . . . allow us to recognize that the healthy sectors of the . . . psyche are reacting with anxiety to a disturbing change in the condition of the self. . .or to the threat of the dissolution of the self."[120] Glendinning regarded them as from God, and, taking them very seriously, found them enormously therapeutic. They both heralded change and supported change. After a long period of succumbing to his demons, Glendinning's dreams enabled him to act to protect his self first within his visions and then in his waking life. His dreams scripted his return to preaching, and he followed this script. His experiences fulfill Christopher Bollas's evaluation of the dream as "the origin of vision, the place where the subject plays with objects, moving through potential patterns, setting up fields of imagined persons, places, selves and events—to be there as potential actuals for future use."[121]

While dreams often played a very significant role in helping an individual attain a new sense of his or her self, shared dreams were part of the life of both the new churches and the new state.[122] They helped develop common symbols, webs of meaning, expectations for the future, and common patterns for self-development. Elizabeth

Drinker, whose pacifist Quaker community had to prepare itself for trouble, recorded that "George Churchman was reading to night to us a Dream of a woman friend, he did not tell us her name, it was of scourgeings that the people were to experience." There is ample evidence that many others recounted dreams in church and family circles and at more public places. Dreams were entered as evidence in court trials and were published in newspapers. Dreams played an important role in letters, were preserved in diaries as well as the narratives, and were created for fictive autobiographies in early novels.[123] In *The Prodigal Daughter*, a very popular chapbook of the Revolutionary period, an angel appeared to a mother and father in their dreams and warned them that their daughter, angered over their refusal to fulfill her extravagant demands, was planning to poison them.[124] This dream warning led them to act in order to save their lives.

In the Revolutionary period dreams served as a conduit to bring radical wishes to consciousness. *A Dream to All Friends of Zion*, published anonymously in 1775, was a "night vision" that expressed the anger of the poor and gave God's approval to radical social change. The great were seen as using all the "good flour" for their own purposes, leaving only "the Gudgings and Bran for the poor Labourer. . . ." In heaven, the words "LIBERTY! LIBERTY! LIBERTY! . . . were written as in Sun Beams, by the inimitable Skill of Him whose Fingers wrote the Ten Commandments."[125]

The potential power of dreams as a catalyst for social change was widely recognized. Revolutionary magazines printed many fictive dreams, clearly hoping to establish the bona fides of the revolution as a God-sent event, and approval for a new future. At the same time, supporters of the new state, apparently fearing this uncontrolled source of legitimation, raised modern objections to reliance on dreams, much as the medieval church had. In 1776 *The Pennsylvania Magazine* printed a well-researched essay on the history of dream interpretation that expressed deep concern with current regard for the predictive nature of dreams:

> It appears strange that men of such improved understandings should be slaves to so ridiculous a fear. . . .There are still many who are frequently tormenting themselves and their neighbors with their ridiculous dreams, and their still more ridiculous interpretations of them.

This anonymous essay concluded that a dream should be regarded as *"a known liar, who, though he generally tells falsehoods, may sometimes, possibly, tell the truth."*[126]

FIGURE 8. Dream Scene, drawn by Isaiah Thomas, from a popular chapbook of the period, *The Prodigal Daughter*, Boston, 1772.

In colonial and early national America, dreams had proven useful to many people. Many were directed by dreams and visions to find wealth. In the record of treasure hunts kept by Silas Hamilton in Vermont in the 1780s, the location of nineteen out of thirty-two treasures had been established by dreams. African American William Grimes (born 1784) gave away lucky dream numbers to those who bought his lottery tickets, and claimed many had won with them.[127] Others felt they were warned of impending dangers, and of deaths. In an attempt to check their veracity, Benjamin Rush made a collection of dreams predicting death and found that only some were proved true.[128] Other individuals only recounted cases that seemed to fulfill such dreams. The Methodist missionary Francis Asbury (born 1745) reported:

Rachel Selby was a professor of religion: she dreamed that within three weeks she should die of the smallpox; she thought she had heard something strike on the top of the house like the nailing up

53

of a coffin; she took it as a warning, went to prayer, was exceedingly happy, sickened, and died triumphantly.[129]

In 1811 Fanny Newell (born 1793) dreamt that a healthy baby of a family she knew well was going to die. She told the parents, who were shocked, which aroused her own guilt feelings. Newell felt a certain satisfaction when the child sickened and died twelve days later, as she felt this death confirmed that God had sent her the message.[130]

Many individuals relied on dreams to guide them, in both their spiritual and daily lives.[131] Jabez Swann (born 1800) felt God "attacked" him with terrible dreams when he resisted becoming a preacher, and he quickly changed his decision.[132] A dream book ritual provided the basis for Lucy Breckinridge's search for surety about her future husband. She "roasted two eggs, then . . . took the yolks out and filled the whites with salt and ate them. I know I ate at least a tablespoonful of the horrid stuff," she reported. "It nauseated me terrible," but it had no positive result. Lucy had hoped to dream of the man who would be her husband handing her water. Her friend Sue, who joined her in the experiment, reported that she did indeed dream that a Mr. Richardson, who was a potential suitor, offered her a drink.[133] Many clearly still sought to rely on this 'liar's truth.'

While many people continued to use dreams in these traditional ways, work with dreams increasingly enabled people to recognize their enemy others and to make new submissions and commitments to change their selves. Commitments made in dreams led to life changes of great significance, especially when the dreamed-of alien other was targeted in waking life. Although racial and sexual projections became far more significant in this period, dreams also played a contradictory role and helped many to reclaim parts of their rejected selves that they had cut off and demonized. The ways in which whites, blacks, men, and women began to use their dreams to alter their selves are explored in the chapters that follow, each of which focuses on one central enemy other.

Chapter Two

Whites' Black Alien Other

> [S]elf must bee left behind, and . . . lett
> black negroes or pots alone.
> *Robert Pyle*[1]

I N 1698, Robert Pyle, a member of the Chester, Pennsylvania, Monthly Meeting of Friends "owned" that he was brought to recognize the iniquity of slave owning only after he had contemplated buying a slave, and that it was a dream that brought him to the recognition that he dare not do this:

> [A]s I was lieng upon my bed as in a sleep I saw myself and a friend going on a road, and by the roadside I saw a black pott. I took it up, the friend said give mee part, I said no, I went a little farther and I saw a great ladder standing exact upright, reaching up to heaven up which I must go to heaven with the pott in my hand intending to carry the black pott with me, but the ladder standing so upright, and seeing no man holding of it up, it seemed that it would fall upon mee; at which I steps down and laid the pot at the foot of the ladder, and said them that will take it might, for I found work enough for both hands to take hold of this lader, it being so exact upright; at the foot of this ladder I saw a man that gave those that goeth up this ladder sumthing to refresh them. At this sight I was concerned, and asked the man what this ladder was. Hee said the light of Christ Jesus, and whoever it bee that his faith bee strong in the Lord, God will uphold that it shall not fall; upon which I awoke.

Pyle awoke certain that the message of the dream was that "self must bee left behind, and to lett black negroes or pots alone." His expectation that he would fall indicated that he himself believed that God should punish him for his thoughts and plans, while the pot image suggests that Pyle had intended to buy a black *woman. The Universal Dream-Dictionary* did not contain a listing for "pot," but it did include "basin" and suggested that this image betokened a female servant, noting that to eat from a basin "shews you have a love to the servant-maid," and to be in a basin indicates the dreamer "shall have children by a servant-maid." The fact that Pyle felt he had been sent a message to let the pot "alone" may well indicate that he had planned not to let her alone but "to fall"—to have a sinful sexual relationship with a black chattel servant. After this dream experience with a black pot, Pyle quickly moved in the opposite direction from the one he had planned: rather than purchase a slave he formulated a plan for manumission that he pressed the Quakers to adopt.[2]

When white narrative writers began to record changes in self-perception they often did so by distinguishing the self from a black oppositional figure, a "not me" that encompassed all they overtly thought was negative. Positing the other in opposition can constrain and in a sense control the self-fashioner to become what the other is not. At the same time as the black alien other was seen in negative opposition to the self, however, it also had a profound affect on the self-development of the narrator as an attracting force. In most cases where such self-change took place it was within parameters set by a sect or church that legitimated and fostered aspects of the new self-construction. When no such authority was recognized, self-fashioning was far more likely to have been limited or to have involved the individual in inner contradictions and conflicts.

Among the group of white narrators who developed a black alien other, almost all had intimate long-term experiences with African Americans. Many were from slave-owning families, others were laborers who worked with the enslaved. These whites, who shared important life experiences with blacks, often exhibited a deep attraction to and a need for certain emotions, culture patterns, and ideas expressed by or projected upon African Americans, at the same time that they generally regarded Africans as dangerous and feared them. This process has long been understood as resulting in part from the projection of rejected aspects of an individual's self onto the other. These aspects are therefore potentially or actually in the self. There is much evidence to support this view, as many whites openly indicated that they were jealous or envious of what they saw as blacks' free and easy ways at the same time that they feared and opposed blacks as alien others.

While in many cases white introjection of African's emotions and values can be seen as a borrowing, which sometimes occurred without either party consciously recognizing what was happening, in other cases whites took by force, generally through psychological manipulation, that which had belonged to blacks through the process that Christopher Bollas has termed "extractive introjection."[3] Evidence provided by the life narratives suggests that a broad range of adaptive and extractive processes was underway and that white worldviews were undergoing change in part as a result of the introjection of Africans' values and emotions both by emulation and extraction.

In the period between 1740 and 1840 it was not rare for whites to have long-term intimacy with blacks, and many white lives were extraordinarily interconnected with those of blacks. Narrative re-countings of ordinary events indicate this. Whites and blacks often worked together on farms and on boats, hunting, drinking, eating, and dancing together, attending revivals and church meetings to-gether, and sleeping together. The evidence of normative, day-to-day, interaction, as well as special interracial events, is found throughout the narratives written by whites. On a slaving journey to Africa in 1766, and while in a cabin with an enslaved African, John Benson (born 1744) experienced a vision of travel to the other world that was an amalgam of African and Christian spirit journeys.[4] James Collins (born 1763) wrote that when in midlife he had a major health crises and leading white doctors failed to cure him, he turned to several different African healers but could not bring himself to follow their instructions. Nevertheless, he went to a third African healer, did what this man told him to do, and credited him with bringing about his recovery and changing his life.[5] William Glendinning, mentally ill from 1785 to 1790, described in passing how he was housed in a slave cabin and was apparently nursed back to health by blacks.[6] When Edward Donnelly (born 1775), living in Carlisle, Pennsylvania, described the day in 1808 that he murdered his wife he noted the mixed-race group with whom he had spent that fateful day (and pre-sumably many others): "My wife, my eldest son, 7 years old, a woman of color, and myself, went out to rake and bind rye in the field."[7] Brantly York, born into a very poor family in Virginia in 1805, revealed his daily contact with Africans when he recorded the future change predicted for him by a traveling fortune-teller: " 'Brantly, you will not always be in the field working with Negroes.' "[8] Samuel Green (born 1760) was a jailed criminal when he participated in plan-ning a breakout with a group of black men. When a black prisoner informed the authorities of their plans, Green murdered him and was executed for this act in 1822.[9] Andrew Oehler (born 1781) claimed to have taken an important part in the black revolution in Haiti, leading black troops.[10] James Pearse, born in the North in 1786, re-ported that he went South to find employment and became a planta-tion overseer working and living with the enslaved, with whom he became ever more violent.[11] Mary Arms (born 1836) who had been "put out" as a young child as a result of her mother's death, later turned to the black woman who had been enslaved in her mother's family for her memories of her mother's past and in the hope of getting the Bible her mother had left to the black servant.[12]

Many whites, deeply involved with blacks, began to record the psychological impact of Africans and African values on their selves. John Taylor (born 1752) described his life as largely spent with blacks, both his slaves and his parishioners. Blacks were central to his self-definition as well as the self-definitions of James Jenkins (born 1764), Henry Boehm (born 1775), and many others. Rachel O'Connor (born 1774) held that several of her slaves "were a part of myself." She wrote: "I cannot part from my Negroes. I have raised all but a few and I love them."[13] Africans brought about the dramatic conversions of Ann Page (in 1800), Sarah Hamilton (in about 1801), and many others.[14]

Many whites knew blacks as nurturers and lovers. When William Byrd II (born 1674) poetically fantasized a love life, he envisioned "tawny nymphs," and in his Commonplace Book he recorded that black progeny could be made white if a white man had a daughter by a black, and then incestuously mated with his own daughter by this union and later with his granddaughter. While he is not known to have had any long-term sexual relationship with an enslaved woman, his diary records indicated that he committed an occasional aggressive sexual act against women of color.[15] Over the next century myriad whites were emotionally and/or sexually involved with blacks: records of marriages, cohabiting, and rapes can be found in church and legal documents, letters, diaries, and narratives.[16] In the narrative of his life, Madison Jefferson recounted that his mother, Sally Hemings, told her children that Thomas Jefferson was their father. "My father" as he termed him in this document "was not in the habit of showing partiality or fatherly affection to us children." Jefferson never publicly acknowledged his paternity. Given the new DNA evidence of Thomas Jefferson's relationship to Sally Hemings' offspring and therefore with Sally, several of the statements Jefferson did make take on new meaning. Jefferson acknowledged, "All my wishes end where I hope my days will, at Monticello" and noted that "I am happy nowhere else and in no other society." Moreover, in May of 1824, when asked what he thought of "the character of the Negroes," Jefferson revealingly answered "they are possessed of the best hearts of any people in the world."[17]

Figure 9. William White turning to "Uncle Jack" for spiritual guidance, as pictured in White's *The African Preacher*, 1849.

Occasionally, whites did openly acknowledge both the relationships and the children they had with blacks, but the normative behavior of most whites who had intimate relations with blacks was to refrain from mentioning anything about them in public. Much of the knowledge we have of such relationships comes from evidence left by African Americans. From such evidence we know that Dr.

James Norcom secretly (but now infamously) pursued the enslaved Harriet Jacobs. Jacobs' writings describe his verbal attacks, which began when she was about fifteen (1828): "My master met me at every turn, reminding me that I belonged to him, and swearing by heaven and earth that he would compel me to submit to him."[18] She also reported that in the night Norcom's wife sat at her bedside in the hope that while dreaming she would utter some words that would reveal a sexual relationship with James Norcom. Clearly, both Mr. and Mrs. Norcom were emotionally involved with Harriet Jacobs, both often very angry at her and, in their different ways, determined to exert their power over her. As a result, both spent a good deal of time with her.

White Samuel Busey, born into a very different family constellation in Maryland in 1828, remembered growing up under the protection of an enslaved fictive family, black people who managed to give him nurturance that stood in stark contrast with the distant and oppressive behavior of his widowed white mother. In his life narrative Busey memorialized black uncles, aunts, siblings, and most particularly a fictive mother, Charity Martin. He held "her memory in grateful remembrance for her many sly favors and gentle kindnesses."[19]

Cassius Marcellus Clay, born in 1810 to "the largest slave-owner in the State" of Kentucky, grew up with George, an enslaved "playmate." Clay recounts that he challenged George, who was the stronger of the two, to a fight but set the fight up so that George was on a ledge and easily pushed down. Clay, for whom honor was always as important as physical prowess, was changed by this cowardly act. He felt that "[t]his fight with an African was one of those instrumental influences by which Deity shapes the ends of life." While Clay had seemed to win, he felt certain that "God decided in . . . [George's] favor," and that it was this act that led Clay to become a Garrisonian antislavery activist.[20]

Interactions with blacks were affecting many whites at a very deep level, as shown by both the attraction and the fear they expressed. Many whites both desired to emulate and at the same time were terrified of African Americans. Many experienced complicated combinations of these emotions. Some whites came to envision the devil as a black man: in 1746 Moravians at Nazareth, Pennsylvania, reported that "a young German girl" who was "dreaming and speaking about the devil . . . describes him to the other children as a black man, who is going to burn them unless they love the savior."[21] Robert Bailey (born 1773) grew up with his mother warning him that if he stole, lied, or swore "there was a great black ugly clubfooted man called the Devil that would take me and all bad boys and put them in hell, and burn them up."[22] A twelve-year-old southern girl called out while she slept "that there was a black man coming to kill her." The following day she had a vision of a man in white who informed her that "the black man she saw was the devil."[23] Others envisioned black spirits protecting them: Theophilus Gates (born 1786) believed that when he was fifteen he was warned against immoral behavior by the figure of a black man that only he could see. When he was nineteen a similar figure, serving as the messenger of God who was sitting in judgment, appeared to him in a crucial dream of heaven.[24] While some were making the rejection of the alien-otherness of Africans the center of their lives, Gates and others came to see their attitudes toward Africans as a test of their own worthiness of God's love.[25] In both cases interaction with African Americans, involving both projection and introjection, played a very significant role in the development of the individuals involved. In many cases, perhaps in most, the process of setting the self against a not-me involved a triangulation of interrelationships: whites often used blacks to help establish their relationships with other whites, much as men often made use of women to establish their relationships to other men. White men often used black women to establish their power over black men as well as over white women.[26]

The black alien other thus emerges as extraordinarily significant in the development of white selves between 1740 and 1840. In the figures considered here there was a reverse progression in their self-fashioning from the 1740s to 1840:

1. *Radical self-fashioning by means of coming to see the black as an (almost) equal other.* This was exhibited in the remarkably full self-refashioning of a cohort born long before the Revolution, John Woolman (born 1720), Freeborn Garrettson (born 1752), and Sarah Hamilton (born 1754), and it was contingent upon their taking responsibility for their own acts and their revolutionary recognition of blacks' humanity.

2. *Post-Revolutionary dramatic narrators who partially realized that they were dependent on blacks for crucial aspects of their selves but were determined to restrengthen hierarchies and "keep blacks in their place."* The experiences of this group span a long period, from about 1785 to 1820, and are manifested in the narratives of John Taylor (born 1752), James Jenkins (born 1764), and many others who were dependent on blacks but repressed this recognition as they were determined to see blacks as dependent upon themselves.

3. *Conflicted self-fashioning in which whites were more actively demeaning blacks to achieve a sense of unity and superiority and were not overtly conscious of the fact that they were dependent on*

them for crucial emotions and values. This can be found in experiences dating from 1810 to 1840. This conflicted interaction involving hatred and attraction was crucial to the self-view of dependent white workingmen like William Otter (born 1787), who desperately sought independence in the economically and socially unstable 1820s and 1830s.

RADICAL SELF-FASHIONING: BY MEANS OF COMING TO SEE THE BLACK AS AN (ALMOST) EQUAL OTHER

The complicated use of blacks to cement relationships between whites can be found in the history of the Quakers, the first organized actors on the antislavery scene. The Society of Friends, or the Quakers, had begun their self-definition in the 1640s by positioning themselves in opposition to other Englishmen. They had begun as *not* Anglicans, rejecting much that was central to that church. But they had also defined themselves in opposition to much that was central to English culture as a whole. They did not accept traditional gender roles (fostering much that was seen as female in their males, and male in their females). They rejected traditional deference to authority. To emphasize this (and mark themselves off from the generality) they rejected traditional speech patterns that expressed deference and traditional "loose talk" in general, valuing silence. They rejected as well traditional concern with establishing inequality through dress, again making themselves other in a very obvious fashion by wearing uniform and distinctively plain clothing. All of these patterns set themselves off as not that which they would not be.

By the mid-eighteenth century Quakers in Pennsylvania, New Jersey, and Rhode Island, having by and large succeeded both economically and politically, were no longer in opposition to common norms; rather, they were living by their own evolving patterns, which had become close to those of the others around them. When a small group sought to return the community to a path that would set them apart from the world, they again sought a core set of rejections to establish that which they would not be. In the context of the different society they now lived in the key marker chosen was that they would not be slave owners. This value grew in response to widespread Quaker slave-owning and even wider involvement in the slave-based economies that surrounded them, which had led Quakers as well to be both attracted to and to reject African Americans.[27]

George Fox, the founding father of the Society, had come into a troubling confrontation with the reality of the lives of the enslaved in his visits to the West Indies and the American South in 1671–1673. As a result of these visits Fox came to advocate the manumission of slaves "after a reasonable Service," but he did not enjoin manumission upon Quakers.[28] As their community grew and prospered in the West Indies and in the mainland colonies, Quakers increasingly became owners of slaves and/or traders with slave owners. Given their custom of intense self-analysis, slave ownership by members of the Society of Friends played a very significant role in both their individual and collective development, and in bringing them to oppose slavery.[29] The journals of Friends who became antislavery advocates often reveal their troubled involvement with slaves. Their reactions generally indicated guilt about their previous behavior and involved a deep level of attraction to and rejection of Africans that affected both their inner and outer selves. Dreaming often brought about a dramatic new awareness of the meaning of their acts to the dreamers, as it had for Robert Pyle.

Most Quakers were, however, becoming ever more successful traders and thereby ever more deeply involved in the institution of slavery even when they did not own slaves. Ralph Sandiford was another successful Quaker merchant who at first did not deeply consider the evils of the system or seem conscious of his own role in it. A trip he took to the West Indies and South Carolina stimulated a change in his awareness; his personal observation of the cruelties endured by the enslaved led him to turn down a business venture directly based on slave ownership. Over time he came to realize that all his trading ventures were deeply dependent on slavery. By 1729 he reported that a "sense" of the sin of slavery "burdened my Life Night and Day," leaving him feeling as if he was "under a mountain." He decided to immediately publish an attack on slaveholding, and as he did not wait for a Quaker editorial committee to approve his writings, he was expelled.[30]

Quaker Benjamin Lay experienced a similar change in consciousness, although he only became fully aware of his complicity after having lived and worked in the West Indies for some time. Lay and his wife were, for a long period, shopkeepers in Barbados, where "the poor Blacks would come to our shop and Store, hunger-starv'd, almost ready to perish with Hunger and Sickness." He rhetorically asked, "Shall I ever forget them?" It is clear he could not, nor could he forget his wife's reaction, meant to help but clearly reeking in his own recollection. He wrote that his "tender-hearted" wife Sarah would be very often giving them something or other; stinking Biscuits which sometimes we had in abundance, bitten by the Cockroaches; or rotten Cheese, stinking Meat, decayed Fish which we had plenty of in that hot Country."

Lay chose to move to Philadelphia, where he became a radical antislavery activist. He would not visit with any slave-owning family, and he spoke out against slave owning on every possible occasion. Lay once absconded with a six-year-old white boy, hiding him for a day in order to bring home the effects of man stealing to white slave owners. When he returned the child to his despairing parents he told them, "You may now conceive of the sorrow you inflict upon the parents of the negroe girl you hold in slavery, for she was torn from them by avarice." Lay, who was a dwarf, and as a result was no doubt often made to feel an outsider, wanted to see himself as one with the enslaved. He claimed that "they seemed to love and admire us [Lay and his wife], we being pretty much alike in Stature and otherways." It was his own coreligionists that he came to see as other, charging them with apostasy. In 1738, one year after he published his lengthy attack on all slaveholders, the Friends disowned him, too.[31]

John Woolman (born 1720), one of the best known of the Quaker antislavery activists, can perhaps be viewed as *the* archetypal figure of a moral antislavery activist in the second half of the eighteenth century. His antislavery pamphlets of 1754 and 1762, approved by the Society's committees, played a significant role in moving the Friends to clean their own house of slave owning, an act that reverberated into the whole of the Western world. Woolman nevertheless mounted a major attack on himself that was centrally concerned with the morality of his relations to blacks. His alien other was tied to the enslaver within and yet also (in part through projection, in part through extraction) connected to the black without. It was the ambiguous ground that reversed color, much as he chose to substitute white clothing for the proper Quaker drab so that he would not use dye produced by slaves. Although he accepted that whiteness stood for purity and knew that others took it as a badge of his antislavery stand, he recognized that it did not cover his own impurity but rather constantly reminded him of it. Woolman's narrative, and the dreams he included in it, allow us to know for a certainty that personal guilt and the introjection of aspects of blacks into his own self played a very significant role in changing his life.[32]

Woolman's narrative does not mention Africans in his household. Other Quakers, living with enslaved servants, have left evidence of experiences that help explain their relationships to African Americans. For example, Quaker Warner Mifflin recorded that a few words said to him by an African owned by his family were the catalyst for a long-term process of change. This event occurred in 1759, when he was fourteen years old:

> Being in the Field with my Father's Slaves, a young Man among them questioned me *"Whether I thought it could be right that they should be toiling to raise me, and I sent to school, and by and by their children must do so for mine also?"*

Mifflin records that he was deeply shaken by this question. His parents owned a large number of slaves, and he no doubt had relationships with African Americans both young and old, yet this was the first time that he consciously thought about what their future held and what his role in it might be. This comment reframed his reality. He decided he would never own slaves. However, as he continued his comfortable life as a plantation owner's son, he slipped into the role of plantation owner himself: at his marriage, he was given land and slaves and fooled himself into thinking that the enslaved chose to be with him. He built his life around them, "until at length I became almost persuaded I could not do without them." It was only when he began raising a family of his own that the words that had shaken him in his youth, no doubt reinforced by the antislavery Truth being circulated by Woolman, Churchman, Evans, and others, came to dominate his thoughts again. In 1774 and 1775, in his own private revolutionary act, he freed both the slaves that had been given him by his wife's family at his wedding and those he had regarded as "volunteers" from his father's plantation, and he began to make restitution to them for their labor. Mifflin had repressed both his concern for the enslaved and his own guilt, and he had to learn to reown these emotions.[33]

Was there anything comparable to Mifflin's experience in the life of John Woolman? Woolman certainly had contact with blacks and with slave owners. There were slaveholders in his mother's family, and there is evidence that a black woman, Negro Maria, worked for the Woolman family. At some point she may have been the slave of someone in the wider family. When she died in 1760 she was a free woman, and John Woolman was the executor of her estate, although he never mentioned her in his narrative.[34] In his life narrative Woolman did write of his guilt for once having written a bill of sale transferring the ownership of a "Negro women" from one Quaker elder to another and of the many subsequent occasions when he refused to write such documents and thereby caused others to give thought to their behavior. He left the strong impression that writing this bill of sale was his most significant sin in relation to the enslaved.[35] Woolman, however, actually committed what he regarded as a far more damaging act that he at the same time revealed and yet hid the full significance of. He referred to it only long after it had occurred, when he was about to try to make restitution for it, and he shielded himself from a more comprehensive revelation of his reaction to it by parceling out the description of the affects of this act, noting some in proper order and some as reflections on the past. Taken together, the evidence signals a crisis of major proportions.

When he came to write about this act, Woolman described it as having occurred "in the time of my youth" and confessed that he and another Friend, serving as executors of the will of a deceased Quaker, had "once sold a Negro lad till he might attain the age of thirty years," nine years longer than a white youth would have been indentured.[36] Woolman's personal record, his "Book of Executorship," reveals that it was in 1753 that he and Henry F. settled the estate of Quaker Thomas Shinns and wrote "Indentures binding Gamaliel and Aquilla to trades" until the age of thirty.[37] (It is probable that one of these young men was either freed or dead by the time Woolman wrote about the incident, as he mentions only one "lad.") When Woolman sold these indentures in 1753, he was thirty-three years old, no longer a youth even by contemporary standards, which sometimes extended the period of "youth" to thirty.[38]

Woolman never forgot this act, which he had carried out long after he had begun to write about the evils of slaveholding, although it was only in the following year, 1754, that his first essay on enslavement, written much earlier, was published. The more he thought of slavery, the more he came to believe it necessary to exercise "pure righteousness" toward the Negroes, and the more he came to see his own behavior as sinful.[39]

Woolman had a constant reminder of this sin in his life. In June of 1769 he noted in his journal that one of these young men, who was "upward of twenty-four years of age and now a servant, . . . frequently attends the meeting I belong to sitting in the uppermost seat." Woolman revealed that he sat at these meetings (with Gamaliel or Aquilla above him) "with abasement of Heart."[40]

Woolman's guilt led him to try to make a direct repayment for his sin. Since he and his coexecutor had together "sold this lad nine years longer than is common for our own children to serve, so I should now offer a part of my substance to redeem the last half of that nine years." Assuming half the guilt, Woolman signed a bond to pay the owner for half the extra term, so that Gamaliel or Aquilla might go free by 1771 at twenty-five and a half.[41] Woolman did not really let himself off the hook so easily, however. He knew "that a heavy account lies against us . . . for oppressions committed against people who did not injure us."[42] He turned his heavy, unpaid account into a new commitment. In order to confront the issues in starker terms, he chose to journey to centers of slaveholding in the South as well as to the major slave-trading ports in Perth Amboy, New Jersey, and Newport, Rhode Island. In these places he observed and talked with the enslaved, and after 1766 he traveled by foot "that by so traveling I might have a more lively feeling of the condition of the oppressed slaves." He voiced his "scruples" about slavery in talks with slave owners and wrote a series of condemnations of slaveholding.[43]

Woolman became one of the central figures in the Quaker movement to end Quaker slaveholding and to influence the wider public. His two essays on slaveholding were circulated to virtually every Quaker meeting in America and England and reached a much wider audience as well. He made his concern with slavery central to his extensive travels: both his speaking and his silences were directed toward bringing about change in this regard.[44] However, the Quaker decision to exclude all Friends who did not manumit their slaves did not come until four years after his death in 1772. As his dreams inform us, he went to his death believing he had not done enough.

John Woolman would not have thought of himself as a Joseph or a Daniel, as others in this period did, but dreams were important in his life and in his written narrative. He recorded ten dreams in his spiritual journal: seven of his own and three that others told him. They span his spiritual life, the first remembered from his first awakening at age nine, and the last perhaps a leave-taking from his mother, before his own death. Woolman pondered their meaning and left us some indication of his dream work. He clearly used his dreams to help him become a self-fashioner.[45]

The one dream Woolman recorded from childhood, which he dated 1729, suggests that he was undergoing radical change. Theories of personal growth often posit a metaphorical "door or threshold through which the stream of consciousness must pass when it 'leaves' one phase behind and 'enters' another phase."[46] Woolman actually saw himself in the doorway or limen of his father's house (on the threshold of change) observing awe-inspiring events outside.[47]

In this dream Woolman pictured himself as a silent observer, the stance that he was to take in most of his recorded dreams. In this first report, however, unlike most of those to follow, he was open to see beauty and awesome change and to place himself on the verge of moving out of his father's orbit, perhaps into the dangerous arena of

Figure 10. Dream ladders drawn by John Woolman in his Journal, April 1754.

his heavenly father. His dream posited masculine and feminine globes moving in an east-west trajectory, while the "sun worm," or son, was ready to take his own path, choosing to move resolutely from north to south, avoiding competition with them. Multiple states of being are apparent in this dream, which strongly suggests an individuating self.[48]

Woolman did not report another dream until April 1754, a year after his indenturing of Gamaliel and Aquilla. In his narrative this second dream report is preceded and followed by important references to slavery: his refusal to write a Friend's will bequeathing slaves and his decision to publish his first antislavery tract, suggesting that he associated this dream, too, with slavery. The dream, however, seems to be about other affairs and has been seen as a prescient comment on the colonial warfare of that year.[49] Soldiers, preparations for war, and others' scoffing at the resigned position taken by Woolman are all in this dream, as are red streams. In fact, these streams were the dominant image of this dream and were so important to Woolman that he made a drawing of them—a singular act.[50] There are no other drawings in his journal. Woolman reported:

> I sat down alone by a window, and looking out I saw in the south three great red streams standing at equal distance from each other, the bottom of which appeared to stand on the earth and the top to reach above the region of the clouds. Across those three streams

went less ones, and from each end of such small stream others extended in regular lines to the earth, all red and appeared to extend through the whole southern firmament.[51]

Woolman associated the color red with the blood of the enslaved, as he explained in relation to a dream entrusted to him by a dying Friend, Peter Harvey, in 1771. Harvey (and Woolman) understood "that . . . the pool of blood" in Harvey's dream "represented the state of those hardhearted men through whose means much blood is shed in Africa and many lives destroyed through insupportable stench and other hardships in crossing the sea, and through extreme oppression bring many slaves to an untimely end." Woolman thought that red also betokened the natural will, which he believed must be crucified. He associated it with Esau, who was "a child red all over," and with the red heifer that was to be slain for purification.

In his own dream of 1754 Woolman may have conflated the Seven Years War with his own war against slavery, and the blood of soldiers with the blood of slaves, which filled his dream screen and "the southern firmament."[52] Woolman's acts regarding the black youths he had just sold no doubt had a deep impact on his thinking at this time, but he was not alone in associating the guilt and blood of this war with the guilt and blood arising from slave owning: Quaker John Churchman openly voiced the conviction that the Seven Years War was a just punishment for the sin of man stealing. When, that same year, Churchman dreamed of a rainbow-colored light and a huge angel whose skin was the color of an Indian's, he interpreted this to mean that God considered "that all colours were equal," a commentary on whites' relationship to both Indians and blacks.[53]

After a lifetime of concern with slavery, several of Woolman's dreams directly confronted the issues raised by his behavior and attitudes toward blacks. In these dreams Woolman can be seen to have attacked parts of his inner self, the unnamed blackness within. One of his most moving dreams revealed the nature and depth of his conflict:

> On the night between the 28th and 29th, 5th month, 1770, I dreamed a man had been hunting and brought a living creature to Mount Holly of a mixed breed, part fox and part cat. It appeared active in various motions, especially with its claws and teeth. I beheld and lo! many people gathering in the house where it was talked one to another, and after some time I perceived by their talk that an old Negro man was just now dead, and that his death was on this wise; They wanted flesh to feed this creature, and they

wanted to be quit of the expense of keeping a man who through great age was unable to labour; so raising a long ladder against the house, they hanged the old man.

One woman spake lightly of it and signified she was sitting at the tea table when they hung him up, and though neither she nor any present said anything against their proceedings, yet she said at the sight of the old man a dying, she could not go on with tea drinking.

I stood silent all this time and was filled with extreme sorrow at so horrible an action and now began to lament bitterly, like as some lament at the decease of a friend, at which lamentation some smiled, but none mourned with me.

One man spake in justification of what was done and said the flesh of the old Negro was wanted, not only that this creature might have plenty, but some other creatures also wanted his flesh, which I apprehended from what he said were some hounds kept for hunting. I felt matter on my mind and would have spake to the man, but utterance was taken from me, and I could not speak to him. And being in great distress I continued wailing till I began to wake, and opening my eyes I perceived it was morning.[54]

This dream can be seen as a reflection of the troubled life-space Woolman was still living in, revealing aspects that he did not discuss in any other way in his narrative. The associations he gave and the symbols he explicated provide a good "feeling sense," as Friends said, of what it might have meant to him. In the margin of this manuscript he wrote, "A fox is cunning; a cat is often idle; hunting represents vain delights; tea drinking with which there is sugar points out the slavery of the Negroes, with which many are oppressed to the shortening of their days." Woolman's limited gloss, when applied to the dream, suggests far more. The dream report notes "A man had been hunting," which Woolman associated with "vain delights," and the catch, which he brought to the town where Woolman actually lived, was a "a living creature." Slave catchers generally caught living creatures. The creature caught in the dream was described as unnatural, half cat/half fox, suggesting that it betokened a mixed race figure. (As the most important Quaker founder was George Fox, the fact that the creature was part fox might suggest that one parent was Quaker, or that the creature's values were not fully Quaker.) Woolman's gloss tells us the creature was lazy but cunning, and the dream warned that it was dangerous, with sharp "claws and teeth". *The Universal Dream-Dictionary*, citing Artemidorus in both cases, saw the cat as "an adulterer or harlot" and the fox as sometimes betokening "an enemy . . . , and most often, deceit by a women."[55]

Whites often regarded mixed-race and black individuals as both lazy and dangerous. Their bodily characteristics were seen as indicating these traits. In the "Register of Free Negroes" kept in York County, Virginia, 1798–1831, which included brief physical descriptions, two-thirds were of mixed race, and many of these people were described as having "fierce black eyes." In his description of "The Negro Character" (published in 1701), John Saffin wrote, "He that exasperates them, soon espies/ Mischief and Murder in their very eyes." A vivid report from 1820 in a Massachusetts life narrative told of the nighttime appearance of a figure with "sable countenance" and frightening "fiery eyes" that the visionary remained in terror of.[56] Woolman's gloss on his own dream suggests that he too was frightened. It is likely that it was his own self that frightened him. He may well have feared that he too wanted to take "vain delights" as the hunter had. In his dream report, Woolman twice repeated that the persecutors "wanted flesh" and noted that the "mixed breed" was "active in various motions," all of which indicate that he feared that these "vain delights" involved sex with the other.

Ladders appear in many recorded dreams, from Jacob's through Woolman's, and the image has stimulated extensive discussion. Jewish commentary has seen it as a symbol of Jacob himself, being trampled on and held up by angels. Christians have seen it as the tree of life, as the cross of Jesus, as well as Jesus himself. The ladder gives itself to standing for anything that rises and falls. Sigmund Freud saw ladders as representing the sex act. James Fernandez has suggested that "ladders are good to think with. . . . The ladder has polarity, a satisfying binary quality. It has mediation. And best of all it has . . . measurement along an equally divided continuum." Ladders appear in many published woodcuts from the colonial period: they were often shown as leaning against the gallows on which a criminal was to be hanged, yet a ladder was often seen as a symbolic measure of virtue.[57]

Woolman was fairly certain to have been aware of Quaker Robert Pyle's dream report of his fear of ascending a ladder to heaven while he was carrying a "black pot," which Pyle believed betokened an enslaved black.[58] Woolman himself drew the blood red streams he had seen in the sky much like ladders. It is also likely that Woolman associated a ladder with the particular African blocking his own route to heaven: the black servant Woolman had indentured sat "in the uppermost seat" of his meeting house, and he probably had to climb a ladderlike stairway to reach it. In Woolman's dream the fact that the body to be eaten was hung on a ladder was a blatant statement that it blocked the guilty from heaven.[59]

Figure 11. The association of ladders and hangings is illustrated in "Elhanen Winchester's Execution Hymn," by Levi Ames, c. 1773.

When the whites murdered the old black man in Woolman's dream report, it was not because he was dangerous but because he was weak and unproductive, and because his body was wanted for food. As an executor of a will, Woolman had sold a black child to make money for a white family; he too had been an executor of the weak.

In his dream Woolman "stood silent all the time." He was a silent witness to crimes against humanity, but he was also silent about his own crime in indenturing two blacks. Silence was central to Quakers, and Woolman had often used silence as a tool, sitting quietly with slave-owning Quakers who had to do inner battle with his unspoken criticism. However, this dream is evidence that he was deeply ambivalent about silence. While he had put off publishing his first work on slavery for some years until he could gain the Quaker publishing committee's approval, he knew that Ralph Sandiford and Benjamin Lay had not waited for approval, nor had they been careful in what they wrote. They had harshly criticized Quaker slaveholding and had been willing to risk (and did incur) punishment. His dream suggests that while he ostensibly accepted that he should be silent and patient, he had a deep need to cry out and to act. His dream indicates that he was in psychic pain over his own silence.

The cannibalism of the whites in his dream caused Woolman to break his silence. He woke screaming or wailing, "like as some lament at the decease of a friend." Part of his own self, possibly a part that Africans had enriched, was being killed. He was the Friend who was dying, but he was also the executioner, participating through his silent presence in the preparation of a human body for eating. This planned act of cannibalism was the key image in this dream. It is likely some event of the previous day, a "day residue," had sparked this image, as, in the morning, when Woolman shared this dream with his close friend Thomas Middleton, Middleton in turn told him that he too had dreamed of black human flesh that was to be eaten. Middleton had envisioned an old smokehouse on his plantation (which Woolman was visiting) filled with tainted bacon (which belonged to people "now living") as well as "one whole creature . . . and though it had some resemblance of bacon, yet it appeared to stand upon its feet, and there was in it some resemblance of a living creature."[60] Woolman and Middleton recognized that slavery was the central theme of both their dreams, and no doubt felt that the Inner Light in each of them had purposefully brought them both to see these painful images on the same night in order that they might help each other move towards the Truth.

George Fox had warned of meaningless and evil dreams, but he had accepted that dreams from God were essentially nonverbal enactments, "signs and wonders . . . from the Lord of hosts" (Isaiah 8.18). The early Friends had performed signs publicly, such as going naked to signify that Christians were " 'not being clothed with the spirit of the Lord,' " but they had changed their behavior in the 1670s when leading Quakers decided they should turn away from such provocative enactments.[61] The signs and portents in dreams, however, continued to be taken very seriously. If they were believed to be prophetic signs, they were now seen as demanding acts in life, rather than enactments of their imagery. What acts in life did this dream demand of Woolman? Woolman responded by voicing a plea to be "witnessed against": in "the words of that righteous judge in Israel [Samuel]: 'Behold here I am; witness against me before the Lord and before his anointed. . . . whom have I oppressed?' "[62] Even though he had displaced his guilt onto others in the dream, the dream enabled Woolman to accuse himself.

Artemidorus had claimed that he had "learned from experience that the best and most auspicious dream by far is the one in which a person eats human flesh." He saw such eating as betokening mutual assistance or the "partaking of one another." Perhaps Woolman's dream can be understood as expressing his tacit knowledge that whites were partaking of blacks' vital spirits, but Woolman clearly did not read his dream in this positive fashion, and it is likely he would have thought such an interpretation from the Evil one.[63]

Woolman's next dream report, from mid-1770, which can be seen as part of a series about the enslaved, indicates development in the way he dealt with his problems and with himself.

> In a time of sickness . . . I was brought so near the gates of death that I forgot my name. Being then desirous to know who I was, I saw a mass of matter of a dull gloomy colour, between the south and the east, and was informed that this mass was human beings in as great misery as they could be and live, and that I was mixed in with them and henceforth might not consider myself as a distinct or separate being. In this state I remained several hours. I then heard a soft, melodious voice, more pure and harmonious than any voice I had heard with my ears before, and I believed it was the voice of an angel who spake to other angels. The words were, *"John Woolman is dead."* I soon remembered that I once was John Woolman, and being assured that I was alive in the body, I greatly wondered what that heavenly voice could mean. I believed beyond doubting that it was the voice of an holy angel, but as yet it was a mystery to me.
>
> I was then carried in spirit to the mines, where poor oppressed people were digging rich treasures for those called Christians, and heard them blaspheme the name of Christ, at which I was grieved, for his name to me was precious. Then I was informed that these heathens were told that those who oppressed them were the followers of Christ, and they said amongst themselves: "If Christ directed them to use us in this sort, then Christ is a cruel tyrant."[64]

In this report Woolman, who was almost always a silent observer in his dreams, and who, in his previous dream report, had become a tormented and immobilized observer, became a member of a social group for the very first time.[65] *His social group was a dull mass of miserable, oppressed heathen slaves.* While Woolman shared in their labor, he was still separated from them (or superior to them) insofar as he recognized that he was a Christian and he did not accept their harsh judgment of Christ. When he awoke, he understood the dream to be about enslaved Africans, and that the Truth he had been shown was that he must view himself as one with them, but he did not know how to interpret the angel's voice that had proclaimed, "John Woolman is dead."[66]

After he had this dream, Woolman spent a year in what today would likely be judged a severe depression. He did not talk at meetings during this year but cried frequently. He found that his "mind . . . [was] very often in company with the oppressed slaves."[67] Neither

Woolman nor his colleagues saw this as a sign of psychological illness. In fact, Woolman welcomed this state as a gift from God. He considered it a fulfillment of his dream's prophetic message.

Woolman also came to closure in relation to the statement about his own death, concluding, joyfully, that it signified the death of his own will and his readiness to do Christ's will. He did not consciously know that this image was borrowed from the African tradition, although in his dream life he had seen that he was a part of this mass. In this dream, he had undergone part of an African American conversion, joining the blacks who heard themselves called by name and witnessed their own death. In the black conversion process, individuals heard themselves called by their private names—Mary, John, or Moses—and then they described how God "struck them dead." In their vision travels they then went to the brink of hell, where they often had a breakthrough recognition of the twofold nature of the soul, very African in its character. They saw "a man in a man," or "a little me inside me," recognizing that an eternal spirit had existed before the life of the person and would continue after death. For many African Americans this was a crucial act of integration, bringing the African spirit into the Christian cosmos and helping African Americans reach a spiritual wholeness and an integral self.[68]

One white man from this cohort, Joseph Thomas, reported that when he was converted at a great revival meeting in Virginia in 1806, he dreamed that the prophet Isaiah gave him "a piece of wood near the size and shape of a small man, and it was apparently deeply stained all over with blood, and said 'you have a long distance to travel, . . . and you must carry this all the way.' "[69] Thomas seems to have envisioned an African little me being put into him.

Woolman did not experience a separable soul, but he had, without his knowledge, absorbed the black understanding of spiritual death. He was called by his name and had died. He had traveled to an underworld filled with blacks, and he came back to life. This dream journey was extremely significant. It prepared him spiritually for an epiphany of redemption, which, as many other whites had, he experienced separately, although close in time to this dream. He reported that he soon "saw . . . the seventh seal . . . opened" and was enjoined "to trumpet." For the first time he was commanded to make a joyful noise. He was to trumpet the news that the opening of the seventh seal brought an invitation to a "safe . . . inwardly quiet" habitation. This was both a new means and a new end for Woolman.[70]

It would appear that Woolman achieved a new sense of assurance with this last vision, but given who he was he could not absorb African American techniques for achieving joy. While he had seen himself in the mines with blacks and was commanded to make a joyful noise, he could not envision himself at a shout, or as one of the heavenly choir. The closest he came to pleasure in a dream was when he later pictured himself going to England and favorably compared his understanding to that of George Fox, as "he saw the different states of the people as clear as ever he had seen flowers in a garden." He didn't allow himself much time in this garden, however. Perhaps he saw it as too prideful on his part to think he could rival Fox and judge people's inner states. In his dream he prophetically saw that he stopped suddenly and broke into tears. Woolman did embark on a trip to England after this dream, and he died during it.[71]

Woolman recorded only one dream in which he interacted with other individuals. His report from July 26, 1764, recounted a dream of a peace mission to Indians, paralleling the dangerous journey he had actually taken in 1763. This dream is shockingly different from all his other recorded dreams: in this dream he had two guides (one an armed trickster), he talked with people, and he accepted their advice. He was also physically active, shaking hands and moving from one group to another. He had a clear goal—to make peace—and was willing to learn about and work with other people in order to carry it out. The dream may have reflected the inner peace with which Woolman could approach Indian-white relations, even when they were dangerous, in contrast to his inner guilt, which immobilized him in dreams about blacks. While the dream ended before he could actually begin his peace negotiations, he was pursuing a solution to a problem and was planning to speak, rather than remain silent as he always had previously. He had also been given an invitation to a meal, the only time this simple and most basic social exchange was mentioned in all his dreams.[72]

Woolman looked to the time "when our minds are thoroughly divested of all prejudice in relation to the difference of colour, and the love of Christ in which there is no partiality prevails upon us."[73] It is unlikely that even Woolman could have achieved this state, but what did happen to him was extraordinary. Woolman worked with and through his guilt, fear, and alienation of the black other and, through empathy, placed himself with the enslaved blacks. He was in the mines in his mind, and mourned. He used this painful empathy to make himself into "a major instrument of the transformation" of modern values, leading to the rejection of slavery.[74] In the process he moved from being a tormented and immobilized observer to being a seer in a beautiful garden of souls. He had become a self-transformer of major proportions.

Woolman and the other eighteenth-century Friends who grew up before the 1770s lived with slave-owning Quakers and often with the enslaved. A number of his contemporaries have left narratives of the trials that they experienced in regard to slave owning and the treatment of Africans. As with John Woolman, the development of their selves was deeply tied to their development of private and public positions on slavery. They all knew Woolman and each other, and they often traveled and worked together. John Churchman (1705–1775), John Woolman (1720–1772), Joshua Evans (1731–1798), and Warmer Mifflin (1745–1798), although spanning almost a century between them, shared a worldview and lived through many historical experiences together. They experienced the increased prosperity of Quakers, obviously related to slavery, as well as the affect of Africans' bearing the burdens imposed upon them by Christians. Their joint perception of the reality was much like Woolman's dream. It is not surprising that they all experienced guilt over their responsibility for Quakers' treatment of the enslaved as well as deep emotional attachments to and crucial sharing of values, emotions, and behavior with Africans. Joshua Evans in a sense spoke for all in this group when he wrote that he held himself guilty for long having been willing to "wink" at the conditions under which the enslaved lived. As his awareness changed he found himself tormented: "It seemed as if the cries of the slaves in the West-India islands reached my ears both day and night." In 1761 Evans began "to plead" with his fellow Quakers to give "liberty to the black people" they held in bondage. He too stopped using goods "procured through their labour." He too journeyed South to work with slaves and slave owners. He came to "believe the land mourns on account of the barbarous and cruel usage of the poor slaves," a view Woolman, Churchman, and Mifflin shared.[75]

Woolman, Churchman, and Evans, as well as Anthony Benezet and others not discussed here, had become both self-transformers and social transformers. They were truly responsible for leading the Quakers to dismiss slave owners from their midst. Quakers born after the Society had excluded slave owners were less likely to have intimate personal experiences with Africans and less likely to feel the burning need to change the social fabric in this regard. This personal change in Quakers' lives meant that after the Revolution young Quakers were less likely to develop a love/hate relationship with an internalized black other and less likely to feel guilty about their own feelings and behavior toward blacks. These factors played a significant role in reducing the number of Quakers who chose to dedicate their lives to this project in the nineteenth century, although a minority still did and made their positions known through their work with black people. Most Friends stepped back from political involvement with the antislavery movement and gave Quakers who continued to devote their lives to this cause a great deal of difficulty, ostensibly because they feared their actions would lead to violence.[76]

By the end of the 1770s individuals in other churches, particularly the Baptists and the Methodists, were facing the dilemma of slaveholding in their midst. In the decade before the Revolution, the whole of white society became far more conscious of blacks' own demands for freedom, especially the vocal demands of black Baptists and black Methodists. As many more blacks left slavery or attempted to, often in violent ways, whites, especially Baptists and Methodists, but Congregationalists and Presbyterians as well, became increasingly concerned about black freedom.[77]

A large number of the white individuals in these churches who became concerned about slavery at the time of the Revolution had also been slave owners at some point in their lives. For example, both Sarah Osborn and her Congregational minister, Samuel Hopkins (who lived in the important slave-trading community of Newport, Rhode Island), came to see slaveholding as the central sin of Americans and the cause of their suffering in the Revolutionary War, and both became committed to changing that reality. Osborn was instrumental in converting a large number of African Americans through a very emotional revival that took place in her home. During 1766 and 1767 one hundred blacks initiated and actively participated in this extraordinary awakening, which reverberated from the black "class" to white people. Hopkins, in part as a result of Osborn's influence, became a very vocal antislavery activist. Both had been slave owners.[78]

Of course, most slave owners at the time of the Revolution did not come to advocate manumission, but many of those who hoped that the institution could be preserved also had complex love/hate relationships with blacks, and significant aspects of their selves were tied to their introjection of African values. Landon Carter, for example, built his sense of self around his role as controller, in so far as he was able, of both blacks and whites. When Moses and six other enslaved African Americans took their freedom in July of 1776, he dreamed that while on their own they were reduced to uncivilized behavior, and that they returned and pleaded with him to protect them:

> July 25, 1776. A strange dream this day about these runaway people. One of them I dreamed awakened me; and appeared most wretchedly meager and wan. He told me of their great sorrow, that

all of them had been wounded by the minutemen, had hid themselves in a cave they had dug and had lived ever since on what roots they could grabble and he had come to ask if I would endeavor to get them pardoned, should they come in, for they knew they should be hanged for what they had done. I replied a good deal.[79]

Carter's dream life tried to return him to idealized pre-Revolutionary conditions, placing Carter in a savior's role and the enslaved in the role of those he had to save. Carter was resisting self-change in the face of radical external change.

Unlike Carter, there were some slave-owning whites who, in submission to an authority, learned to use their response to the black other to bring themselves to both an avowed acceptance of repressed parts of themselves and to fuller ownership of their own values and responsibility for their own actions. In the Revolutionary period, Methodists, like the Baptists after the First Great Awakening, responded rapidly to the extraordinary spirituality of Africans. Methodist revivals appealed to and were dependent upon blacks from the first outreach of Francis Asbury and Thomas Rankin, who arrived in America in the 1770s. African American Methodists (like the black Baptists before them) used African methods as well as English Christian ones and integrated an African sacred cosmos with a Wesleyan one. Whites who joined with them in worship were willy-nilly exposed to a new mixture of values and of practices that affected their sense of self.

Freeborn Garrettson (born 1752), was the son of a slave-owning Anglican family in Maryland. He chose to join the Methodists in June of 1775, after several years of being both attracted and repelled by them. Having lived through what was becoming the fairly common pattern of early childhood awakening, falling away, and second crises near the end of the second decade of his life, he had come to a parting of the ways and felt he had to make life-determining choices. At this point, Garrettson experienced the series of disturbing dreams and visions discussed previously; his developing interpretation of them and his reactions changed his life. Above all, his understanding of his dream life stopped him from being pushed into behavior he did not feel morally committed to and supported him in acting in socially unacceptable ways. He was called on to "chuse" and began to make a series of critical choices.[80]

Through submission to the outside authority met with in his dream and vision experience, Garrettson began to attack parts of his inner self and to change his life. Preaching to the enslaved, he heard the voice of God telling him, "You must let the oppressed go free." Claiming he had not read or heard any objections to slaveholding, he nevertheless freed his own slaves immediately: "It was God, not man [that] taught me the impropriety of holding slaves." In response to this act and to his preaching to the enslaved, he was beaten by a slave-owning relative.

Garrettson also decided that he should not "have any hand in shedding human blood." Freedom for himself meant opposing the War of Independence. He took the dangerous route of resisting the war publicly and faced a violent Patriot mob with passive resistance. Notwithstanding these heroic acts, which were precipitated by his dream commitment, in his dreams he was again attacked by the devil, much as he was being attacked by friends and family in his daily life. He decided that he had to resubmit to God in order to free himself from the devil's threats. He interpreted the dream that followed as a demand that he renege on a marriage proposal he had made, so that he would be free to devote his life to preaching the word. A dream informed him that he had to be "chased [chaste] almost to death" but would eventually be received by a "person."[81]

A dream of "sharp and terrible weapons" that were "turned into feathers" (discussed in chapter 4 of this book) supported Garrettson in his adoption of passive resistance, which was regarded as a feminine means of protection, helping him to develop a more androgynous self than was generally approved of. Nevertheless, while "Cornwallis was ransacking the country" Garrettson bravely waged a campaign "against the practice of slaveholding," facing angry mobs of Southern white males who were committed both to waging war and to maintaining slavery.[82]

Garrettson emerged from this time of inner turmoil and outer conflict with slave owners, Revolutionary mobs, and the temptation of a sexual and family life as a recognized leader in the new Methodist Church, a man free to dedicate all his time and all of his self to his oppressed people, black and white. Through opposition to the self that was considered proper for white southern males (one that aggressively displayed superiority over slaves and women and was ready to use violence), and through the incorporation of alienated parts of himself, he became more loving toward other males and toward himself and more open to female figures of authority within the church, as well as to blacks.[83]

With the words, "You must let the oppressed go free," the voice of God had spoken to Garrettson as though he were both Pharaoh and Moses. He responded by freeing both his own slaves *and himself.* Afterward, he spent much of his free time with the enslaved and was often deeply moved that "many of them," believing themselves near God, "were amazingly happy." He did became aware that he was adopting shouting and other African patterns to bring himself to that state, in part because his critics pointed it out to him, but he did not indicate that he was conscious of the inner work he had undertaken. Nevertheless, he had changed his self, achieving freer emotional expression and broader moral commitments through his use of his enslaved black (and female) alien others and through dreamed commitment.[84] Garrettson had achieved his own personal revolution through his rejection of the national revolution.

Garrettson did eventually marry, but only (at age forty-one) after he felt he had fulfilled his commitments and only when he became convinced that God wanted him to take this action. It was the dreams and visions of Catherine Livingston that convinced him and allowed him to take on the roles of husband and father as well as Methodist preacher. She was the "person" who received him.[85]

The narrative of Sarah Beckhouse Hamilton (born 1745) describes a transition similar to that of Garrettson, but very different inasmuch as it was written by a relatively powerless woman, albeit one who also chose neither to be a slave owner nor to marry in order to succeed in her own war of independence. Hamilton recounts that some time after the Revolution, during which she had been widowed, she was preparing to marry a Georgia plantation owner. She had visited what was to be her new home, and her fiancé visited with her as they moved toward marriage. During his visit (perhaps in 1801) he informed her that one of his slaves was to join the Baptists that very day. Hamilton was appalled that he was allowing this (i.e., not taking control as Carter would have tried to do). A family member offered to "flog" the "dirty wench" in order to satisfy Hamilton, but in place of that Sarah Beckhouse Hamilton suddenly decided to attend the baptism ceremony herself, although she claimed, "I hate the very sight of them."[86]

What brought Sarah Beckhouse Hamilton to do this? Sarah Beckhouse had been a motherless child of seven when her wealthy father brought her from Frankfurt to Charleston in 1752. Once in Charleston, it is likely that she was cared for by an enslaved African American. It is also likely that she attended Baptist services with her, or with some other enslaved African American, perhaps secretly, as her father was Catholic. Thus the thought of a black baptism ceremony may well have sparked memories of pleasant or secretly exciting times from her past. There was attraction mixed in her acknowledged hatred.

Hamilton did attend this slave baptism, and on seeing the white Baptist minister, she recounts that she fell to the ground in a fit as she recognized him as the man who had rescued her in a disturbing, recurring, dream. In Hamilton's dream, which had been sparked by a play about the Revolution, she had seen herself "in a beautiful place as ever I saw; where there was all the most truly delightful and fashionable things in the world; also cards and dice, play that I had been familiar with in my younger days." There she drank wine out of "golden bowls" while wearing an "extravagant head-dress." The Georgia plantation reminded her of the setting of the dream, but parallels and similarities might not have been enough: she felt she was given a direct sign that her dream was being fulfilled when her betrothed "brought me just such a headdress as I dreamed about." In the dream Hamilton had been warned that to "go through [to heaven] . . . I must take off my extravagant head-dress which I had on," and she had thrown the headdress into the fire. (Women often saw ostentatious clothing as the symbol of all they had to give up to prepare themselves for God's riches.) When her betrothed actually proffered the gift, however, Hamilton accepted it. In this act the stage was set for the entire drama: it was to be one of repeated turnabouts.[87]

In her dream a "great sea" had blocked Hamilton's way to heaven. She had stood immobilized before it until "a negro came and pushed me into it." A black had given her the crucial first push on her journey to salvation! Further along the way she fell into a deep pit, which the white minister rescued her from by means of a ball of thread.[88] Once in heaven, she saw "a great company of shining people in white robes, with white palms in their hands. They all sung with melodious harmony, such singing as I had never heard before." All these references suggest that Hamilton saw the heavenly host as African American: "Singing such as . . . never heard before" was a response often made to Africans' singing, and the "white palms in their hands," can be understood as a pun which conflated the palms of Palm Sunday with the white palms of Africans' hands. The "shining people" may well have been another reference to Africans, who used oil to anoint their skin.[89]

After seeing her dreamed-of savior at the slave baptism ceremony, Hamilton fell ill. Neither a Catholic priest nor a minister of the Church of England was able to bring about a positive change in her condition, and her family very reluctantly called in the Baptist minister, whom they regarded as an evil magician. He spent time praying and talking with her and showed her a New Testament, "the first that I ever saw." After his visit Hamilton had an ecstatic experience in which Christ on the cross spoke to her of her salvation. She decided to be baptized by this minister. "The next Lord's day morning . . . when I came down to the water side, I related the dealing of God with me, which account proved instrumental in God's hands of the awakening of fifteen souls." Hamilton's fiancé, father, and friends rejected her while she followed the words she had said in her dream: "I must be gone." Hamilton left her home to go to live with the Baptist minister's people in North Carolina and shared in the life of their mixed-race congregation. She was "gone" as well from the existential place she had been and believed that, as in her dream, she was on her way to salvation.[90]

Hamilton's recurring dream suggests that she had been troubled by her life and her values for some time; that she had felt that her desire for riches and easy living obstructed her spirituality; and that she believed that enslaved blacks could help her in her blocked spiritual development. She had, however, been deeply ambivalent about blacks. Even at the outset of her dream she had seen her evil self and her evil companions, including the priest and her family, as "black and very disagreeable."[91] In this dream, however, blacks became white-clothed figures who were at God's right side. Envious of their "melody, union, and harmony," she gave up her social position and potential wealth to associate with the enslaved and outcast. Having been on the verge of becoming mistress of a slave plantation, she became a lay leader in a black and white congregation. Whites, a husband, and wealth were rejected for blacks, independence, and poverty.

At first successful in her rejections, Hamilton was in the end a virtual runaway, forced to escape from the South when her father, whom she had sought out once again, tried to capture her and, as it were, deprogram her away from her alignment with the Baptist magicians, the "dirty wenches," and other poor outcasts.[92] Hamilton's relationship to blacks, who had changed from hated others to beloved sisters and brothers in Christ, had played a very important part in her self-change, which clearly occurred under the aegis of an outside authority. Her writing of her life narrative more firmly established her new identity and broadcast it to the world. She was a person who had remade her self, using the legitimation of a dream seen as a message from God. She had been empowered to leave father and friends, fiancé and slave plantation, wealth and whites. She had taken responsibility for herself, for her values, and her acts, at the same time that she gave it to God.

Hamilton's black other was in her dream and in her self. Turning from attack on this figure she sought to unite with it, going to live with her savior-preacher's black and white congregation. However, after some three years she ran away from the South, ostensibly running from her father but in doing so abandoning this congregation as well. She was not willing to allow her move to be seen as such a rejection; her publication of her autobiography after a trek North was a public affirmation of the blacks and of the change in her self that she had brought about through her new commitment.

In the greater Revolutionary generation the enslaved played a significant role in bringing about a change in self-perception among white people. As these narratives and dreams indicate, many white people had deep and very significant relationships with Africans, and the inner work done by whites as a result of these relationships was an important factor in bringing about change in themselves. Very often this was an "unthought known." Many "knew" their changed values and changed selves in ways they would not or could not acknowledge or think about consciously. When Thomas Jefferson wrote "All men are created equal," this "unthought known" slipped through his conscious censorship. In 1773 the holder of one slave published a direct judgment on all slave owners in which he declared that the "keeping a slave after you are convinced of the unlawfulness of it" is a "crime [that] stands registered in the court of Heaven."[93] Benjamin Rush, the author of this statement, had probably come to believe this as young man but had put it aside and acted as though he did not believe it.

Benjamin Rush had grown up with several enslaved Africans in his father's house, but after his father's death he had a mentor who no doubt led him to question the institution. Samuel Davies, who taught Rush at the College of New Jersey and who made a deep impression upon him, had earlier made a special effort to reach out to the enslaved while he was a preacher in Virginia. More than 300 blacks had come to attend his services, and 150 had asked for and received baptism. Davies firmly believed that God would ask the enslaved to testify about slave owners' behavior. He held that in heaven, "They who lived or conversed together upon earth, and were spectators of each other's conduct, will then turn mutual witness against each other."[94]

In an important position paper on slavery, published in 1773, Rush echoed the words of Davies that he had heard in his childhood, and wrote of God judging slave owners in the "court of heaven" based on the words of those they had wronged. Notwithstanding this strong antislavery essay, when Rush was planning to marry and establish a household, perhaps in 1775, he purchased William Grubber, an African slave. Rush held this man in bondage for many years, probably until 1794. During this very period Rush was establishing his credentials as a Revolutionary antislavery idealogue.[95]

Benjamin Rush had complicated and ambivalent feelings about Africans. While he left no note of those he grew up with in his parents' home, his comments about William Grubber indicate that Grubber played a complex role in Rush's adult life. Rush felt he had reformed and improved Grubber and that Grubber was deeply dependent upon him, while Rush's writings suggest that it was Rush who was in need of Grubber's affection. When William Grubber died in 1799, Rush memorialized him with his memories of Grubber's love for Rush:

> In a fit of sickness which I had in [1788] it was expected I should die. William refused to go to bed on the night in which he expected that event would take place, and added, "If massaw die, put me in de grave with him. He be de only friend I got in dis world.[96]

While Rush could not express his own attachment to Grubber, in that same year he did write of his unusual appreciation of a black "practitioner of physic," James Derham, noting, "I expected to have suggested some new medicines to him, but he suggested many more to me." In that same year Rush did come to recognize the broad emotion that all Africans seemed to arouse in him, noting that

> I love even the name of Africa, and never see a Negro slave or freeman without emotions which I seldom feel in the same degree towards my unfortunate fellow creatures of a fairer complexion.[97]

Davies' message and his own argument that a man who continued to hold another in bondage when he knew it to be wrong would pay for his crime in heaven did their work in Rush's inner life. In 1788, over a decade after publishing his attack on slaveholding, Rush anonymously published a dream report in *The Columbian Magazine* describing how he had found himself in heaven in a "Paradise of Negro Slaves." In this dream he found that dead Africans, who were judging whites' eternal fate, had decided that they would admit only one white man to heaven, Quaker Abolitionist Anthony Benezet. Benezet had stimulated Rush to write his attack on slavery, and his death had been the catalyst for Rush's dream. Rush reported that the Africans in heaven told him that his color "is to us a sign of guilt in man." Rush tried to pacify their rage at whites by suggesting that the pain whites had inflicted on them had eased their paths to glory. Rush printed the grueseome life narratives of these Africans in heaven as well as his own attempt to convince them that the "afflictions" imposed on them by their white "task-masters" had led to their "present happiness."[98] He did not succeed. Rush's dream report of paradise indicates that he knew blacks hated whites, that he feared the consequences of their just anger, and that he used his dream life to cope with his recognition that he did not measure up—not to Benezet and not to what he himself knew was right.[99]

Post-Revolutionary Dramatic Narrators:

Who in Part Realized they Were Dependent on
Blacks for Crucial Aspects of their Selves,
but Were Determined to Restrengthen Hierarchies and
'Keep Blacks in their Place,' c. 1785–1820

White introjection of black emotions, values, and culture patterns continued throughout the greater Revolutionary period. After the war the very whites who were attracted to blacks, who both borrowed and stole African values and culture, and who were likely to want to continue to live with the enslaved now widely found it desirable to legitimate the institution of slavery and their own slave owning. This can be seen in myriad Baptist and Methodist narratives written in this period.

The Baptist outreach in the South appealed to poor whites and blacks from the very start, so that virtually all who became Baptists in the eighteenth century were involved in an integrated church life. The Baptist churches rapidly came to depend on black techniques for achieving ecstasy and soul travels, which meant that white members were adopting African patterns at the same time that Africans were becoming Christians.[100] Some early Baptists and Baptist churches came to oppose slave owning, but after the war (which involved their co-option to the cause of the elite) Baptists too generally accepted a world with enslaved Africans. The effect of these developments on an individual born to a plantation and slave-owning tidewater family is illustrated in the narrative of John Taylor, born in Fauquier County, Virginia, in 1752. Taylor's family lost their wealth and slaves during his youth. Taylor blamed this failure on his father's excessive drinking, which had led to a loss of his emotional support as well. This suggests why Taylor may have felt a need for a supportive religious community and why he might have turned particularly to Africans: It is likely that he grew up longing for the lost emotional support of blacks who had been in the family in his childhood.[101]

John Taylor came to see himself as a dramatic narrator. He charted turning points in his life at which he could have gone in different directions, each one marked by the crucial presence of black people whose behavior and nature he saw as other but also as highly desirable. At age seventeen (1769) Taylor went to a Baptist service "as if to a frolic" to observe the "strange exercises." To his apparent surprise, the words that he thought he would listen to as an entertainment suddenly "pierced my soul as quick and with as much sensibility as an electric shock." His immediate associations, however, suggest that childhood involvement with African spirituality had prepared him for this event:

> From that time I felt a particularly tender affection for all I could think were religious, though it might be an old African negro, and had the world been mine, I would have given all to have been one of them, though with it a slave for my life.[102]

In this extraordinary statement Taylor reveals that he was, in part, deeply jealous of the enslaved but saved blacks: he *would have given all to have been one of them.* Taylor spent the rest of his life with blacks, trying to be one of them. He was baptized with blacks, preached to blacks and whites, came to own black slaves (and for a time lived with them in one small cabin), and shared preaching tasks with blacks. He lived through the Revolution and the postwar turmoil, however, without consciously considering the possibility that slavery should be abolished, while with his actions he supported its further development.

Dreams marked turning points in Taylor's life. A lucid dream in which he decided that the figure trying to dissuade him from preaching was a messenger from the devil led him to become a preacher. Visionary dreams also preceded the two great revivals he participated in, and the second led him to the fulfillment of his youthful desire to be one with the black community. When he dreamed of catching small fish he awoke certain that this meant he would succeed in a revival among the enslaved. When a revival did begin at Clear Creek Church in Kentucky in 1823, Taylor joined "the poor blacks" who were

> now stirred up to a devotional spirit; they flock together and in the dead time of the night you may hear them at a distance praying to; and praising God with charming sound. And as you travel the road

in the day time, at their business, you hear them singing with such heavenly melody, that your heart melts into heavenly pause.[103]

Taylor took special sustenance from this African American spiritual revival. He found that he was able to share "a heavenly feast among the black people" as he had never been able to do before. He "partook with the utmost pleasure . . . thankful that our God was no respector of persons." This experience of "exulting joy" among the blacks led Taylor to believe that he was living in the last days and that he was reaching fulfillment of what he had first hoped for in their presence fifty years earlier: "Say, 'O happy day's long looked for, the comforter is come.' I have almost forsaken my home, at fifteen or twenty miles distance, to be among them."[104]

Taylor was not a particularly introspective man. When hit earlier by blows of death in his family, destruction of his property, and failure in his church, he did review his actions but concluded that he "could see nothing of which I could accuse my self." He did, however, accuse his slaves of selling his goods at market, which "placed everything I had in jeopardy." Taylor projected onto the enslaved his own fears and behavior: it was he who sold the goods they produced. It was he who put everything they had in life in jeopardy. Taylor did not recognize this. He saw no conflict between his desire to participate with blacks in their ecstatic worship and his ownership of them as slaves. He would not have been called a "white negro," a phrase later used to refer to white antislavery activists: he was apparently unaware of how much he wanted to be an African, and of how much African culture he had finally appropriated.[105]

As a young convert, Taylor had voiced his longing to be a religious black, and he kept this memory alive in his narrative. His church had helped him deal with this need by justifying his introjection of African values at the same time as it legitimated his exploitation of Africans' labor. Taylor's submission to an outside authority, the Baptist church, helped him openly recognize the beloved other in what was for so many others primarily the hated other. His self grew in the process, but not enough to take full ownership of his emotions, his values, and his actions.[106]

Henry Boehm (born 1775), like Garrettson, Hamilton, and Taylor, chose to leave his father's church. Boehm, like Garrettson, joined the black-white communion of the Methodists, where he was immediately caught up in the mass conversion of both black and white people that was underway. He "preached against slavery" and convinced many white converts to free their slaves. When he converted those still enslaved, he regarded them as "made 'free' by 'the son' " to enjoy "the liberty of the soul." He believed that the conversion of Africans "gladdened the eyes of angels and thrilled the heart of the Savior." Boehm was also thrilled to be taking part in these exercises, which were unlike anything he had ever experienced before:

> The people got so happy and shouted so loud they drowned my voice, and leaped for joy, and sometimes they would fall, lose their strength, and lie for hours in this condition, and then come to praising the Lord. At several funerals many were awakened and in several instances loud shouts were heard at the grave. This was something entirely new to me.[107]

It was not new to the masses of Africans participating. Henry Boehm, Richard Whatcoat, William Capers, James Jenkins, and many other white people ended up shouting, although they had never expected they would. James Jenkins recorded how shocked he was when in 1790: "I shook like a man with the ague; and rising from my seat, I shouted and exhorted with all my might." Other whites criticized him for his behavior; a dream gave him solace and God's approval.[108]

Many whites were willing to follow the lead of blacks, which is likely to have had a deep affect on their sense of self. At a camp meeting near Wilmington, Delaware, in 1802, a white participant reported that "about sunrise a negro man, belonging to brother Bell, commenced praying near one of the tents; some of us soon joined him—his master among the rest—and the people having collected from every quarter, the work broke out and spread through all the company. . . . Many souls professed sanctification".[109]

In many cases the fact that a black exhorter or preacher could not read led whites to conclude that God spoke directly to the African as " 'none but God could cause him to pray so.' "[110] And if God was speaking to Africans, then clearly whites should listen to them. Boehm wrote that "about 100 preachers" listened to Harry Hosier (commonly called Black Harry) "with great wonder, attention and profit" when he preached "with great eloquence" in Philadelphia in 1803. Illiterate, he nevertheless quoted the Bible "with great accuracy" and attracted great numbers of whites wherever he preached, both in the North and the South. Frances Asbury, Thomas Coke, and Richard Whatcoat welcomed him as a coworker, clearly not displeased that his preaching brought white and black crowds to their meetings and led to emotional arousal. Hosier and other black preachers had a deep affect on the preaching and responses of white Methodists. The African dialogic call and response between preacher and congregation became a common white Methodist (and Baptist) form, although few made note of its origins. The African shout was, as noted, widely adopted by white Methodists: like many others in the period, Bishop Whatcoat "Shouted" on his way to his death on July 5th, 1806, and his coreligionists advertised this widely as the proper way to die.[111]

African metaphors and folktales came into the white religious tradition as well. Garrettson, for example, wrote the following comments in his journal while on a preaching tour with Hosier: "[T]he morning appeared very beautiful, and I was very much delighted with the prospect when the natural sun had arisen and illuminated the earth with his bright beams, but one much brighter Sun doth arise to cheer the mind, even the Sun of righteousness." Garrettson did not report that this image was from Hosier's sermon, but it is very likely that it was, as two suns were important in African American iconography. Garrettson may very well have knowingly taken it from Hosier without acknowledging the source, as Garrettson had a troubled, competitive relationship with this black preacher. In Providence, Rhode Island, in July 1790, one thousand came out to hear Hosier preach, but only three hundred of this crowd stayed on for Garrettson's sermon. After this embarrassing experience, Garrettson decided not to preach when Hosier was scheduled to do so.[112]

Henry Boehm's narrative confirms that he heard this metaphor used by an African American. Boehm was very taken with this image when he heard a black brother's testimony about his conversion in Camden, South Carolina, in 1808, which he recorded as follows: " 'Bredren, I cannot exactly tell it, but when I was converted two suns rose dat morning sartin.' " Boehm found it "a beautiful figure," but he had to explain it to himself didactically: "He was converted just as the natural sun was rising, and that moment the Sun of Righteousness arose with healing in its wings and shone into his dark soul and he was all light in the Lord."[113]

William Hayden, born a slave in Stafford County, Virginia, in 1785, remembered all his life that as an infant he had seen two suns every morning—one in the sky and one reflected in the Potomac. His mother saw this as a sign that he would have special powers, and, indeed, Hayden grew up believing that a spiritual voice accompanied him and foretold his future.[114]

After Lewis Clarke, born into slavery in 1812, took his freedom and traveled to Canada, he used the sun as a metaphor for his self and his condition, writing, "It was a long time, before I could make the sun work right at all. It would rise in the wrong place, and go down wrong; and finally, it behaved so bad, I thought it could not be the same sun."[115]

Figure 12. The figure of two suns can be found on many
African American tombstones. The grave of G. L. Galloway is dated 1924 and is in Baxterville, Mississippi.

The figure of two suns can still be found in black graveyards in the
South, and it also has a documented African provenance. Vusamazulu Credo Mutwa, a Zulu shaman, describes ancient rock carvings
depicting two suns, and retells a traditional trickster tale that begins
"Long ago there were two suns in the sky, a male sun and a female
sun" and goes on to explain that as a result of the transgressions of
demons on earth, the female sun fell and caused havoc.[116]

Boehm consciously tried to use this and other black "figures"
whenever he preached to blacks, and that was very often. He told
one large black congregation that "if a man was plowing and he
should look back, he would make a very crooked furrow." He saw
many black people smile, and a black brother responded, " 'I have
put my hand to the Gospel plow, and I am determined to plow my
furrow clean up to glory.' " This dialogue was a significant exchange,
the white using what he thought were black figures and the black
speaking as a white speaking to whites might. They both clearly
knew that Jesus had used much the same figures (Luke 9:62).[117]

Black figures, or metaphors, were widely used by white Southern
Methodists. One of the earliest remembered dreams of James Jenkins
(born in 1764), who grew up in a slave-owning family, was of "the
devil in the shape of a great bird" whose "aim was altogether at me,

because I was so bad." Birds play a central symbolic role in African religions. The Yoruba, for example, believe that God comes down in a feathered form, and a bird is the symbol of Osanyin, the god of herbal medicine. The bird also symbolizes that which "God places in the head of man or women at birth as the emblem of the mind." That Jenkins adopted a devil-bird with a very African quality is not surprising. In the area of the Little Pee Dee River in South Carolina, where Jenkins grew up in the 1760s and 1770s, there was little Christian worship, but whenever a slave died Jenkins attended "what they [Africans] called a play for the dead."[118]

It is also not surprising that Jenkins's early idea of conversion was that it came about through "a dream or some strange sight," which also suggests African American influence. His eventual rejection of this idea was part of his changing relationship to the black other. By the time he was a young man, Jenkins felt he had suffered at the hands of his black and white family, that he was "the least loved of all" the children in his family, and that "even the negroes" made him "the butt" of their anger. He turned his hurt and anger against himself, and thought of killing himself. Perhaps the death of his father during the Revolutionary War allowed him to take a different turn. At the age of twenty he was given the responsibility of overseeing Africans, and he behaved violently toward them. At this juncture he heard an antislavery sermon given by a Methodist preacher; as a result he became convinced of his own guilt and dreamed that God was warning him that he deserved to die, but that He would give him one more year in which he could change his behavior.[119]

Within the year (1789–1790), Jenkins was reborn at a black and white revival, and much about his life changed, although his relationship to blacks and slavery remained a very complicated one. He came to regard slave trading as immoral, but he never rejected slavery and continued to own Africans until his death. James Jenkins's lengthy tale of the death of an African who had long been in his family suggests the complexities of his relationships with blacks. This man and Jenkins's infant daughter, Elizabeth Asbury Jenkins (named for Bishop Asbury's mother), both died in 1810.[120] Jenkins wrote nothing more than a brief note about his daughter's death but followed this note with a very lengthy comment about the African, informing us that he and the enslaved man had shared an intense social and religious life that meant a great deal to him. He even recorded this man's dream report, in which he saw Jenkins preparing his body for burial. He did not, however, record the name of this African American he had known since childhood. He wrote:

We also lost an old African servant, the first that my father bought. He was a remarkably faithful, and good old man. In his country he was a follower of Mohammed; but embraced the religion of Christ about the same time I did, and enjoyed it in no scanty measure until his death, which took place in his ninetieth year. I never saw him out of temper, or knew him to neglect fasting on Fridays, sick or well. He was quiet in his religion, and never seemed to enjoy himself so well as when he saw the Lord's work prospering. If he had no money, he would beg some to give to the "blessed preachers;" and, like the widow in the gospel, he always gave all that he had. I found him every morning at the door, waiting for prayer, when he was able to get there; but the time had come for the good old man to die; and the same religion that comforted him in health, and amidst various infirmities, cheered him now in the immediate prospect of an exchange of worlds. Yes, he was happy, and could speak of death with as much composure as if he were going to sleep. On visiting him one morning with my son James, he said to me "Budder, (for so he always called me,) I dream last night you shave me, to bury me;" and then, taking James by the hand, he said, "Good by, budder, your old dada going to die, and leave you." His last hours were spent in praising God aloud, though I never knew him to shout much before.[121]

Old Dada (perhaps this was what he was called) was clearly a significant other for Brother Jenkins and his family, at the same time that he was enslaved by them. Jenkins was a poor man but apparently had slaves even at his lowest point when he hired out his own very young son so that he could "procure the common necessaries of life." Apparently he regarded slaves as a common necessity. But, like Taylor, he also recognized that enslaved Africans caused him much difficulty, claiming that it was slaves belonging to his neighbors who "were often doing me private injuries, such as killing my stock, burning my rails, & c." The damage he did to Africans was never consciously considered.[122]

Jenkins preached to African congregations all his life, down into the difficult 1830s, after the Nat Turner rebellion. Even then he acknowledged that "some of my best meetings were among the coloured people." There had been an exchange of methods and values as Africans participated, for it was at such meetings that Jenkins had learned to shout and to "fly away" in ecstasy. Jenkins, for his part, felt he had brought Christianity to these black congregants. He, too, had a dream of catching many fish and believed it was fulfilled when blacks responded. He came to feel that it was his conversion of Africans that justified his life: "From among the coloured population the Lord has given me some precious souls for my hire."[123]

While Jenkins had come to deny that conversion came through dreams (probably blaming blacks for this error), he always accepted that both he and his mother, whose significance in Jenkins' life is suggestively alluded to, had been religiously awakened by dreams and that dreams brought important messages. Some messages he could not speak about. When he had his first religious crisis, what he did not articulate, but clearly knew, was that there was a relationship between the dream's message that he needed to reform, and his harsh punishment of blacks. By connecting his description of his ill treatment of the enslaved with his report of his conversion, he made evident his unspoken understanding. Becoming religious did turn him both in the direction of accepting black religious methods and towards reevaluating Africans and his treatment of them. However, neither his appreciation of Africans nor his appreciation of the gospel brought him to advocate manumission. He had always preached, "Stand fast therefore in the liberty wherewith Christ has made you free," but he understood this to mean freedom of the soul and thought it could be achieved without reference to the body. He cited as justification words he attributed to Francis Asbury: " 'I am called upon to suffer *for Christ's sake*, not for slavery.' "[124]

Asbury's words reflected the changing Methodist ethic amidst the changing American reality. By the second decade of the nineteenth century, the institution of slavery, which had been attacked by Baptists and Methodists as well as by Quakers, and which had been undermined by the war and the taking of freedom by myriad slaves as well as by the first abolitionist wave that swept through the North and Upper South, was once again expanding and was reaffirmed widely by white southerners. While blacks earlier had played a very central role in the lives of non-slaveholding Methodist preachers such as Boehm, by 1814 a very large number of black Methodists had left the church to join the African Methodist Church, and many more white Methodists had become slave owners. In 1816 a Methodist committee on which Boehm served concluded that "little can be done to abolish a practice so contrary to the principles of moral justice." With this, Boehm and most of the white southern Methodists relegated the issue of enslavement and their concern with the enslaved to the periphery of their consciousness. They had incorporated African spiritual methods and African values during the heady intermixed days of the Second Great Awakening. These remained part of their individual selves and their church life. They had come to see them as their own and had little overt awareness of how African they were.

Jenkins, who remained a slave owner and a preacher to blacks, was in far more significant contact with blacks in the 1820s and 1830s than was the non-slave-owning Boehm. When Jenkins was old and nearly blind he had a year of great "affliction" in which he "lost two grandchildren, and one of our coloured ones." He noted, "I think they have all gone to a better world." He did not really think through this conclusion, but he knew its truth. In the less-good world he lived in he had learned to project some of his angers outward, especially when he still felt he was the "butt" of both blacks' and whites' anger. Jenkins didn't often express his own emotions, but he often borrowed others' expressions of emotion to reflect his own. He quoted and no doubt shared the reactions of another Methodist preacher, George Dougherty, who had been teaching a black class and felt that he suffered for it. Jenkins reported Dougherty's comment on his low public esteem: " 'The epithet of negro schoolmaster added to that of Methodist preacher makes a black compound sure enough.' " The community no doubt marked Jenkins similarly for his work with the enslaved, and Jenkins no doubt also felt burdened by "a black compound." Jenkins, however, also shared Dougherty's more positive reactions to (and psychic need for) blacks: after a period of persecution following the Vesey plot, when blacks stayed away from the "white" Methodist churches, Dougherty was " 'again cheered at the sight of some black faces in the galleries at night.' " Near the end of his ministry Jenkins did write directly about himself, although it was what others were saying. He was proud that "They say I am harsh and rough." He apparently was, and blacks no doubt were among those who said this with good reason. Jenkins made those who were close to him but whom he saw as rejecting or injuring him pay for his pain. He injured them.[125]

The difficulty Jenkins and many others had with expressing emotions other than anger and rage helps explain why southerners found Africans' expression of positive emotions enormously appealing. When Africans accepted Baptist and Methodist Christianity they helped whites be religiously happy in a totally new way. This change can be seen in the life of Methodist Thomas Smith (born 1776). Smith began his preaching career in 1801 with a dire message to the enslaved emphasizing "the wicked . . . torments of the burning world," to which they responded with silence "solemn as death." By the time Smith died in 1844 he had changed so remarkably that he was memorialized as if he had been an African: it was said that "[t]o *have* religion with him was emphatically to be happy in religion; and being happy in religion, he not infrequently gave vent to his full soul in exclamations of praise and glory to God."[126] Smith's change exemplifies the fact that under the influence of Africans, joy was given a new religious framework, and the use of expressive body movement for religious purposes was legitimated in a totally new way. Music and movement became an integral part of white religious rituals, and white Baptists and Methodists rocked and rolled in ecstasy.

Not only southerners changed under black influence. Much like Jenkins and many others in this study, Theophilus Gates, born in Connecticut in 1787, was, at the age of twenty, quite depressed and had thoughts of taking his own life. At that point he dreamed that he had already died and was near God when "a coloured man came toward me, and told me it was my turn to be judged." (The image of a black guarding the gates to heaven appeared as well to Clark Moorman, who owned two slaves. Moorman manumitted his slaves the next morning.) Gates, who had earlier imagined a black as a protective spirit but who had no apparent understanding of what this imagery might mean for him, nevertheless left Connecticut and began a trek South. While working as a tutor on a Maryland plantation Gates struggled with a call to preach to the enslaved and dreamed of the South as warmed by "the sun of righteousness"; he saw the North as frozen "and unfit to receive the word of grace," reflecting his negative view of both his own family and the wider community he had grown up in. Gates, in rejecting his own past, was attracted to what he believed was the warmth of Africans' religious life.[127]

Gates, along with Woolman, Taylor, Hamilton, Garrettson, Boehm, and Jenkins adopted affective processes from Africans by sharing in what blacks were doing as well as by appropriating elements of their psychic life through "extractive introjection." This term, as used by Christopher Bollas, identifies a process "in which one person invades another person's mind and appropriates certain elements of mental life."[128] Using the African process of shouting, many whites achieved religious ecstasy. African spirit travels brought some whites to be called to God by name, others to come in contact with a little me or with aspects of spirit that they had not known before. Others were brought to see themselves with Africans in heaven, at the right hand of God.

CONFLICTED SELF-FASHIONING:

In Which Whites Were More Actively Demeaning
Blacks in Order to Achieve a Sense of Unity
and Superiority and Were Not Overtly Conscious of
the Fact That They Were Dependent on Them for
Crucial Emotions and Values, circa 1810–1840

As Gates's life indicates, and as blackface minstrelsy confirms, non-slave-owning whites who grew up in the North were also deeply affected by African Americans. Blackface minstrelsy has been widely seen as expressing the most vulgar racism, but Eric Lott has recognized the fondness and even love that were part of the early blackface of the 1820s and 1830s; he recognizes, too, that there was also "theft" of emotions and styles, parallel to what can be seen to have happened in the shared religious life of the South. W. T. Lhamon Jr. further argues that in taking on the role of blacks young white workers were purposefully identifying with all that the evangelicals and other moralists hated: that playing the black allowed a young white man to play at adopting values and behavior that were forbidden to him.[129] David Roediger, who has focused on the role that blackface played in creating a sense of whiteness, also holds that young white laborers who were being pressed to internalize a new work ethic envied and longed for "the cool, virility, . . . [and] abandon, . . . that were the prime components of white ideologies of black manhood."[130] By the end of this period this envy and longing were often mixed with rage and aggression against African Americans, and this anger was expressed in both language and behavior by whites playing blacks in minstrelsy as well as by many white laborers.

An extraordinary example of such a longing for "the cool, virility, . . . [and] abandon" projected onto blacks (or found there), mixed with "the affirmation of white male superiority" and a desire to share in the life of blacks, can be found in the narrative of the white laborer William Otter (born 1787).[131] As Roediger emphasizes, "independence" was a particularly "powerful masculine ideal" for Otter's generation of white men, most of whom found themselves increasingly dependent while trying to live out the heritage of the Revolutionary ideal of independence.[132] Otter and others found that the black/white stage of action allowed them to appear independent of controls and to assert their manliness in what they regarded as a properly violent and humorous fashion that appropriated the trickster behavior often associated with blacks and yet demeaned the black other. This was reenacted on the stage in blackface minstrelsy, and in life by Otter and many others.[133] That Otter was subconsciously aware he was playing a blackface role in his "real" life is suggested by the subtitle he gave his autobiography: *Musical Incidents Altogether Original*. He wrote his narrative as though it were the script for a blackface minstrel show in which he played the lead role of master trickster.[134]

Otter projected an anti-self or not-me onto blacks at the same time that he craved interaction with these others. Playing the roles of jester and later slave hunter allowed him to damage blacks as well as to act the savior and throughout maintain contact with blacks. Both as jester and as slave catcher Otter acted on a public stage and elicited laughter at "their" expense. Otter caught slaves, shared drinks with them, made irons to hold them, and turned their travails into folk stories to entertain whites. Otter, like the blackface stage minstrels, produced plays "in which improbably threatening or startlingly sympathetic racial meanings were simultaneously produced and dissolved."[135]

Otter conceptualized his life as a series of violent "sprees" in which he acted out whatever emotions appealed to him. He felt no guilt for these often violent enactments. It is clear that he saw them as a form of public entertainment and himself as a performer. He did take responsibility for these acts, and was in fact proud of them, but morality was not an issue for him. Otter never suggested that he believed God was involved in his life at any point, neither in setting his values nor in determining the outcome of his life. He viewed providing entertainment, primarily through causing major discomfort and often violence to alien others, as the most desirable activity, and he left evidence that friends and the public greeted his actions with approval. He found the trickster aspects of his self used to humiliate blacks served him well in drawing the attention of his audience. The approval of other white men was central to Otter's concerns, a need that may be related to his troubled childhood.

At the age of eleven, after being beaten by his father for not working properly, Otter ran away from his home in Hull, England, and began his independent working life. He came to America four years later looking for his parents, who had migrated during his absence, only to declare his independence from them when he found them. In New York City he moved from trade to trade but finally stayed apprenticed to a plasterer for a year and a half, perhaps because during this time he became involved with a local gang in "sprees" of violence and destruction. When he and his friends beat a group of Negroes who were at work shucking oysters and were not punished for this act, it marked a significant point in his life: Otter realized that the wider society welcomed such acts as entertainment. Otter became part of a group of fifty young men who regularly crashed parties and dance-house balls and crashed the heads of others, often blacks. This clearly became an important part of his life: it gave him a social group, excitement, and a sense that he had power.[136]

In 1807, after the death of his parents, Otter broke his indenture and ran away to Philadelphia. Claiming to be a free and fully trained plasterer, he worked steadily at his trade and continued his sprees. He wrote of what he did as "fun," but he reveals that he was an angry young man, angry at his family, at the Irish, at women, and especially at Africans. Many others in the community were angry at blacks as well. His gang of "butchers, ropemakers, carpenters, plasterers, and bakers" was approached by householders in a neighborhood where the Quakers had "erected a house of worship for Africans, who, after some time, became so numerous as well as clamorous in their worship, that they were estimated (at a fair calculation) by the neighborhood as a nuisance, and to rid themselves of their noisy blackies, they fell upon the plan to get the boys and let them make a set upon them."

Otter took pride in the fact that his group was both "ready" and "willing" to set upon the Africans in trickster fashion: they tied up and blindfolded a goat and daubed the animal with excrement, creating a goat/devil in blackface. They locked the church doors, and just after the preacher said, " 'Don't you see the devil a coming" they set the goat loose in the crowded black church. As the black men and women fled through the windows, the white "boys" beat them with ropes and metal "tails."[137]

Otter's relationship to blacks became even more bitter and violent after he learned that a watch he had purchased from a black man had been stolen from a white. In helping to catch this black man, Otter found his second calling. While he was now very proud of his speed at plastering, he became a slave hunter as well, making additional money, but, more importantly, enhancing his self-esteem. As a hunter of blacks, he felt he was a man to be feared.[138]

Otter's account of his slave catching provides evidence that it involved him intimately in the lives of blacks. He went to "Negro dance houses" and work sites and to mixed-race hostels to find the men he was looking for. He paid blacks to spend time with him and help him find the people he wanted. When given a handbill describing a black man being sought as a slave, it took him no more than "a moment's reflection" to know "where Congo was harbored." Otter rented a pallet for himself in the loft where he knew that Congo slept, and overpowered him with the help of a black man he had hired.[139]

In a second revealing case, when he met another slave catcher who had taken a black man prisoner, Otter ostensibly helped the other slave catcher by tying up the black man. At the same time, however, Otter began playing his tricks on all the actors in this real-life tragedy. He told the black man that he was to be sold South to Georgia but could save himself by making a break for the mountains. When the black man did free himself and began to flee in the direction that Otter had recommended, Otter followed. "I hissed my dog Ponto on him, and as soon as the hiss was out of my mouth, my dog flew at him, and seized him, and held on to him until I came up to him."[140]

Otter often wrote of himself as a diabolic jester, performing for his social set. Rarely alone, he generally involved others in his actions and claimed that they joined gladly. In an important tale, he recounted that he had once met "a black woman of uncommon size [who] carried blackberries about for sale."[141] (Otter, too, was of uncommon size.) In this case he told the friend he was with that "if he would engage the black woman in a conversation, that I would pour a bucket full of the whitewash soup over the blackberries."

Otter tells us that she cried out "Who the hell done that?" His friend and the readers know that Otter carried out his trick by pouring whitewash from an upper window. The lime covered the berries that were in a basket on the woman's head as well as covering the face of the black woman. Otter then ran down and pretended to be a helpful bystander: "In commiseration for the poor wench, we took her to one of the hydrants and washed her." This was part of the musical script he was acting out. He now played the servant and "washed her," bringing himself into physical contact with the black woman.

> I began by pitying her, and told her, that it was a tarnel shame for any body to play such a trick upon her, and proposed to pay her in part for the berries. Some of the by-standers followed my example by giving her some little change, and made up as much money as to pay her for her blackberries. She washed her blackberries at the hydrant, and gave Smith and myself half a peck of them for the money raised for her, as a mark of respect and reciprocity for our kindness.[142]

While Otter seemed a kind savior and a positive role model, he was clearly anxious that others should know his true role and appreciate the play he had enacted. The audience for this tale consisted of white males, and the trickster role Otter played with the black woman served to bond him with this audience.[143]

100

On another occasion Otter was clearly jealous of two black workers who socialized with a young white woman, and he turned the tale of their punishment into a folk story that gave him (and no doubt his audience) great pleasure. Otter recounted that while working, he saw these two young men steal some bacon from his employer, after which they gave it to a young white woman

> whose name was Elizabeth; the two negro boys and Betsey they took a three-handed reel, and of course Betsey was the Jack for both sides; she was in the middle dancing to one, and then presently the other would say, dance to me Miss Betsey, and she would turn herself around to her sooty companion and dance to him awhile; and as they danced, the other would call and say, dance to me Miss Betsey, and so they kept up the sport in this way.

Otter recounted that on the next day the black workers were beaten for their behavior, and between blows the slave owner interjected the refrain "dance to me Miss Betsey."[144] Otter had probably informed the owner of his workers' actions. Otter repeated the mantra-like phrase "dance to me Miss Betsey" many times as if it had magical qualities, and for him it no doubt did. It signified that blacks who thought they could call a white woman to dance with them were just as surely calling down the wrath of white men upon themselves. He would give them a "dance to me Miss Betsey," as he replayed this drama on his own blackface minstrel stage for his white male audience.

Otter did not seem to be aware of an inner self or of any immorality in his acts. He remained throughout a cruel trickster, proud of his physical girth: he was six feet four inches tall and weighed about 250 pounds, with very powerful hands, all of which marked him as "Big Bill." He used his physical power to control blacks and to create white social play that put him at the center of attention. Otter's self remained dependent on his audience of boys and men. His inability to develop a more individuated inner self was tied to this as well as to the fact that he respected no authority outside this group. When a Pennsylvania employer had invited him to a Quaker meeting he noted, "I felt a pretty strong predilection never to get myself much into that habit, [they] being a kind of motley crew of all sects of Christians."[145] But no other sect of Christians ever attracted him either, nor did any ideology. He played to a different tune, one he saw as uniquely his own. He did not recognize that he was part of a chorus in a very popular stage show.

Without expressing it, however, Otter was in dialogue with Quakers and others around him, challenging their values by his acts. Elected to the local governing board in the town of Emmitsburg,

Maryland, in 1835, he was apparently seen by most of his neighbors as representing something in themselves as well. Their election of him gave Otter strong support for the racist self he had developed; in his autobiography (published a year later) he in turn gave them a clear message that the community should expect him to provide support for others' racist acts.[146] As Thomas C. Holt reminds us, "[T]he self is fashioned in social space, in relation to others, and in relation to historical time."[147] All around Otter white males were participating in acts of violence against blacks. A major race riot had occurred in Philadelphia in the summer of 1834. It began after a group of blacks had bested a gang of whites; a mob of whites retaliated by beating blacks brutally and demolishing much black property, including two African churches. Young white laborers, much like the groups Otter had once been part of, were held responsible.[148] These acts were part of a much larger wave, with violence against blacks erupting in Cincinnati and New York as well as in Philadelphia. In September 1835 *Nile's Register* reported there had been five hundred recent incidents of mob violence and social upheaval: "*Society seems everywhere unhinged*, and the demon of 'blood and slaughter' has been let loose upon us. . . . [The] character of our countrymen seems suddenly changed."[149] Otter had participated in similar mob violence in his youth, and as a man he had continued to take joy in social upheaval. Now many more in the society seemed to be acting (out) congruent with his ways.

Writing a year after his election Otter praised himself by stating that he had, "as far as my ability allows, discharged the duties entrusted to me, without favor, affection, or partiality."[150] It is not likely that his "ability" allowed him to be impartial when it came to African Americans; it is also unlikely, however, that he saw this as an issue at all. Otter's election did bring him to evaluate his behavior and to assert that he would change, claiming he had "sowed all my wild oats." He held that inasmuch as he was forty-six, he had "arrived at an age when all men become grave."[151] Otter had been involved in violent acts against blacks, women, and the Irish since he was sixteen; they marked every phase of his adult life and almost every page of his narrative. Inasmuch as Otter did not undergo any traumatic emotional experience at this point, it seems unlikely that he changed radically. There is no reason to believe that he ever developed a persona much beyond that of the white male "boy" who loved to go on sprees with his gang.

Otter, however, apparently came to think of himself as a modern character, in part through narrating his life as a drama in which he had been the main actor. His positive appreciation of his own self and his ownership of his actions on the public stage, as well as his modern racial other, do mark him, in part, as a modern youth/man. However, he was controlled by his angers and not in control of them, and while he was always highly dependent upon the approval of his social group, he had no moral authority to guide him.

Otter's worldview encompassed what Lott has aptly termed "the social unconscious of blackface."[152] Just because he was attracted to Africans and their style of manliness, it was particularly important to him to best them in fights and to outrun them in their flight. He deeply resented blacks' attentions to white women, and punished blacks who threatened him in this way. He could show pity to a black woman and help her in her distress (making contact with her in the process), but only after he had shown his audience that he had really been the powerful trickster who caused her distress.

White men who, like Otter, were demeaning yet jealous of blacks knew they risked retaliation or unconsciously feared it, and these anxieties were sometimes expressed in compelling imagery in dreams. In March of 1835 a tale was printed in *The Southern Literary Messenger*; it centered on a white man's dream report in which the dreamer saw himself as a dishonored victim who was being dismembered by several slaves. Asleep in a crowded steamer cabin on the Hudson River, filled with the noise of many snoring men, the dreamer reported a terrifying nightmare:

> I plainly perceived two large, gaunt blackamoors (whom I well remembered to have seen at home in Richmond, pursuing their daily toil in Meyer's tobacco factory,) descend the cabin stairs, and approach the spot where I lay. The obstacles of a crowded room did not seem to impede them; and I soon felt their iron grasp on my limbs. I was lifted by them from my pallet, and borne, I knew not how, up the stairs, past the engine, to the forward desk. I endeavored from the moment they laid hands on me, to struggle with them, but my limbs were powerless; I endeavored to call out, and awaken my fellow passengers; but my voice had lost its sound, my tongue seemed paralyzed; I could not articulate a syllable. The cold sweat of terror stood upon my brow. I had a presentment that some awful fate awaited me, but I could form no conception of what it was to be.
>
> At the place where they halted in their progress, I saw a huge grindstone, from behind which a little black urchin leapt up, and seizing the handle, commenced turning it with surprizing velocity, looking into my face and laughing with that hearty glee so peculiar

to the c[m]achinations of his race. I knew the imp too well, for I
had seen him in his tatters an hundred times, hopping the gutters
in front of the Eagle Hotel. A horrible consciousness of my fate
now flashed upon me.

The narrator (perhaps Edgar Allen Poe) had prefaced the dream by
noting that on the previous day he had heard news of the lives of his
childhood friends in Virginia, as well as a warning sent by his Aunt
Deborah that "unless he [the author, "E."] studies prudence and
economy, sooner or later, *his nose must come to the grindstone."*
His dream clearly built on this day's residue, as well as his awareness
of (snoring) noses in the common cabin, but it also drew on a lifetime
of concern with and fear of blacks: they would be the ones to bring
his nose to the grindstone!

Scarce had the imp commenced turning the instrument upon
which I had now become aware that I was to be tortured, when the
Titans in whose grip I was held, forced my head downward, until
my proboscis rested upon the revolving stone, and I felt its horrid
inroads upon that sensitive member. The first excoriation was severe. I writhed and struggled to free myself, but the power which
held me was indomitable. Gradually the urchin relaxed the rapid-
ity of his motions—the stone revolved slowly, and I saw that my
torment was to be a lingering one.

In the midst of their task the inhuman wretches began to chant
songs and incantations adapted to the horrid ceremony. I remember some snatches of the ballad they sung. Never shall I forget
them for their cruel mockery of their fiendish merriment was
more galling than the pain I endured, or the awful reflection that
I must pass the rest of my days the noseless object of pity and
contempt. One of the stanzas ran thus:

> De man who hold he nose too high
>   Mus' be brought low:
> Put him on de grinstone
>   And grind him off slow.
>   Wheel about and turn about,
>   And wheel about slow;
>   And every time he wheel about
>   De nose must go.

The writer of this dream report, while far more self-conscious and
far more intellectual than Otter, revealed himself as his compatriot.
It was "the cruel mockery" that the author felt he had suffered at the
hands of blacks that most hurt him. Their hearty African laughter

dishonored him and spurred him to break his bonds. The noseless dreamer awoke "covered with perspiration and in a mortal tremor." He closed his tale with a strong inversion, angrily charging the blacks with theft, claiming that the words and music he had heard them sing during this "ceremony" had been *stolen . . . from the white black-face minstrelsy stage.*[153]

This dream report, which may well have been based on a true dream experience, turned reality on its head, much as Otter had. The writer seems to claim that the enslaved are thieves, that they have stolen the blackface culture of whites. But, unlike Otter, he is clearly charging that the whites, in parodying black culture, have stolen from the enslaved blacks. The dream report, true or fiction, reveals that the writer believed that the enslaved would make another "gigantic effort" to achieve "freedom and revenge," as Nat Turner had done four years earlier. Their anger and strength frightened him, as did their access to spiritual powers he could not really explain. The small black figure he claimed to recognize from his past can be seen as representing an African spirit figure whom he believed had the power to torture and unman him.

Chapter Three

Blacks' White Enemy Other

"When I was a slave I hated the white people."
Sojourner Truth[1]

What he most dreaded, that I most desired.
What he most loved, that I most hated.
That which to him was a great evil, to be
carefully shunned, was to me a great good
to be diligently sought.
Frederick Douglass[2]

IN WRITING his life, Frederick Douglass (born 1818) remembered that when he was eight years old, and Hugh Auld decreed that learning to read would "harm him," he recognized that it was crucially important for him to adopt an oppositional stance to all his white owner's values. Douglass had come to a realization that was central to personal development in his own and later generations of African Americans.[3]

Although in the early seventeenth century the relatively small number of enslaved Africans brought to North America had to adjust to living as a minority among English people and English culture, by the close of the century their numbers had increased significantly and the process of cultural interaction had changed. By the time the South became a society based on the labor of enslaved Africans in the eighteenth century, many African Americans were living in fairly large enclaves and had formed families and extended kin groups. In the Lower South there were extended areas in which the population was mostly black and where the culture of the enslaved was largely African; however, in large areas of settlement in the Upper South, where whites and blacks were almost equal in number, they deeply influenced each other. By the close of the greater Revolutionary era, the culture of the enslaved in these areas was the product of an African/American mixed universe of values that had grown out of extensive black and white interaction.[4]

Most white migrants had come to the colonies as indentured servants, serving some four to seven years, while a significant minority had been prisoners sent to serve seven to fourteen years in the colonies. In America a very large number of white children were "put out" to serve other whites until they were twenty-one. As a result, all through the colonial period a large number of whites were unfree. The enslaved worked with, lived with, and clearly interacted with these unfree whites as well as with free white field hands, artisans, overseers, and owners. Whites were being influenced by blacks at the same time that Western culture was affecting African Americans, most of whom began to speak some English and some of whom became Christian. By the time of the Revolution the interplay was very significant for both groups. Revolutionary ideals deeply influenced African Americans, who widely recognized that concepts of individual liberty and the right to "pursue happiness" could and should apply to themselves. Thousands of the enslaved contributed to the Revolutionary turmoil and took their freedom. We now know that massive numbers of the enslaved, perhaps some one hundred thousand out of less than seven hundred thousand, freed themselves, and that a significant number joined the British.[5] A great many of these people died of illness; some of the others were re-enslaved by the British or the Americans; some achieved liberty. Thousands more were legally manumitted in a wave of Revolutionary abolitionism that led to the eventual end of slavery in the North and the enormous growth of the free black community in the Upper South.[6] For some African Americans there seemed to be what Shane White and Donald Wright have termed a "small window of opportunity" between the Revolution and about 1810.[7]

After the war, much changed. Although white children were still put out, far fewer whites were indentured or otherwise "unfree," which contributed to a change in black/white relationships. There was as well a white backlash against the moves of blacks to share in the promise of the Revolution. By 1815 the substantial growth of racism led the northern and new western states to impose ever harsher limitations on quasi-free blacks. This was accompanied by the revitalization of southern slavery and its westward expansion. After a brief time during which there had been some reason to hope that the values of the Revolution might indeed bring about the end of slavery, it was clear that most blacks faced increasingly difficult times. In the 1820s and 1830s, as the urban white working class expanded and experienced harsh economic difficulties, whites saw free African Americans as a growing threat. Although the oppression of African Americans increased, and no doubt African American rage grew in response, blacks knew that the expression of their rage at whites would trigger more violent repression.[8] One means of self-protection was to reinforce the African American sense of community. While many whites were opposing blacks in part to develop a new sense of a superior, independent self, blacks used their white alien other to renew a quasi-African communal self. New communal institutions, "African" churches and *landsmanshaften*, played an important part in legitimating life changes, supporting new roles, and above all, keeping people alive.[9]

John Beattie has suggested that in traditional African cultures, much as in those of the Europeans, lineage and clan were central, and that "the rights and duties entailed in group membership" were emphasized. In traditional African cultures the self was generally regarded both as many-faceted (with separate, shadow, or double souls) and "open, . . . rather than something closed and private."[10]

With enslavement and transport to the Americas, Africans' sense of self came under severe attack on all counts. The slave trade itself largely destroyed lineage and clan. As close to two thirds of those transported to North America were male, the polygamous family structure, the basis of most African societies, was virtually wiped out, and whites treated attempts to re-create it as uncivilized. Owners rejected outright African conceptions of gender roles , but while European gender definitions were seen as proper they were denied to the enslaved. Males were not allowed the authority they had either in England or in Africa, and females were generally assigned heavy field work, in violation of the English norm, and were not protected from sexual violation, a breach of both African and English values.[11] Whites regarded the belief in separable souls and spirits that was an intrinsic aspect of African worldviews as demonic, and spirit workers were seen as evil magicians. For Africans, having children was a crucial aspect of ensuring that the spirits of the parents would be properly revered after death. New African Americans suffered a blow to their expectations for eternity as only a small percentage of the first generation of the enslaved achieved marriage and parenthood, and both institutions were systematically violated by whites afterward.[12]

African religious life was also extremely difficult to reconstruct under the conditions of enslavement, leaving the enslaved in desperate need of "a source of power and communal values." The Baptist and Methodist outreach to both blacks and whites came at a point when a significant percentage of the enslaved African population was ready to accept a new "enabling institution."[13] In 1757 the white Baptist preacher Samuel Davies recognized that as a result of the enslaved's loss of their old society their need for something new was deeply felt but inchoate: "Many of them [the enslaved] only seem to desire to be, they know not what: they feel themselves uneasy in their *present* condition, and therefore desire a *change*."[14] Many were far more than uneasy: a number of the black narrators recorded that they considered suicide, while many more noted that they were seriously depressed.[15] By the second half of the eighteenth century many Africans had begun to adopt and adapt a minimally significant portion of English culture so that they were able to consider joining the Baptists and later the Methodists. These congregations held a particular appeal; they approached the life of the spirit in ways that Africans recognized and were, at the outset, made up of the poor and disadvantaged who were living in conditions very close to those of the enslaved and often working with them. Africans early had an impact on the practices and beliefs of these two faiths, making them far more attractive to other African Americans.

As blacks became Afro-Christians, the Baptist and Methodist Churches were in part Africanized. As noted, whites as well as blacks were hallowing, shouting, and entering ecstatic trances that brought them to experience spirit travels to hell and to heaven. While African and European techniques and goals were being shared by both groups, significant group differences were maintained. During spirit travels Africans were more often accompanied by a spirit guide; became aware of several souls or "a little me in me"; envisioned spirit as white or light rather than Christ or God; were convinced that once they were saved, they were saved for ever; and expected heaven to be a homecoming to an African clan. But many images and ideas were shared. Individuals in both groups, black and white, saw hell as biblically pictured, with fire and brimstone and tormented people. Whites increasingly joined blacks in spirit travels in which blacks and whites often experienced heaven as filled with white sheep, ecstatic music, and a beautiful home awaiting the homecoming of the believer.[16]

While African culture played a crucial role in the development of the Baptist and the Methodist Churches, and while almost all early Baptist and Methodist congregations were of mixed race, after the Revolution Christian blacks came to experience life in these very churches, which had welcomed their membership and participation, as increasingly racist, and many felt a strong need to create African Christian institutions of their own.[17]

Once there was an enabling Afro-Baptist or Afro-Methodist congregation or class in place, together with a developed white alien other, the enslaved could reaffirm selves based on communal control of both the means and the goals for the proper life. Once a communal self was reaffirmed and strengthened, more individual change could be supported. However, when some African Americans developed more individualistic selves they risked being castigated by both blacks and whites; blacks were likely to see them as abandoning their people, while whites were likely to regard them as too assertive, violating the self-serving white fantasy that African Americans were childlike dependents.

BLACK INTEGRITY VERSUS WHITE DISHONESTY

A key method used by enslaved Africans to develop and protect themselves was to consolidate an image of the white enemy other. Both consciously and unconsciously, this became that which they would not be, a fierce white enemy that was hated and was to be attacked whenever possible and whose characteristics, if found in the black self, were to be destroyed. One of the earliest narrators to draw a picture of what he saw as central to white character (and what he himself would not be) was Broteer, or Venture Smith (born 1729), who published his life account in 1798. Smith placed special opprobrium on white people's thievery and trickery of Africans, behavior that he believed they saw as *"good enough for the black dog."* In opposition, he treasured his own "truth and integrity" and viewed himself as " 'so habituated to keeping his word that he would sacrifice even his life to maintain it.' " He firmly believed that he had been "habituated" to this morality as a child in Dukandarra, Guinea, where he was captured and then sold to a slave ship's steward as his private "venture." Smith asserted that he had acted on these African values from his first moment in Rhode Island when he was only eight years old, and he was proud of the fact that even at that age he had been willing to be punished by a white man in order to keep a promise he had given another white man.[18]

The image of the white as a liar and a cheat played a very strong role in reinforcing Smith's need to be an upright man of his word. He emphasized that throughout his life he had been robbed by white men, citing key cases from his early days in America to his old age. Once he had lent money to his second master's brother, but this master broke into his trunk and destroyed the note, ending the white man's obligation. Years later, after Smith had purchased his freedom and much property as well, a wealthy white man falsely prosecuted him for payment of damages for goods lost. Smith had been a passenger on a small boat transporting these goods but had not been responsible for the boat or the goods. However, he did have money, while the boat's owner did not. After several white men whom he respected advised Smith that the rich man was likely "to carry the matter from court to court till it would cost me more than the first damages" Smith paid for the rich white man's losses. He was nevertheless made to pay many times over for the unjustness of this case, as his rich white adversary "has often since insultingly taunted me with my unmerited misfortune." Smith knew that many blacks had cheated him as well, but his rage was reserved for those whose white skin color legitimated their actions and allowed them to laugh at him derisively.[19] Although Smith was able to voice his rage at the white other, he apparently did not commit himself to any outside authority or institution, which may well account for the fact that he found no direct way of channeling his anger into assertive action.[20]

In contrast to Smith, George White (born into slavery in 1764, just about the time that Smith was purchasing his own freedom) recorded how, through a painful personal campaign, he became part of a "white" institution that enabled him to change himself and use his anger in extraordinarily constructive ways. George White joined what was known as the white Methodist Church and fought a very hard battle with the white clergy to become a licensed preacher.[21] George White only mutedly voiced his anger at whites; he had learned how to control his anger in order to make use of it.

White wrote a very brief account of his life in slavery, but he did note that he was "torn" from his enslaved mother in Accomack County, Virginia, before he was two years old and that he was sold at age six and sold again at age fifteen. He contrasted his first two owners, from whom he "received much better treatment than is usual for Africans to meet with, in this land of human oppression and barbarity," with his last master, who imposed upon him "all the severities of the most abject slavery." White gave no description of beatings, rapes, or murders, as many ex-slaves later did. On the contrary, he recounted that when he was nineteen his brutal master gave him permission to take a one-week journey to Virginia to seek out his parents. White asks the reader to participate in his reunion: "As my mother knew not what had become of me, the reader will easily imagine the affecting nature and circumstances of the scene of the first meeting, of a parent lost, and a child unknown; and both in a state of the most cruel bondage, without the means, or even hope of relief." Fulfilling his image of himself as an honest man even when it served the needs of his brutal white "master," White left his mother (never to see her again) and returned to what he assumed was to be a lifetime of enslavement, as he had given his promise that he would. Seven years later he was manumitted in the will of this same harsh man, an event that he did not attempt to explain. We know that the percentage of free black people in Maryland rose from 7 percent in 1790 to 16 percent in 1800. Revolutionary ideology, Methodist enthusiasm, and economic pressures, which led many farmers to abandon labor-intensive tobacco production and plant wheat instead, were key factors. Notwithstanding the growth in manumissions, White feared re-enslavement by those who had hoped to inherit him; he opted to leave Maryland, working his way slowly up to New York City, which he reached by 1791. As a free black man in the alien environment of a big northern city George White began to seek out a community and a commitment. He began to get serious about religion. In the process he replaced the image of threatening enemy whites with a new enemy other, the devil. He came to believe that it was the devil who was seeking to re-enslave him by means of his "rage." White tried to control both the rage of the devil and the rage within himself through use of "the light" of God's spirit.[22]

George White decided to become a Methodist and worked hard at achieving his own salvation: "I set out with my whole heart to seek a saving interest in Jesus Christ." Throughout his spiritual journey White used the techniques of fasting and praying for long periods, and he was rewarded with visionary experiences that both shocked and sustained him. He experienced a vision of hell that was "perfectly answering the description given of it in holy writ—a lake burning with fire and brimstone." It was, however, also a very personal gendered image. He saw the hell/lake as decidedly feminine and sexually enticing: "*she* . . . has enlarged her mouth without measure, and is moved from beneath, to meet the wicked at their coming." The one who was enticed revealed himself as male and involved in a sexual act: he was small but grew to be "the size of a man." He was a devil, with "flames of fire" coming out of his mouth.

White saw other devils leading "gay, modish" people in their fine coaches down into the lake. Although White burned his feet at the rim of this lake, his spirit guide indicated he was not to go down into hell but was to return to the living. The guide ordered him to "*Go, and declare what you have seen.*" While White's dream seemed to be informing him that neither sexual contacts nor material wealth would bring him peace, the dream also indicated that he had to deal with his memories and with the rage he felt toward the white devils who had mistreated him and his people, a rage that was betokened by the flames that came from his own mouth. *His dream adjured him to talk about what he had seen in slavery.*[23] George White, however, understood his dream to mean exactly the opposite: he thought he should sublimate his own rage and talk of his vision of hell. He decided he should become a preacher. This was a choice that would provide him with an opportunity to do both, as he could (and would) conflate what he had seen in slavery with his vision of hell.

White began a protracted and emotional contest to win a license to preach from the white church authorities. At first he began preaching in a "broken way," and although he was given permission to be an exhorter, in trial after trial he failed to gain a license to preach. After each trial sermon he underwent spiritual trials as well, during which he again fasted and prayed. He was rewarded with dreams of "union with God" and saw himself shepherding God's flock. He experienced a midnight vision of "three forms, like doves, . . . who, for some minutes looked me full in the face. A peculiar brightness, or light, surrounding each of them." Most African Americans thought doves betokened sorrow and death, and White originally shared this view; he was at first quite frightened by this vision. However, Africans also saw doves as ghosts or spirits of those who had died, while white Christians held that doves betokened the Holy Ghost.[24] George White Afro-Christianized his associations and came to see the doves as spirits of angels and " omen[s] of good," redeeming his vision. Another young black Methodist envisioned a similar change within a dream: In 1822 Frederic Swan dreamed of "the largest white bird I ever saw." In his dream it became an angel who brought him wine to commemorate the loss of his sinful nature.[25]

At his next trial George White initiated a direct confrontation with his white judges and found the words to voice his rage. When the judges turned him down once again, he turned the tables on them and assertively questioned them: Did they object to his sermon? Or to his character? When they replied that they found fault with neither, he refused to accept their decision to deny him a license. "I cannot rest without greater liberty than I now enjoy," he maintained, as he insisted that he "wished to be at liberty to speak from a text." This enraged one minister, who warned him "that it was the devil who was pushing me on to preach." At this White too became "extremely agitated . . . [and] cried out . . . 'for God's sake, brethren, do not talk thus.' "[26]

White was shaken but not broken by this encounter. He requested yet another trial and preached his sixth test sermon on April 12, 1807. Although a minority remained strongly opposed, he finally won majority support at this meeting and was given a license to preach. His previous confrontation with the white governing board and his open demand for more liberty had altered his relationship to

113

those in power. His self-assertion had also changed his own self-image, and when he became a licensed preacher he changed his life. Previously, White had preached to both "the coloured, as well as the white people." Now he recognized that "the former being my own blood, lay near my heart; so that my chief happiness consisted in seeking to promote their spiritual welfare." His life finally became his text. In the years after he wrote his narrative White began to associate himself with public outcries against slavery. Over time, he moved toward total independence from white authority: in 1820 he opted out of his old alignment with the so-called white Methodist Church, which was actually very mixed, and joined black Bishop Richard Allen's African Methodist Episcopal Church. White had brought hatred of the white other with him out of slavery, but he had also been ready to share in an emotional religious life with whites in the Methodist Church. It was in that church, however, that he found his rage nurtured by the continuing trials that white men put him through, both literally and figuratively.

White had arrived in New York City in a period when blacks were encountering growing working-class opposition, which he no doubt met with while working as an oysterman, and he found a similar opposition expressed in the church.[27] Using African-style practices he had achieved visions that strengthened his resolve to fight for liberty in the church. In the same church he learned to use his rage at the white other in a controlled way and recognized that he did not have to eliminate it.[28]

INNER RAGE AND CHRISTIAN LOVE

Christianity called upon believers to love their enemies. If blacks, increasingly becoming Christians, tried to live by this Christian concept of love, they had to absorb an inner contradiction of enormous proportions. Most did not. When Doctor John Hall died in January of 1801, Benjamin Rush recorded the reaction of his unnamed servant, who had probably been "his" for over half a century: "His black woman whom he had emancipated twenty years before, said he had been her master, father and mother. 'If,' said she, 'any man had taken him away I would tear him to pieces, but as God Almighty has done it, why I must submit.'"[29] In this one brief statement we have evidence of a black woman's acceptance of this particular white man (John Hall, her former owner) as her fictive kin rather than her enemy other; of her submission to the Christian God; yet perhaps also her memorial to the African idea that almost all deaths are caused by humans; and evidence of her overall rage not far below the surface: *she would tear any man—or every man—to pieces* to avenge the death of her fictive white parent.

The life story of Swema, a young woman enslaved in East Africa in the mid-nineteenth century, has come down to us with pertinent detail about her anger. When she was too ill to be of value to the Arab who owned her, he buried Swema alive. Rescued by others and given to a Catholic mission, she converted and eventually became a nun. During the conversion process she had "a dream in which she saw her self as a crow tearing away with her beak at the flesh of the bleeding Arab [who had owned and buried her] and beating him with her wings in the middle of a burning desert." This dream "awakened her to the depth of her hatred." She knew that to become a Catholic sister, she had to rid her soul of this anger.[30]

Very few Africans in America were offered refuge by a closed religious community such as the one that gave Swema the psychological and physical protection that enabled her to seek to rid herself of her anger.[31] Many were, however, given enough support by their new churches to lead them to try to follow Christ-like ways of dealing with their own rage and that of their opponents. Young Frederic Swan, an African American Methodist, ill and close to death in 1822, succeeded when he dreamed that he "saw the devil come to fight with me; I thought I had a sword, but did not fight with that, but kneeled down and prayed . . . he seemed to give back and went toward the window, and gave a dreadful shake and went off."[32] Others also felt that they could fight off the inner and outer enemy by pacific means, but a growing number of African American Christians, among them George White, came to see ways they could use this anger to help themselves if they left the "white" churches and worked with their "own" people.

Many, however, became conflicted about their inner anger. Some could neither give up their anger nor find acceptable ways to use it. In 1797 Benjamin Banneker, the free black surveyor, mathematician, and almanac writer born in Maryland in 1731, who had appealed to Thomas Jefferson to appreciate his and other blacks' achievements, dreamed of the devil as a figure that kept returning to him and vanishing. He finally "let in the infernal Spirit" and began to fight with it, "but all in vain." Part man, part beast, this devil revealed his interest in blacks by declaring he was "concerned" with a Becky Freeman. While this Becky Freeman may have symbolized the feminine aspects of Banneker to himself (he was the free son of Robert Banneker or Bannakey), Elizabeth (Becky?) Freeman was also the name taken by an African American woman, Maumbet, after she won her freedom in a well-known case in Massachusetts in 1781. In Banneker's dream the devil was apparently after a black female who fought for her freedom. Banneker sought to burn this devil in the fire and held him there, but the devil told him that "he was able to stand it." Perhaps this devil represented the white other; or perhaps he betokened Banneker's troubled concern with feminine aspects of his self, or with women; or all these things confounded together. What is clear is that although Banneker had tried to burn out the devil, he remained at risk. It would appear that he still felt that both the devil and the flames of hatred were inside him.[33]

The hopes and expectations of both enslaved and quasi-free African Americans, aroused in the period of the American Revolution and dampened by its outcome, were rekindled by the Haitian Revolution. These ideals and hopes found extraordinary expression in the plans of Gabriel [Prosser], born 1776, who sought "Death or Liberty" in Richmond, Virginia, in August of 1800. Gabriel apparently expressed racial hatred fairly openly (virtually all whites encountered were to be killed), but it was tempered by ideology: "friends of liberty"—Quakers, Methodists, and French people, as well as poor white women without slave property—were to be spared. Gabriel was not able to carry out his plans, as they were made known to whites (by blacks); their exposure led to his execution. His plans, however, did generate immediate results among whites: whites' fears of black violence escalated. Both the oppression of blacks and black hatred of whites increased.[34]

A contemporary of Gabriel's, Charles Ball, born to enslaved parents in Virginia in 1781, recorded that all the enslaved maintained a hatred of all whites, although Ball distanced himself from "their" perception:

> Heaven will be no heaven to him [the slave], if he is not to be avenged of his enemies. I know, from experience, that these are the fundamental rules of his religious creed; because I learned them in the religious meetings of the slaves themselves. A favorite and kind master or mistress, may now and then be admitted into heaven, but this rather as a matter of favour, to the intercession of some slave, than as a matter of strict justice to the whites, who will, by no means, be of an equal rank with those who shall be raised from the depths of misery, in the world.
>
> The idea of a revolution in the conditions of the whites and the blacks, is the corner-stone of the religion of the latter; and indeed, it seems to me, at least, to be quite natural, if not in strict accordance with the precepts of the Bible.

Ball reported that the enslaved held that "[t]hose who have tormented them here, will most surely be tormented in their turn hereafter."[35]

While indeed it seems certain that almost every enslaved person would have come to regard whites as the external enemy, and in some fashion would have internalized whites as an alien other, only occasionally did black narrators such as Charles Ball and William Wells Brown risk acknowledging this so openly. William Wells Brown, born in Kentucky in 1815 to Elizabeth, and fathered by George Higgins, the white half-brother of Elizabeth's owner, published his open avowal of this view in his 1847 narrative, testifying, *The slave is brought up to look upon every white man as an enemy to him and his race.*[36] Brown reported that he had heard the cries of both his mother and his sisters when they were being "tortured." He revealed that when this owner was ill, he had "prayed fervently for him—not for his recovery, but for his death." Taken by this owner to Missouri, Brown suffered through twenty-one years of dreadful hardships, particularly in the long period when he was hired out to a slave trader. Brown dreamed of freedom and came to feel that he was "on a hunt" to achieve it. On his second attempt he succeeded in liberating himself, but during his trek north he became quite ill and was in great danger of being recaptured. It was then that Wells Brown and his wife, white Quakers, took him into their family home and nursed him for fifteen days, "treating me as kindly as if I had been one of their children." Both the fact that he had freed himself and the fact that white people—his alien enemies—were treating him as a man and as kin, shook him to his core. He was able to acknowledge that "all this made me feel that I was not myself." Over a decade later he knew he had not yet come to terms with these changes: "On different occasions, when telling these facts, I have been asked how I felt upon finding myself regarded as a man by a white family; especially just having run away from one. I cannot say that I have ever answered that question yet."[37] The fact that he took Brown's full name (which Wells Brown offered him) as his own, adding the Christian name William—the name his mother had given him, but which his owner had refused to call him—answers the question in part. But the part that relates to his acknowledged hatred of whites is not fully answered by this story. William Wells Brown knew that he had come to feel a very special respect, perhaps even love, for a few whites but that he retained his overall hatred of "them."

Most blacks found it too dangerous or painful to allow themselves to express hatred of whites openly to a white audience, but more than the issue of public expression was involved. Black communal support of rage at whites meant that there was less need for each person to develop an individualized white alien other. Most grew up knowing that all whites were their enemies; they didn't have to work hard to demonize this other. Some African Americans, however, faced with the often overwhelming need to protect themselves and their families, displaced their anger from the white other and denigrated both their own selves and other blacks, falling victim to what has been termed identification with the aggressor.[38]

Sojourner Truth publicly acknowledged that she had hated all white people, but she did this only after she felt she had changed this hatred into love. She realized that accepting Jesus as her master had enabled her not only to change her attitude toward white people but also to chose to live among them rather than in a black community:

> When God gave me that master [Jesus] he healed all the wounds up. My soul rejoiced. I used to hate the white people so, and I tell you when the love came in me I had so much love that I didn't know what to love. Then the white people came, and I thought that love was too good for them. Then I said, Yea, God, I'll love everybody and the white people too. Ever since that, that love has continued and kept me among the white people.[39]

Truth did not really explain, and probably didn't understand, why her hatred turned to love "kept" her largely among whites.

Whatever the consciousness, in writing it was generally wise for African Americans to be very careful, as it was to be expected and even desired that written narratives would be read by whites and could have serious consequences for the lives of the narrators.[40] The autobiography of William J. Anderson (born 1811) reveals both a powerful hatred of the white enemy other and what Anderson accomplished through use of this figure, but these revelations seems to have been made against Anderson's conscious will and came only after he first presented a rational analysis of racial problems and an unemotional, moderate suggestion of solutions.

Anderson first maintained that facts would convince "the Christian reader" that slavery was "wrong" and that it had to be ended. He provided the cold facts—names, dates, and crimes—from his own experience of the evils of slavery. Born in Hanover County, Virginia, Anderson's status at birth, according to the law, was not that of a slave, inasmuch as his mother, Susan, was a free woman when he was born. Moreover, he was the son of a Revolutionary War soldier, a fact in which he took bitter pride. His father, John Anderson, had expected to be free at the war's close, but he had not been manumitted. Neither John Anderson's status as a slave nor his status as a Revolutionary

FIGURE 13. Sojourner Truth. "I used to hate white people so . . ."

War veteran had any legal bearing on his son's status, but he may nevertheless have been a source of protection; it was only after John Anderson's death in 1816 that William J. Anderson's mother bound him out as an indentured servant. Anderson grew up on the plantation of a Mr. Vance, where he was "whipped up, starved up, kicked up and clubbed up." Notwithstanding his mistreatment by this white Christian, he openly sought to be a Christian and covertly sought to learn to read and write. Some white children helped him with this second goal, a fact he remembered into old age. More importantly, he remembered exactly when his "free" life came to an end: on November 8, 1826, Mr. Vance took him into Richmond and sold him for $375 to a slave trader taking a coffle of twenty men to Tennessee.[41]

119

FIGURE 14. Willam J. Anderson. perhaps playing a trickster role: smiling and very serious. Frontispiece of Anderson's *Life and Narrative*, 1857.

Anderson, like Brown, was a victim of the second great displacement of families and kin networks, when one million African Americans were resettled or sold from the Old South to the Southwest in the long period between the end of the Revolution and the end of the Civil War.[42] Unlike White, Anderson recounted the horrors of his twenty-four years as a slave in great detail. Without the network of real and fictive kin he had built in his early years on a Virginia plantation, he was in even greater distress than he had been as an indentured child. Whites were his enemies, although many slaves inflicted damage upon him as well. A white man promised to help him run away and then turned him in, but blacks also informed on him. Although he suffered as a result, he showed understanding for the crimes of the enslaved: "It should be remembered that slaves are sometimes great enemies to each other, telling tales, lying, catching fugitives and the like. All this is perpetuated by ignorance, oppression and degradation." He did not explain the behavior of whites: it enraged him. He witnessed white overseers and owners seeking satisfaction of their "hellish passions": "These acts, heinous as they are in the sight of God and man, were considered right, and therefore nothing was said; not even in the church to which they [the perpetrators] belonged. It seems truly, as though there was nothing too bad for some slaveholders to do."

Anderson longed for freedom, "mother and friends." "I made up my mind to run away, let the consequences be what they would. Patrick Henry's words became my motto, viz.: 'Give me liberty or give me death.' " This motto, which had been emblazoned on Virginia black troops in Dunmore's Brigade, signaled that Anderson was determined to fight his own revolutionary war, essentially alone.[43]

In a litany of horrors, Anderson's narrative moved through several failed attempts to free himself and described being "sold eight times . . . , in jail sixty times . . . , whipped three hundred times!!!" This brought him down to July 4, 1836, which he chose as his day to achieve liberty. (Some enslaved blacks did mark Independence Day, and it seems likely his father had. Nat Turner had originally planned to begin his rebellion on July 4.[44]) Throughout this period Anderson preserved a secret power: "No one knew that I could either read or write." He wrote himself a pass to Vicksburg and told those he met on the journey that he had been hired to cook an Independence Day dinner. His pass didn't stand up to the close scrutiny it was given after he took passage on a boat going north, and he was "found out"; however with the help of both black and white seamen he made a break to Indiana and freedom.

At the moment Anderson freed himself, he experienced a sense of rebirth and a markedly changed sense of self that led him to feel "Sure this is not me."

O, then I had a time of rejoicing. I laughed and cried. I tried to pray and return thanks to the Lord for His goodness to poor me. I am not able to express my feeling then or now. When I remembered that just a few days ago I was down in a slave state, under the lash; that only a few moments ago I was a slave on yonder boat, but now free! free forever! O, I was like the Indian who went out and

121

FIGURE 15. "Portrait of a Man," probably a Virginia slave owner, c. 1810. Subject and artist unknown.

painted himself, and, returning to camp, his own dog bit him, he said, "Sure this is not me." Those were my feelings truly. O, reader I can never forget that morning.[45]

Although Anderson had made this change in his self happen, he at first experienced a sense of unreality. He was no longer his old slave self. His actions had tied him to his father's fight for freedom but brought him beyond it to personal success, an Independence Day that celebrated a new self that he did not at first recognize.[46] This sense of having immediately become someone different as a free person was widely shared. William Wells Brown testified, "The fact that I . . . could walk, talk, eat and sleep as a man, and no one to stand over me with the blood-clotted cowhide—all this made me feel that

FIGURE 16. "Virginian Luxuries." Dreamlike hidden painting on the reverse side of the "Portrait of a Man." These two sides picture the two faces of slave owners much as William J. Anderson pictured them in his narrative.

I was not myself."[47] Anderson, like so many others, danced to celebrate this radical change. Dancing marked important occasions, and no doubt led him to feel like himself again.[48]

Anderson came to take a controlled pride in the person he became after achieving freedom. Beginning his new life as an unskilled hod carrier, it was not long before "among both white and colored citizens my credit was in fair repute and my honesty and steadiness of purpose was acknowledged." Anderson followed Venture Smith, George White, and many other Africans in his choice of key values: pride in "honesty and steadiness of purpose." These were values, however, that were most problematic for the enslaved; theft from slave owners was regarded as moral, while "steadiness of purpose" that served the slave master's interests was immoral. While Anderson and most other ex-slaves generally legitimated any theft or subversion of purpose that harmed the master and helped the slave, these values could also complicate the life of an ex-slave, as Anderson learned when ex-slaves stole from him as well. Anderson felt that in slavery, theft from whites was a positive good, "a kind of first principle," inasmuch as "they that *worked* had a right to eat." When

123

his black customers stole from him, Anderson did not feel rage against his own people; he held white people responsible for the African American's condition and behavior.[49]

Deeply feeling the need to belong to a free family, Anderson married a woman he called "Miss Sidney" and whom he described as "a worthy, industrious and estimable woman." These words suggest the distance he wanted to establish from his slave life, where a black women was never called "Miss" and rarely regarded as estimable. Anderson also chose an enabling institution that served him well: he had himself baptized and joined the Methodist Church, soon becoming a class leader; an exhorter; and a licensed preacher. He built his own church and became active in helping the enslaved escape. He worked as a grocer, bookseller, and an abolitionist lecturer. All through this period he participated in church activities with whites as well as blacks, but, without explanation, he recorded a fateful parting of the ways: "At length I came to the conclusion to withdraw from the Methodist Episcopal Society of Whites, and join what is now the African Methodist Episcopal Church."[50] His narrative indirectly reveals his motivation for making this break.[51]

Anderson's ostensible views did not violate those of many white Methodists. In the body of his narrative Anderson proposed a "Simple Plan for Abolishing Slavery in the United States": Congress should compensate slave owners by providing them with western lands in exchange for slave manumission, and at the same time set up a separate western territory for free blacks to emigrate to. His calm voice thus said that the "owners" should be paid off so they would accept the loss of their property; however, at the end of the same text an enraged voice said, "[S]end the devils to their death."[52]

In a coda to his autobiography Anderson exposed a rage and an anger that were close to the surface. He revealed as well a worldview far different from the one he had ostensibly shared with white Methodists. Anderson believed that the first Adam was black—made of the "dust of the earth"—and that white skin first appeared when God changed the skin color of Gehazi, Elisha's servant, as a just punishment for his lies. The Bible reveals what Anderson had in mind: when Gehazi lied about taking goods and money that did not belong to him, the prophet Elisha warned him that although he might use these for buying slaves and property, he and his "seed" would always be diseased (II Kings 5:27.) Anderson believed Gehazi's progeny inherited this mark of sin: whites' skin color was their punishment for lying and slave owning. Anderson viewed all whites as both wicked and diseased.

Anderson apparently also believed that whites had a small black devil inside them, as in this tale he told about a white overseer:

In my boyish days, in old Virginia, there lived a very rich man by the name of Garland, in Hanover county, the place of my birth. He owned a large number of slaves. His overseer's name was King, who was an awful tyrant—a monster among the Negro race— whipping and driving both men and women, and cohabiting among the women, both married and single. So Mr. King flourished for a time; but his cup of iniquity got full, and one day while he was counting rails in the woods, two brother slaves named Humphrey and Thornton, knocked him down with their axes and killed him. Just before he expired, some little black thing or devil made his appearance and said, "If he is not dead don't kill him." They did, however, kill him and placed him on the road side. This Mr. King, they supposed, dealt with the devil, and this was his black brother, who came to relieve him. But the slaves were too strong for the devil.

Although Anderson maintained that the original *pure* skin color of human beings was black, he also believed that the color of the devils in white men was black. Many Africans shared the view that evil spirits have a black aura. Anderson also held what Ball had identified as the universal African American Christian's view: he wouldn't choose to go to heaven if white masters were there. Anderson revealed that his worldview and self-view conflated both cultures. He accepted Christ but did not "turn the other cheek." He sang and prayed for the death of all "tyrant masters" and very likely for all whites. Anderson clearly saw the white as his enemy other, and part of him sought the destruction of this other, but in hiding his rage from whites, he in part hid it from himself, and lived with a bifurcated worldview.[53]

The fact that it was extremely dangerous to express anger at whites openly was always a serious problem for the enslaved. A critical process in the socialization of the enslaved by their parents and kin involved teaching children to hide or displace this anger, which led, at times, to its use against themselves and other blacks. Josiah Henson, born in Maryland in 1789, had as much good reason and as many bitter memories as any other black in this study to react to whites as his alien other. His mother was raped by a white overseer; his father was brutally beaten for attacking this overseer and was then sold South to Alabama; and the rest of the family was sold off separately after the white owner's death. All this happened before

Henson was six, but the memory of his mother's sale and his rage at the white people involved stayed with him for the rest of his life.

> I seem to see and hear my poor weeping mother now. This was one of my earliest observations of [white] men; an experience which I only shared with thousands of my race, the bitterness of which to any individual who suffers it cannot be diminished by the frequency of its recurrence, while it is dark enough to overshadow the whole after-life with something blacker than a funeral pall.

While this memory overshadowed Henson's life, he was also ruled by an extraordinary desire to excel and to be judged as honest and honorable by his white owner. His diligent work and his compliance with his owner's demands led his owner to assign him the role of overseer. This placed him in a position that while ostensibly better than that of the field slave, was also fraught with danger. This danger was realized when, in 1825, his owner, faced with bankruptcy, gave Henson the responsibility of taking his enslaved wife, children and eighteen other African Americans to Kentucky, in order to protect the white man's property from his creditors. Henson followed his orders: he did not allow the enslaved to take their own freedom, nor did he take his own. He did this because he had given his word that he would, and like Venture Smith, he believed he had to keep his word. After Henson's extraordinary act of loyalty to the enemy other, this very owner tricked Henson out of his own self-purchase, keeping the money Henson had paid him. By the time Henson wrote his narrative he had come to view what he himself had done as evil, but wrote, "I console myself with the thought that I acted according to my best light, though the light that was in me was darkness." Only when he had been repaid by treachery after acting in the best interests of his people's oppressors did he begin to recognize both his own interests and his own angers.[54]

Henson's relationship to a white enemy other had been complicated by the positive or ambivalent roles several white people had played in his life: when he was eighteen a white Christian had convinced him that Christ had died for him, and this changed his life; his owner had given him the position of overseer, strongly bolstering his sense of self; and in 1830, after he had finally taken his freedom, a poor white sailor saw to it that he and his family made it to the shores of Canada by paying for their passage across the Great Lakes. This white man told Henson that "as soon as your feet touch that [soil] you're a *mon*."[55] Once he felt he had become a "man," Henson clearly tried to redress his earlier moral failings by undertaking several dangerous journeys back to the slave South to lead family and friends to Canada.

WHITENESS AND BLACK SELF-FASHIONING

Some African Americans seemed to come to a self-acceptance that allowed them to make sophisticated and complex judgments about whites and white behavior. Moses Grandy, born in Camden, North Carolina, in 1796, had good reason, as did every other slave, to hate whites. He saw his father and his siblings sold away from him. He learned that his wife, who lived on another plantation, was sold when he saw her in a slave coffle, about to board a boat heading south. He painfully acknowledged his deep attachment to her in a rare manner for this period: "I loved her as I loved my life." Yet he could do nothing to protect her life or their marriage. He himself was whipped and half-starved; he had seen his mother severely beaten and witnessed the flogging to death of both a twelve-year-old boy and a young pregnant woman. He vowed to seek freedom.

Grandy showed great will all his life. Taking his mother's protective actions as a model (she had managed to hide some of her children to prevent their being sold), he early learned to try to change his situation and his life, seeking out renters, owners, and business opportunities. He now became determined to buy his own freedom, and he amassed sufficient funds by working nights and Sundays. Over the years he paid for himself twice and was tricked out of the money (a total of $1,200) by two different owners. While these two major setbacks literally took years from his free life, he nevertheless overcame his deep depression after the second event and was able to turn to a white man whom he felt he could trust, Edward Minner. It is amazing that Grandy could maintain such trust after what whites had done to him, but this third time he did turn to a man of honor. On hearing Grandy's story Minner offered to put up the money to buy him and allowed Grandy to work for himself while he was repaying him.[56]

> By the end of three years from the time he [Minner] laid down the money [$650], I entirely repaid my very kind and excellent friend. During this time he made no claim whatever on my services; I was altogether on the footing of a free man, as far as a colored man can there be free.

When Grandy got his free papers, Minner pressed him to go North to Providence, Rhode Island, and to establish residence there as a free man. Grandy did go, but within two months he felt compelled to come back to his second wife and children, as well as to his fictive white family, in North Carolina:

On my arrival, I did not stop at my own house, except to ask my wife at the door how she and the children were in health, but went up the town to see Captain and Mrs. Minner. They were very glad to see me, and consulted with me about my way of getting a living.

Grandy knew that without Minner as his protector his situation in the South would be intolerable. Indeed, when Minner died a year later Grandy immediately decided to go North again. Once there he dictated his autobiography, which was to be "sold for the benefit of [purchasing] his relations still in slavery."[57]

In the North white people who got to know Grandy thought he was without rancor. George Thompson, a white abolitionist who wrote of Grandy as "my colored brother," noted that "his benevolence, affection, kindness of heart, and elasticity of spirit are truly remarkable." Indeed, in his narrative Grandy did not express ill will toward whites (although he was no doubt constrained by the fact that his kin were still in bondage and he was planning to buy their freedom), but he did not hesitate to reveal the physical and psychological annihilation that was carried out by whites. Grandy did imply that blacks had expectations that whites would be punished by God, but he projected these expectations onto other African Americans.

Grandy's one reference to his dreams reveals that he too had experienced an almost instantaneous conversion-like experience after he achieved freedom:

When, at length, I had repaid Captain Minner, and had got my free papers, so that my freedom was quite secure, my feelings were greatly excited. I felt to myself so light, that I could almost think I could fly; in my sleep I was always dreaming of flying over woods and rivers. My gait was so altered by my gladness, that people often stopped me, saying, "Grandy, what is the matter?" I excused myself as well as I could; but many perceived the reason, and said, "O! he is so pleased with having got his freedom."[58]

Inasmuch as reporting and interpreting dreams were "seen as part of the description of self" in much of Africa, it is not surprising that most African American testimonies and narratives reported dreams, nor is it surprising that Grandy, like so many black dreamers, experienced flight through the air. In some communities in Africa, flying in dreams was interpreted as signifying good fortune; in other groups it signaled communication from spirits who might be either propitious or dangerous.[59] The enslaved Phillis (or Philesh) Cogswell, who converted during a revival in Ipswich, Massachusetts, in 1764, reported to her white minister that when Christ took away her "Burden" of guilt, "I felt so light as if I could fly."[60] Elizabeth, born enslaved in Maryland in 1766, recorded that she flew (and saw bright light) in her early dreams and visions: "I was often carried to distant lands and shown places where I should have to travel and deliver the Lord's message."[61] She felt she later fulfilled her dream flights in her extensive journeys, as did Harriet Tubman and Rebecca Cox Jackson.[62]

Jackson, born free in Pennsylvania in 1795, was an extraordinary black visionary and Shaker leader, one of a small number of free blacks who were able to make use of their rage against whites to expand themselves and their possibilities of action. Her alien other was a mixed figure—both white and of the opposite sex—which helped her find allies on several fronts and to change her self radically.

Jackson was overtly concerned with white spirit figures and her spiritual absorption of pure whiteness. Although the influence of the values of white people must be considered, it should again be strongly emphasized how African her color-coded view of purity was.[63] In Africa, priests color their faces white, holy buildings are painted white, white objects signify purity, and white in dreams foretells joy and happiness. African Americans retained much of this symbolism: the dreams of Frederic Swan, the thirteen-year-old black Methodist convert, recorded in 1822, were filled with white objects—spirits, angels, men, sails, birds, buildings, and a high pole— all of which he took to signify his acceptance by God, as Sea Island interpreters would have.[64]

The continuing valence of the African concern with white objects does not rule out the possibility that the power held by white people also influenced the black interpretation of white images.[65] Rebecca Cox Jackson, for example, who was born into a free black family, lived her adult life in a world of blacks *and whites*, spent many years as a disciple of white Shakers, living in an essentially white community, and then became the founder and spiritual leader of a primarily black, but decidedly mixed, Shaker community in Philadelphia. Her outer and inner worlds were inhabited by figures of both colors.

Jackson's life was expanded by her mixed-race (and mixed-gender) visionary experiences. Her earliest dream memory, dating from 1805 when she was ten years old, was of a white witch killing her siblings. In this dream Rebecca was already protecting herself: she "flew faster" than the white witch and reached heaven safely. In heaven Rebecca found her dead African grandmother, who was busy tending white children. She probably wanted to stay, as God (whom she did not look at, and so could not report on his color) sent her back to the earth saying, "You must go, for I have a great work for you to do."[66]

When she later returned to memories of this dream she saw it as her first anointment, but she did not begin to follow a special path until after she had married and was caring for her husband as well as her widowed brother (a prominent black Methodist minister) and his children. Her spiritual call in 1830, which came to her during a thunderstorm, required a commitment from her to be chaste. From this point on her dreams and her life involved significant power struggles with black men and whites of both sexes.

Jackson's first spirit guide was a female, whom she gradually drew near to in her dreams. In 1834 she envisioned this female spirit guide merging with her soul. On January 1, 1836, in a dream she called "Three Books and A Holy One," she experienced extraordinary interaction with a white man who promised "I will instruct thee—Yea, thou shall be instructed from the beginning of all things to the end of all things." Over the following months she often saw this white man "as plain as I did in my dream." She believed that he taught her to read and understand very difficult texts, led her through deep meditation, and gave her "understanding."

Jackson's next spiritual advance came at midnight on Easter Sunday 1836, when, after three weeks of fasting and prayer, she had a crucial vision in which "[a] white ball . . . entered into my heart. As soon as it entered it became a man, and my heart an arch, and a chair in it. He had a mantle on him. He raised himself up three times, wrapping his mantle around him every time. Every time he wrapped his mantle, it caused black specks to rise up out of my heart and pass into nothing." With this union Jackson felt fully redeemed. A Sea Island dream analyst would probably have shared her recognition that the white object that came into her heart in her dream signified her "coming through." Africans would have recognized the chair in her bosom as a throne for one of high office, important in African societies and re-created in the African American visual universe in gardens and folk sculpture. The disappearing black specks of evil are reminiscent of Western visualizations, such as that of Ezra Stiles, which he had painted in his self-portrait. These very varied symbols suggest the richness of Jackson's signifying universe as well as her acceptance of the color white as betokening the pure and of black as evil.[67]

At the outset of her mission, Jackson had to overcome very strong adverse feelings before she could preach openly to whites, but she came through this and later worked closely with white Perfectionists and Shakers. She envisioned that she slaughtered parts of her inner self in order to continue on the path she had chosen. She dreamed of killing her senses: her feeling, hearing, seeing, smell,

130

taste, and even her "understanding." Perhaps she understood that were she to continue to feel, hear, see, smell, and taste her hatred of whites, she could not continue to function spiritually. In an epiphany of death and resurrection, she saw whiteness come out of her mouth "like the purging of a dead body." She emerged with her taste, mouth, and chest "clean as a little child's." It was her hatred of whites that had been purged.[68]

In an important study of the process of change, Watzlawick, Weakland, and Fisch maintain:

> There can be no doubt that a large part of the process of socialization in any society consists in teaching the young that which they must *not* see, *not* hear, *not* think, feel, or say. Without very definite rules about what should remain outside one's awareness, an orderly society would be as unthinkable as one that fails to teach its members what they must be aware of and communicate about.[69]

Clearly, Jackson's socialization as a young person had brought her to see, hear, and think of too many disturbing aspects of white/black and male/female relations. Jackson had many trials over accepting (white) absolute power and could not fully submit until she retrained her senses and greatly enlarged the arena of "what should remain outside [her] . . . awareness."[70] It was only after she had purged herself in her dream vision that she could act as if she had purged herself of the enemy figure she had been pursuing. Only after her hatred (of whites and males) had done its work in creating her strengthened sense of self was she able to submit, both to God and to her white (female) superior in the Shaker order.

In one of her dreams, Rebecca Cox Jackson heard words from God directing her to change herself: "Thy make must be unmade and remade, and thou must be made a new creature." She "also learned what was in me, and how to overcome it." She felt she was given "power" and "great wisdom and knowledge" from her white male guide and from white spirits that became part of her self.[71]

Jackson did remake herself: after she believed her black sins were gone Jackson came to feel it was time to dedicate her work to her "people in bondage." Inner whiteness remained her mark of purity, but having purged herself, she no longer had to attack an internalized enemy. Now she became more aware of whiteness as marking her people's outside enemy and could work to help them. She was then enabled both to accept absolute (white) authority and to become an authority on her own, eventually leading a community of blacks and whites, females and males.

While Jackson seemed to blame her African culture for her ignorance ("For I was [so] buried in the depth of the tradition of my forefathers, that it did not seem as if I never could be dug up"), her act of total submission to God, which committed her to follow in the spiritual paths revealed to her, enabled her to dream and to act in new and different ways, combining the three traditions that she lived within—the African American, the black Methodist, and the Shaker. She seems to have seen the Kongo cosmogram of "four quarters of the earth, which represents the spirit world," merged with the four aspects of the Shaker Godhead: the Father God, betokening faith; the Mother, wisdom, or charity; the Son, mercy; and the Bride, peace. Jackson envisioned the Father God in the Northeast, or in the upper right quadrant of the mandala, probably with the son to his left, and Mother and the bride below. In Africa, as Robert Farris Thompson notes, the top half of the cosmogram is seen as male and the bottom female.[72]

THE CALL TO VIOLENCE

Many other African Americans also used their hatred of the white other to reaffirm quasi-African values in a Christian matrix. However, in the Christian context they were increasingly called on to follow Christ in meekness. Nat Turner (born 1800), an enslaved second-generation Virginian who had become a Baptist, felt he was following Christ both in his life and in his death, but Christ did not lead him where white slave owners had hoped. He reported that

> On the 12th of May, 1828, I heard a loud noise in the heavens, and the Spirit instantly appeared to me and said the Serpent was loosened, and Christ had laid down the yoke he had borne for the sins of men, and that I should take it on and fight against the Serpent, for the time was fast approaching when the first should be last and the last should be first.

Turner believed he was to "arise and prepare myself, and slay my enemies with their own weapons."

> I saw white spirits and black spirits engaged in battle, and the sun was darkened—the thunder rolled in the Heavens, and blood flowed in streams—and I heard a voice saying, *"Such is your luck, such you are called to see, and let it come rough or smooth, you must surely bear it!"*

132

It is very likely that Turner took white to betoken purity and "white spirits" to refer to those of African Americans, while the "black spirits" were those of slave masters. Nat Turner followed this vision to a bloody conclusion in the rebellion he led in August of 1831. It is not surprising that when, awaiting his execution, he was asked, " "Do you not find yourself mistaken now?' " he unhesitatingly answered, " 'Was not Christ crucified?' "[73] Turner, whose attitude toward whiteness and visions seems African, was clearly a Christ figure in his own eyes, and read his Christianity as demanding of him an African warrior's attitude toward defense and honor.

Many blacks were calling for violence in the 1830s: two years before Turner's rebellion, David Walker (born free in 1785), challenged all black Americans to act violently:

> They [the whites] want us for their slaves and think nothing of murdering us to subject us to that wretched condition—therefore, if there is an *attempt* made by us, kill or be killed.[74]

After the Turner rebellion, waves of fear spread over the white South, and suspected slaves were murdered without trial; thousands were sold "to Georgia"; white riots disrupted the already precarious urban life of free blacks in Cincinnati, Philadelphia, New York, Providence, and Boston. African American people were both more likely to need to express their rage and more likely to fear its repercussions.[75] A few blacks, among them Maria Stewart, Samuel Cornish, David Ruggles, and Henry Highland Garnet, were ready to follow David Walker and openly advocate violence.[76]

In March 1833 Maria Stewart (born free in 1803) announced that she believed that God would violently punish whites and that black people in America would be the agents of his wrath:

> [M]any powerful sons and daughters of Africa will shortly arise, who will . . . declare by Him that sitteth upon the throne that they will have their rights; and if refused, I am afraid they will spread horror and devastation around.[77]

Garnet, whose enslaved parents brought him out of slavery at age nine in 1824, was shamed by the seeming compliance of most of the enslaved. In a talk he gave in Buffalo, New York, in 1843 (which he published as an "open letter to the enslaved"), he charged, "You act as though you were made for the special use of these devils." Although he was a Presbyterian minister Garnet was nevertheless trying to goad the enslaved to take violent action by calling their honor into question, and reminding them that their African fathers and forefathers advocated violence. He told them, "Your dead fathers speak to you from their graves," and he asked them, "[A]re you men?" Men, he maintained, would take the Revolutionary slogan of "*Liberty or Death*" to heart. "Nathaniel Turner, Denmark Veazie, Joseph Cinque, and Madison Washington" were his heroes, and Garnet told the enslaved blacks to model themselves on these men, adjuring them, "Let your motto be resistance! *resistance!* RESISTANCE!"[78]

Garnet, who as a young man had pledged that he "would go [back] to the South and foment slave rebellions," did not do this, but he did give voice to the rage that so many felt they had to keep hidden.[79] It is probably true, both today and in the period of slavery, that virtually "[e]very black person carries around a reservoir of rage. For some it is always full, sloshing around and overflowing at the slightest provocation. For others, . . . its level tends to stay low. But it is always there."[80] The most common object of this rage was (and probably still is) the white enemy other.

Chapter Four

"Making Men What They Should Be"

"In the name of God, we ask, are you men?"
David Walker[1]

"ARE YOU MEN?" was a challenge openly posed to black men in the greater Revolutionary period. However, as in other periods of great turmoil, gender roles became increasingly unstable in this era, and many white men became less sure of what it meant to be a man.[2] Once the Revolutionary War began many came to feel that they could improve their insecure sense of manhood by becoming soldiers.[3] This chapter will explore ways in which white and black male insecurity and desire for strength was turned against the feminine, both within males and in women.

BE A MAN!

In the period of the Revolution many of the sects and churches, the very authorities that so many were looking to for direction, shifted their demands and their acceptance of male (and female) behavior. Jacob Ritter's narrative, recounted in chapter 1, testifies to the pressures he and so many others felt: Ritter's Lutheran minister, and probably his father, pressured him to join the army. He responded but could not fight; captured by the enemy, he felt defeated and ashamed of his behavior and was convinced that he was a deserter. Only dream work, and his new commitment to the Quaker fellowship allowed him to move on with his self-development and his life.[4]

In his narrative, James Collins (born 1763), another very young man in the Revolutionary army, admitted that he too would have run away from the fighting if such an act would not have publicly shamed him. After a battle in North Carolina in October of 1780, Collins was horrified by the "heaps" of dead bodies around him and described himself as having a "shake." He was ready to desert when he was stopped by a public ritual:

Each leader made a short speech in his own way to his men, desiring every coward to be off immediately; here I confess I would willingly have been excused for my feelings were not the most

135

pleasant—this may be attributed to my youth, not being quite seventeen years of age—but I could not well swollow the appelation of coward. I looked around; every man's countenance seemed to change; well, thought I, fate is fate, every man's fate is before him and he has to run it out, which I am inclined to think yet.[5]

Collins quickly retreated from his readiness to take self-preserving action, passively accepting "fate." Fear of humiliation as a publicly shunned coward turned him around.

The narrative of Joseph Plumb Martin (born 1760) presents a very different account of the war experiences of a young man who developed a strong code of honor and "proved" his bravery and loyalty to his comrades on many occasions. Martin's self-view developed not out of fear or shame but out of his reaction to day-to-day problems, his unthinking responses that added up to a code of honor. Martin would not leave a sick comrade to die on the road, but carried him with great difficulty to a field hospital. He defended men who fled to save their lives as well as those who died in acts that other soldiers saw as "foolhardy." He did not follow orders when he saw no reason to, and he was pleased when honest soldiers were not punished for their mistakes. While he often was "starving and freezing" and ill from eating rotten garbage that he had foraged for, he was proud that "my conscience bears me witness that innumerable times I have suffered rather than take from anyone what belonged of right to them, even to satisfy the cravings of nature." But he also reported that other soldiers sought plunder and fought each other, rather than the enemy, over issues of honor. For Martin it was a point of honor to work very hard for the new nation:

> I always fulfilled my engagement [to my country] however she failed in fulfilling hers with me. The case was much like that of a loyal and faithful husband, and a light-heeled wanton of a wife. But I forgive her and hope she will do better in the future.[6]

While Martin's sense of self demanded that he honor his promise to fight, and while he was proud of the fact that he grew from a rebelling sixteen-year-old youth to an honorable man during his seven years of war service, he felt that he had suffered much, and that he and his mates were badly treated both during the war and after: "no one cared."[7] Nevertheless Martin clearly recognized that he had a commitment, a marriage contract to the new state and its army, and that he had to be faithful even if "she" was not.

There was great dislocation during the war, and many narratives witness the hunger, the deep pain at the deaths, and the fear. For some whites it was "a time of captivity," and life never returned to "normal."[8] Given the numerous traumatic experiences, it is not surprising that great anger at women marks many of the life narratives of men in this period.[9] In a world that too often seemed out of their control men often focused on women as particularly dangerous, as well as potentially controllable. Before the Revolution there was a new concern with the carnality and dangerous behavior of "poor, laboring, Irish, and black women."[10] During the Revolutionary War, while many men were busy doing the manly work of fighting the external enemy, many women running farms and households were playing more independent roles than they had previously, and men were more often forced to rely on them in new ways. Carroll Smith-Rosenberg maintains that after the Revolution "middle-class men displaced onto middle-class women criticisms the gentry had leveled against them" earlier.[11] This was no doubt true, but after the Revolution white males of all classes who tried to return to their old roles found that they were compelled to renegotiate their positions of dominance and were often unsuccessful: they increasingly focused their anger on women as well as blacks.

The very revealing correspondence of Anne Huntington and her husband, Benjamin H. Huntington, of Norwich, Connecticut, provides ample evidence of Benjamin Huntington's virtual abandonment of family in order to fulfill what he took to be his responsibilities to the new state, as well as evidence of Anne Huntington's personal growth. A lawyer who between 1775 and 1798 was a member of a Committee of Safety, the Continental Congress, the first U.S. Congress, and the Connecticut legislature, and was as well a mayor of Norwich and a judge of the Connecticut Superior Court, Huntington later wrote, "I have been a Slave to the Public these 24 Years Pass'd." When he first left home, his wife began their correspondence with requests that he make decisions for her, but she soon came to act on her own, noting in her letters that she was sure her husband would have acted as she had. Although Anne Huntington became quite ill while her husband was away, he saw it as his responsibility to continue serving the new state, and he did not stay at home during the extended illness that preceded her death. During that time Anne Huntington continued to expand her sphere of authority.[12]

The rapid change in values, the increasing acceptance of public hostility toward women, and the increasing sexual license in the period of the war (when many young men were freed of familial and

FigURE 17. "John R. Shaw as a Soldier"
well illustrates Shaw's own simple sense
of self. From Shaw, *A Narrative of the Life
and Travels of John Robert Shaw, the
Well Digger. . .* (1807).

community oversight, and brothels for the army proliferated) encouraged more men to seek illicit sexual pleasures, but they were
not without guilt about such activities. Many men claimed that sol-
diering had changed their morals. John Robert Shaw blamed his gam-
ing and drinking on his companions in the British and American
armies. Meynard Sampson (born 1756) also felt that he learned to be
"wanton" in the British service, and he too continued swearing and
drinking afterward. These were relatively minor crimes they admitted to—essentially inflicting harm on themselves. While some ostensible patriots passed bad money, enlisted several times (for the
bounties), and simply took anything they could from anyone, as
Samuel Green (born 1760) confessed he had, there were, however,
widespread reports that "both loyalists and rebels went about plundering and killing all who joined the opposite parties." James Jenkins
(born 1764) voiced the widely held view that many people "became
very dissolute and abandoned in their habits during the war."[13] Anxious about their own indulgence of "fleshly gratifications" and
"worldly pleasures," male narrators in all the religious groupings
spoke of themselves as having become "carnal" as young men.
Clearly frightened by the sexual disorder, marked by the rise in pre-

marital pregnancy, some sought an authority that would help them exert control over their own "wicked madness" and were attracted to the new sects that demanded individual self-control.[14]

After the war, it did not take long for men, having lost their political enemy, to turn back with greater intensity than before to their old collective social enemy. Most were determined to reestablish their position at the same time that they were under increasing pressure to assert their independence in new economic roles; they often failed at both. Their needs and their angers grew. Christine Stansell's research on New York City provides substantial evidence that "male license for sexual aggressiveness increased in the two decades after the Revolution, especially toward women in public."[15]

While lower-class men (and women) faced a different reality than the emerging middle class did, they shared in some of the basic attitudinal shifts toward women. Poor women generally worked to support themselves and their families, both within and outside the household, and poor men knew they had no choice but to depend on the work of their wives and families. They always had, but it became more evident as work moved outside households and women received pay rather than bartered goods. While lower-class men and women often had a rough companionship that seems to fit a more modern mode than did the increasing separation of the middling sort, nevertheless when some working men organized and became vocal in unions in the thirties, they by and large opposed the laboring of women and pictured working women as victims. While most had to accept that their wives worked this did not seem to change their assumptions about male superiority nor reduce male violence against women. Working class men, much as most others in the society, "saw hostilities between the sexes as normal and even natural."[16]

Although most men felt that their manhood was being challenged in a new way, it is clear that black men, especially enslaved black men, faced special hardships in proving their manhood to themselves and others. In 1830 African American David Walker drew a devastating picture of the manhood of the enslaved:

> You act as though you were made for the special use of these devils. You act as though your daughters were born to pamper the lusts of your masters and overseers. And worse than all, you tamely submit while your lords tear your wives from your embraces and defile them before your eyes. In the name of God, we ask, are you men?[17]

139

While white men increasingly denied them their manhood, black men (like white men)continued to place much emphasis on physical strength and bravery and displayed both in their relations with one another. It was more difficult to display either against whites, but this certainly was done. In 1703, in the protocol of a Massachusetts court case that has been considered the first American slave narrative, Adam, slave of John Saffin, was reported to having returned a white man's push with a similar push, and with having warned the white man that "if he struck Adam, Adam would strike him" as well.[18] While it was far less likely that a southern slave would have made such a public statement, after African American G. W. Offley, born into slavery in Maryland in 1808, became a free man at age twenty-one, he became a teacher of the "manly arts" of wrestling, boxing, and fighting. When he became a Methodist, and a preacher, Offley recognized that there was a conflict between his Christian values and his advocacy of the martial arts, but he found that he could live with both of them, holding that "no one is so contemptible as a coward. With us [African Americans] a coward is looked upon as the most degraded Wretch on earth, and is only worthy to be a slave."[19] Very much the same view can be found in the narrative of ex-slave William Grimes, who held that to be manly meant not to be cowardly; Grimes also felt that he had to push down anyone who pushed him.[20]

Many other black men were ashamed of what they saw as unmanly cowardice exhibited by the enslaved, and sought to display their own manliness through physical prowess. Frederick Douglass came to feel this was critical when, in 1835, he fought Edward Covey, the slave-breaking farmer to whom he had been hired out. Douglass, as usual, was conscious of the existential significance of his act:

> I was a changed being after that fight. I was nothing before—I was a man now. It recalled to life my crushed self-respect, and my self-confidence, and inspired me with a renewed determination to be a free man. A man without force is without the essential dignity of humanity.[21]

Douglass sought to follow through on this recognition in his life. This was not what the white abolitionist William Lloyd Garrison concluded when he observed Douglass as a free young man in the North. In fact, Garrison described Douglass as fulfilling a contrary Christian ideal, noting, "He has borne himself with gentleness and meekness, yet with true manliness of character." This was a description of Garrison's ideal black man, meek and yet manly, and not the

FIGURE 18. Frederick Douglass. Frontispiece from Douglass, *My Bondage and My Freedom*, 1855, which well illustrates his own sense of himself as a "man of parts" but also suggests his militancy through his almost fist-like hands.

more challenging reality, as Garrison was to learn. Meekness did not enter into the ideal of African American manliness, although most whites would have preferred that it did.[22]

During the Revolutionary War the British army mobilized blacks, who flocked to a manly service that they believed would also free themselves. Thousands of black men did serve in the two opposing armies, but many of these men soon died of illness, or were reenslaved. Others served themselves directly by taking their own freedom.[23] Of this number, one whose accomplishments stood out was David George, a second-generation African American, born into slavery in Essex County, Virginia, around 1742. George changed his life and fulfilled his dreams. He first began changing himself in slavery, welcoming the possibilities for revision of goals and self in the Baptist outreach. He went through a period of inner turmoil, seen as "sin-sickness," and he emerged ready to commit himself to self-change and community change by becoming a Baptist elder while yet a slave. With the war, he recognized that possibilities for freedom had opened, and he fled the South with the help of other blacks who, like both George and his wife, had set up small businesses in British-held Savannah. Arriving in Nova Scotia in 1782, he became a charismatic leader, establishing seven churches, and a decade later he led virtually all the membership, more than one thousand migrants, to Sierra Leone. The brief autobiographical essay that he left indicates that he believed that his self and his life had been made over.[24] Both whites and blacks were witnessing a "new Negro," but before they could come to terms with the changes, much had changed for the worse again. The Revolutionary War, however, remained a symbolic referent of the promise of freedom in black narratives for several generations.

THE EXPRESSION OF ANGER

Over the course of the greater Revolutionary period the expression of anger at women was generally increasing, but it was also often combined with a complicated desire to emulate women. This may well have been related to the fact that much of what had been a part of the common sense of self was increasingly being denied to males, especially the familial and communal imbeddedness and interdependency, as well as "soft" virtues such as sympathy. Increasingly, these attributes were seen as feminine.[25] The change in regard to crying can be seen as an important marker of the overall change. Men had been expected to cry both publicly and privately in the eighteenth century: it was seen as a mark of true emotion. By the mid-nineteenth century, it had become a mark of weakness in a male, while it remained a proper feminine attribute.[26] As individuation became the key to ideal male development in the nineteenth century, it was coupled with new demands for males to show strength in their fight through life. As this became too difficult for many, they vented their rage at the women closest to them.

Jonathan Brunt, a fear-ridden madman, expressed the most open anger at women of all the men in this study. His was an extreme expression of what the sane were very worried about as well. He saw women as the cause of all his problems. In his short life narrative, which he published three times over the last decade of the eighteenth century and once in the first decade of the nineteenth, he maintained that by accusing him of insanity, "She-Cains," or "wicked women," had caused him to lose both his English inheritance and the chance of citizenship in New York. He believed that women had given him potions to induce him to marry against his will: "Some depraved miscreants, preparing some unfortunate bodies [for burial] and then castrating them, gave me the unlawful contents to eat secretly." He thought they wanted to increase his libido and have sexual relations with him. Hinting at what now would be seen as sexual abuse, Brunt railed against adults "playing with children as equals," and thereby weakening their morals. He prayed for God to bring about a "Christian Revolution" that would end all such "domestic disorders."[27] These were the very disorders that were deeply frightening to sane men: They were losing their English citizenship and not secure in their new state. Sexuality had become more problematic, and women seemed to be far more independent and demanding, choosing their own husbands and evaluating them, often publicly. Too much seemed in disorder.

Many of the men convicted of violence against women wrote accounts of their crimes prior to execution, revealing both the disorder of their lives and their rage at women. Before his execution in 1776, Thomas Powers wrote an account that indicates that although he was a free African American, he was never without constraints, and was always violating those constraints. Powers was put out by his "pious" father by the time he was three. He quickly came to expect that his masters would return him as they found him "naturally too much inclined to vice." His narrative suggests that he accepted that their judgment was accurate, but blamed women, who early figured as his ensnaring enemy. Powers claimed that when he was about ten years old, "a young Negro women who lived in the house, she, enticing me to her bed, . . . soon taught me the practice of that awful sin." From that time on, "I played my pranks, with the young black girls about the streets." When he was moved from the town of Norwich, Connecticut, to a much smaller New Hampshire community where there were no "black girls about the streets," the race of his female other changed and his "pranks" led to his death. He was charged with "ravishing" a young white women, and though white men were rarely if ever executed on this charge in this period, Thomas Powers, a black man, was.[28]

William Gross, a white man born in 1796, *was* executed for the violence he did to a woman. Gross, whose mother had died before he was three, had been put out to "cruel and inhuman" masters, and early began a dissolute life, becoming a drinker and a gambler. He married a woman he met at a dance house, but left her to live with another. When his new partner, Kezia Stow, began going to dance houses without him, he became enraged. When she announced that she "intended to go where she pleased and do as she pleased," he attacked her with a knife and killed her.[29] Kezia Stow's words, which led to her murder, may be taken as emblematic of what was making some men so angry. Women seemed, increasingly, to be going where they pleased and doing as they pleased.

Brunt, Powers, Gross, and many others, regarded themselves as witnesses to the evil acts of women. They felt they had been tempted, enticed, goaded, fooled, and punished by females. Each witnessed his own downfall and essentially viewed his female victim as responsible for his own lack of control.

CONTROLLING THE "WOMANISH PART"

The radical shifts that were made in gender roles in utopian communities of this period support Frank Manuel's view that utopian visions are the collective dreams of a society. "Free love" as at the Oneida community, celibacy as among the Shakers, and the new family structure at both, suggest both what men of this period were frightened of and what they were dreaming of.[30] The Quakers, the Shakers, the followers of the Universal Friend (Jemima Wilkinson), and later the members of the Oneida Community all shook up established roles and alterity, and continued to change these roles over time. Baptists and Methodists also began by radically increasing the status and power of women, but both groups came to a point where they shifted direction and reconstructed patriarchal power. The Quakers and the Shakers also shifted ground in this area, which had been basic to their self-definition. The Mormons, organizing at the close of the period under consideration, represent the clearest shoring up of patriarchy in the face of the period's threats, particularly in their institutionalization of polygamy, but in theodicy and church polity as well. As these groups moved toward church status, most retreated from their deviant gender demands, sometimes leaving members of the transitional generation confused about how they should behave and what they should become.[31]

The Quakers originally maintained the most extreme deviation from the ruling concept of manliness. Partly by choice, they remained a sect into the nineteenth century, but in their outreach they confronted most Americans with an alternative that, while rejected, had an important although often negative effect. From their beginnings in England in the seventeenth century, the Quakers believed the inner light to be in both males and females, and they accepted that "Truth" was voiced by both sexes. In the seventeenth century Quaker men had been relatively free "to use the verbal and body language of femininity," and they did.[32] Over time, acceptable language and behavior changed; men became far less likely to adopt androgynous patterns, although women continued to talk publicly with a voice of authority. In the nineteenth century this seemed to alter as well.

While certain androgynous patterns were approved of and adopted, both male and female Quakers had always been adjured to annihilate "the woman within the self." As John Churchman (born 1705) explained in his narrative, "the creaturely will, would choose and would be busy with questioning, is it not, or may it not be so and so; that is the womanish part, which is not permitted to speak in the church, [as] it runs first into transgression."[33]

Churchman felt he had been given early personal assurance that if he could control the "womanish part" of his own self, which he identified as his desire for sensual pleasure, he would become a "child" of God. Along with other Quakers, Churchman regarded sensuality as the basic cause of evil and thought it might well bring about the destruction of the world. He believed God had given warning of this when he had sent the flood as a punishment for those "who chiefly aim at gratifying their own sensual appetites." When Churchman had a dream in which he heard Quakers singing, he associated this with "David's rejoicing before the ark," when David had lept and danced in public and his wife had accused him of exposing himself to his female servants or slaves (II Samuel 6:20). When, soon after this dream, Churchman heard singing at a Quaker meeting, he felt certain that God had sent him the dream so that he would be ready to warn Quakers to change their behavior. Recounting his dream in public, Churchman adjured these Friends to mourn rather than sing joyfully, and to recognize the sins of the community.[34]

Churchman wrote an account of his own personal concern with sensuality: in his life narrative he recorded that at the age of twenty-five he "accomplished marriage," revealing that it was a very difficult accomplishment for him. He chose a woman "whom I had loved as a sister for several years because I believed she loved religion." Their love for each other was expressed in the Quaker way—a disregard of outward concern with the other's presence. Soon after his marriage, Churchman began traveling to distant Quaker meetings, journeying, as was customary for Quakers, without his wife. His travels to England and Ireland kept him away from his sister/wife for more than four years, although he was in contact with other Quaker sisters and brothers, some of whom became close friends. Margaret Brown Churchman, his wife, also became a traveling minister, and in their travels they sometimes met in passing. All women who were Public Friends were presenters of spiritual Truth and were, in the process, harsh critics of men, many of them heads of families and established leaders. These women were behaving in ways that some men in the Society may well have found disturbing.[35]

Churchman's own sexuality remained a problem for him, as his dream life indicates. In 1753, when he was in London, he often met with the English Quaker minister Catherine Phillips, who became very attached to him and regarded him as her mentor. At that time he dreamed of a dangerous invasive attack, and of his fingers being cut off:

> I thought I beheld two armies set in array against each other, one of them well armed with swords and muskets; the other had no formal weapons for their defense; but a charge given them by their general to keep their ranks, and gently to march directly forward as he should lead, no man reaching forth his own hand to defend himself; they joined in battle, and when one of the unarmed soldiers was borne hard upon his opponent, he reached forth his hand at arms length, when a sword took off one of his fingers, and the blood sprinkled on several of his fellow soldiers; whereupon knowing the orders given, I cried out, if that had not been so stretched out, this wound would not have been received, and so I awakened.

This dream can be seen as a gloss on Churchman's life at many levels. It depicts an armed male army, facing gentle (perhaps female) opponents, as Quaker men seemed to face female Public Friends. But the dream, with its references to being "hard" and "stretched out," to blood, a wound, and an extended finger being cut off, also suggest concern over the dangers of sexual excitement and the fear of punishment by castration. Churchman wrote that he thought the dream referred to a colleague who had been trying to defend himself against opponents and brought about attacks "on himself and some others." Churchman believed it was this colleague's concern with "self" that led him to his dangerous and in effect evil acts.[36] His interpretation indicates his displacement of concern from his own self to that of others and may well reflect his inability to face his involvement with Quaker women, an involvement that he may have subconsciously recognized as dangerous "combat" that had a sexual component. It suggests as well his sense of rivalry with female Quaker leaders and his worry over pushing forward his own self. Quakers had accepted a new role for women, but their roles were always being renegotiated, as this dream indicates.

EMBRACING THE "WOMANISH PART"

In early Methodism, gender roles also shifted and women took on many tasks that they were excluded from in the Anglican Church, including preaching; young men were nevertheless regarded as the core group of activists, and in making a significant outreach to the colonies before the Revolution much of the English openness to new female roles was downplayed. The young men attracted to the Methodist ministry were expected to remain single and to refrain from sexual activity for a far longer period than was then customary in the colonies. Their role model was John Wesley. While Wesley's sense of mission was crucially influenced by a young woman, Sally Kirkham, with whom he spent much time, he did not propose to her. He did have a very serious correspondence with her both before and after her marriage, in which spiritual practices and reading (particularly Thomas Kempis's *Imitation of Christ*) figured significantly. Over the course of time several other women were important in his spiritual life, but he never married.[37] Bishop Francis Asbury, the central figure in the establishment of American Methodism, believed that each preacher should support a widow or a woman in need, but he strongly advised against marriage for men in church leadership, and he did not marry. When Asbury surveyed the American Methodist Convention of 1809, he noted with pleasure that only three preachers present were married, while eighty-one were single. He described "many of them" as "the most elegant young men I have ever seen in features, body, and mind; they are manly, and yet meek." Asbury revealed that although he recognized that marriage was honorable, for him it was "a ceremony awful as death."[38] By these acts and judgments Methodists were choosing to violate basic white Protestant values, which held that men should choose to dominate women in marriage and become patriarchal authorities. Methodist men were expected to value brotherhood over fatherhood, and service to the new communal family more than mastery over wife and children.[39]

How was a Methodist to be "manly, and yet meek"? Freeborn Garrettson's attempts to fulfill this goal provide answers to this question. His attitude toward the female in himself and toward females was central to his behavior. His mother had been the first to awaken his spiritual yearnings. As a child, he had been convinced that "the blessed Spirit was with her," and not with him. He had come to long for sainthood, and dreamed of a saint as a "most beautiful" person. His mother's early death probably brought him even closer to conflating sainthood and femininity.[40]

A most significant turning point in Garrettson's life occurred when he felt his moral convictions and bravery had been tested and he did not behave in what was considered a manly fashion in his Maryland community. He was present when a mob threatened violence against a Methodist preacher, and he did not defend the man under attack, although he wanted to. This failure to behave as he believed an honorable man should played a role in bringing him to his submission in June of 1775. His choice of the Methodist Church and his subsequent freeing of his slaves and opposition to the war aroused great anger among local white men, and he was attacked and beaten several times. He responded with totally passive or feminine behavior, "singing, praying, and praising God." This was not proper manly behavior in the southern tradition, which called for violence in response to violence, but it did fulfill the new Methodist demands.[41]

Garrettson, however, also decided to get married: "The object was soon determined on, and I made her a visit, told my errand, and set a time when I should expect to have her answer." The night before Garrettson expected "the object" to reply he had another fateful dream, which he interpreted to mean that "the hand of the Lord was against" his marrying. "During the night it was as if some person was telling me, 'You are about to do your own will: I have a greater work for you: You must go out and preach the gospel.' "[42] In this period when men were increasingly trying to follow their own will, Garrettson chose to abandon his own desires. On the night of February 26, 1780, Garrettson dreamed: "[M]any sharp and terrible weapons formed against me; but none could penetrate, or hurt me; for as soon as they came near me they were turned into feathers, and brushed by me soft as down." Garrettson, under attack by other white males, was trying to build his faith in the Methodists' advocacy of passive resistance to all attacks. He did not imagine that this dream, in which penetrating weapons became feathers, might reflect any fear of sexual association with males or females.[43] On the contrary, Garrettson interpreted his dream as a prophetic description of exactly what would happen to him. He felt prepared when the very next day armed men invaded the congregation he was preaching to, and a pistol was put to his "breast." He believed that the transformation of guns into feathers that he had seen in his dream indicated that the pistol would not harm him. He exhorted his followers not to resist, and he meekly allowed the armed men to take him to prison. He was being "meek but manly" in the proper Methodist way. Preaching from his jail cell, Garrettson sparked a revival in which "hundreds both white and black . . . experienced the love of Jesus." This reassured him that his dream had foretold this turn of events and that God was pleased with his behavior. Garrettson never recorded any fears of penetration of his body other than in such attacks on him for his Methodism.[44]

In a dream on Good Friday, 1780, the Devil pelted Garrettson with stones and daubed him with dung, *making him black*. Christ, who appeared to Garrettson then as "the most beautiful person that ever my eyes beheld," reassured him that "your enemy is chained," and that as a result, an "innocent creature," although "chased almost to death," would be saved. Inasmuch as sexual desire was Garrettson's chief personal enemy, the dream can be seen to contain the message that a very feminine Christ had "chained" Garrettson's sexual desire (seen as excessive, which he may well have associated with the black man he had become in his dream), and that Garrettson would remain "chased" (a pun on "chaste") for a very long time.[45]

Garrettson did remain chaste for another two decades. Much like the followers of Jemima Wilkinson and Anne Lee, he and many other Methodist men conflated what they saw as female qualities with Christ-like qualities and found it difficult or impossible to contemplate marriage.[46] Garrettson never again discussed any overtly sexual issue in his narrative, and he closed his account before his marriage to Catherine Livingston, which took place on June 30, 1793, when he was forty-one years old. Livingston, a convert to Methodism in 1787, had experienced deeply rewarding dreams and visions in the period between her conversion and her marriage. She had seen herself crucified and had enjoyed "as much of the love and presence of the deity as I can at present bear." It is likely that Freeborn Garrettson, with whom she shared these dreams, came to view her much as the saint he had longed to be. Her own self-presentation, as her portrait suggests, was that of a laicized *religieuse*. (See the portraits of Catherine Livingston Garrettson and Freeborn Garrettson in chapter 6.) Her assurance that God had willed their union enabled him to overcome his long-lasting conviction that he should not marry.[47]

In the Revolutionary period, a number of people publicly acknowledged that they recognized a woman as the incarnation of the divine spirit, reinforcing the conclusion that this period saw a significant category change in gender roles. The public visions of followers of

Anne Lee (the Shakers) and of Jemima Wilkinson were matched by the private dreams of individuals who saw a female Christ and were empowered by her.

One of the men empowered by a female Christ figure was Levi Hathaway (born 1790). Hathaway's life followed a new life pattern that was becoming common. After a very early religious experience, Hathaway had "fallen away," but as a young man he became "serious" again and experienced visions and trials. After extending help to a distressed young woman who was also seeking salvation, Hathaway dreamed that he volunteered to sit by a dead woman's body and pray for three days in the expectation that she would live again. In his dream his prayers were answered: the dead women "arose and stepped to the floor, and to my real surprise, she was immediately changed into an immortal being!" On awakening, Hathaway's dream experience with this Christ-like female figure empowered him to take on the role of preacher, which he had not previously felt he deserved and which the male authority structure had not seen as a proper role for him.[48]

Many bachelor Methodist preachers had live female spiritual guides, whom they termed "Mothers in Israel," but the preachers generally lived with other men, with whom they developed deep emotional ties. Bishop Francis Asbury publicly acknowledged his intense relationship with Henry Boehm, who was with him from 1808 to 1813: "For five years he has been my constant companion. He served me as a *son*; he served me as a *brother*; he served me as a *servant*; he served me as a *slave*." At Asbury's death in 1816, Boehm referred to him as "our venerable father" and remembered "the many times I had slept with him; how often I had carried him in my arms." When Asbury had been ill, Boehm had been the one to "bathe his limbs, dress his blisters, and nurse him like a child."[49]

Much as David Leverenz noted about the relationship between Puritan sons and their biological fathers, the Methodist fictive sons also seemed to "erect the [fictive] father to absolute authority and give themselves a homoerotic wish fulfillment of cooperative submission."[50] Boehm indeed saw himself as the submissive son, while Asbury fulfilled Boehm's desire by asserting absolute authority over him. Asbury finally used this authority to push Boehm out of his bed and out of his roles of son, servant, and slave in 1813, when he directed his fictive son to return home to care for his ailing biological mother. It is not clear if he was punishing Boehm or was trying to help him grow spiritually; probably both were true. Asbury certainly was critical of Boehm, noting in 1810, when Boehm was thirty-five, that "Brother Boehm is greatly taken up with his friends, his horses, and temporal burdens."[51] Boehm left Asbury's service but rejected the future that Asbury had ostensibly planned out for him and chose to move in with a young bachelor preacher in Philadelphia and engage in more active church work. Perhaps this was what Asbury really wanted anyway.

Asbury made his values very clear: itinerant preaching was to come before family and all other attachments. He warned his next fictive son, Jacob Gruber, "The rich are coming in, they bring their daughters. Methodist preachers marrying, falling! Oh Lord help . . . [those] *leaving the work*, never counting the *cost*. Lay these things together my son!" Asbury, who did not seem to recognize his own double entendre, did not mince words. When preacher Thomas Coke's wife died in 1811, Asbury plainly told Coke she might well have died because Coke "loved her more than God."[52] It is not surprising that it was only after the death of Asbury that Boehm was able to marry.[53]

Like Boehm and Garrettson, a good many of the Methodist preachers married in their forties, when they could claim that they had fulfilled their roles as itinerant preachers and should therefore be allowed to take on the roles of settled preachers, husbands, and fathers. Those few who married at an early age were generally punished. One was a promising young preacher, who, as a colleague noted, was treated with great "severity" by the Conference of 1811:

> No one of his class stood fairer than he for piety, zeal, diligence in duty, and usefulness as a preacher. Not the shadow of an objection was there against him but that he had married a wife; who was in all respects a suitable person, and of an excellent family. And yet for this sole reason he was neither admitted into full connection nor elected deacon.[54]

Most Methodist preachers of the early period learned this lesson well and withstood the enemy embodied in women. They accepted the wisdom of young Garrettson, who had recognized marriage as "the snare of the devil."[55] The Methodists substituted a new, jealous family for wife and children. An unmarried Methodist preacher was likely to have a Mother in Israel, who helped him to achieve conversion and remained a significant spiritual supporter afterward; a fictive wife (a widow whom he supported); spiritual godchildren, who were named after Wesley's mother or himself; and many houses that he called homes, places where he was welcomed on his circuit. He also had his class, where he and his brothers exchanged experiences, and mixed love feasts in which sisters played a significant role.[56]

The Mothers in Israel who often supported young men in their quest for a spiritual life resocialized them with a value structure that included what were seen as feminine virtues and encouraged them to use emotional means also seen as feminine, particularly the ability to cry and to have compassion. The relationship between these Mothers and their spiritual children was in some ways like that of the courtly love relationship between ladies at court and knights. The lady was often married to a lord, and the relationship with the knight, if consummated, was adulterous, but "from his service to his lady, the lover was supposed to learn how to be faithful and self-sacrificing—the primary virtues of any vassal."[57] Among the Methodists and Baptists the ideal relationship to the Mother in Israel clearly proscribed the sexual act; the young man was expected to learn that the best love did not involve sexual relations, and he, like the knight, was to learn to be faithful and self-sacrificing. Moreover, the Mother in Israel was to serve the acolyte as well, providing the model of religious experience and direction as well as solace and security during his spiritual trials. These relations were often very intense at the same time that they were ostensibly asexual.[58]

CONTROLLING "DEVIANT" MALE SEXUALITY

In the colonial period, while many men were known in their communities to have had long-standing sexual interest in other men, few were prosecuted. Richard Godbeer distinguishes between the attitudes of the hierarchy and the ordinary people toward these men, claiming that while the people recognized that individuals had "an ongoing sexual interest in members of the same sex," those in power regarded "sodomy as a sacrilegious and disorderly act but not as an expression of desire or sexual identity." As a result, there were few trials for sodomy, and most communities eventually allowed those few men convicted of sodomy to return to their previous roles, provided they were contrite and expressed a desire to reform. In New London, Connecticut, for example, Baptist minister Stephen Gorton was accused of sodomy in November of 1746, and his ordination was revoked, but it was restored just over a decade later after he made a public confession expressing contrition.[59]

In the post-Revolutionary period, the number of cases dealing with what was regarded as personal misconduct rose significantly, and by the 1830s the issue had become one of excited, widespread concern. Sylvester Graham, whose basic principle was that "stimulation led to debility," held that "masturbation, sodomy, fornication, . . . adultery . . . [and] ordinary sexual intercourse performed by husband and wife" were all injurious to health. Among the middling sort, a "pervasive and obsessive masturbation phobia . . . took hold."[60] One of the men prosecuted in this new wave of anxiety over autoeroticism and homosexuality was the prolific narrative writer Eliezer Sherman.

In 1815, when Sherman was a poor twenty-year-old cabinetmaker living in Taunton, Massachusetts, a visionary experience changed his life. He heard Jesus asking him a question much as a Methodist class leader might have: "Are you willing to . . . forsake carnal Pleasures . . .?"[61] When Christ asked, Sherman declared that he was prepared to commit himself to this path. In order to do so he chose to join the Disciples of Christ, a church that viewed illicit sexuality as well as drinking, smoking, eating to excess, and dressing richly as unacceptable to God.

Sherman had joined a marginal church that, unlike the Methodists and Baptists of the early nineteenth century (who were becoming far more mainstream), actively sought equality for women. Sherman himself held, "If a woman has a gift, she has as good a right to improve that gift as a man; and she has examples in scripture to support her." A Mother in Israel helped him through his first crisis after his conversion, and a number of women played important roles in his revivals, exhorting as well as praying and singing. "I do not expect the women are in silence in heaven," he maintained, "nor that their number is smaller than that of the men. I expect there will be no difference between them there."[62]

Unlike most Methodist preachers, Sherman married young (at age twenty-four) and did not report that he was conflicted about the act, although he only lived with his wife and children from 1819 until 1828. During that time vivid dreams directed his action, leading him to towns where he converted hundreds of working-class people. In June of 1828, just after he led a very successful three-month revival in Newport, Rhode Island, he recorded that in the middle of the night, perhaps in response to a dream, he pledged that he would "give up all." In the morning he told his wife that he had to leave the family and become an itinerant preacher. He wrote that she accepted his decision, which was tantamount to abandoning her and the children, as "she seemed perfectly satisfied it was my calling."[63]

Sherman was a man with a clear social vision and a willingness to devote his life to bringing it about. He was committed to a just society: he opposed slavery as well as the inequality of women; he dreamt of Christ sending him to convert the poor; and he went out to the new factories to speak with black and white, male and female workers. His message that "the spirit of the gospel brings all on a level" was embraced by many of the young factory workers he appealed to. When he was ordained, a vast supportive crowd that included hundreds of his working-class converts attended the service.[64]

In the midst of this success a dream ominously warned Sherman of trials to come. In this dream a thirty-year-old messenger (the age that Jesus was when he began his mission) appeared to Sherman and told him, "[T]here is a great work to be done here, and you must not leave this place. And I further tell you, that you have been under trials about some things, but they will not hurt you; those who try you shall be tried themselves."[65] In his several autobiographies Sherman never suggested why he might have had reason to fear troubles, but this dream indicates that even if unthought, in his dream life he knew that aspects of his behavior were likely to provoke violent opposition.

It was Sherman's relationships with young men that came to arouse violent reactions of members of the wider community. Rumors led a local newspaper to interview a group of males and to print their claims that Sherman either had or attempted to have sexual relations with them. Given the new popular concern with homosexuality, the community responded rapidly. In July 1835 a special interdenominational council was convened to sit in judgment. After the young men cited in the newspaper repeated their stories, Sherman was found guilty. He was reported to have broken down at this trial, accepting the verdict that he give up preaching and pleading that he did not know what to do with the rest of his life. Afterward, however, he challenged the decision and published a denial of all charges, except for one, that of masturbation. In this regard he defended his actions, writing at length of his practice of "self-gratification" and acknowledging that he did talk with young men about such activities. He believed that he reassured these troubled young men when he told them that masturbation, practiced in moderation, was healthy, although "any thing of this nature carried to excess, was hurtful to the constitution, and a species of intemperance." He also acknowledged that "I might have put my arm around Br. White and have kissed him after we got in bed. I hope, if I did, it was no more nor less than a holy kiss; if so, it was fulfilling the scriptures. I do not recollect, for a certainty, anything further."[66]

Sherman suffered for his actions because social values were changing. With the new concern for the self, acts of sodomy, which had previously been seen as separate acts much as the body was seen to be made up of separable parts, were now being regarded as reflections of the inner self. Thus Sherman and others were newly thought of as homosexuals whose contrition was not adequate to restore them to their previous position.

Overall, white men who were coming to view sexuality as dangerous increasingly saw sex as what the other did, and increasingly feared the sexuality of white women, and all blacks. They projected their rejected sensuality onto these other figures, and found it there, fulfilling their expectations.

TAKING PLEASURE IN PASSION WHILE DEMEANING WOMEN

In an unacknowledged dialogue with Graham's views, as well as the earlier negative views of sensuality held by Quakers, Shakers, Methodists, and other religious groups, a few of the growing group of secular men began to take more open pleasure in their passions and write narratives of their sexual adventures. At the same time they expressed hatred of and disdain for women. Some wrote with open pride of their profligacy and their abandoning of women.[67]

Robert Bailey (born 1773) was one of these men who came to regard women as his chief enemy and was determined to punish them. Born to a very poor family, in post-Revolutionary Virginia, he was always deeply concerned with his class standing. Mistreated by his stepfather he apparently blamed his mother for remarrying and putting him in this man's hands. He left home and was on his own by the age of nine, working as a ploughboy. His standing remained very low. In this context a minor event took on major significance: when he was not yet thirteen, a rich girl refused to dance with him at a social event. He left in a rage at her and all women. He became determined to change his class standing by educating himself for something better and dreamed of becoming a doctor. He did not manage to do this, however, and when he was nineteen decided to marry a thirty-year-old woman because he thought she was a rich widow and assumed he would become owner of her property. What actually became his, however, was the responsibility for her first husband's debts, which further embittered him. He became addicted to gambling, which he now looked to as the best way to change his social standing, and he also became "addicted to going to houses of bad fame" in which he acted out his dreams of mastery over women. Bailey claimed that he had "double" Solomon's 700 wives and 303 concubines. He was particularly proud of the fact that his "girls of pleasure" generally dealt with "upper class men" and that a young society woman "became violently in love" with him.[68]

Bailey's life narrative was structured around his compulsive gambling and "womanizing." He established himself as a gambler at Berkeley Springs, Virginia, and thought he was climbing the class ladder, but he was rudely thrown down when once again an upper-class woman would not dance with him in public, reawakening his childhood pain. This time he reacted by taking control of the immediate situation: he stopped this woman and all the others from dancing by purchasing the slave fiddler "on the spot," much as he purchased and used women to take his revenge. But he did not gain respect or honor for this act.[69]

Bailey's definition of his calling expressed his attitude toward women and toward himself: it was very important to him that he be considered a sportsman rather than a gambler. He defined a sportsman as "a high minded liberal gentleman attached to amusements regardless of loss or gain." The gambler he saw as "inventive in schemes to allure and seduce" others for profit. He saw the first role as proper for an upper-class man, while the second he regarded as a lower-class and feminine role. Bailey wanted to be the upper-class male, the sportsman, but he often felt he was masquerading and clearly feared that he was marked as lower class and effeminate. He revealed that "[p]owdered and elegantly dressed . . . , I was always esteemed one hundred per cent or more than my intrinsic value," while he "felt himself no other than little Bob Bailey, the plough boy of old Captain Walker."

Bailey was certainly not playing the role of innocent boy with women; rather he was the alluring, seducing rake. He left several women who were particularly attracted to him with a miniature of himself, together with a lock of his hair. Giving them this icon as if he were a dead saint, he went on to "allure and attract" others. His actions in abandoning many women, as well as his violent treatment of his longtime lover, were expressions of his extreme anger at women but also may reflect his hatred and fear of the "womanish part of himself."[70]

At the center of Bailey's life was his relationship with a Mrs. Turnbull, another widow he had thought rich; again he found he had to support her, reaffirming his role as a trickster who consistently found himself tricked. He remained deeply involved with this woman for a long time but eventually beat her and found that after this act he could no longer have a sexual relationship with her. Perhaps he felt he had violated her as he had been violated as a child, and she came to betoken what he regarded as the weak/womanish part of himself that he hated. He abandoned her, as he had abandoned his wife.

Bailey recounted a revealing folktale about a slave who aspired to be a doctor, much as he himself once had. In this tale, in order to dissuade the enslaved Tom from wanting to better himself, his master tricked him into eating excrement while treating a sick woman. Bailey, like Tom, felt he had been tricked into eating "shit," but unlike Tom, he held women responsible for all his sufferings, and he was not "cured of his longings" for high status. He tried running for political office but was forced to flee when his debts were called in and he faced imprisonment. Nevertheless, at the end of his narrative, when he was living in a small cabin, much like that of a slave, together with his new young lover and their twins, Esau and Jacob (suggesting that he saw himself as an aged Isaac), he claimed to be happy. He maintained that he was beginning a new life as a responsible husband and father, ready to live in relative poverty around a hearth in a small cabin, where he often read the Bible. Although his narrative indicates that he had felt no guilt when he abandoned women or children, at its close he attributed his problems in life to what he now termed the "crime" he was guilty of when he left his first wife: "Upon a retrospective survey of my life I am filled with fear and trembling."[71]

Much of what Bailey did to women can be understood in the context of his desire to establish his position in relation to other men.[72] He desired women desired by rich and powerful men, and he was broken when slighted by such women. He could not touch a woman who had been beaten. He sought to ensure his status by "masquerading" as a rich and powerful man, by playing at "their" leisure-time games as a sportsman, but he failed. At this crucial juncture he tried to turn back to a myth of an idyllic family, back to a home in a small cabin with a young woman chosen for love, with whom he could redeem his sinful life by becoming a responsible husband and father. It is highly unlikely that he became either one, but his desire to do so indicates his conviction that these old values were the proper ones, even though, or perhaps especially because, he himself had never been able to live his life by them.

When H. H. Brown published a pamphlet detailing the "scandalous" evidence that had been presented at Eleazer Sherman's trail for sodomy, he defended his action by stating that he was moved to do so to "extend correct knowledge." This, he claimed, was "our only hope of making men what they should be." Neither the tribunal that tried Sherman, nor H. H. Brown, ever raised any question about Sherman having abandoned his wife. It was how men treated each other that was at issue in "making men what they should be."[73]

How they treated their wives (and their slaves) was left in their own hands, which they often used to vent their anger and establish their superiority.

WHITE AND BLACK WOMEN AS THE ENEMIES OF BLACK MEN

Many black men also centered their rage on women, thus sharing a key value with white males. Black men often regarded white women as their central enemies. William Grimes, born a slave in Virginia in 1784, was one of those who seemed to center his life on his hatred of women, primarily white women. He remembered that when he was a small child his first owner's wife "would beat me until I could hardly stand." Although Grimes became a Christian, he did not learn to turn the other cheek and he openly hoped to carry his rage against this white women into the afterlife. "She is dead, thank God," he wrote in 1824, "and if I ever meet her again, I hope I shall know her." When another white mistress had him severely beaten for showing weariness after he had worked all day and most of the night, he added her to his list for afterlife revenge: "It seems as though I should not forget this flogging when I die; it grieved my soul beyond the power of time to cure."[74]

Grimes's anger at women was not restricted to whites. Sold away from his mother at age ten, he became a houseboy on a large plantation where he had no kin or friends to protect him. There he was certain that Patty, a black women, jealous for her own son's sake of his position, adulterated the coffee he served with a drug. Grimes was severely beaten for this repeated offense. He believed that another enslaved woman bewitched him, and he accused her of "riding him" all night in a "night-mare" and causing him great difficulties with his owner.[75]

After Grimes had freed himself he continued to find black women evil others. He claimed that one black woman led a court to suspect that he was the man who had raped her, while she knew the guilty man and was simply getting back at him for having run a very noisy shop in the room over hers. In another case Grimes was accused of running a brothel when he employed a white woman who was a known prostitute. He claimed she worked for him as a laundress.

Grimes repeatedly maintained his innocence of the crimes he was charged with, but there is no doubt that he found most women hateful. In his life narrative of 1824 he noted, "I do rekon the generality of girls are sluttish, though my wife is not." Grimes had little else to say about his wife and did not even mention her name. It was only in an 1855 addendum to his narrative that he praised her as having been very "fruitful" (she had borne eighteen children) as well as very smart, and revealed that she was called Clarissa Caesar.[76]

Clarissa Caesar had earned his praise for a lifetime of support; he probably hoped that she would continue her efforts. She had stood by her husband in the early 1820s when the southern white man who claimed ownership of Grimes found him in Connecticut and took all his property in exchange for his freedom. By 1855, when Grimes wrote well of her, she had gone off to California to prospect for gold, leaving their eight-year-old child with him. Grimes, who had been a successful laborer, barber, and entrepreneur, was aging and in need of support at this point, and while he wrote in praise of her, he probably feared she had abandoned him.

Late in life Grimes sold lottery tickets and gained fame for arriving at winning numbers through the use of his dreams: "I would often have dreams, and of course I told my friends of them, and then they would greedily seize the lucky numbers, and be *almost* sure to get a prize." This was a traditional use of dreams in Africa and among African Americans. Use of such numbers fit Grimes's voiced attitude toward life. Although he was a man whose own narrative shows how he had changed both his self-image and his life, he claimed to believe that fate and fortune were responsible for everything that had happened to him. He often visited fortunetellers and thought they told him his future in exact detail. He also had faith in God and in prayer, but he hid much of this. He reported, for example, that as a slave he had once heard God's or a spirit's voice. He revealed only that "I heard a voice from heaven, saying, 'Be of good cheer; *and other words, which I do not conceive necessary to mention in this history.'* "[77] What might he have chosen to keep secret? Grimes heard this voice from heaven when he was imprisoned in a slave jail and suffering dreadfully. He may well have heard a heavenly promise to punish harshly the evil white people who had put him there. With varying degrees of passion, Grimes hated white women, white slave owners, Jews, black slave drivers, and many black women, and was certain all would be punished. White women, however, were at the top of this list.

In the brief addendum to his narrative, written when he was in his seventies, Grimes claimed that he wanted to "forgive" and "forget" all the evil done him. His sense of his self had grown, and its reflection was very large in his own eyes: he noted he had "often been called one of the most remarkable personages of modern times." But the expression of old angers and hatreds was not altered. Grimes republished his powerful and bitter 1824 conclusion:

> If it were not for the stripes on my back which were made while I was a slave, I would in my will leave my skin as a legacy to the government, desiring that it might be taken off and made into parchment, and then bind the constitution of glorious, happy, and *free* America. Let the skin of an American slave bind the charter of American liberty![78]

Black men who wrote narratives increasingly took the route to self-development described by Douglass: they would become exactly what their enemies would not have them become. Many of these men recognized that they were "assigned to play" a role in society, and that, as Marion Starling has noted, it was "the 'bad part.' "[79] Most knew that if they were to change their selves and change their status, they had to aggressively defend themselves. Torn, at times, by the demands of the Christian churches that they increasingly joined, and by what they saw as actions congruent with their own self image, they widely managed to legitimate controlled aggression in their worldviews, and when they could not hold church and use of force together, many were willing to change churches, or accept expulsion, or simply go their own way, sometimes violently. Some, of course, did this without consciousness of any choice.

Grimes had been able to use his anger to help himself to flee slavery in 1814 and to respond protectively to his being threatened with reenslavement in 1820. He would not accept the " 'bad part' assigned him to play" by the white community.[80] When he framed his life in his narrative he saw it as an almost constant battle, with a hierarchy of enemies, in which women figured significantly. He had responded with manly aggression.

MANLINESS AND FAILURE

Manliness was being redefined by the sectarian groups, but for many, especially the poor, both black and white, physical prowess and proven bravery remained central. The demands of the Revolutionary War reinforced this traditional view.[81] When anyone meddled with William Otter, a white man, or with William Grimes, a black man, they could expect a strong physical reaction. Most visions of manliness were still based on physical strength, and strong reactions were generally expected to follow abuse of either honor or the body, the traditional boundaries of the male self. Like the Methodists, many of the sects introduced more permeable body boundaries, enjoining men to adopt passive resistance. The majority did not do so, however. As the Baptist and Methodist sects became churches and more

160

white men of the middling sort joined, these churches' values changed, and increasingly their calls for meekness were made to black others, who widely rejected this call. African American Christianity continued to honor the physical strength of men and expected a man both to protect himself and cause bodily harm to those who damaged his body or his honor.

In the sects, the mainline churches, and the culture at large, the separation of the spheres of action and differences in ideal values and behavior for men and for woman were increasingly emphasized. The crying that the Methodists had encouraged men to do did not become part of the common ideal, and the Methodists themselves turned away from it. Its rejection had symbolic importance. By the end of this period it was generally accepted that men, and manly boys, should not cry, nor should they exhibit the debilitating sympathy that crying stimulated. They should not approach life as weak figures in need, not even in need of God, but as strong men who could control themselves and dominate others. Ideally, they were enjoined to leave the crying to women, who were seen as both necessary facilitators of their success and major obstacles to its fulfillment.

Economic dislocations and depressions in 1807 and 1819 caused failure for many of those trying to succeed. This period closes with the depression that followed the crisis of 1837, in which myriad working men were discharged and landowners and slave owners were dispossessed. Bruce Laurie regards the 1837 depression as the "great depression" of the nineteenth century, holding that it "marks a watershed in the making of working-class culture."[82] It ensured that the fear and hatred (as well as the jealousy and emulation) of women would play an ever more significant role in men's lives. Many of the men who lost jobs or land were forced to rely on their wives and families for support and realized "that they had to compromise their ideals of independence." They often deeply resented this need to compromise and saw women, from whom they demanded dependence, as further robbing them of manliness by supporting them when they had failed.[83] White working men increasingly viewed women as dangerous competitors for their jobs, since they would work for less, and were determined to keep them out of the workplace. But while there was a rational basis to this fear, their opposition to women had far more emotional roots. By adopting the white male middle-class view of women as the weaker and purer sort, who needed to be protected from "moral injury" in the workplace, working-class men took male superiority along with whiteness as part of their symbolic payment for becoming dependent wage workers in an increasingly regulated world.[84]

In this same period during which the self-respect of black men was consciously attacked by virtually all whites in the society, black women also often played an ambivalent role for black men. Many black women achieved independence from black men, often fostered by whites both because this worked well in the economy of slavery and because it played a role in unmanning black males. While black women widely became central sources of strength and power in newly formed extended families, to "be" a black man became increasingly difficult.

In looking back to the pre-Revolutionary period there seemed to have been a "widely accepted coherent set of values: a man could know what it was to be a man." Ideally, a white man of the middling sort or the elite had hoped to hold patriarchal authority in a household that respected his rule and in which he took responsibility for most aspects of the life of everyone in the household. By the close of the greater Revolutionary era the new ideal for a middle-class white male centered on his using strength of will to become a self-made man in the marketplace "at the expense of his obligations to other human beings." Middle-class white men were expected to make their mark outside the home and to use what were now regarded as their valuable natural aggressive and competitive feelings, while the poor were enjoined to be independent in a world in which they only barely had enough to eat. The reality for all men did not match the ideal. This was a period in which many landowners, masters, and journeymen were reduced to being laborers; laborers were often reduced to penury by the depressions that followed the crises in 1819 and 1837; and the enslaved were increasing in number at the same time that their overall condition deteriorated. Independence was thus growing as an ideal while dependence increased in reality.[85]

This radical shift in goals and opportunities occurred together with a marked new emphasis on sex-role differences. As Alexis de Tocqueville noted in the 1830s, "[I]n no country has such constant care been taken as in America to trace two clearly distinct lines of action for the two sexes and to make them keep pace with the other, but in two pathways that are always different." There is strong evidence that many men were deeply troubled by this cutting off of a range of their capabilities. Mark C. Carnes argues that the hidden message at the heart of the Masonic mysteries was "that men possessed traits defined as female." Thousands of men—the same men who protected spheres of proper male behavior from the intrusion of women—sought out the Masons by the mid-nineteenth century. The popularity of the Masons may well have reflected men's hidden desire to be more like women, to reaffirm aspects of themselves they had denied in order to develop more aggressive and rapacious behavior. These strict limitations had meant that for most men "it became harder to be a man" at the same time that "it became vital to prove one's manhood."[86]

Chapter Five

Women Seeking What They Would Be

I N THE NARRATIVE of her life, Olive Cleaveland Clarke, born in Northampton, Massachusetts, in 1785, reported that once, when Governor Caleb Strong was on his way to Boston, bad weather forced him to ask for hospitality at the home of her neighbors. She recounted that

> He took supper with the family. A large dish of bread and milk was set in the center of the table and each had a spoon and dipped from the same dish. The Governor told the matron that he would prefer a dish by himself, as he might get more than his share, but she thought there was no danger, and did not gratify him.

I think we can take this single tale as emblematic of what Olive Cleaveland Clarke wanted to communicate about her own self feelings: that she had not allowed a man (the ostensible governor) to get more of herself than she was willing to share with him. It is likely that she, as she noted an ancestor had been, was "a proud, high spirited women," but she nevertheless saw herself as having porous boundaries. She told a story about her neighbor in order to tell something important about herself. She, too, ate, both literally and figuratively, out of a collective bowl.[1]

In the colonial and Revolutionary periods, patriarchy was the ostensible ruling system, but under certain conditions women found room for much negotiated and unnegotiated independent activity. In New England, for example, "wives as well as husbands traded with their neighbors, . . . young women felt themselves responsible for their own support, [and] . . . matches were made in the tumult of neighborhood frolics."[2] The work of Cornelia Hughes Dayton shows that women were also often active players in courtroom dramas until mid-century.[3] At that point, as women were being closed out of the courts, women in the new Baptist congregations in New England (which developed widely after the First Great Awakening of the 1740s) were taking on new roles. Susan Juster's research demonstrates that between the 1740s and the 1770s Baptist women participated in decision making at many levels, "admitting and rejecting members, choosing and dismissing pastors and deacons, establishing or abolishing rituals, and determining modes of worship." Although they were not ordained, many women exhorted and played a significant role in bringing others to religious experience.[4]

In the Middle Colonies some communities were more patriarchal than in New England, but many were far less so, notably those of the Quakers in Pennsylvania and the Jerseys, which more closely resembled the Quaker communities in Rhode Island, in which women preached to and criticized men and advised on political activity. In the South, however, extensive slavery negatively affected the roles and freedom of virtually all women both by degrading work and by allowing white men to violate black women at will. Slavery had an overwhelmingly pernicious effect, primarily, of course, on the enslaved but also on the male and female enslavers and their children, as well as on the process of social development. As a society based on slavery, the white South had to be wary of boundary changes at all times, as they threatened an always potentially unstable order.[5]

Some enslaved and quasi-free African American women, however, developed more individuated selves than most white women did.[6] Enslaved women knew they were valued for their ability to produce income as well as to reproduce slaves, and because their families were so often broken, they widely became the key strength of their kin. They recognized they had an enemy they had to oppose or risk loss of self. However, they were also concerned with rebuilding a supportive community, which they had strong need of, and those women who were able to often invested part of their selves in an imbedded black communality.

In all areas some women moved toward increased self-development, although more white women probably did so in New England and the Middle Colonies than in the South. Overall, the new eighteenth-century self-view, while seen as the work of men, was in good part made by myriad women who aspired to and achieved a modicum of independent self-development.[7] The reality widely violated the male-centered ideal, but did not vitiate it.

The greater Revolutionary era can be seen as a period of "category crises" in which the national, class, race, and gender boundaries, which had been widely accepted as ideals before, were being altered, both by design and by happenstance. Many borderlines were more permeable, making this a dangerous time that left many insecure, even those who thought they wanted revolutionary change of one kind or another.[8] The response given by John Adams to his wife Abigail's oft-cited serious plea to create a new code of laws that would "not put such unlimited power in the hand of the Husbands," because, as she reminded him, "all men would be tyrants if they could," indicates that he sought to make a joke of what was his serious discomfort over changing boundaries.[9] John Adams was determined to maintain a gender wall at all costs, while all else was shifting:

As to your extraordinary Code of Laws, I cannot but laugh. We have been told that our struggle has loosened the bands of Government every where. That Children and Apprentices were disobedient—that schools and Colleges were grown turbulent—that Indians slighted their Guardians and Negroes grew insolent to their Masters. But your Letter was the first Intimation that another Tribe more numerous and powerful than all the rest were grown discontented.—. . . . Depend upon it. We know better than to repeal our Masculine systems.

Adams warned his wife that should women gain a change in status, "I hope General Washington and all our brave Heroes would fight. I am sure every good Politician would plot, as long as he would against Despotism, Empire, Monarchy, Aristocracy, [or] Oligarchy." Thus, while John Adams claimed that his wife's letter caused him to laugh, he responded with a threat of violence, indicating how deeply it touched a very serious concern. Abigail Adams was not pleased with her husband's response, but she did not consciously continue the debate with him. She may well have continued an unvoiced argument, however; her subsequent behavior, especially as wife of the President, suggests that she was determined to take more into her own hands than he would have allowed women through the increasingly male oriented law.[10]

This recognition of anger is apparently a critical aspect of change. As Carolyn Heilbrun emphasizes, "If one is not permitted to express anger or even to recognize it within oneself, one is, by simple extension, refused both power and control." Abigail Adams recognized her anger and did suggest to her husband that she would find ways to get around his "[a]rbitrary power." In the growing conflicts of the Revolutionary era, more women openly came to recognize their rage at the other sex as the enemy that should be "marked for attack." Others, however, made an enemy of the traditional woman; or of the mother, the one closest to them who played this role; or, more ominously, of themselves. But recognizing an enemy and expressing anger against that enemy are not sufficient for self-development. Only those who accepted an authority that directed their anger and approved and assisted their own development in opposition to their alien other moved in the direction of creating a more individuated self. Those who had no authority to give direction and legitimation to their anger often could not cope with their own powerful hatreds and found that their anger was dangerous to their selves. As gender roles became more polarized, more women came to have significant conflicts over their own gender, and some chose to act the role of the other. Some came to adopt the hatred of the other for their own sex, while many women,

166

although better educated than those in the colonial period and more often involved in social reform work within the framework of the churches, continued to develop a communal sense of self.[11]

By the nineteenth century, a white woman of the middling sort was expected to be a virtuous and relatively passive wife and mother who would remain embedded in the family and a sodality of women. Henry Poor (born 1812) summarized in one sentence what he and many others thought was women's proper role and life: "The chief end of women is to make others happy."[12] Sexual appetites, seen before this period as voracious for both sexes, with women viewed as quite aggressive and dangerous, were increasingly assumed (by middle-class white men) to be primarily male, and courtship shifted from a shared aggressive drama to dependence on male initiative. Burton Carr (born 1792), who was planning to move west in 1829, saw his future wife as just such a compliant women, noting that she was "willing to do as I would have her do."[13] The household, which had been the workplace for all, was increasingly viewed as an enclosure for women, while children, who had been assumed to need firm discipline and had been widely under the guidance of fathers, were now often believed to be naturally pure and in need of the protected environment that women were to service.

Early modern society was moving toward a more structured life cycle, and white males were being pressed into conformity with this new pattern, especially by means of lengthened schooling. White males were eventually promised a proper self without the emotional turmoil of a new birth or radical self-change, but part of the price was that they had to become "what they should be." This involved becoming less androgynous and more determined to root out female "weakness" from their character. This was the ideal. The reality was more complex for both sexes.[14] A minority of women, although far more than are commonly known, rejected both the commonality and "weakness" and fashioned themselves anew. A small minority chose to act as if they were males in order to function more freely on the social stage.

Eighteenth-Century Quaker Women Eliminating Their Womanish Parts

In the eighteenth century, Quaker women were the first white women who could rely on a supportive network to back them if they chose to become itinerating public ministers, an individuated and public leadership role that was positively encouraged for a leading minority. Quaker homes and meetings were open to these women, and local Quaker individuals (generally females, but sometimes males) often offered to accompany them on their journeys. Quaker women preachers, or Public Friends, exerted a wide influence on the Quaker community.[15] They took upon themselves the task of voicing harsh criticism of Quakers' practices, even (or perhaps especially) those of male elders and leaders. An attack on male others formed a subversive subtext of their mission, which was ostensibly geared to eliminating womanish values, particularly sensuality and other "natural emotions" from both males and females.

Analysis of the narratives of a group of Quaker women who were active in eighteenth-century America suggests the central symbol they adopted in their self-development: prophet in Israel. Most renamed themselves symbolically after biblical men—Jacob, Joseph, Daniel, or Christ—symbolizing the new level they had achieved in spiritual development. They virtually never thought of themselves as the namesakes of women, since women were not their role models. The closest they came to this was when they saw themselves as Mothers in Israel, in the tradition of Deborah, but the honorific was used for heroes of God's laboring force, not for exemplary mothers of children. Their personas were quasi-male, in part because the freedom they took to talk publicly was based on the Quaker demand that both sexes eliminate the womanish parts of themselves.

A second shared symbol of self was to become wayfarers. Travel stood, as it had traditionally, for spirit travel and growth. These women did not particularly seek visionary travels, although they accepted them if they came to them in dreams, but they actually chose to travel physically, unmooring themselves, placing themselves in very new and trying circumstances. They traveled stations of the cross, as it were, metaphorically. They had to travel a large circle before they could reach home again, and on the way they had to stand up to trials. They had to be willing to fight symbolic and real battles to find the Truth, which in the Quaker view was the "ultimate spiritual reality."[16]

It was very important to these women to demonstrate that they were a means to express Truth, which became a sign of the self they hoped to have. To do this, they had to find hidden faults, or sins, in others and expose them. They had to prove their worth as critics and seers, and play the role of judges. The selves that were constellated around this symbol, Truth bearer, and the others, prophet in Israel and wayfarer, were very different from the ideal of the female self posited in the more normative colonial and Revolutionary communities, and involved critically attacking men and competing with men.

When Catherine Payton [Phillips], born in England in 1727, came to the colonies from England in 1753, she was treated as a Truth bearer and played this role with great strength. Although she traveled to America together with Quaker minister Mary Peisley, who had been born in Ireland in 1717, she often journeyed alone or, when in the South, was accompanied by an enslaved African, traveling in difficult backcountry and living under harsh conditions. Payton and Peisley realized that "[n]o women ministers had visited part of this country before us, so that the people were probably excited by curiosity to attend some of the meetings we appointed." They welcomed this curiosity, and during their travels from South Carolina to New England, in which they spoke to every Quaker meeting they could find, they also spoke on ferries and at inns to whoever would listen. They were pained by what they saw as "a dark carnal spirit" among the people and claimed that even the Quaker children sought "vanity and earthly riches." Many non-Quakers listened to them, and they thought they influenced some deeply. On quite a few occasions, however, particularly in the towns, when they suspected that many had come for the novelty of hearing women speak, they were silent, expecting that their silence would have a more significant effect. Once "Ranters," whom Friends in Hampton, Massachusetts, had disowned for accepting idiosyncratic revelations, came to disrupt a meeting at which Payton [Phillips] was expected to talk. She reported the incident as if she had been a passive witness whom God spoke through: "I had no view of what was given me to speak before I stood up; but I was immediately and mercifully clothed with such a degree of authority, that it might be said the truth was over all, and the meeting ended in awful solemnity." That she was by then actually an assured self-fashioner was made clear by her subsequent behavior: she fearlessly went to the Ranters' meetinghouse and aggressively called on them to give up their "enjoyments, visions, and revelations" and "to return" to the orthodox Quaker way.[17]

Payton [Phillips] "thought there was need of weight to counteract the light frothy spirit which appeared in the people," and to that end she harshly criticized those who came to meeting for "company and conversation." Both she and Mary Peisley were "led to find out some hidden works of darkness" and criticized the sexual behavior of male and female Quakers. Payton [Phillips] may have been projecting her own guilt when she decreed that "young women who travel in the service of the ministry," as she and Peisley did, must adopt some "cautions, . . . toward those of the other sex, who are also unmarried." While she recognized that it might be proper for them to provide services for the males, she cautioned that it must be "free from a mixture of natural affection." Perhaps this criticism was directed at Mary Peisley, as they separated again for a time. But perhaps it was an unvoiced recognition of her own affections. Her narrative provides evidence that Payton [Phillips] herself had an attachment to her mentor, John Churchman, the married Quaker minister who had been instrumental in her decision to journey to the colonies. She sought him at his home but was disappointed to find he was still in England. Later, when they met in their separate travels, "We were mutually refreshed in beholding the faces one of another, our union in the Truth being strong, which was now renewed in the fresh springing up of its life." Payton [Phillips] framed their relationship as a spiritual union, and was not conscious of any other implications, but the dream of mutilation reported by John Churchman (discussed in chapter 4) indicates that he may well have sensed its emotional aspects, and was punishing himself for them.[18]

Payton [Phillips] was opposed by some of those she criticized, and was depressed when she did not seem to have influence, but the French and Indian War mobilized her to action and to success. Early in 1755 she organized a special meeting of all Quakers in the Pennsylvania Assembly, at which she spoke strongly against their support of the war and for their intervention in the peace process. She took pride in the results: "I think it worth remarking, that the termination of this Indian war, was at last effected by the peaceable interposition of Friends."[19] She clearly counted herself as one of the important voices in this process.

Payton [Phillips] was always sensitive to the roles women were playing. She was pleased to learn that the silent Indian women who attended the Quaker peace meetings in Pennsylvania played a role in Indian councils, and when she returned to England she thought there had been a relative increase in Quaker women's activism there. She reported that at the 1756 yearly meeting at Penrith, God "lay the weight of the service upon the females; who, though the weaker vessels by nature, are at times rendered strong through his Divine power."[20]

The pride that Payton [Phillips] took in other women's assertion of authority was part of a matrix of self-perception that would not allow her to accept male authority over her self. She worked hard and long to create her self and her ministry and clearly felt that she herself had been "rendered strong through his Divine power." Although born a Quaker, as a young woman she, as so many of the young men in other churches, felt that she had transgressed and that her heart was "an uncultivated wilderness," as evidenced by the fact that she had written poetry and essays, and read widely. She abruptly gave all this up, suggesting a crisis, and left a girls' school in London to return home, where she faced far fewer outside temptations or influences. She now read only the Bible and no doubt had religious experiences; she was soon ready to state that "the dealings of the Almighty with me . . . have been singular." By the age of twenty-three she began traveling as a Public Friend and continued on such journeys for the next twenty years, enlarging their scope and her stature. Early in her ministry William Phillips, a widower (with children) whom she converted, sought to marry her. She was not prepared to become a wife and mother, claiming it was because she planned to continue traveling as a minister, although many Quaker women combined both roles. (She also was not very impressed with Phillips's spiritual development.) She did eventually marry this man, but not until twenty-three years had passed. By then both her self and her role were far more firmly established and the children were grown.[21] She continued to travel after her marriage, both with and without her husband, noting pointedly that God "chuseth whom he pleaseth. . . . He appoints, of both male and female, 'some apostles, some prophets, some evangelists, and some pastors and teachers.' "[22] Catherine had come to appreciate William, but he was none of the above, while she was indeed a woman of great authority.

Mary Peisley [Neale] also recognized her own significance, although she too was worried about pride, and always gave credit to God. Peisley [Neale] feared that it was her concern with "self" and the competition between herself and Payton [Phillips] that had led them to separate while in America. Nevertheless, the positive reactions to her preaching reassured her that God was with her and allowed her to state pridefully that "the light went before me . . . till I was become as a sign and wonder to myself and others." On this journey she came to feel like "a mother in Israel," as well as "one nailed to the cross."[23] Both Peisley [Neale] and Payton [Phillips] felt they had changed significantly during these travels, and while they both credited the Light, they recognized that they had to use will and dedication to achieve their ends on their difficult journey.

The life journey of Quaker Elizabeth Sampson Sullivan Ashbridge, born in England in 1713, was, on all counts, far more arduous than those of Payton Phillips and Neale Peisley, and the result was an even stronger public expression of an individuated self. While the Quaker faith of the natal families of both Payton Phillips and Peisley Neale made it more difficult for them to consciously acknowledge their own negative views of males, Sampson [Ashbridge] began life as an Anglican and early was aware that she regarded males as her enemy. She apparently had a difficult relationship with her father, who as a ship's surgeon was rarely home during her childhood, but he returned to live there when Elizabeth was twelve. Perhaps his new presence upset the family politics and placed new limits on Elizabeth, who chose to leave home two years later, when she was fourteen, eloping with a poor stocking weaver who was "the darling of my heart." When he died five months later, her father would not countenance her return. Her mother, however, arranged for her to go to live and work with her Quaker relatives in Ireland, where she began a difficult, essentially unvoiced, dialogue both with her father and with Quakers, a dialogue that centered on the issue of her self-development. In both cases she began by doing what these others would not have her do or being what they would not have her be. In Ireland she became more "lively," singing and dancing in the face of Quaker belief that she should desist; and when she decided to leave for America it was consciously to become the rejecter (of her father) rather than the rejectee. In both ways she was asserting herself and enslaving herself. She thought of her father at crucial turning points in her life, and the critical response she expected he would have made influenced her choices. She often chose to do what she believed he would not have her do but on other occasions seemed to choose not to do what he objected to, seemingly more to violate his expectations than to fulfill his demands.

Samson [Ashbridge] was, like many in this study, a seeker, and was both attracted to and repelled by the faiths she came into contact with—Anglican, Catholic, Presbyterian, Baptist, and Quaker. She tells us that even as a young child she had wanted to be a minister "and sometimes wept with Sorrow, that I was not a boy that I might have been one." Her anger at the limitations imposed on her gender, which upset her from an early age, and her longing to be a minister explain one level of the satisfaction that Quaker faith could provide. Before she could free her self to make a full commitment to any church, however, she had to punish her self far more deeply, as she recognized. She never revealed what she felt to be all her sins, but an important vision provided her with a dark list.

> While I was sitting as in a trance, I beheld a long roll, written in black characters, hearing, at the same time, a voice saying, "These are thy sins," and afterwards adding, "And the blood of Christ is not sufficient to wash them out. This is shown thee that thou mayest confess thy damnation to be just, and not in order that thou shoudst be forgiven."[24]

When Samson [Ashbridge] decided to leave Ireland, she played a significant role in indenturing herself: she was first "deluded away," onto a ship but was freed by the intervention of friends. Nevertheless, she went back on board of her own free will, only to be indentured by the captain before landfall. After working three years for a harsh and possibly sexually aggressive master in New York City in the early 1730s, she contemplated, but rejected, going on stage as a singer and actress. She knew that this would have fulfilled her father's worst expectations, since actresses were widely regarded as little more than prostitutes. She managed to buy herself free of her last year's work through much overtime labor, yet when she was free, and probably for the first time truly on her own, she apparently became panicked by this state and she very quickly entered what she regarded as "slavery for life" by marrying "a man [she] had no love for." She revealingly commented that she married her second husband, Sullivan, because "I was not Sufficiently Punished."[25] Although she at first traveled from job to job with her husband, an itinerant teacher, she decided to travel alone to visit relatives in Pennsylvania, ostensibly unaware that they were Quakers. She was clearly longing for both an embracing family and a faith, and probably for the Quaker faith in particular. When she found that her relatives were indeed Quakers, she was at first "mortified," but soon realized that their faith attracted her deeply. She yielded, and desired to commit herself, again for life. First, however, she punished herself again by inviting her husband to join her. On arrival, Sullivan was appalled to hear that she had adopted the Quaker use of "thee" and "thou," but he was soon deeply upset as well by her serious depression. In the face of her conflict between her growing commitment and her husband's orders not to become a Quaker (which she had no doubt expected when she invited him to join her), Elizabeth gave up food, drink, and sleep and took to wandering in the woods. Her husband then took her on a forced march of many miles to get her away from the Quaker hothouse of her family and new friends. On the way, he attempted to force her to dance and thereby publicly signal her fall from Quaker ways. Eventually, he brought her to a house where they were both to teach and lodge; strangely, it was with Quakers. Sullivan acknowledged that he, too, had changed and had become ambivalent about his wife's faith, but he apparently told her that his fear of public ridicule held him back from making a further commitment. Drink protected him, and in a drunken bout in 1740 he enlisted to go as a soldier to Cuba. There, his wife tells us, he refused, on Quaker principles, to fight, was badly beaten, and was sent to an English hospital where he died.[26]

Most of the people described in Elizabeth's narrative were men, and she regarded virtually all of them as untrustworthy in one way or another. Once she had left her father's house at age fourteen, he would not see or help her. Her beloved first husband died within a few months, abandoning her, as it were. The ship's captain on the boat to America repaid her help to him (she revealed a mutiny plot) by indenturing her and selling her to a harsh master. She saw her second husband as weak, a hard drinker, and sometimes brutal. In dealing with all of these men and events, Elizabeth followed a fairly common path noted by Carl Jung, wherein the "[t]he right way to wholeness is made up of fateful detours and wrong turnings."[27] Repeatedly, she escaped from one enslavement only to turn to another. While she was suffering under her harsh indenture, and having contemplated suicide, a dream helped her recognize the possibility of a different future:

> Soon after [considering suicide] . . . I had a dream; and, though some make a ridicule of dreams, this seemed very significant to me, and therefore I shall mention it. I thought I heard a knocking at the door, by which, when I had opened it, there stood a grave woman, holding in her right hand a lamp burning, who, with a solid countenance, fixed her eye upon me and said, "I am sent to tell thee, that if thou wilt return to the Lord thy God, who created thee, he will have mercy on thee, and thy lamp shall not be put out in obscurity." Her lamp then flamed, in an extraordinary manner; she left me and I awoke.[28]

While Elizabeth's dream confirms many things she wrote about herself in the narrative, it does lead to some new insights. It is not surprising that a woman rather than a man came to help her. This was a strong confirmation of her view of her life experiences, in which she saw the men as treacherous and only her mother and her Irish aunt as reliable figures. It gave her hope that she, too, could play a significant role. This woman was grave, rather than lively, as the Quakers had long been trying to convince her was best. And she spoke in distinctive Quaker language, informing the dreamer that there is Truth in the Quaker way. What is surprising, in terms of the position that the narrator held by the time she wrote this, is that with the phrase "thy lamp shall not be put out in obscurity," she recorded (and the Quaker editorial committee allowed the printing of) extremely strong support for the dreamer's ego, or self. This pledge of an inner light and fame was highly unusual in a Quaker narrative. Elizabeth Samson Sullivan [Ashbridge] was not yet ready to follow through on this promise, but she harbored the memory and eventually brought it to realization.

"Self" was often directly taken note of by this narrator, as it related both to her physical body and her soul. When Elizabeth first rose to speak at a Quaker meeting, "the power attending made me Tremble, & I could not hold my Self still." Near the end of her reports about her marriage to Sullivan, Elizabeth quoted herself as having said she would try to improve their relationship, but that where his commands "imposed upon my Conscience, I no longer Durst: For I had already done it too Long, & *wronged my Self* by it." By becoming a Quaker, Elizabeth found an institution to help her *right her self* and focus her anger: she could become a critic of men as well as of women and establish her authority over them. As was the case with Phillips, she became a minister, while her third husband, Quaker Aaron Ashbridge, whom she married in 1745, did not.[29] She became a respected Public Friend, and in 1753 she decided to travel to England and Ireland, without him, in order to preach. She was returning full circle to the places where she had been a confused seeker to show what she had achieved. She left no record of her reactions to this journey, nor do we know if anyone in her family was still alive to hear her new voice, but at age forty she was once again speaking to her (dead) father, now with great authority. She had become capable of holding her "Self" still.[30]

Payton Phillips, Peisley Neale, Samson Ashbridge, and many other Quaker women, found ways to develop their own voices. They, like their male counterparts, were denying the womanish parts in themselves, but for women this clearly had a different valence than it had for men. These women sought to root out "natural affection" while following their calling, and this meant, in part, putting off or never becoming mothers of children. Those who had children left them for long periods of time: Susanna Hatton, for example, "was frequently from home traveling in the service of Truth." In 1760, when her daughter Susanna was seven, she left her on the family's Irish farm while Hatton went off for a two-year mission to American Friends. As her father had died the year before, young Susanna bore many responsibilities for the family. When her mother returned, it was in order to uproot the family and take them to Pennsylvania, to live with her new husband, whom she had met on her travels. In stark contrast to her mother, who was a very self-confident Public Friend, the daughter was often overcome with self-doubt and "a sorrowful spirit." After the daughter married Hugh Judge, who had been deeply influenced by the preaching of her mother, he admonished his wife that "we must not always expect to draw as from the breast, and be dandled as on the knee." It is unlikely that she had been so spoiled, but while it may be suspected that she harbored anger at her mother, she punished herself, as may well have become more common among late-eighteenth-century Quaker women.[31]

TAKING ON THE MANTLE OF CHRIST, 1740–1840

While women who were Congregationalists or members of the Church of England may have expressed anger at men more readily (as court and church records indicate), they did not have the ideological frame to see these as God-given criticisms nor the institutional supports for self-expression that Friends did. It was therefore far more difficult for a non-Quaker woman to find an acceptable way of expressing her anger at males and developing her self.[32] Much like Ashbridge, Sarah Haggar [Wheaton Osborn], born in England in 1714, a Congregationalist who grew up in Rhode Island, began her narrative by recounting angry acts she had done "contrary to my parents' commands." From her early youth she had acted in ways that suggest she was determined to take both physical and social risks, and above all to violate gender restrictions in order to develop a self that was not immersed in a feminine communality. She went boating alone at midnight and literally walked far out on thin ice. She did much the same in her social behavior, at eighteen keeping company with and marrying a sailor, Samuel Wheaton, against her parents orders. It is not surprising that at this point "every one seemed to be enemies to me." By the time she was twenty her husband had died at sea and she had a young son to support. As a widow with a young child she both elicited more sympathy and made herself more socially acceptable than she had as an independent young woman who was breaking social rules.[33]

After the death of her husband, Sarah Haggar Wheaton [Osborn] went through a deep crisis, during which she herself realized that she had long been angry and in revolt against social norms and that she now wanted acceptance. She longed to find a new figure of authority and become part of a community. She emerged from this depression when she had an ecstatic experience of Christ being with her: "Thus . . . was I brought to lay down my arms of rebellion, which I saw I had held as long as I could." Soon after she wrote a personal covenant committing herself to do God's will, and she again experienced God's presence. She recognized the part she played in this drama and felt that it was reciprocated: "My heart reached forth in burning desires after the blessed Jesus. O. how I was ravished with his love."[34]

From this point on, Sarah Haggar Wheaton [Osborn] managed to direct her life in new paths, to take initiative and to take enormous risks that violated the accepted gender limits, and yet to retain the approval of leading members of her congregation and community. In accepting the rule of her male Lord Jesus she had markedly freed herself to defy other males and many male-imposed restrictions.

From the outset she wanted to play a significant role in other lives, but as she tells the story, this came about as if she had no hand in it: "For soon after this [her conversion] a number of young women, who were awakened to a concern for their souls, came to me, and desired my advice and assistance, and proposed to join in a society; provided I would take care of them." However, Wheaton also records that she had established her special qualities by personally approaching both the local minister whom she had chosen, Nathaniel Clapp, and the visiting revivalists George Whitefield and Gilbert Tennant. Their positive personal responses to her singled her out in the community of women, establishing her as special. This process confirms that she played a significant role in determining her calling. She headed the female religious society organized in 1741 until her death, some fifty years later. At its peak, some sixty women met once a week to confess their sins, be criticized and punished, and came together again to fast and pray on the Saturday before the monthly Lord's Supper. They formed a permanent family, with Osborn at their head, and she did take care of them, as they had requested, much as a minister, father, or husband might have.[35]

Sarah Haggar Wheaton [Osborn] tried to support herself and her child by teaching, but she left this when she married again in 1742, in the expectation that Henry Osborn, a widower with two children, would support her and her son. But Henry Osborn soon went bankrupt and became ill and infirm, and by May of 1744, she had opened a school that was to support the family for more than thirty years. Sarah Osborn was now the leader of women in the community, the head of what became a fairly large school (with seventy students, including ten who boarded with her), and the sole support of a large family. Her own psychological support through all this extremely taxing work was not her second husband, whom she barely mentions in her published narrative, but her dearest friend and partner in "Emanuel," Susanna Anthony. For many years, these two women supported each other in public works but had a more competitive private relationship. They shared their raptures with each other and intertwined their identities, but they also competed for Christ's attention. When Anthony longed to die, to be with Christ, Osborn felt this as a deep rejection, and when Anthony had ecstatic experiences, Osborn feared that she was not her spiritual equal and that she could not follow her all the way.[36]

Anthony and Osborn worked together in the women's society and also set aside private time each week to be with one another. When apart, they exchanged letters of love and rapture. (Anthony to Osborn: "Pray for me . . . who am, I trust, yours in the bonds of an everlasting relation; members of one body, Jesus the head." Osborn to Anthony: "My Dear One, my heart has been yearning towards you."[37]) Their relationship, which was known to the community, did not arouse criticism. On the contrary, they were praised for their unusual dedication to each other. After the deaths of both, Samuel Hopkins, their minister, who edited and published both their narratives and their letters, wrote, "It is not known or believed that there is to be found, or has been in this century such a union and happy christian friendship between two such eminent christians for so long a time." He was certain they were together in heaven, where "with . . . high delight and rapture have they met among the spirits of the just made perfect."[38]

Osborn spent several hours each day writing extensive biblical commentaries and keeping up her correspondence with several ministers. She came to engage these men, who had begun as her mentors, as colleagues. On one occasion, for example, she sent the Reverend Joseph Fish, who was in bitter conflict with the New Lights in his congregation, an almost priestly blessing, which she felt was proper as "My trials bear some resemblance to yours":

[I] wish the Lord may be with y[ou] and grant you much of his gracious presence. My heart aches for the many troubles I hear rushes in upon you. . . . The Lord support and comfort you and grant you may patiently wait his time for a deliverance from all your troubles, and be strong and of good courage for god will glorifie himself not withstanding all these strange confusions and by and by wipe all the tears from your eyes. Tis but a little while eare the wicked shall cease from troubling and the weary be at rest. Blessed be God, this is not our home. We are but travelers and strangers here.[39]

Osborn had apparently played a decisive role in convincing her own congregation to hire Samuel Hopkins and in her subsequent interaction with Hopkins played a role in bringing him to publicly oppose the slave trade and then slavery itself.[40] Both had been slave owners, and Hopkins was reputed to have suffered deeply over the fact he

had sold a slave rather than manumit him. Hopkins went on to become one of the pillars of the manumission movement, and then of
the colonization idea, having come to believe that the sins of white
people against blacks made it impossible for Africans to work out a
decent future in America.[41]

Between 1765 and 1768 Osborn was involved in a public activity
that of all her actions most disturbed gender roles and her local community. As Hopkins facetiously wrote, "[T]here was an uncommon
attention to religion, which turned the thoughts of many to Mrs.
Osborn." In fact, a revival had begun in the Osborn home, which at
its height attracted more than five hundred people a week, and Sarah
Osborn was at its center. When Osborn described the beginnings of
this movement in her letters to her mentor/colleague, the Reverend
Joseph Fish, she again drew the picture of others bearing primary
responsibility, and she denied that she was acting as a minister. In
April of 1765 she wrote that "there is several Ethiopians thotful who
Having their Liberty to go where they like on Lords day Evenings
have ask'd Liberty to repair to our House for the benefit of family
prayer reading etc. and I Have thot it a duty to Encourage them."[42]
Perhaps this began with six of the African Americans in her own
family singing, giving testimony, and responding to her prayers.[43]
With her encouragement, forty-two slaves were soon attracted to
what became weekly meetings. When a number of free black and
white youths began coming as well, bringing the number to over
seventy, it made it difficult for some of the enslaved to find room. In
an attempt to preserve Sunday evenings for the slaves, who could
not come at any other time, Osborn divided the people attending by
race, status, gender, and age, setting aside different times for heads
of families, young white women, young white men, free blacks, the
enslaved, and a catechism class of children. Significantly, the whites
were divided by gender and age, the blacks only by legal status: chattel or free. The blacks had come first, and kept coming long after
others dropped away. Their singing was central to their evenings,
and to attracting others as well, and explains in part why Osborn
found that these meetings "seem then to refresh recruit and enliven
my Exhausted spirits."[44]

But more than refreshed spirits were involved: Osborn believed
that in conducting these classes she was doing the Lord's work. She
was made to suffer for it as well, losing much of the friendship and
support that had been extended to her previously, which added to
her conviction that she was bearing a cross. She noted that her home
had gained the epithet of a "Negro House," and that she was seen as
its keeper. Nevertheless, she chose to continue with this task, rather

than "creep into obscurity," suggesting thus that being in the public eye, even if under opprobrium, was very important to her sense of self. Leading five hundred each week in singing and prayer, and speaking with them, was heady stuff, and not easily given up. She knew there was a "Line" she should not pass, and yet she had succeeded in doing just that by labeling it as school, as she said the blacks called it, rather than a meeting.[45] But both she and Fish knew that she had passed the old accepted line and established a new one. She was playing the role of a minister but calling herself a teacher.

Osborn did not voice her attack on the male as an alien other, she enacted it. She became the sole support of her family, and an unmarried woman became her strongest emotional support, her helpmeet. She resembled most of the men in this cohort in rarely ever mentioning her marriage partner in her narrative. She ran a school, a large religious society, and a revival. She interacted with ministers as their spiritual equal. Nevertheless, when she wanted to get things done outside the institutions she had established, she had to rely on influence as she did not have power outside these institutions. Much as she had influenced her congregation to hire Hopkins, she influenced him to oppose slavery and to support the education of several Africans in order to prepare them to be missionaries. She could not convince the ministers she knew to directly support her own role as a preacher, but she did reduce their opposition to her serving the spiritually needy. However, while she had made a life for herself, she did not pave the way for other women to follow her.

Prior to the Revolution some Baptist women had come far closer than had Osborn to full participation in their churches' decision-making process, but when the Baptist churches sought to join in the Revolutionary movement they began what Juster has characterized as a "steady, quiet retreat . . . from . . . commitment to sexual egalitarianism." In accepting the authority of the new state, Baptist men lost a primary enemy other, and after joining the patriarchal Revolutionary movement they moved rapidly to reemphasize the feminine as that which they would not be. Many values that Baptist men had begun to share with women were redefined as feminine and were increasingly regarded as dangerous and sinful.[46] Because the Baptist churches also accepted more middle-class members in this period, they more rapidly changed to parallel the mainline churches by limiting women's roles at the same time that they redefined much that was evil as womanish.

Dreams were a source of power to women in these trying times. Baptist convert Chloe Willey (born 1760) had a powerful series of dreams in 1788 that gave her "spiritual discernment, whereby I could discover the difference between a faithful and a carnal christian, and between a real saint and a hypocrite." While she did not go out to preach, she offered to tell anyone who came to see her the "truth" about their nature. Many did come to hear this seer.[47]

Even in this more limiting period some Baptist women became preachers, among them Salome Lincoln, born in Massachusetts in 1807, who began to preach when she was twenty. A poor factory worker, she held that "God hath chosen the *Weak Things* of the world, *to confound the things* which are MIGHTY." She preached three or four times a week, primarily to the poor, both in factories and at churches. A radical activist who fought against slavery as well as for the rights of women, she chose to marry as well as to stay within the church, and managed to hold together all these roles until her death after childbirth at age thirty-four.[48]

Women had also played a significant role in English Methodism from the 1740s to the 1790s. During Wesley's lifetime more than forty women, who were regarded as "extraordinary messengers," had been accepted as nominal preachers, but they were rapidly excluded after Wesley's death in 1791. English Methodism was also returning to a more patriarchal order.[49] When the Methodists extended their outreach to America in the late 1760s and the 1770s, they did not seek to establish sexual equality, but in this early period, women such as Barbara Heck (1734–1804), the founder of the John Street Methodist Church in New York City, did testify publicly, and she and others adopted roles that were quite different from those of women in the Church of England.[50] Many consciously sought "liberty" and found that the Methodist classes gave them a direct opportunity to embody this value. There, among other women, they began their exhorting. Some moved far beyond the segregated classes.[51]

One of the women who simply took her liberty was Methodist Fanny Newell (born 1793), who was anointed in a dream in a manner that, as a women, she could not expect in waking life. In this dream she was given a cross to carry and told to wear the gown of her dead mentor, Preacher Henry Martin. When she awoke she said aloud, "[B]ehold the handmaid of the Lord, let the mantle of an Henry, or rather Elijah, rest on me."[52] She took on the role of preacher and prophet (recognizing that it made her a surrogate male) without a public anointment. She held that the dream anointment was binding.

Many other Methodist women felt they had to develop new public roles that in part hid their assertiveness. Methodist convert Catherine Livingston (born 1752), who was painfully trying to work out a different future for herself while pressed to conform to her wealthy mother's social aspirations, dreamt "that I was going to be crucified, that they were raising the cross up on which I was stretched, and I was in expectation of great sufferings."[53] It is clear that Livingston, who had also seen herself walking on water, envisioned herself as a female Christ, but she did not make any public claim to this role and so avoided punishment.[54] When she did take a public role, it was as the wife of Methodist minister Freeborn Garrettson, whom she married against her mother's wishes in 1793, when she was forty. Their joint home became an open haven for Methodists, who saw her as intensely religious and self-denying. Her premarital dreams and visions, while recorded, were not widely known, nor was her "rage at her mother," who became her negative role model.[55] Livingston became what her mother most wanted her not to be: a Methodist and a mystic, who experienced union with Christ. Livingston also had female spirit guides, including a black girl, and a "Spirit of Wisdom," seemingly much like that female figure important to Shakers. This spirit brought Livingston the knowledge that she would follow a difficult path but achieve "happiness here, and hereafter."[56]

One woman who did announce her role as Christ, enslaved Aunt Katy, was indeed punished for this act. In the first decade of the nineteenth century, while at an African American Methodist love feast in Wilmington, North Carolina, Katy "with many extravagant gestures, cried out that she was 'young King Jesus.' " In angry reaction, the Reverend Joseph Travis, who was white, charged her with blasphemy and "publicly read her out of membership." While he regarded her behavior as "fanatic," he was ready to reaccept her when she gave evidence that she "felt it [her guilt] deeply," and formally repented. She may, however, have felt her exclusion more deeply than any guilt.[57]

During the greater Revolutionary period both Ann Lee (born 1736) and Jemima Wilkinson (born 1752) read themselves out of the traditional roles of women and out of traditional churches. Both apparently saw themselves as sharing in the Godhead with Christ.[58] Both opposed a male alien other and both created institutions to support themselves and others in achieving a new sense of self. While male Shakers in the following generations exerted much authority, certainly some Shaker women with a strong male enemy other, such as Rebecca Cox Jackson, still found the Shaker community a supportive and nurturing institution in which, after severe trials, they could come to a new sense of self.

Jackson knew that she and Mother [Ann Lee] had their significant but negative others in male figures, although she did envision a gentle white asexual but male spirit guide instructing her. Sex, rather than having a male body, was *the* sin. "In this respect," she wrote of sexuality, "they [men] have fallen below the beasts, for these know times and seasons, and after that they remain still, until the time of nature's season returns." Men, she believed, knew of no limits.[59]

When Jackson had a most terrifying "Dream of Slaughter," she knew her violent enemy was a man who

> took a lance and laid my nose open and then he cut my head on the right side, from the back to the front above my nose, and pulled the skin down over the side. Then he cut the left, did the same way, and pulled the skin down. The skin and blood covered me like a veil from my head to my lap. All my body was covered with the blood. Then he took a long knife and cut my chest open in the form of the cross and took all my bowels out and laid them on the floor by my right side.[60]

Jackson believed that she stayed alive in this dream because God commanded her enemy "not to touch me again." Given Jackson's overwhelming desire for celibacy it is likely that she conflated sexual relations with her husband with the trials she underwent in this dream. However, when Jackson interpreted this dream she explained that the enemy was a Methodist minister (whose color she did not specify) who four years later "persecuted me in as cruel a manner as he treated my body in the dream." When he died shortly after mistreating her, she believed that God had punished him for his cruel behavior.

Other women who wrote and published narratives of their lives in this period also came to what seems an intuitive understanding of the fact that personal development was tied to both commitment and focused oppositional self-development. Some succeeded in achieving such change because they managed to operate outside male controlled institutions. The experience of the enslaved girl Elizabeth (born 1766) is a remarkable example. In 1778 Elizabeth, who had been separated from her parents by sale a year earlier at age eleven, and was suffering from this traumatic break in her life, had a vision of the Lord asking her if she was "willing to be saved?" She replied yes but the question was asked again. She then experienced a developmental change in her dream as she came to the recognition that it was not enough that she willed to be saved. She suddenly realized that she could only be saved if she followed "the Lord's way." Only acceptance of an authority beyond herself would bring her to a point where she could act by and for herself. In her dream she made the decision to submit fully.[61] Her dream confirmed the critical importance of this decision:

> Immediately a light fell upon my head, and I was filled with light, and I was shown the world lying in wickedness, and was told I must go there, and call the people to repentance, for the day of the Lord was at hand; and this message was as a heavy yoke upon me, so that I wept bitterly at the thought of what I should have to pass through. While I wept, I heard a voice say, "weep not, some will laugh at thee, some will scoff at thee, and the dogs will bark at thee, but while thou doest my will, I will be with thee to the ends of the earth."[62]

Elizabeth lived a life that fulfilled this promise. Although persecuted both in the Methodist Church and outside it for her determination to break the boundaries set for women, she became a preacher and a teacher. Referred to as a "speckled bird," she was perhaps seen as unnatural, but nevertheless succeeded in her life's work. Manumitted at thirty (in 1796) she traveled extensively, stood up to threats and dangers, and accomplished much both as a missionary and as an educator. She apparently never married, nor did she submit to the authority of any male-run institution.

Although both enslaved and nominally free African American women were exploited and oppressed, and were threatened with virtual "soul murder," many were able to achieve remarkable self-development.[63] African American Jarena Lee, born free in 1783, was a converted Christian and a member of the African Methodist Episcopal Church in Philadelphia, but when she heard a voice adjure her to " 'Go preach the Gospel!' " she feared that the Devil was after her. She certainly did not intend to take this call seriously. The following night, however, she began preaching in her dreams.

> I took a text and preached in my sleep. I thought there stood before me a great multitude, while I expounded to them the things of religion. So violent were my exertions and so loud were my exclamations, that I awoke from the sound of my own voice, which also awoke the family of the house where I resided.

Her visionary experience convinced her that her call was from God, but the Reverend Richard Allen, a leading black Methodist preacher, refused to recognize her call. She was at first actually relieved, but then became tormented by her own willingness to give up the cross of preaching so easily. In 1807, a vision of "a man robed in a white garment" who told her, "Thou shalt never return from the cross," convinced her that no matter who opposed her, she would have to try to become a Christ-like public preacher. She was again stopped, but this time it was by her own decision to marry. Her husband was a preacher, and Lee moved to his community, where she began an eight-year moratorium that ended only after her husband's death. At that point her interpretation of a dream during a period of severe sickness encouraged her to attempt once again to preach.

> I thought I saw the sun rise in the morning, and ascend to an altitude of about half an hour high, and then become obscured by a dense black cloud, which continued to hide its rays for about one-third part of the day, and then it burst forth again with renewed splendor.

Accepting the African American interpretation of the sun as symbol of the self and avoiding any reference to the men who had blocked her ascent, Lee set out to fulfill the promise she felt was embodied in the radiant sun that had reappeared in her dream. The Reverend Allen and her husband had formally and informally blocked her way. Rendered independent once more by the death of her husband, she reframed this loss as God's way of setting her on the road, and she began to forge her own way, disregarding Allen's objections and welcomed by both women and men. After 1815 she traveled widely in Pennsylvania, New York, and New England, preaching almost daily, and repeatedly reported, "We had a blessed outpouring of the spirit among us—the God of Jacob was in our midst—and the shout of heaven-born souls was like music to our ears."[64]

Women Attacking Men and Damaging Themselves; Seeking to Become Self-Protective, but Often Floundering, 1775–1840

In the half century after the Revolution, as the working class grew, conditions for working-class men and women deteriorated. Men who were having increasing difficulty in supporting themselves and their families did not want the competition of women in the marketplace or in the home. As working men lost ground and could not support wives and families during the hard times they all suffered, their sexual aggressiveness increased. At the same time, the number of white women who never married rose significantly, with at least some of them finding that "Liberty [was] a better husband."[65]

Some women came to believe that there was a possibility of obtaining more freedom. In the same process some came to see their fathers and their husbands as particular oppressors. Some found

Figure 19. Jarena Lee. African Methodist Episcopal writer, preacher and "instrument of God." Frontispiece of Lee's *Religious Experiences*, 1849.

support in political theory, tying their search for liberty to the Revolution's promise; many, however, lacked communal or institutional support, and often damaged themselves rather than the males who oppressed them.

Elizabeth Munro Fisher (born 1759) provides an example of a women with a powerful male alien other who had no institution to focus her hatred and support her self-development.[66] The narration of her childhood suggests that from a very early age she saw her father as uncaring and oppressive. Her mother had died at Elizabeth's birth, and her father, Harry Munro, placed her with a wet nurse. He soon remarried and brought his new wife home; she also died in childbirth, and Elizabeth and her new brother were left with the same nurse when her father, a chaplain in the British army, went off to seek ordination in Scotland. Elizabeth's brother died while her father was abroad, adding to the already harsh impact of deaths on her life. When her father finally returned, he brought a second stepmother with him, who often whipped Elizabeth and put her in the cellar without food. Her father soon boarded her out again.

Elizabeth Munro [Fisher] claimed that when she was sixteen, her father pressed her to marry a forty-five-year-old "toothless and gray-haired" man from his regiment, informing her that "if you refuse your consent, you must not expect forgiveness from me."[67] She rejected his control, chose to marry a young man, also from the regiment, and was indeed disowned by her father.

The Revolutionary War turned her world upside down. When her house was burned in a battle that led her husband's unit to retreat to Montreal, she followed the army, carrying her young child with her. In Montreal she became an independent businesswoman, supporting herself both by selling merchandise and by renting out space in her log cabin. Her marriage, however, was not successful. When, after the war, her husband took the family back to the Lake Champlain area where they had previously lived, she chose to return to Canada and began an ongoing conflict with him over their possessions. One of these possessions was Jane, her slave girl, the only person Elizabeth Fisher ever described as loving her. (Elizabeth never described herself as loving another person.) When her husband negotiated the sale of Jane, Elizabeth took Jane from her husband's house in the middle of the night, and when slave catchers took Jane, Elizabeth "rescued" her again. Elizabeth was clearly a very independent woman who was willing to violate the law to take what she believed to be hers. Years later, in a dispute over inherited possessions, her half-brother formally charged her with forging documents relating to the ownership of their father's land. Convicted, she was sent to prison in New York State in March of 1805. When released in June of 1806, she was at a loss to know what to do with her life: "I felt nearly as bad coming out, as I did going in." Her father, her husband, and her brother had been her enemies, but she had not found a legal way to oppose them and to help herself. She wrote her narrative at this point in an attempt to reframe her past, but she did not have an authority to demand her commitment, and could not conceive a new life plan. No dream had brought her anointment and she did not respond to any individual or movement calling for commitment and change. Her hatred of males had led her to inflict damage on her self.[68]

When she was young, Ann Baker Carson followed a path similar to Elizabeth Munro Fisher's. Carson "learned to scorn and despise" the husband she had married at sixteen, "only regarding him as a slave does an austere master whom *he* is compelled to obey, and to whose authority *he* must submit." (Here, describing the outset of her development, Carson pictured herself as a male slave, i.e., one who was more likely to become a rebel.) When her husband, a sailor, returned from his long journeys, he demanded her subservience. While he was gone, she freely entered into many amorous involvements, at the outset blaming others for enticing her. While she did not follow a mentor or join an institution calling for commitment, Ann Carson nevertheless experienced a sudden and unexplained change: "for the first time a love of liberty arose in my heart." She refused to become again what she now termed her husband's "Turkish female slave," and presented her argument as an extension of Revolutionary rhetoric:

> To this kind of conduct, I never could or would, bend. I was an American; a land of liberty had given me birth; my father had been his commanding officer; I felt myself his equal, and pride interdicted my submitting to his caprices.

Carson claimed that "my own spirit had emancipated me from thralldom, and I considered myself as free as the bird that cleaves the air."[69] Carson had become a daughter of the Revolution, and for her the political was personal.

In the years following her declaration of freedom, Carson thrived and became an independent businesswoman while her husband went into a physical and spiritual decline and became an alcoholic. When he went on a long sea journey once again, Carson resumed her liaisons with other men and eventually married one of these men, although she later claimed that she was tricked into this act. When her first husband returned and demanded the return of his wife, her second husband got into a violent confrontation with him and killed him. Ann Carter was charged with conspiracy in this murder, but in a trial held in Philadelphia in November of 1816, she was acquitted. She was, however, convicted of bigamy. Her declaration of freedom as an American was clearly not accepted as legitimating the "liberty" she had taken in her personal relations, and for this she was punished. She died while in jail.

Lucy Richards (born 1792) never married and did not recognize a male alien other, but her account of her life in her narrative makes it likely that she focused much anger on her father and the other male authorities in her life. Richards was a hard working child ("I . . . had spun upward of ninety runs of yarn before I was seven years and a half old") who grew up in the burned-over district in Oneida County, New York. Although her father had been converted by Freeborn Garrettson, she was "lively" as a young woman, and unconverted. It was the conversion of friends, not her father, that brought her to religion. In fact, after she did convert at a very emotional camp meeting on September 22, 1809, she chose not to join her father's church. This was clearly an act of independence, but not of outright rejection. Richards took another independent act by going away from home to school when she was eighteen. Over the next decade she taught school, experienced "a fuller baptism of the Holy Spirit" in which she was "swallowed up in God," converted women and children, and went off to study with the Reverend George W. Densmore, a very successful itinerant minister. Through all this activity she was often ill and described her ailments and weak feelings in great detail. The pattern of her illness, which often was at its worst when she was at home, suggests that it was tied to her relationship with her father and that she may well have been punishing herself for her acts of independence. She even seemed ready to give up her independent life when both her personal and her family's loss of funds in the depression of 1819 led her to return to teaching.

Teaching was an acceptable role for an unmarried woman, but when Richards chose to become a missionary to the Oneida Indians she marked her independence in a crucial way. She was enabled to do this by framing her choice as God's choice, not her own. She had pledged that if she were cured of her illnesses, she would devote her life to a mission, like the wife of a missionary she had heard of. When a simple herbal medicine gave her great relief from all her symptoms, she announced that God had decided her future. Having no husband, she went off as a missionary on her own. This brave act, taken in 1829 when she was thirty-seven years old, changed her self-perception and her life. "I feel there is a great work before me," she recorded at the outset of her missionary journey to the Oneida. She found her young students "bashful" and the elders "suspicious," but they responded to her enthusiasm and interest, and she soon succeeded. "The desire of the natives to learn exceeds any thing I ever saw before." She instructed eighty students, to whom she taught reading, writing, religion, and her ideas of proper cleanliness and decorum. Isolated from whites, she immersed herself in Oneida culture and life. She participated in their customs and wanted to learn their language. For the first time in her life Richards was willing to acknowledge that "I am contented and happy." She was also well!

Richards was not allowed to continue in this state. In 1831, in view of her success, the church sent a man to take over the institution she had established. She left, and became depressed and ill again. Recognizing that she had left her life's work, she chose to return to the Oneida Indians in the only role the church would allow her and which she now ostensibly accepted: as a teacher of domestic economy, and, as she wrote, "such other kindred branches as would fall more properly within the range of female instruction." We can read her comment as an ironic expression of her psychic pain at their decision, the only criticism she allowed herself to make. Her illnesses returned and did not leave her this time, and in great physical pain she left her "dear people" again. Dreams came to her, and while she believed that "the good Lord often communicates himself to me in the night watches," she was not sure that she understood them, and she could not act on them. They may well have expressed anger at the turn she had been forced to make. She did not record their content, perhaps because she could not allow her self to face her own anger. She died on September 10, 1837, with the words "God is love." When she left the Oneida she had prayed "the Lord comfort and sustain them, and grant us a final union of spirits in 'the region of pleasure and love.' " Oneida Indians occasionally visited her during her last years, and she no doubt retained the hope of union after death with those who had been the light of her life. Richards had found commitment and a calling and had remade herself, but she had been cut down by the male-run institution she sought to work within.[70]

Transvesting, 1775–1840

All of the women who succeeded in taking on authority—Ashbridge, Payton, Paisley, Osborn, Lee, and Jackson—played roles that had been defined as male, yet they claimed to be acting as women and marked themselves as such by wearing clothing that defined them as females. Nevertheless, they each found their own voice by speaking as a Joseph, a Jacob, a Daniel, or a Christ. Jemima Wilkinson's persona was more anomalous than all the others; she apparently claimed to encompass both the male and the female aspects of God and chose clothing that signified her change but did not actually violate accepted gendering: she did not wear trousers, but her robe was much like a minister's and her hat and hair style suggested those of a male. She did drop her gendered Christian name and chose to be called "The Universal Friend." Other women who wanted to play the roles that men were allowed or expected to play adopted the guise of men or transvested themselves. While we cannot be certain, it would appear likely that this practice grew in the greater Revolutionary era. Certainly awareness of the practice grew.[71]

Marjorie Garber maintains that concern with cross-dressing indicates the existence of "a *category crisis elsewhere*" in the society, with the "resulting discomfort" displaced onto the marginal figures of cross-dressers. Garber thus sees concern with "cross-dressing as an index . . . of many different kinds of 'category crisis . . . ,' " which she defines as situations in which borderlines, such as those between male and female, black and white, or rich and poor, "become permeable."[72] The Revolutionary period certainly was one in which all these categories were being shaken up.

The most important figure among the transvesting or passing women of the Revolutionary period was Deborah Samson (born 1760), whose name so strangely combines those of two biblical figures, a female and a male, both emblematic of strength.[73] Samson had to abandon these powerful names in order to pass as a man, which she did when on May 20, 1782, she enlisted in the Continental army under the colorless name of Robert Shurtleff. There she passed as a "blooming boy," one who had not yet begun to grow a beard, until her sex was revealed during an illness in October of 1783.[74]

Samson's story comes down to us in a volume written by Herman Mann, who talked at length with Samson but wrote his own version of her narrative, although he stated that part was in her own words. This makes it extremely difficult to use this document, but the extensive historical research done by Alfred Young has provided a broad basis of facts to rely on. We now know that Deborah's father had abandoned her; her mother had put her out at age five and later indentured her until she was eighteen; and her master had burdened her life and belittled her abilities. He may also have attacked her sexually, or failed to protect her from attack. While Deborah is likely to have harbored great anger at many of those around her, in view of her history it is not surprising that males seem to have been singled out in a very special way.

The written narrative of Deborah Samson's experiences includes an extensive dream report that is very likely authentically Deborah's. She was certainly able to write: her first job after obtaining freedom was as a schoolteacher, and there are references to a lost journal. The fact that she lived in a very dream-conscious culture in which people widely wrote down, shared, and worried about their

Figure 20. Deborah Samson, depicted as strong yet female. Frontispiece of the narrative published by Herman Mann, *The Female Review*, 1866.

dreams increases the likelihood that she would have recorded and later remembered such a dream. In the narration the claim is made that when she was fifteen years old she dreamed this dream on three different nights, thus establishing that it fulfilled the traditional requirement for a dream from God that would come true and that was well worth remembering.[75]

The dream report opens at sunset, with the "Sun . . . declining." In the symbolic universe of this period, the sun stood for "felicity," and its decline signaled a bad turn was coming. Before it declined, however, Deborah found herself in a garden of delights, where she smelled "ravishing odours" and climbed gently "ascending ground" until she reached a peak, all close to overtly sexual descriptions.

Suddenly all was reversed. The sun became clouded over, while the stench of sulfur and the sounds of lightening, thunder, and an erupting volcano made for a new scene whose images were recognized as symbolic of hell. Samson had gone from a garden of Edenic pleasures to a roiling hell in which a bloody snake, moving at great speed, sought to attack her. In panic, she reported that she looked back at what were now the bloodied streets of her town, an act similar to that of Lot's wife in Sodom, a turn back to the past, an act often punished in folklore and in life. Samson was not made into a pillar, but she was *drenched in blood* and "fell into a swoon."

From ancient times, snakes were extraordinarily complex emblems. The serpent could betoken male sexuality, or temptation, the devil and evil, but it was also seen as a symbol of wisdom and often assumed to represent the power to heal.[76] For Samson (and later for Nat Turner) the snake was not bivalent: it was the enemy that had to be annihilated.

Her "apartment" did not protect her, the door opened and the serpent, "of immense bigness," with a "sharp sting" at the end of his tongue, tried to enter but found the room "too small." In the modern world most analysts would see these symbols as overtly sexual. Samson's contemporaries recognized dreamed of homes as emblems of their souls and were likely to have suggested that the snake was trying to pierce her very self. If she consulted a dream manual or spoke with others who had, the suggestion was probably raised that the serpent represented her enemies. Had she failed to destroy the snake it would have been regarded as "very disastrous, betokening an enemy that is not yet overcome." While she did eventually kill this snake, when she originally confronted it in the dream she covered her head and "tried to call for assistance, but could make no noise."

Samson's description of the snake's attack supports an interpretation that the dream was a response to an attack on Deborah, either physical or psychological, and alerting her to her desperate need to defend herself properly. In her dream she was suddenly gifted with words of encouragement and strength that gave her a holy task and the power to carry it out: *"Arise, stand on your feet, gird yourself, and prepare to encounter your enemy."* In a dreamed rite of passage, as in a knighthood ceremony, she began in a position of submission, was anointed and told to rise, and was then given a weapon. This was a "bludgeon," which she then used in a "severe combat with the enemy," in which she hacked the snake to pieces, providing a dream scenario of good portent: she would overcome her enemies.[77]

The fear, rage, and blood in Deborah Samson's dream suggest that she may have been deeply injured as the result of such an attack. She may well also have felt guilt over an attack made against her: the snake that she bludgeoned suddenly became fish-tailed (did the attacker swerve sneakily?), and on each part of its tail "were *capital letters* of yellow *gilt*." This gilt can be easily read as a pun on *guilt* for a *capital crime*. Deborah no doubt wanted to expose the guilt of her attackers but perhaps was also afraid that she would or should be blamed for her own behavior, as many women who were raped were. (As rape was a *capital crime*, accusing the victim was one means of escaping death.) Her dream scripted a relationship begun with rapture that turned into an attack on her self. Only her anointment saved her, as the pieces of the snake took on a second life as a goring ox (another traditional phallic symbol), but the now heroic Deborah found both the weapon and the will to bludgeon the ox into a "gelly."[78]

The words Deborah heard in her dream, "Arise, stand on your feet, gird yourself, and prepare to encounter your enemy," echo the Biblical words of Deborah the prophetess, who called on Barak and his ten thousand men to prepare for war with the cry: "Up! This day the Lord gives Sisera [your enemy] into your hands." The Israelites sang a similar song to Deborah: "Rouse, rouse yourself, Deborah, rouse yourself, lead out the host." (Judges 5:7, 12) The biblical Deborah then accompanied Barak to battle, although another woman, Yael, was responsible for killing Sisera. Deborah Samson, brought up in the Congregational Church, which she attended along with her master, Deacon Jeremiah Thomas, had to have known this biblical story very well and no doubt was told many times that her biblical name was expected to affect her character and life. It did.

Deborah Samson followed the command to "gird yourself," and bandaging her breasts to her body, she was able to pass as a male. (To gird oneself apparently connoted the hiding of one's sex. The association is confirmed by Elizabeth, the black Methodist preacher, who reported that when she went to the Bible for advice on whether to continue as a preacher, she opened it to a verse stating: "Gird up thy loins now like a man, and answer thou me. Obey God rather than man." Elizabeth was apparently referring to Job 38:3.[79]) As a putative male, Samson succeeded in enlisting and was given a "weapon of defense." In the army, she acted in ways that did not violate the expectations of the men in her unit for the proper behavior of a young man.

Taken together, Deborah Samson's dream and her subsequent act of joining the army indicate deep anger at the opposite sex, accompanied by ambivalence about her own sex. In her dream she feared penetration and being bloodied, but after anointment she had the strength and determination to bludgeon her attacker to a powerless pulp. She could become a warrior in life only after bandaging up her body and hiding her sex. She could become a Deborah and a Samson only when she played a male role. Transvested, given a proper weapon, she entered into combat and acted the role of a proper man, protecting both herself and others.

Mann suggests that Deborah Samson also attracted females, and perhaps even pursued them.[80] While this remains unsubstantiated, it is clear that by playing the role of a man she protected herself from sexual relations with men. Samson had come to maturity in a period of rising illegitimacy and premarital pregnancy. The war years, with the increased sexual activity of both British and American soldiers, added to the changing morality.[81] By imposing a chastity belt on herself Samson placed a moratorium on acting the role of a woman. Even after being discharged she apparently continued to wear men's clothes for a time, a most unusual act for a woman whose transvesting was disclosed.

For Samson, the enemy was both the inner fright that was considered feminine and the aggressive male without. She had roused herself and subdued her enemies, both within and without, by becoming the enemy. Although the biblical Deborah became the archetype for the "mother in Israel" ("Champions there were none left in Israel until I, Deborah, arose, arose a mother in Israel." Judges 5:7), unlike the many religious women to whom this term was applied, or who called themselves by the term, Deborah Samson was never seen as such a mother, because it was hard for people to call her a woman. There was no proper category for the self she had established.[82] In a sense, she had bludgeoned the old categories out of existence for herself. Senator William Ellis, who claimed to know her well, could find no better category for her than "diplomatist." While he termed her

195

"a woman of uncommon native intellect and force of character," he felt constrained to note that she seemed a mixed being. "Her countenance and voice were feminine; but she conversed with such ease on the subject of theology, on political subjects, and military tactics, that her manner would seem to be masculine."[83] The culture had no acceptable slot for a woman of Deborah Samson's strength, character, and experience, which were defined as male. She herself found it hard to put herself back into the symbolic and real fetters of female dress and acceptable female roles.

In other narratives of transvesting women that were published in the opening decades of the nineteenth century, the women acknowledged that they knew of Deborah Samson and that in a sense they had adopted her dream as their own. Several of these narratives may well have been fictive, written and published by men as business ventures, but "it would have been difficult for contemporary readers to be sure." Although they were probably fictive, they played a role parallel to those played by "true" life narratives providing individuals with role models and ideals. These books read as though they were written by women who had experienced life as transvestors, and they drew on the experience of others who had really had such experiences. The fictive works ostensibly written by Eliza Bowen (whose birth date is given as 1790) cite Samson explicitly as a role model. In this narrative the author "recounts" that, using the name of Lucy Brewer, she had become a prostitute in Boston around the year 1807; and that a customer of hers, an officer on a privateer, told her that Samson had "served her country . . . without a stain on her virtue and honour." Putting himself in Lucy Brewer's place, he said that "were I a female and disposed to travel, I would . . . garb myself as a male, and for such pass." The narrative tells us that this idea reframed Lucy Brewer's sense of herself and her possibilities: "From this moment I became dissatisfied with my situation in life."[84]

Silvia Prince, a young African American, was a prostitute in Boston in this same period.[85] Her sister, Nancy Prince, in her life narrative, described the conditions in which Silvia lived: she maintained that Silvia was held in virtual slavery by a madam who claimed that Silvia owed her money. Nancy Prince and a male friend, who was armed with a "large cane," came to Silvia's rescue, dragging her from the arms of the madam. This act helped change Nancy Prince's self-evaluation, and she soon took control of her own life, but it did not rescue her sister Silvia for long.[86]

The fictive Eliza Bowen Webb/Lucy Brewer figure is described as having used Samson's book as the weapon to release herself from just such bondage. She "thoroughly studied" it and treated it both as a magical object and as a practical guide. Brewer is quoted as saying, "By a strict adherence to the precautionary means by which she (Samson) was enabled to avoid an exposure of her sex, I was too enabled to conceal mine." Brewer is described as having worn tight "underdrawers," and, like Samson, a "bandage around my breast." Her sex was like a wound that she had to hide: were it known, she would have been in serious trouble. She had signed on a frigate, the *Constitution*, and was taking part in military actions, and she knew that it was widely believed a woman endangered such a ship at sea. The narrative asserts that she completed her service without being found out and that after three years she was honorably discharged and given both wages and prize money.[87]

In this fictive life story the author "relates" that after her military service she purchased an officer's uniform in order to impersonate a more important male and that she switched back and forth from female to male clothing and roles. It was only in the second edition of the narrative that is was "revealed" that she had been seduced when a young woman, and that when she found herself pregnant she went to Boston to seek work. Like Silvia, she claimed she had been tricked into working in a house of prostitution. (In 1831 a Boston grand jury "focused attention on the way 'the young and unwary' were 'decoyed' into pernicious brothels.") The narrative described her youth as a series of distressing events for which she took no responsibility and revealed that she had absorbed ideas and values without giving them much thought: she was proud that she had worked in one of the better houses of prostitution, one that only white clients came to. She shared the popular fear of racial mixing both in brothels and outside.[88]

Only when the narrator put on a man's clothing and took on the role of a man was she pictured as taking responsibility for her actions. In one case, it was claimed that she defended a young woman who was being pursued aggressively by a man by challenging the man to a duel. The man is described as having withdrawn dishonorably, consonant with his behavior toward women, while the ostensibly female narrator is described as having become both a "first-class shot" and a person of honor. Dishonorable men were her enemy, but she found it possible to attack them only when playing the role of a man.

Although this narrative claimed that the narrator was a woman, it also claimed that she was continuing to play the role of a man; that she put on a skirt again only to pay a brief visit to her parents. Once that was over she supposedly returned to wearing pants and playing the male. It was claimed that she was writing in order to warn "youths of *my sex* never to listen to the voice of love, unless sanctioned by paternal approbation."[89] However, the true message of this fictive narrative seems to have been that life as a man was full of adventure and honor, that when playing the role of a women the narrator was passive and dishonored. The narrative (which was apparently believed to have been true) suggests that it was eminently possible for a woman to follow in Samson's path and become a self-fashioner, but only while playing the role of an honorable and adventurous male.

Emma Cole [Hanson], who was born in the 1780s, followed this same path, although she wrote that the act of putting on male clothing was an enormous hurdle for her to overcome. The wearing of male clothing seems to have had an almost magical quality, which, to all intents and purposes, was an operation that changed one's gender. Leonora Siddons also felt that by wearing pants she was "launched forth in the world as it were another being."[90] Notwithstanding this magical protection, these women feared exposure, and often kept a set of women's clothes at hand should they be found out. Indeed, it was reported that Elmira Paul, a transvestor who had been found out while riding in a stagecoach, was rushed into a house by her female fellow travelers so that she might immediately change her clothes and resume her "proper" gender markings.[91]

Emma Cole's life began in ways parallel to Samson's. Having been orphaned by the age of five, she, too, was then put out. She wrote that as a young servant girl a young man whose sexual propositions she had refused put stolen goods in her room, much as in the biblical story of Joseph. As a result, she was thrown out, and when she was on her own in Boston she wounded a man who was molesting her. Fearing she had murdered him, she ran for cover in male attire. Once in pants, she "so well acquired the air and tone of the sailor, that the character seemed familiar to me." She claimed that she lived through three years at sea during which she was taken prisoner by pirates and was jailed in England, all without detection. While she remained accepted as a man, she nevertheless became increasingly nervous about discovery. She took the occasion of a display of bravery as the opportunity to reveal her true sex. Rescuing a child who fell into the water at dockside in Boston, Cole responded to the parents' warm approval, and potential interest in "him" as a suitor, by being honest with them: "I thought best now to come out in my own true colors, and discover who and what I was. But this was a delicate business." Cole herself clearly had to "discover who and what" she was and it was a delicate and difficult business for her as well. The

THE CABIN BOY WIFE;
OR,
SINGULAR AND SURPRISING ADVENTURES OF
MRS. ELLEN STEPHENS,

Who, having been compelled to marry against her will, after experiencing much cruel treatment, was deserted by her husband, and in pursuit of whom, (and her infant child) dressed in *male* attire, and obtaining a berth on board of one of the Steamers, on the Mississppi River, as *Cabin Boy*, in that capacity made several passages up and down the river in 1839 and '40, without her sex being known or suspected.

Figure 21. Ellen Stephens as a "blooming boy." Frontispiece, *The Cabin Boy Wife. . . .*

rescued child's family turned rescuers and saved Cole. They supported her as fictive kin and provided her with female clothing, false braids, and a home. She found this transition as difficult as her first change: "My dress now appeared as odd to me as when I first put on male attire." Cole [Hanson] claimed that she made this transition

Figure 22. Emma Cole, begging to be spared sexual violation.

with success and eventually married a Mr. Hanson, a wealthy Boston resident, had four children, and lived thirty-three years as a woman before she wrote her revelatory narrative.[92]

The issue of sexual relations with women was raised in each of these narratives. Mann claimed that women were attracted to Samson/Shurtleff and suggested that the emotion was reciprocated. Brewer played the role of a "gallant," and enjoyed the appreciation when she/he was taken up by a young woman's family. Hanson came out as a women when it became likely that she/he would be seen as a prospective husband. Another transvestor, Almira Paul, wrote of enjoying being pursued by a woman.

Paul, supposedly born in 1790, suggested that it was economic need that led her to become a transvestor. The narrative states that she had been left with two young children when her husband, William Paul, was killed at sea on a British privateer in February of 1812, and that she put on his clothes and signed on the cutter the *Dolphin* in June of that year. "So well did I act the man, that I am confident no one on board had any suspicion of my being a woman." A "tight waistcoat" or "sementers" was her protection, which saw her

Figure 23. Emma Cole, captured by pirates, but persevering.

though a public whipping and imprisonment on an Algerian ship in the Mediterranean. The narrative claimed that Paul acted like a man in many roles: that she fought with others, and threw a seaman overboard; that she squandered her money like the rest; and that she successfully wooed an English widow.[93]

While Cole Hanson's narrative suggests that as a young woman she had a very strong dislike of females as well as males, acting the male, and living a life that allowed her to develop her self through acts of bravery and honor brought her to a point where she was able to reaccept her self as a woman. Brewer is depicted as not wanting to "come out" as a women, while, in the eyes of others, Samson, who became a wife and mother, always remained somewhat differ-

201

Figure 24. Lucy Brewer pictured as proudly serving as a U.S. sailor.

ent from other women. Paul is depicted as a male rowdy and a scoundrel. The range of views expressed by the narrators suggests a range of gendered selves, including lesbians, transvestites, and those who chose to play the male role on the basis of ideological motivations. But the computations were often very complex, and they changed for each woman over time. The women played roles, but also became different, often recognizing that their selves had altered. With all these differences, these narrators, whether fictive or real, shared one message: as a male each one had become a stronger and more individuated human being.

The ambiguous sexuality of a female viewed as a male in the post-Revolutionary era was most fully explored in the narrative of the life of K. White (born 1772), who, in her unwillingness to provide her full first name, perpetuated the ambiguous image of herself that she gained in her life. White was not a transvestor in dress. She wore women's clothing throughout her life. It was her body and her body language, as well as her voice and her behavior, that led many of the people she came in contact with to assume she was a man wearing woman's clothing. Accused of this many times, she came to play this role with pleasure, enjoying it when others assumed she was a man dressed as a woman. Writing at the age of twenty-nine, she explained the situation as due to factors out of her control:

> Although in my younger years I was of slender form yet as I advanced in age, I became large in stature somewhat of a masculine form, of a robust strong complexion, so that upon the whole I would not make a bad appearance as a *man* were I dressed in masculine attire. . . . Nature had so "ordered it" and I could not remedy it.

In contrast to this assertion, White's narrative suggests that she played a significant role in her sex "change." As a young girl, she was viewed as properly feminine, but her childhood had been marked by several traumatic events. Brought to America from Edinburgh in 1775, her father, a Tory, abandoned his family because America was unsafe for him, and returned to Europe. In what reads like a dream sequence, the only one in her narrative, White recounted that her world then became unsafe for her. Sent to a boarding school in Stockbridge, Massachusetts, she recounted that she was captured by Indians, "poked and taunted," witnessed the torture and death of another captive, and was then befriended by an Indian youth who took her on a four-day trek back to white society.[94] Whether or not this was a real event, no doubt the feelings were real and may explain in part who she became. Abandoned by her parents, she felt that her body was "poked and taunted" and that she was in danger of death. She came to be armored against such attack by her girth and the impression she gave of being a male. This gender confusion became central to her self-definition and her life.

White recounts that in 1789, on the day she was to have married an officer (identified only as H. G.), he committed suicide, and that she then learned that he was already married. Pressured by her parents, she soon married a distant relative, S. White, who had a child by her maid and then abandoned K., leaving her pregnant. White responded to her new situation by acting like a man. She chose to become a merchant, so that "I might acquire an independency, or at least a competency." She became embroiled in adventures in which time and again she was seen as some kind of impostor: a forger, a spy who was a Frenchman or an Englishman, or a man pretending to be a woman—a spy in enemy territory. A man accused White of having an affair with his wife. A woman pursued her, and White finally agreed to marry her. White broke this engagement, fulfilling another male role by becoming a rake much like her hated husband.[95]

White was "content to wave the distinction with which society has marked the walks in life of the two sexes." She was pleased she could use this gender confusion to gain both financial and personal independence. Widely assumed to be a man, she chose to act as a man in women's clothing. She would never become dependent on a husband again.

> Hence Hymen; then, thy alter ne'er shall know
> Again a victim once deceived by thee;—
> Here I proclaim aloud, "I am they foe,"
> And death shall only end our enmity.[96]

Once K. opted to play the role of a man, she, like each of these women, felt empowered. These women recognized that they were responsible for their new selves. They chose to go to war or to sea, to duel or to fight, to go into business or to write. They were playing roles (as transvestors) that it was believed God did not approve of, but God did not seem to play a role for them. Although Deborah Samson was a role model for all of them, not one of the other transvesting women cited an anointing dream. They seemed to change their lives themselves, and seemed to lack a sense of commitment to any outside authority. They were bent upon traveling to new places, not spirit travels; upon adventure, not overt reform of society.

There was an unvoiced ideology, however. They saw themselves, much as African Americans did, as enslaved. They were enslaved by men, and enslaved by bodies that forced them into unfree lives. With breasts bandaged and self-imposed chastity belts in place, these transvesting warriors battled for themselves by battling against themselves, with freedom their goal.

Coda

"In Dreams Begins Responsibility"

Use Any means at Your Disposal to Protect Your Self

On the night of the fifth of December 1791, Being a deep Sleep, I
dreamed that I was in a public Company, one of them demanded
of me the limits of Rasannah Crandolphs Soul had to display itself in, after it departed from her Body and taken its flight. In answer I desired that he shew me the place of Beginning "thinking
it like making a Survey on Land." He reply'd I cannot inform
you, but there is a man about three days jorney from Hence that
is able to Satisfy your demand, I fortwith went to the man and requested of him to inform me place of beginning of the limits that
Rasannah Crandolph's Soul had to display its self in, after the
Separation from her Body; who gave me answer, the Vernal Equinox, When I returned I found Company together and I was able
to Solve their Doubts by giving them the following answer Quincunx. Benjamin Banneker[1]

IN THIS dream Benjamin Banneker (born 1731), the free African
American farmer, mathematician, clock maker, surveyor, astronomer, and almanac writer, seems to have faced a key problem assessed in this study: the "limits" a self had to develop in, and
he recognized that public perceptions of both gender and race were
central to his answer.

Assuming that the problematic self that Banneker dreamed of was
his own, the dream ostensibly does not deal with his racial problems
but rather with the limits or extent to which he had developed his
feminine side. It suggests that he felt that the "public" was troubled
by this part of him. Banneker, who never married, may well have
been concerned with this question, as it seems to have been raised
in several of his dreams, but the solution he first suggests makes it
clear that race was a hidden subtext.

Banneker's dream posed two solutions to the problem. The first,
which he found by going back to "the place of Beginning," perhaps
to childhood, perhaps to Africa, was "the Vernal Equinox."[2] This is
the day in the year in which light and darkness are equal. In the mind
of an African American astronomer the vernal equinox might well
stand as the symbol of equality of black and white. This solution

206

suggests that Banneker realized that black and white had an equal place in his soul, much as his white grandmother and his mixed-race mother were reputed to have had in his early life. But he traveled in spirit to consult "a man," and it was this man who gave him the answer suggesting basic equality for "Rasannah." Perhaps male and female aspects of his self were to be given equal space as well, but his dream suggests that Banneker was to be "a man" of courage and publicly acknowledge his mixed heritage.

In his dream, however, when Banneker returned to the "public Company," he gave them a different answer. They, the others, the whites, apparently had 'demands' that would not be satisfied by equality. Banneker "was able to Solve their Doubts" by telling them "Quincunx." What can quincunx have suggested to Banneker in this context? The word is built on the Latin root for five, a quincunx being either "a five-twelfths weight marked with four spots or balls at the corners and a fifth ball or spot in the middle; or a similar planting of five trees."[3] Such markings were believed to have mystical symbolism.

While these meanings may well have influenced Banneker, the arrangement of five items at four corners and in the center, which had come to be called a quincunx, was also a very significant and power-laden arrangement in African American conjuration lore. When graveyard dirt, salt, candles, or other markers are placed at the "FOUR CORNERS OF A BED, ROOM, HOUSE, [GRAVE, OR] ANYTHING, AND [AT THE] CENTER [THIS] IS CALLED A QUINCUNX, [WHOSE] MAGIC DESIGN DIAGONALS FORM A CROSS TO PUT [A] SPELL ON [A] VICTIM OR TO PROTECT YOURSELF[;] INTENTION IS THE POWER."[4] It is very likely that Banneker's intention in his dream was to protect black and/or feminine aspects of his self by putting an African American spell on his (white?) enemies. When he awoke Banneker the scientist might well have thought 'You are defending yourself with outmoded weapons,' but he left no record of any of his thoughts about this dream and much else.

Banneker was sixty-one when he had this dream, and, in order to take part in a public endeavor, he had, for the first time, recently left the area of his rural Maryland home ten miles from Baltimore. From February through April of 1791, he had been involved in surveying land for the Federal Territory of Washington as an assistant to the chief surveyor, Andrew Ellicott. There, the press took note of him when the *Georgetown Weekly Ledger* reported that Ellicott "is attended by *Benjamin Banniker*, an Ethiopian, whose abilities, as a surveyor, and an astronomer, clearly prove that Mr. Jefferson's concluding that race of men were void of mental endowments, was without foundation."[5] Under new public scrutiny, Banneker, living in the field with the white crew of engineers, negotiated a public persona whose nature we have a small clue to: while working with them he chose not to accept their invitation to sit at their table but ate at a separate one at the same time and place. This may well have been the demanding public company that Banneker dreamed of.

Banneker had also taken up the argument made in the newspapers himself: in August of 1791 he had written to Jefferson suggesting that his and other Africans' accomplishments belied the common prejudice. Although he replied politely, Jefferson, much like the company in Banneker's dream, was not so easily convinced, and although Banneker proudly reprinted this correspondence, it is likely that he was unconsciously aware of Jefferson's negative view.[6]

By December of 1791 Banneker's life was in the process of further change. His almanac was being considered for publication and his self was under greater scrutiny than it had ever been before as questions were raised as to whether this was actually his own work. Abolitionists were particularly anxious to establish that he was an African and that he had written the almanac without help. He was indeed the son of an African father, who took the name Robert [Banneker] in America, but his mother, Mary, was the daughter of white Molly Welsh and her husband Bannka or Bannaka, an African she had purchased and manumitted. Banneker's heritage was a mixed one.[7]

Although he often attended Quaker meetings, Benjamin Banneker apparently did not formally belong to any church. However his dream life confirms that he had experienced the classic Afro-Christian journey to the other world. In what he recorded as "A Remarkable Dream" of the 10th Month, 1762, Banneker reported seeing himself dead and then being called to follow a spirit guide who led him up to a white building where there were very bright beings all wearing the same long bright shirts: "I look'd to see if I could Distinguish Men from Women but could not." Banneker was very reluctant to leave this wonderfully 'sweet and composed' asexual company in heaven, but he slowly followed his guide down to a room painted with many beautiful colors, populated by richly dressed people whose clothing clearly distinguished the men from the women. Among them were several he had known, including an old white "gentlewoman." Although these people were very well dressed, all was not well: they had "blackness on their lips" and smelled of brimstone. Banneker's guide confirmed that this was hell.[8]

Banneker's dream of the other world taught him that in heaven men and women would lose all markings of their earthly sex and would be regarded as equal while in hell gender differences were retained. What of their color? All those he saw in hell seem to have been white people. Perhaps Banneker shared the view widely held by African Americans that heaven was reserved for blacks. Certainly, with the name "Rasannah," it is likely that the female in heaven in his quincunx dream was black.

Banneker's dreams provide rich evidence of his concern with boundary renegotiations, problems that were troubling so many in this period, and they indicate his inner desire for radical change. His dreams seem to acknowledge that he was on a spiritual journey to reassess his white and female aspects but also warn us that he felt the need to protect his self by traditional means. This may have reflected a part of himself that he was not consciously aware of. While in his quincunx dream he was protecting himself with what he consciously thought of as an outmoded weapon, he recognized that his self was in grave danger and that he must use whatever means he had to protect it. He found the solution in a spell based on a traditional African American conjure pattern.

Many narrators in this study who were concerned with boundary renegotiation left evidence that their self-development was conceptualized in oppositionally gendered terms, this most often by women who saw themselves as men. In 1824, Ann Byrd (born 1797), a Quaker, envisioned herself as a Jacob, asleep in the wilderness, provided by God with a ladder to climb.[9] While she overtly desired to increase her selflessness and saw "the path to heaven . . . [as] a narrow path . . . of self-denial," at the same time she desired to climb this ladder rapidly and achieve a very high status. She could only envision doing this as a man: "[W]hen I reflected upon myself, and how wonderful is man,—when I considered that so noble a creature must have been formed for some great purpose, my heart longed that his purpose might be effected in me."

In her inner life Ann Byrd encompassed the crises and contradictions of the new sense of self that she shared with so many in her generation. She feared following her own "self-will" to be a great "man" and yet longed "for some great purpose." While attracted to the new, she saw the city as a maelstrom of evils and longed for the Edenic qualities of her parents' home in what is now probably the lower Bronx. While she wanted to be independent, she strongly resented the fact that the economic turmoil of the 1820s and 1830s, and the death of her brother, meant that she had to work in order to support her ailing parents. While she felt sympathy for the poor workers she saw on the docks, she felt a strong call to reform them, presaging the organized reform work of some women in the 1830s. She did work with and help to set up a school for poor New York

City girls, but she was appalled by their earthiness and brutality and fell into using harsh methods with them and felt she had to censure herself. In 1831 she was recognized as a Public Friend, or minister, but she died in that very year, and although she had achieved much, it is unlikely that she believed that she had truly climbed that invisible ladder. Rather than her accomplishments, it was her knowledge of her own longings that marked her changing self.[10]

One can imagine many of Banneker's and Byrd's contemporaries together figuratively on a Jacob's ladder, longing to climb up, to achieve more individuated selves, but also pulled back by fears of punishment for self-concern. Many men and women who had "male minds" began to make their own way, often aided by their dreams as well as by a new patterning of life that helped them to find a legitimating institution.

CREATING A NEW LIFE PATTERN

My parents became poor, and [in 1739] when I was four years old, the family, then consisting of five children, were obliged to disperse and throw themselves upon the mercy of an unfeeling and evil world. I was bound out to a farmer in the neighborhood. As is too commonly the case, I was rather considered as a slave than a member of the family, and, instead of allowing me the privilege of common hospitality, and a claim to that kind of protection due to the helpless and indigent children, I was treated by my Master as his property and not as his fellow mortal. Solomon Mack

Large numbers of the narrators in this study were, like Solomon Mack, put out at a very early age, while others remained at home until late marriages.[11] Many never went to school; some went for several months a year over a period of years; several started to go to school only when they were as old as eighteen or twenty-one.[12] Some married at fifteen and some at forty or later. Some had children over a much longer span than is now common. Many of their mothers had died in childbirth or soon after; other mothers and fathers died while their children were very young, although some outlived all their children. The great majority of narrators seem to have spent much of their youth in homes other than those of their parents, but some spent all their lives in their parents' homes.[13] Taken together, the two hundred narratives selected for this study present very varied life patterns.[14]

210

Before the modern period, death was far more likely than it is now to occur at a random point in the life span, and this reality cast an enormous shadow over life.[15] Children in this group lived through the deaths of siblings, parents, servants and slaves, as well as more distant kin, friends, and neighbors. Thomas Smith (born 1776) was three when his mother died, and three and a half when his father, two sisters, and one brother died after inoculations for smallpox. "I barely escaped," he recorded. He went to live with a married half-brother, but this relative, together with another half-brother and a sister, and an uncle who took him in after the half-brother's death, were all dead by the time Smith was sixteen. Smith was quite disturbed by all these deaths and considered suicide but sought religious assurance to enable him to continue living.[16] At the age of eighteen he had a dream of a dove taking him to heaven and returning him to the world because "the Lord has work for you to do." Smith distrusted this call, but within a year he was a Methodist preacher to blacks and whites in the excited areas of Maryland and Virginia. Dreams later confirmed his role as a harvester of crops for God.[17]

This eighteenth-century world, which seems so close to ours in many ways, was also very far from it: deaths were widely seen as serving God's purpose. When Sarah Osborn's step-granddaughter Susanna died, her close friend Susanna Anthony suggested to her that God had brought about the death of this child, who was Susanna Anthony's namesake, so that Osborn would devote herself fully to her God-given role. Anthony wrote, "I thought, perhaps this young plant would have drawn too much sap from that spreading, yet aged oak [Sarah Osborn], and so eclipse her beauty, mar her importance, and weaken, at least, her shady influence."[18]

For a large number of the narrators, the deaths of close relatives and friends precipitated personal crises, and religious awakenings often followed. (This was true of Sarah Osborn after the death of her only son.) From the time of the First Great Awakening, a new life pattern, often involving a series of such awakenings, was in the process of being established. Many in this study experienced a very early childhood conversion, which generally occurred between the ages of five and ten and after the death of someone close, and a second conversion between eighteen and twenty-five. The two conversions demarcated the period of youth.[19] In the years between, the young individual often reported living a "carnal" life.[20] Young people experiencing this might well have increasingly expected that they would "come through" again and reach the next marker event. Lives were beginning to have more regular changes, tied to age, and a future different from the present was more clearly imaginable. Such change often involved much conflict with parental expectations.

Theophilus Gates (born 1787) was, as a young child, "wonderfully afraid of death" and dreamed of dying and being "confined in a small place in the middle of [a] . . . rock, about four inches square." Gates, like so many others, became less concerned about dying and turned to "worldly ways" for many years. When he was seventeen, the death of his "very promising" four-year-old brother precipitated his second crisis and conversion. Dejected, depressed, thinking of suicide, he dreamed of being in heaven and awaiting God's judgment. In this dream he saw "a retrospective view of my past life, and I seemed to know everything I had transacted," much of it evil. On awakening, Gates was overwhelmed by this experience: "It appeared to me as if I had really died, and just as I was to receive my final due, I was remanded back to earth again." He wanted to change, but did not know how. In July of 1806, at age nineteen, he left home to try to preach, and wandered southward, penniless, jobless, and ill. It took him several years to lose his feelings of unworthiness and become a man with a clear mission.[21]

During such periods of crisis, dreams often gave young people "retrospective" reviews of their lives and sensitized them to their "need" to change their selves before they died. John Leland, who regarded himself as "almost in all evil," was a "leather apron" working boy when he dreamed he heard a voice telling him, "You are not about the work you have got to do."[22] Many others interpreted dreams as sending them this message. Many felt they had to begin new tasks, and in doing so, become new people. Some, Gates and Leland among them, went on to devote themselves to churches and to reform movements, hoping to change the world as well as themselves, but never lost the sense of having stepped beyond what they still accepted as their given class positions.[23]

After the Great Awakening of the 1740s, Christian rebirth was increasingly recognized as an event that could be sought by the individual. A common method of "seeking" was widely accepted by the late eighteenth century. Individuals widely chose to fast, and to spend sleepless nights praying and crying. African American seekers wore white clothing and white headbands. A "serious" person thus chose to be different—in behavior, clothes, and even in expressed emotion. Popular attitudes seem to have gone further than most theological formulations in accepting that individuals were able to prepare themselves for conversion.

During this process individuals were encouraged to own their emotions and use them to break old bonds and cement new ones.

Laughter and crying were regarded as the literal expressions of inner states: laughter was a sign of frivolousness, crying of seriousness. When, in 1785, Hugh Judge, a Quaker, wanted to praise a young Friend whom he thought was "as solid a young man as I have lately met with," he noted that "he has been with us for several days, and I have seldom seen a smile on his countenance."[24] When Eleazer Sherman, who had his first awakening at age six, in 1801, turned sixteen, the death of a friend precipitated another "serious" turn. In the period between these awakenings, he had moved back and forth from "what is called civil mirth and recreation" to being "serious." When Sherman was moving toward this second conversion, he "tried to be as cheerful as possible, fearing my companions would discover I was serious." When they did discover him to be concerned with more than frivolous issues, they said "he is going to be religious, and we will laugh him out of it."[25]

If laughter, or even a smile, was seen as a sign of frivolousness or worldliness, dancing was an even more significant act.[26] In the eyes of Puritans, Quakers, Baptists, Methodists, and others, dancing committed one to a nonreligious path.[27] When Elizabeth Sampson Ashbridge was becoming a Quaker, her husband attempted to break her attachment by forcing her to dance in public.[28] Dancing was, for some, paralleled by banjo playing. In the South, the display of a broken banjo became a symbol of religious commitment, a public act that symbolized a private pledge.[29]

A major act of commission that the serious could publicly exhibit was crying. While they might pray for many hours, fast and sign commitments to God in private (although, as there was little privacy in this period, these acts were probably observed and talked about by others), crying was very commonly done in public, and the crying of one or some often led to the tears of many. Africans were particularly noted for crying at revivals, and they were welcomed as "warmers-up" of emotions by many New Light preachers. Africans played a similar role in individual lives: James Jenkins (born 1764) grew up on a South Carolina farm, where he was deeply influenced by African Americans. When he was ten years old he was "induced to cry much" when his fears of death were stimulated by his dreams of "the devil in the shape of a great bird " reminiscent of African spirit birds. Both as a child, and later in life, when he had joint "crying sessions" with a preacher's wife, tears signaled religious turnings in Jenkins's life. His experience and that of many others in the narratives indicates that crying was still acceptable for men and was tied directly to significant events, especially conversions.[30] This view began to change during the Revolutionary War, when young men began to feel "that it was beneath the dignity of human nature to shed tears or to mourn for the dead." Crying began to be that which only women should do.[31]

Converts often recognized their conversions as the New Birth written of in the New Testament and cited their "spiritual Birthday" as the most significant event in their lives.[32] They often memorialized the event—the year, the month, the day, and the exact hour—and celebrated it for the rest of their lives. Lucy Richards, who was born October 3, 1792, had her "spiritual birthday" on September 22, 1809. Each year she took the occasion of her spiritual birthday to make "a solemn review of my past life."[33] This was a pattern many others followed.[34]

When individuals reached a state of assurance of God's acceptance, they often wanted to mark their new state by a ritual act and create a new ritual object that would have a lasting material reality. Seth Coleman and others chose to write and sign a covenant with God.[35] Coleman's conversion in 1761, and his virtual marriage to Christ, no doubt comforted him as he set about making a break with his home and family and set limits on the person he would allow himself to become. In Christ he believed he had found a mentor who would serve as both firm father and tender spouse. He was to be both obedient child and acquiescent lover.

Coleman and many others sought a fictive family in their new church communities; many felt justified in virtually divorcing their natal families. Throughout the Revolutionary era, opposition to the values held by parents and/or the surrounding society provided one of the best routes to a more individuated self for both women and men, blacks and whites. Some converts felt they were engaged in "spiritual warfare" with known enemies. When Sophia Hume (born 1701) became a Quaker, she recognized that "I became singular, and consequently despicable to my children." She, in turn, chose to give up "excessive Love to . . . Parents, . . . Children, Friends," fearing that it was "obstructive" to her love of God's way.[36] When Sarah Beckhouse Hamilton (born 1745) chose to become a Baptist, she was totally rejected by her Catholic father and Presbyterian fiancé, as she no doubt had known would happen.[37] John Leland (born 1754) experienced "how wives stood up to husbands" and saw parents opposed to their children.[38] The son of one of Leland's Baptist converts, viewing Leland as the cause of his mother's alienation from the unconverted family, attacked the minister with a sword.[39] James Jenkins (born 1764), whose father had opposed his mother's conversion, observed, "Frequently a man's foes were they of his own household; wicked fathers, mothers, husbands, & C."[40] When African American

Jeremiah Asher (born 1812) thought of violating his family's tradition by moving from the Presbyterian to the Baptist church, his father sought to take his mind off religion by setting him a double task of work to do. That very day an ecstatic experience confirmed Asher's desire to associate with the more assertive black church. Asher had resented his parent's advice to accept white insults passively, and he found a way to distance himself that was legitimated as God's command.[41]

Secret or closed church societies were important to many of these individuals. They helped protect vulnerable selves in the process of change. They provided a refuge from the family and a bulwark against it. They generally heard confessions and gave criticism, absolution, and support. They allowed for individual participation but structured it and limited its direction. They helped people to adopt new attitudes toward life and death.[42]

Such secret societies as well as the new church communities were often truly enabling: they helped individuals begin a flight to spiritual and/or physical liberty. Both whites and blacks could share talk about this freedom from bondage and act on it, although they often sought rather different ends. When the black Baptist Lott Carey preached a sermon at the mixed-race First Baptist Church in Richmond, Virginia, in January, 1821, he took as his subject the liberty of a believer in Christ. The white congregants accepted his talk as being on the subject of soul liberty, while the black congregants no doubt focused on the fact that Carey was about to embark on a journey to Liberia, where he and those accompanying him would become free in body as well.[43]

Lucy Richards, white, and John Malvin, black, were among the many narrators who became Methodists or Baptists and who held a relatively new Western attitude toward death. They shared the belief that one should go to death "happy"; that a joyful attitude as death approached indicated both faith in the Lord and God's acceptance of the dying individual. James Jenkins had noted a similar view among the people he grew up with in South Carolina, during and after the Revolution:

> [A]mong white and coloured, if any one appeared willing to die, and no remarkable incident (as a storm, &c,) occurred at the time, it was taken for granted that such a one had gone to heaven, no matter what had been his manner of life.

African American attitudes to the afterlife, the expectation that kin were waiting and that there would be a life in heaven for all who had experienced rebirth, as well as the extensive experience with ecstatic trance in which the afterlife was traveled to, had a deep impress on both the Baptist and Methodist faiths joined by so many whites and blacks.[44] Both faiths came to enjoin believers not only to die willingly, but to die with joy. Methodists widely came to accept the black shout as the proper deathbed response to the last significant event in a life, which the believer should leave "happy and triumphant."[45]

Events that led to change in self among the nonreligious (some of whom did become religious later in life) are sometimes more difficult to recognize. While in many cases early breaks with their families resulted from deaths and/or having been put out, many others ran away, or married against their parents' will, or joined the army, or went to sea—often at very early ages. John Griffith (born 1713) left South Wales, and his parents, to go to America at age thirteen. Elizabeth Ashbridge (born 1713) eloped at fourteen. Robert Bailey (born 1773) supported himself as a plowboy from the age of nine. After her mother's death when she was ten, African American Elleanor Eldridge (born 1785) began supporting herself.[46] She long remembered that when she first left home her five year old brother called out, "Don't go, Nelly! I play alone. I be tired. I cry!" This memory suggests that she too probably felt alone and tired, and no doubt cried. It was the end of her childhood, and the only time she recorded black English. Significantly, "I be tired" signifies "I am tired all the time." Work was at the core of her identity and her image of herself.

In the 1770s and 1780s the Revolutionary committees, congresses, militias, and army provided a very important new means for people to consolidate new values and new selves. The large number who signed the nonimportation pact were committing themselves to the new ideology and new movement on a first level, while the many thousands who became members of the Sons of Liberty, the women's spinning associations, the local Committees of Inspection, and the Committees of Correspondence all committed themselves to the Revolution in groups that paralleled the earlier religious societies.[47] Their emotions were similarly characterized as "enthusiasm," which now took on a positive connotation, as a former member of the Continental Army recalled: " 'The soldiers . . . were as strict a band of brotherhood as Masons and, I believe, as faithful to each other.' "[48]

The Revolutionary War remained a symbolic referent of the promise of freedom in black narratives for several generations. Elleanor Eldridge's father, Robin Eldridge, who fought for his freedom in the Revolution, was given a prominent billing in the volume on Elleanor

FIGURE 25. Elleanor Eldridge: Work was at the core of her identity. Frontispiece, *Memoirs of Elleanor Eldridge*, 1838.

that was put together by a group of white women who clearly found a voice for their own hopes in her story. A poem centered on him suggests that "He nobly battled for the right/TO CALL HIMSELF A MAN!" and placed his daughter as his spiritual descendent: a person fighting on the economic battlefield for the right to be called a free woman. Eldridge was free of immediate male control in that she did not marry; she was free of church control in that she professed no religious experience; and she had achieved self-sufficiency, purchasing property with the funds she earned through her own labor as a whitewasher, cheese maker, and weaver. She had, however, been cheated out of much of her property, and her narrative was being published to help her recoup her losses.[49]

217

Nancy Prince (born 1799) proudly established herself as the descendent of Tobias Wornton or Backus, who "although a slave, . . . fought for liberty" at Bunker Hill.[50] William J. Anderson (born 1811) was both proud of his enslaved father's role as a Revolutionary soldier and embittered at his having remained a slave after its close. He wrote, "Patrick Henry's words became my motto, viz.: 'Give me liberty or give me death,' " and he chose July 4 (that of 1836) as the day to take his own freedom.[51] Jeremiah Asher, born only a year after Anderson, memorialized his grandfather's participation in the Revolutionary War. This grandfather had been promised his freedom if he replaced his owner in the army, and after the war he did become free, but only after he paid two hundred dollars for himself. Asher's mentors were three black men who had served in the war: "Champions for liberty," they gave him firm ideas "of the right of the colored man to life, liberty and the pursuit of happiness."[52] Lewis and Milton Clarke, born several years after Asher, were sons of an aging white Revolutionary soldier who died when Lewis was ten. Their autobiographies celebrated him in the very title: *Narratives of the Sufferings of Lewis and Milton Clarke, Sons of a Soldier of the Revolution . . .* ," and the text explained that they had inherited his blood and his dedication to fight for freedom.[53] Well into the nineteenth century, the Revolutionary War remained a symbol of black hopes and black expectations of achieving freedom, at the same time that it also called up memories of promises not kept and battles lost.

In stark contrast, whites, in their narratives, often referred to the war as a time of trials and tribulations and of great sorrows—"a time of captivity." Samuel Hopkins testified that "those who remained in town [Newport] were so reduced in their worldly circumstances, and dejection of their minds, by living so long under the tyranny of the British, that excepting a very few, they had not courage enough to think or do much." Born during the war, Mary Marshall felt that her whole life was ruined by this occurrence: "In time of the Revolutionary War, at that chaos of trouble, when our country was clothed with a robe of mourning, I was ushered into the world, and by certain scenes, in Providence, the most of my days have been veiled with sackcloth." Ebenezer Thomas, eight at the end of the war, never forgot his hunger: he had suffered from the scarcity of all foodstuff, especially bread as "[a]t this period the country was bare of everything." Sally Leland's friends recounted that in Virginia during the war, "Often she was left alone with her little ones, far from neighbors, her husband gone, . . . while runaway blacks who had neither courage to join the British army, nor patriotism to join the American, were hoarded together around her for plunder and sometimes murder."[54]

Joseph Thomas was one of very many who dwelt on the fact that his family's wealth had been "stripped and devoured" in the war. Richard Lee was another. He had just bought land to clear when "the unhappy war broke out in this country and everything being in confusion, I must confess that I did not know what to do." He recorded that without much ardor he "enlisted myself for 8 months in the service," but became ill and, after a brother took his place, turned to trading. Lee took paper money and gave credit, ending up in serious financial difficulty, during which time his wife died and he "hired his [six] children kept." He tried very hard to make a go of it, working as a farmer, a storekeeper, a tanner, a trader, a land merchant, and a button maker, but failed many times. Lee came to the conclusion that the war had been the beginning of his moral and financial decline, and that the lust for gain that he developed during the war ruined him. He made a decision to return to the preaching he had once done and chose to remain poor.[55]

War resisters make up a significant number of these narrators. Opposition to the war provided an important route for individuation, one that was taken by people of all classes, who often chose to fight their own private war of revolution.[56] While for most it meant opposition to members of their families and/or their communities, for Quakers war resistance meant conformity to the values of their sectarian group. Thus, it is not surprising that many Quakers chose to focus on a different oppositional value: objection to slaveholding, which a great many Quakers then participated in.

Quaker John Woolman, one of the central white self-fashioners in this study, grew up in a community of Quaker war resisters, and while he was an active war resister he focused his life on his antislavery convictions. Woolman chose a concrete and "powerfully evocative, multifaceted concrete symbol" for his life task.[57] He clothed his body in white to serve as a public display of his values and his self, but this choice exemplifies the duality, ambiguity, and contradiction that can inhere in such a core symbol. Woolman viewed the use of the indigo produced on slave plantations to stain clothing as the symbol of complicity with the evil institution. He opted to wear unusual undyed or white clothing to symbolize his hatred of slavery, but this also helped him to see himself as pure and white, and not as black and evil. This clothing served as a constant reminder of his moral decision to oppose slavery, and as a symbolic container of his energies for moral purposes. Much like a nun's habit, his clothes were both a prop to help him habituate himself to proper behavior and a visible symbol for others. Clothing was supposed to tie Quakers together, but the color of Woolman's clothes clearly made him stand out. It thereby also emphasized his singularity, and drew attention to his self, violating Quaker values. And, as previously suggested, it also served as a constant reminder to himself of his hidden sin in relation to slavery.[58]

Woolman chose white as a key symbol much as most blacks did; his dreams confirm his desire to be part of the black mass. Yet in his dreams a hunter captured a dangerous mixed-breed figure, clearly with evil intentions; his white Quaker neighbors hung an old black man for food; and Christians enslaved the black mass. Was he not in these figures as well? He knew the worst about himself from his sale of two young black men. The repressor and the slave catcher and the silent wailing observer were all in Woolman. Woolman both feared and wished to be the other; his self, like that of many others in this study, emerged from a conflict with that which was alien.[59]

New Values in New Lives

The Revolution, in part the work of people who had a new self-view, hurried changes already begun and was in turn a catalyst for new change in self.[60] Having to make a decision of such magnitude— whether to join the Revolution—changed individuals and broke apart many families. The impact of the war itself was very widely and deeply felt. We now know that human losses in the war were greater than once thought, and that economic losses were severe. Many participants recorded memories of great suffering in their personal narratives.[61] Many individuals faced crises during the war, and a great many of these people underwent a critical process of self-change. Many came to describe themselves as independent actors both in their own lives and in those of the community.

In the greater Revolutionary period, attitudes toward many core values changed significantly. Perhaps the most significant change in underlying values involved a new understanding of the nature of causality. The perception that God was an immediate cause of both natural and social events was receding, and there was a concomitant growth in the role assigned to human action in the new understanding of change. The new evaluation of the nature and significance of lightening can be seen as a symbol and bellwether of this change in the understanding of causality.

Lightening looms large in the memories of many early modern narrators and was probably a memory marker long before that. Giambattista Vico suggested, in what Robert E. Haskell has termed the "big bang theory of metaphor," that "[I]n some distant and dim past,

. . . groups of men huddled together and *identified* a sudden and loud clap of thunder as *anger*."[62] However, the large number of early modern narrative writers who had an overbearing fear of lightning and thunder did not react to it as a metaphor: they were certain that God made known his displeasure through these events, and they feared that they would be struck with God's wrath. As James Jenkins noted, the appearance of lightning and thunder at a funeral was taken as a sign of God's negative judgment of the dead person. Landon Carter, Ann Page, Susanna Anthony, Jacob Swann, Rebecca Jackson, and many others recorded very emotional scenes involving their own fear of God's judgment when there was thunder and lightning.[63] Page, Anthony, and Jackson all came to see their loss of this overwhelming fear as an extraordinary gift given them by God. Most people remained terrified. Benjamin Abbott, a Methodist preacher, was proud of the fact that he had made use of this fear during a severe storm in Delaware in the 1770s:

> The tremendous claps of thunder exceeded any thing I ever had heard, and the streams of lightning flashed through the house in a most awful manner! It shook the very foundations of the house, the windows jarred with the violence thereof. I lost no time, but set before them the awful coming of Christ, in all his splendor, with all the armies of heaven, to judge the world and to take vengeance on the ungodly! It may be, cried I, that he will descend in the next clap of thunder! The people screamed, screeched, and fell all through the house. The lightning, thunder, and rain continued for about the space of one hour, in the most awful manner ever known in that country, during which time I continued to set before the people the coming of Christ to judge the world, warning and inviting sinners to flee to Christ. One old sinner made an attempt to go, but had not gone far before he fell. . . . [Many] were that day convinced, and many converted.[64]

It was both very practical and symbolically significant that Benjamin Franklin set out to understand and control lightning. This project can be seen as an avatar of Franklin's self-view and worldview: his central concern was to show how a man could learn to control himself (reflecting Franklin's gender bias) and the world. He seemed to suggest that one could gain self-control through affirming humane and moderate values and simple bookkeeping techniques: intention and a record book of self-evaluation of behavior would do the trick. Behavior kept in mind could be changed. Franklin ruled a page for each of thirteen virtues, with a box for each day, so that he could record his progress toward each one, emphasizing one virtue each week. The virtues were listed as temperance, silence, order, resolution, frugality, industry, sincerity, justice, moderation, cleanliness, tranquillity and chastity, with humility added when a Quaker friend pointed out that he lacked this. While the virtues seem to be traditional, his guidelines were very much his own, and nonconformist. His guidelines for chastity, for example, were "Rarely use Venery but for Health or Offspring; Never to Dulness, Weakness, or the Injury of your own or another's Peace or Reputation." He made a plan to begin each day by asking himself, "What good shall I do?" and to close each day with a "self examination" of his accomplishments.[65] Attending to his behavior and writing it down were central, and the result amounted to a cryptic autobiography. Controlling the natural world, or the world made natural, appeared much more difficult, but Franklin simplified this too, when, in his famous experiments of the 1750s, he used a child's kite and a key to establish that lightning was an electrical discharge and found that a simple rod would lead the electricity into the ground. With this, Benjamin Franklin provided a new rational basis for understanding and controlling lightening that gradually became the ruling idea, although many continued to regard lightening as God's wrath.[66]

How difficult and frightening it was for some to change their worldview and self-view can be seen in the narrative of Levi Hathaway, who from childhood had sought to follow God's will, but when he was twenty-two became fascinated with science and determined both to study science and to change himself. After taking this turn he began to suffer, and he came to believe that "the Lord laid his afflicting hand on me" as a punishment for his choosing to follow his own will. When he had a vision of Jesus with "a band that went round his head, and the appearance of flashes of lightning went out of it," he understood this to signal his need to reject modern learning. His vision reaffirmed that Jesus created and controlled lightning and that it was sinful for him to try to learn how to do this.[67]

Quite a few of the narrators in this study were attracted by and then explicitly rejected the idea of changing themselves and controlling the "natural world." Nehemiah Duncan (born 1746) gave up the deism he had firmly held in response to what he believed was a spiritual visit from a friend who had died. As Duncan was reading Paine's *Age of Reason*, the friend's spirit adjured him to "cast away that damnable book." Duncan, who had previously forbidden his children to read the Scriptures, now burned the Paine book, returned to the church, and turned back from fashioning himself anew.[68]

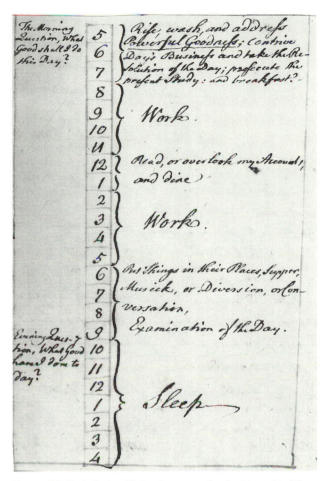

FIGURE 26. To help instill the "precept of order" into his life Benjamin Franklin attempted to follow a set "Order of the Day," as he noted in his Autobiography.

Some premodern ideas, such as the belief that each person had to face different challenges in a series of nine-year periods that reached a critical climax when the age of sixty-three was reached, gave way as people began to believe that if they followed a more regulated life plan, built around increased education, change would follow.[69] With increasing belief in the possibility of making significant choices and changes, a new attitude toward life and death was developing. As Robert Wells and others have shown, death began to be pushed out of first place in consciousness, and new attitudes toward it began developing long before the significant shift of most deaths

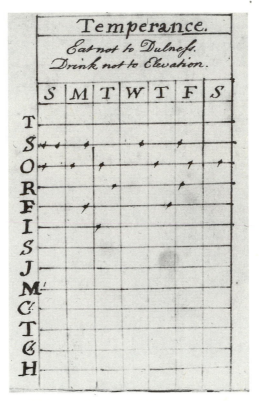

FIGURE 27. Benjamin Franklin's "Temperance Diagram," part of his plan for assessing his behavior in regard to thirteen virtues, each represented by a letter on the left.

to old age took place. Although until the 1850s overall life expectancy remained much as it had been in the eighteenth century, popular ideas about death began changing rapidly in the post-Revolutionary period as more of the population became Baptists and Methodists. The new attitudes toward death involved both welcoming death and the growth of a romantic sentimentality. Both attitudes were radically different from the views that had prevailed in the eighteenth century.[70]

A new attitude toward bringing children into the world was developing in this same period. "Around 1770, a change of major significance appeared in American childbearing patterns, as small numbers of parents began to make deliberate efforts to limit the size of their families." This small cohort grew significantly during this period. "Women who married in the seventeenth century averaged 7.4 children. Those who married in the late eighteenth century and had some of their children after 1800 averaged 6.4 children. Women married between 1800 and 1849 had 4.9 children."[71] Women and men were changing the family in ways that would prove revolutionary.

Attitudes toward raising children changed radically as well. Through the mid-eighteenth century, children were still very widely regarded as being in need of strict control—both of their bodies and their souls. It was widely assumed that they were born with evil desires and needed to have their wills broken in order to save their souls. In the next century, it was widely believed that infants were essentially pure and that mothers should allow for a much more "natural" development.[72] However, this change also meant that children were expected to be "good" and that the pranks and even violent acts that had once been seen as natural were now labeled unnatural. The life of Isaac T. Hopper (born 1771) illustrates how behavior that would later be seen as deviant (including bashing in heads) was labeled "His Love of Fun" and did not mark him as a bad person. He was expected to act peaceable as an adult and indeed went on to a life of devoted benevolence.[73]

Women underwent a similar transformation in the general evaluation: they had widely been seen as inherently evil, with very troublesome sexual urges and subject to difficult and rapidly altering and often aggressive emotional states. In the mid-eighteenth century these once generalized "female attributes' were increasingly associated with lower-class white and black women. By the early nineteenth century women not poor or black were widely assumed to be more moral and sexually passive than men, and mothers were generally accepted as the proper mentors for their children's development. Here too, as suggested, these expectations were also limits that were to be internalized.[74]

Expectations about fathers, who had earlier been seen as the proper educators and controllers of both women and children, also changed. Increasingly expected to make their mark outside the home, they were increasingly distanced from children's upbringing. Both men and women had been part of the communality in the eighteenth century; as individuation became the key to ideal male development in the nineteenth century, it was coupled with new demands for males to show strength in their fight through life. The change noted in attitudes toward crying can be seen as an important marker of overall change. Men had been expected to cry both publicly and privately in the eighteenth century: it was seen as a mark of true emotion. By the mid-nineteenth century, it had become a mark of weakness in a male, while it remained a proper feminine attribute.[75]

225

The shift in Western attitudes toward slavery was a crucial aspect of these Revolutionary changes. In the greater Revolutionary generation the enslaved played a significant role in bringing about a change in self-perception among white people. Both the dream reports and the life narratives provide very strong evidence that the significant relationships that a great many white people had with African Americans led to a change in themselves; nevertheless, this was most often an "unthought known"—a change in thinking and in ways of behaving that whites were not conscious of. When Thomas Jefferson wrote, "All men are created equal," this unthought known not only slipped past his conscious censorship, but, inasmuch as it was adopted as a mantra of the Revolution, it passed the conscious censorship of many others in power and has served as a catalyst for change in the world from that time on.[76]

African Americans, who had played a crucial role in bringing others to see the immorality of slavery, now began to justify their own public demands for their freedom on newly voiced ideological grounds. Virtually all the black individuals in this study were affected by these beliefs. Given the peculiar realities of New England slavery, many African Americans in the North were able to recognize the potential power and personal relevance of Revolutionary ideology and activism, and they used both to petition the new American institutions with a call for the end of enslavement. When Prince Hall and seven other African American men sent a formal petition to the Massachusetts legislature in 1777, requesting that slavery be ended there, they noted that "your Petitioners apprehend that they have in Common with all other men a Natural and Unalienable Right to that freedom." Similarly, when nineteen enslaved "natives of Africa" petitioned the New Hampshire legislature to end slavery in that state in November of 1779, they did so on the grounds "that freedom is an inherent right of the human species."[77] There is strong irony in the fact that the words of Jefferson, a slave owner who did not intend to bring about the end of slavery in his own lifetime, spoke directly to the souls of black folk and were a catalyst for further revolutionary action on the part of the enslaved.

Jefferson's words were directly responsible for moving Maumbet, an African American enslaved in Sheffield, Massachusetts, to petition the courts for her freedom. Catherine Maria Sedgwick, who heard the story from Maumbet, recorded her memory of the events:

> It was soon after the close of the revolutionary war, that she chanced at the village "meeting house," in Sheffield, to hear the Declaration of Independence read. She went the next day to the

226

office of Mr. Theodore Sedgewick, then in the beginning of his honourable political and legal career. "Sir,," said she, "I heard that paper read yesterday, that says, "all men are born equal,["] and that every man has a right to freedom. I am not a dumb *critter*; won't the law give me my freedom?"[78]

" 'If we are all free and equal,' " Maumbet asked, " 'why are we slaves?' "[79] When the courts did indeed declare her free, she proudly took the name of Elizabeth Freeman, signifying the change in her perception of her status that Jefferson's words and her own desires and actions had brought about.[80]

HATRED AND COMMITMENT AS KEYS TO SELF-DEVELOPMENT

The narratives and dreams of two formerly enslaved women, Sojourner Truth (born Isabella Baumfree in about 1797) and Harriet Tubman (born Araminta Ross about 1821), strongly suggest that they, like so many others in this study, developed themselves through powerful hatred of an alien other and by committing themselves to something outside themselves. Truth, as noted above, openly acknowledged, "When I was a slave I hated the white people." This hatred filled her life. At Pentecost/Pinkster in June of 1827, the year she took her freedom, Isabella [Baumfree] Van Wagenen had an ecstatic experience that led her to take Christ for her master. Although she then felt that love filled her heart, she did not want to love white people: "I thought that love was too good for them." However, she eventually found that she could not maintain her previous hatred, and she grudgingly committed herself to this difficult love: "Yea, God, I'll love everybody and the white people too." After she renamed herself Sojourner Truth in 1843, in an unvoiced adoption of the Quaker quest, she increasingly spent her time with white people but became ever more devoted to black emancipation and women's rights. Hatred had played an important role in focusing her oppositional development. During the period when her hatred of whites dominated her life, Isabella [Baumfree] Van Wagenen took several crucially significant decisions that changed her life and her self-view: in 1827 she declared herself free when her owner violated an agreement he had made to free her; and in 1828 she went to court and succeeded in getting one of her sons returned after he had been illegally shipped South. In the 1830s she chose to live in the patriarchal Zion Hill community, run by a white man who beat her to improve her. When this experiment ended dramatically with

227

FIGURE 28. Elizabeth "Maumbet" Freeman, who won her own freedom through the courts. Portrait by Susan Sedgwick, 1811.

the suspicion that one of the founders had been murdered, she was strong enough to initiate and win a case against those who were spreading rumors that she was implicated, and, although she still supported the patriarchal leader, she was able to move on, still seeking a better way.

Isabella Van Wagenen had embodied, in her self, the exploitation and oppression that black women were suffering, and yet as Sojourner Truth she came to voice a most extraordinary vision of the possibilities for development. As she said in 1851, "I am a woman's rights."[81]

228

Harriet Tubman was far more enigmatic. Her words never seemed to match her extraordinary acts, and neither her appearance nor her narrative was magnetic. Her acts were unique, however. She is the only person who, having freed herself, went back into slave territory time after time in order to lead her people to freedom. It was her very ordinariness that clothed her in anonymity and allowed her to pass as a downtrodden slave. No one said of her, as Harriet Beecher Stowe said of Truth, that she displayed "an unconscious superiority." No one said of her, as Douglass said of Truth, that she ridiculed his pretensions.[82] But she did become an extraordinary woman, the only one to lead men into battle in the Civil War. Her dictated narrative does not offer any explanation of how she became this woman, but that she hated slavery and the enslavers is clear. She may well have come to hate her husband, who, although free, opted both to remain in the South and to take another wife after she left for freedom. What she did say of herself only reinforces the questions raised:

> I grew up like a neglected weed,—ignorant of liberty, having no experience of it. Then I was not happy or contented: every time I saw a white man I was afraid of being carried away. I had two sisters carried away in a chain gang,—one of them left two children. We were always uneasy. Now I've been free, I know what a dreadful condition slavery is. . . . I think slavery is the next thing to hell. If a person would send another into bondage, he would, it appears to me, be bad enough to send him to hell if he could.[83]

In slavery, Tubman thought of white men as devils. How did Tubman move from being afraid of every white man to the point where she was able to steal back into the South and out again some fifteen times, with frightened men, women, and children in tow, secretly flouting every white man? A crucial change no doubt dated from the summer of 1849, when her husband and brothers became afraid to leave with her for the North and freedom, and she decided to act alone. But something in her development had given her the strength to make that courageous decision and carry it out.

Dreams played a crucial role in bringing both Tubman and Truth to a realization of their potential. They helped Tubman achieve a different self from the one she described. Tubman reported that while she was a slave in Maryland she dreamed of flying "like a bird" over landscapes that she believed she afterward saw in the North. Such flying was a common theme in dreams of Africans and African Americans: the ZeZeru in Zimbabwe interpret flying in dreams as communication from spirits, while the Temne of north-western Sierra Leone believe that dreams of flying betoken good fortune.[84] African Americans seemed to share both of these positive evaluations: images of flying (especially flying back to Africa) play an important role in many folktales, and later in written literature. In most, the black person who can fly is pictured as a person of great strength.[85] Certainly Tubman (and Truth) felt empowered by these special dreams of flying. Tubman heard an inward voice telling her, " 'Arise, flee for your life!' " In her dreams she began her flight to the North,

> but it appeared like I wouldn't have the strength, and just as I was sinking down, there would be ladies all dressed in white over there, and they would put out there arms and pull me across.

When she freed herself she remembered these visions bitterly:

> I had crossed the line of which I had so long been dreaming. I was free; but there was no one to welcome me to the land of freedom, I was a stranger in a strange land. . . . 'Oh, dear Lord,' I said, 'I aint got no friend *but* you. Come to my help, Lord, for I'm in trouble.'[86]

The color white was very important for Tubman, as it was for many if not all of the African Americans in this study. Tubman's dreams of white people held out the promise of her acceptance by God. After she had seen the white women in her dreams, she had indeed fled for her life. Later, when she found supporters in the North, she came to believe that God had led her to the white women that she had envisioned would help her.[87] It was her use of her dreams and visions that enabled her to become a leader among both black men and women, one who had a price on her head in the South, at the same time that she was sought as a partner by white abolitionists in the North.[88]

Maria Stewart, a free black woman, came to believe that most free black women were in need of the role change that Harriet Tubman and virtually all of the self-possessed women in this study underwent. Speaking publicly in Boston, in 1831, in the face of angry black opposition, Stewart courageously called on "the fair daughters of Africa" to undergo what she described as a metaphorical gender change:

> Do you ask the disposition I would have you possess? Possess the spirit of independence. . . . *Posses the spirit of men*, bold and enterprising, fearless and undaunted. Sue for your rights and privileges. . . . [Y]ou can but die if you make the attempt; and we shall certainly die if you do not.[89]

230

FIGURE 29. Harriet Tubman armed, as she chose to have herself shown in her narrative. Frontispiece, Sarah Bradford, *Scenes in the Life of Harriet Tubman*, 1869.

Stewart had become aware of and voiced what nearly all the women who fashioned themselves anew had unconsciously or consciously done: they had pictured themselves as male or as following male mentors. Independence was seen as a male attribute by women as well as men. The religious women often saw themselves as being like Jacob, Joseph, or Christ. Osborn had felt like a Samson; Elizabeth

FIGURE 30. This painting by the African American artist and preacher Anderson Johnson, "Vision of White Angels," 1994, portrays the vision that led him to fulfill his dual roles. It is in the tradition of Harriet Tubman's dream and suggests the continuing significance of white imagery in the symbolic universe of African Americans.

and Willey like a Daniel; while Byrd felt like both a Jacob and a Joseph and Jackson like a Jeremiah and an Ezekiel. Harriet Tubman became known as the Moses of her people.[90] Women who became more individuated were clearly seen by others as developing in a male way and often were referred to (and referred to themselves) as having "ideas almost masculine."[91] Chief among such ideas was the goal of freedom, which often developed out of hatred for male masters—fathers, husbands, or slave owners. Sylvia Dubois (born circa 1788), who had fought for her freedom (and was a champion boxer), remembered eighty years later that on her first journey as a free woman a man had called out to her, " 'Whose nigger are you?' I replied 'I'm no man's nigger—I belong to God—I belong to no man.' "[92]

Notwithstanding the fact that women often developed themselves on the basis of a strong hatred that might seem to violate the Christian ideal, in the eighteenth century Christian sects provided the key institutional support for women's change in self. By the nineteenth century many of these sects had become churches and as part of established society were reemphasizing patriarchal values. The Baptists retreated from their extraordinary support for female self-development; the American Methodists had always hedged the Wesleyan vision; and while women continued to have a singular role among Quakers, the Quakers' quietist journey led them away from supporting aggressively deviant roles. Nevertheless, women did find new ways in which to take some control both of themselves and of men within the mainline patriarchal churches.[93]

In this same period the growing number of more worldly white men were increasingly focused on attacking their female and/or black enemy others. Apparently, most white men believed that virtually all women were not destined for self-fashioning, a delimitation that became more and more onerous as white men were increasingly viewed as having the natural right to seek self-development. As any significant enlargement of self was categorized as male and was therefore seen as unnatural for a woman, a female who sought such change was marked as an unnatural woman whatever clothing she wore.[94] It was in this context that more women opted to speak as men (they had "masculine minds"), or spoke and acted as unwomanly women (self-appointed preachers, leaders of rebellions, fighters and runaways), and a small number chose to "transvest" and seek a role as males so that they might have more freedom to fashion themselves. Given the situation, an increasing number of women chose to remain unmarried, often voicing the recognition that there was greater freedom in this state.[95]

In addition to the new ideal of the passive women, a new feminine ideal of an assertive women was being developed both in life narratives and in novels.[96] This assertive ideal was voiced in Catherine Maria Sedgwick's *A New England Tale* (1822), which Nina Baym regards as the archetypal tale of this new genre. In this fictive narrative, Jane Elton, a strong, unflawed woman, comes to know her own self-worth and brings about her own success.[97] Sedgwick portrayed Elton's changing self-perception as beginning with a small but crucial act: she was enjoined to help save someone's life but in order to do so had to sneak out of her house in the middle of the night and face the peril of a guard dog, a task assumed to be too dangerous for a woman to undertake. Elton subdued the dog and this single act

233

enabled her to proceed on a new life path: "Now," thought Jane, "that I have stirred up my womanish thoughts with a manly spirit, I wonder what I could have been afraid of."[98]

These words of the fictive Jane Elton echo those in the Revolutionary War diary of Margaret Morris. Morris, a Quaker who was known not to support the Revolution, set out alone on a dangerous journey through territory surrounding Philadelphia that was held by the Revolutionaries. When her horse's harness broke, she was forced to jump from her careening "chair." She found a man to help with the repairs, but she coped with her fears by herself. After the journey she was advised never to undertake such a "perilous" trip again. She recorded that she told her friends that "so far from being a discouragement, [it] was like a whet to an hungry man, which gave him a better appetite for his dinner."[99] Both the real Margaret Morris and the fictive Jane Elton were committed to an institution outside themselves: acts of "manly" courage alone were not enough to change them. Morris was a born and committed Quaker, while Jane Elton was portrayed as believing that, unlike the Calvinists she had grown up among, Quakers demanded that everyday actions should be consonant with moral values. It is not surprising that Sedgwick had Elton choose to become a Quaker.[100]

The independence that Catherine Maria Sedgwick attributed to her as yet unmarried character, Jane Elton, mirrored Sedgwick's own attributes. Never married, she knew that she had "an independent power to shape her own course, and to force her separate sovereign way."[101] But she also believed that her independence of character had been shaped in her childhood, and rather than crediting an institution she credited one individual in particular, a black women who has already appeared in this narrative as a catalyst of black freedom in Revolutionary Massachusetts.[102]

Maumbet, or Elizabeth Freeman (1744?–1829), the extraordinary ex-slave who had won her freedom through the courts with the help of Catherine's father, became the fictive but real mother and often single parent to Catherine Maria Sedgwick. Sedgwick's biological mother was not able to play this role because she suffered from debilitating mental illness; Sedgwick's father was gone from home half of each year, serving the Federalist Party and his country, first in the House of Representatives and then in the Senate. It was Elizabeth Freeman who provided Sedgwick with the role model of a wise, hardworking, independent, and strong woman. Sedgwick spent her life trying to live up to Maumbet's example and expectations.

When Maumbet (or Mumbet) was ill and close to death, Sedgwick recorded the depth of her feelings in her private journal:

29 November 1829: Mumbet—"Mother"—my nurse—my faithful friend—she who first received me into her arms—is finishing her career—a life marked by as perfect a performance of duty—perhaps I should say more perfect than I have ever known. Her talents were not small nor limited: a clear mind—strong judgment—a quick and firm decision—an iron resolution—an incorruptible integrity—an integrity that never for a moment parleyed with temptation—a truth that never varied from the straight line—an unexceptionable fidelity to her engagements—always as she said "up to the mark"—a strong love of justice stern as Brutus—she could not forgive a wrong, but she would sooner have died at the stake than committed it—a productive, intelligent industry—an astonishing capacity of labor and endurance—a severe economy—and affections stronger than death were the riches of her character.

Later in life Sedgwick compared Elizabeth Freeman to George Washington and found her to be his equal in moral stature. This was high praise indeed, especially in view of the fact that Catherine Sedgwick was quite critical of the morality of most other ex-slaves.[103]

Sedgwick did not judge herself so well. Thinking she was near her own end in December of 1854, she wrote: "I am truly overwhelmed with a sense of my *poor* life—of my neglect of gifts—abuse and neglect of opportunities—on my self-indulgence." She also berated herself for having an unspiritual and cold religious life. All these qualities stood in stark contrast to those she attributed to Maumbet.[104] Sedgwick, unlike Elizabeth Freeman, had not been able to commit herself to an enabling institution. While she loved and respected her fictive mother very deeply, she felt she had not lived up to her example.

Maumbet's burning goal to feel " 'I am free' " was adopted by Catherine Sedgwick and remained with her all her life. Sedgwick internalized this and other values held by Elizabeth Freeman, but she was not guilty of psychic theft. She paid for these values with honor and devotion during Freeman's life and by memorializing Freeman as her "Good mother" both on her gravestone and later in print.[105]

DELIGITIMATING DREAMS/REFRAMING LIFE

In the greater Revolutionary period, dreams often served to bring to consciousness the needs and desires as well as the fears of both individual dreamers and groups within the society. Many sought more freedom, and both those who demanded more freedom and their opponents viewed their demands as an expression of "self-will." Even those who called for the subjection of self-will and those who had withdrawn to the borders of society participated in these changes. A prime example can be found in the relatively isolated and previously strongly communitarian Moravian settlements of Wachovia and Bethabara in the Carolinas, where Anna Catharina Ernst, a Moravian settler, observed "the spirit of self-will began about the time of which I am speaking."[106] The year was 1773.

Self-will and self-change often made itself known to these narrators, including Moravians, in dreams that led to change in self and in life. Anna Catharina Antes and her future husband, Christian Ernst, both made the difficult decision to migrate from Europe to Moravian settlements in Carolina only after dreams empowered them to overcome their fears. Christian Ernst had feared "red men, . . . sharp lightening, . . . thunder-storms," and the loss of contact with God. When Christ appeared in his dream and told him that He would go with him to Carolina, Ernst decided he could make the journey. Once there, Christian accepted a communal decision that he marry a bride of their choice, and shared this dream with her as his first act of intimacy.[107]

A dream also brought Catherine Sedgwick, who was moving toward marriage, to act, but she suddenly rejected her lover when her dream brought her to realize that she wanted to retain her personal freedom far more than she wanted to marry him. Many others, reacting to dreams, freed themselves from the constraints of family or tradition in revolutionary moves that were widely viewed as sanctioned by God. Many black people dreamed of flying over the world, a flight that was in itself freedom and often led them to free themselves. Several women dreamed that they annihilated attacking snakes or bulls and were able to attack their enemies in daylight. Several white men dreamed of eating black human flesh and were determined to deal more directly with the sins of slavery when they awoke. Many blacks saw redeeming white visions that gave them assurance of salvation, and often the necessary strength to protect themselves. At least one black man dreamed of the conflict of blacks and whites ending in streams of blood, and realized his dream. At least one white man saw liberty written in the sun's rays, while another saw people of color standing tall before God. Their visions were only partially fulfilled, but they both worked toward their fulfillment.

The eighteenth- and early-nineteenth-century narratives provide evidence that many of those who began to reconstruct their selves found that work with their dreams could be of great support. While dreams first helped to demarcate a new, more individualized self by

FIGURES 31 and 32. Catherine Livingston Garrettson, and her husband Freeborn Garrettson, role models for religious self-fashioners in the greater Revolutionary era.

pitting it against enemy others who were primarily of the other gender or another race, new, more incorporative selves could also be worked toward on the dream screen. John Woolman, John Taylor, Sarah Beckhouse Hamilton, Freeborn Garrettson and Catherine Livingston Garrettson, Henry Boehm, James Jenkins, Elizabeth, Rebecca Cox Jackson, Nat Turner, and myriad others accomplished commitments in dreamed action and incorporated what had been alien parts of their selves or their enemies into new, more inclusive self-images. That blacks were borrowing from whites and women from men has been known and accepted; but whites were also borrowing from blacks, as were men, both white and black, from women. Waking behavior often altered after dream changes, as did self-perception. Writing self-narratives, a new preoccupation of myriad people of the middling and lower sort, served both as a means to help bring people to new self-perception and as an end product to provide proof of their new selves.

After the Revolution there was what has been seen as "a window of opportunity" for change, particularly for newly freed black people, but for many white women and poor white men as well. But this window was soon closed by the rebellions of the powerless and the insecurities of the powerful. Their fears were fed by economic and social unrest and led to a program to reimpose discipline and control the unruly—blacks and women in particular.[108]

Alfred Young reminds us that under Jefferson and Madison elite coalitions sought to "eliminate [the] grievances" of the agrarian rebels and the rising urban mechanics (i.e., the white males), but that "they could not accommodate African Americans in slavery or American Indians, and were indifferent to the new voices among American women." Evidence from the narratives indicates that white males were not entirely "indifferent" to any of these groups: their reactions to blacks, Indians, and all women were a very negative but significant part of their behavior. They defined themselves as *not* these others and were determined to restrain these others in conditions that would support (rather than threaten) their own self-conception. This was a significant part of the way in which they created their self-view and their worldview. At the same time, blacks were increasingly regarding all whites as their enemies, and women were increasingly othering men. The process of othering by those in power has been widely analyzed, but little attention has been focused on othering by the subjected and the introjection of values from the other by both groups. These processes played a significant role in the development of early modern Americans. As part of the program to reimpose discipline and control, the reliance on dreams was denigrated by the new ruling elites in the society and the 'ruling ideas' in the culture. Much as in the medieval period, when the Church saw dream interpretation by laymen as a threat to Church discipline, the new elites' unvoiced recognition of the threat that popular dream interpretation held led them to discredit dreams.[109] Dreams increasingly came to be viewed as part of a premodern irrational worldview, and narrators became far less likely to cite dreams as the legitimation for particular actions in life.[110]

However, when fears were very powerful, their expression in dreams was sometimes still acknowledged publicly. In April of 1831, *The Liberator* published two dream reports submitted by a white northern supporter (T.T.). The first dream report is a lengthy description of the dreamer's visit to a future United States run by a very successful black president who is the symbol of the extraordinary integration that has taken place. In the dream, the "revolution" in racial relations that led to social integration was brought about by violence between whites in which many fought and died. A black man comments that it was very "fortunate" that this had been the case:

> Because in no other way could the seeds of jealousy and ill-will [among the blacks] have been so completely destroyed. But now,

the good they [the whites] have done us, and the kind and noble feeling they have shown towards us, have neutralized the effect of former wrongs.

While creating a scenario of a future when whites would not fear blacks, this dream recognizes the depth of black "ill-will" against whites in the 1830s. T.T.'s own fear of black violence was not assuaged by this dream's "utopian" vision of equality, in which black women were sexually available to white men and black men were more polite and dignified than whites. Two weeks later the same individual contributed a second dream report in which a successful and violent revolution was carried out by blacks against all whites, and in which he himself became a suffering slave. T.T. now reported that he dreamed that northern militias had been sent South to help crush a slave insurrection, and that his own family, left unprotected in the North, was killed by savage slaves. He and other whites were taken captive and enslaved by blacks. When, a few months later, on August 22, 1831, Nat Turner led more than sixty enslaved African Americans in the bloodiest slave rebellion in American history, both blacks' and whites' dreams and nightmares seemed to be coming true.[111]

Certainly, not everyone rejected dreams at the close of this period.[112] Margaret Fuller (born 1810), the New England translator, editor, and writer, and her close friend, James Freeman Clarke, exchanged and analyzed their dreams. Fuller believed that she " 'learned to read strange secrets in the hearts of others' " by analyzing their dreams, while her own dreams reinforced her self image. In 1839, when she dreamed of a female figure comforting her, she wrote, " 'As I have masculine traits, I am naturally relieved by women in my imaginary distresses.' "[113] When, in that same year, Ralph Waldo Emerson recognized that dreams revealed the dreamers' inner life, it may well have been because Fuller had brought him to this realization. Emerson asked:

What part does he [the dreamer] play in them,—a cheerful, manly part, or a poor driveling part? However monstrous and grotesque their apparitions, they have a substantial truth.

Emerson maintained that dreams were not sent by angels or spirits and did not reveal the role of God or fate. Rather, he held "that the reason of them is always latent in the individual."[114] While Emerson held this view intellectually, it is not clear that he understood the emotions in his own dreams, especially what seem to be revelations of his anger at women. The dream of October 25, 1840, in which

Emerson is flying, is clearly a play on the story of Adam and Eve, but one in which Emerson wipes out Eve and makes his own eating of the apple/world a holy act:

> I dreamed that I floated at will in the great Ether, and I saw this world floating also not far off, but diminished to the size of an apple. Then an angel took it in his hand & brought it to me and said: "This must thou eat." And I ate the world.[115]

Fuller's and Emerson's rich understanding of dreams as revelations of character did not become part of the ruling ideas of the 1840s. By this time, the close of the greater Revolutionary period, many of those who regarded themselves as modern among the elite and the growing middle class had come to feel that reliance on dreams was part of an old-fashioned and irrational as well as feminine and lower-class worldview.[116] Often, whites who viewed themselves as superior to this practice took note of black reliance on dreams: putting credence in dreams began to become something the other did. The Moravians had long viewed dreams as a significant marker of God's will; however, in the 1830s Renatus Shmidt, white Moravian pastor to blacks in his North Carolina congregation, "regretted" that blacks based their "conversion so much on dreams, visions and other fantasies." White and black Baptists had also found the word of God in dreams, but Robert Ryland, official white pastor (1841–1865) to the First African Baptist Church of Richmond, Virginia (which was unofficially but actually pastored by Joseph Abrams, a black man), held that blacks' attitude toward dreams led them to respect spirit "as independent of or opposed to the word of God." Blacks, in their own congregations, continued to recount dreams and visions in which they were called to make spirit journeys and traveled to hell and heaven.[117]

Although large sections of the population, including many new immigrants, continued to view dreams as significant, a great many came to regard dreams as "subjective, irrational and illusory."[118] Even those who still emphasized the inner life, such as the Society of Friends, rejected concern with dreams and edited them out of earlier narratives.[119] Those who still relied on dreams were often more self-conscious about this behavior, and far fewer people who published personal narratives advertised any reliance on them.[120]

By the time of the Civil War, dreams were rarely posited as important data to be cherished or studied, except by blacks and women. Abraham Lincoln, who had prescient dreams of success before a number of Civil War battles, and a deeply disturbing dream of his own death in April of 1865, recognized that along with other aspects of character that had been shared by men and women, regard for dreams had become feminized. He noted, "Nowadays dreams are regarded as very foolish, and are seldom told, except by old women and by young men and maidens in love."[121] In losing this supportive technique of the self, the poor and the weak lost an important bulwark in their attempts to act or behave in ways that were not in keeping with the demands of those in power. This loss was a serious one, but other lost aspects of dream use were perhaps more fateful. In the process of fashioning their selves, increasing numbers of individuals were rejecting parts of themselves and responding to these rejected aspects as other and alien. As a result, the need to address dreams actually became more acute among all segments of the population, not only the marginal. Earlier by relating to their dreams, often in ludic or playful ways, a wide spectrum of the population had become reconnected with disassociated parts of their selves. As dreams were increasingly ignored, these aspects became more alien and more dangerous, and selves began to develop in more polarized and menacing directions. The "power of the world of dreams" was by and large lost sight of, ostensibly because of the growth of rationality, while the power of the irrational hatred of the other grew apace.[122]

The use of dreams to change the self, exhibited in the lives of self-fashioners such as Woolman, Tubman, Truth, Ritter, Glendinning, Jackson, and many others in this study, was not widely known in the generations that followed. It was not until the work of Freud and his followers and critics made an impact on a culture that was suffering in part because of hidden inner rages that Western culture began to return to the dream with a recognition that it might serve the modern world in a modern fashion.[123] Dreams, however, had played a crucial although largely hidden role in bringing men and women into the modern world. In dreams, as in waking life, much change was achieved through the development of individuals in opposition to those they regarded as their enemies, and that change often involved theft and introjection of aspects of the enemies' values and behavior. Dreams also helped many to further reframe reality, to reclaim parts of their rejected selves, and thus to behave as fuller selves, whites taking from blacks, and men from women, as well as the reverse.[124]

If racial and gender otherness were central to early modern white male self-fashioning, racial and gender inequality is part of the essence of modernity. The implications of this are of great contemporary concern. Demands for black and female rights have popularly been viewed by white males as attacks on white male domains or territories of the self. In response, many have held that proper value education would alter this reaction. However, if the modern white male self is, indeed, built on the assumption of the gender and racial inferiority of the other and on the rejection of traits projectively identified with the other, racial and sexual equality *are* deeply threatening. Moreover, if such alienation is at the core of modern Western individuation, neither females nor black males were or are protected from it. As individual white and black women and black men moved (and continue to move) from more imbedded to more individuated development, they too shared (and share) in the need to position themselves against clear enemy others.[125] We all share in this history and participate in these developments, and we need to consider ways in which we may be able to alter our binary systems of white/black and male/female, in order to reframe reality. Perhaps the way lies through a new appreciation of individual dreams and collective myths.[126]

Notes

INTRODUCTION

1. Auster, *The Red Notebook*, 107.
2. This "we-self" was apparently similar to the self observed in the present-day societies of Japan and India by Alan Roland, who maintains that the Indian and Japanese familial self is formed by "intensely emotional intimacy relationships" both within the family and in the wider society "where there is a constant affective exchange through permeable outer ego boundaries." In contrast to the West, both libidinal expression and a more private spiritual development are encouraged. Roland, *In Search of Self*, 7–8, 225. On the communal self in the West see Sabean, *Power in the Blood*, 35, referring to German men; and on England Gillis, "From Ritual to Romance," 95–96.
3. The greater Revolutionary period can be demarcated by the First Great Awakening at the start, and the depression of 1837 at the close. Other significant markers of this era were the new sense of "secular pride in provincial citizenship" that can be dated from the Louisbourg Expedition of 1745, and the takeoff of industrialization at its close. See Shortt, "Conflict and Identity in Massachusetts," 185.
4. See L. Kaplan, *A Bibliography of American Autobiographies*. The narratives written by Loyalists attempting to gain compensation from the British for their lost property, as well as those later written by ex-soldiers seeking American government pensions, can be viewed as autobiographical statements encouraged by the state.
5. Moore, *Care of the Soul*, 12. C. G. Jung termed the dream "a theater, in which the dreamer is scene, player, prompter, director, author, audience, and critic." Jung, *Dreams*, 52. Bert O. States suggests that "dreaming is the ur-form of all fiction." States, *Dreaming and Storytelling*, 3. Michel Foucault holds that "The dream is not a modality of the imagination, the dream is the first condition of its possibility." Foucault, "Dream, Imagination, and Existence," 67. See also O'Flaherty, *Dreams, Illusion, and Other Realities*.
6. See Curti, "The American Exploration of Dreams and Dreamers," 391–41. While early American dreams have not been widely analyzed, both David Hall and Jon Butler have taken the historical role of dreams in America very seriously. See D. Hall, *Worlds of Wonder*, 19, 72, 74, 86–91, 106–109, 132, 213, 215–216, 222–223, 229, 274, 331; Butler, *Awash in a Sea of Faith*, 20, 84, 184, 186, 222–243, 295. Butler has very generously provided me with many dream reports he located in his research. Wigger discusses dream reports among early Methodists in "Taking Heaven By Storm," 167–194. Heyrman writes that in this period, "The fascination with dreams was nearly universal," but she goes on to suggest that the belief in dreams was part of a "supernaturalism" that played a negative role. Heyrman, *Southern Cross*, 61–63. For studies of particular dreamers see: McGowan, "The Dream of Ezra Stiles" 181–198; Sleeper-Smith, "The Dream as a Tool

for Historical Research," on William Byrd, 49–92; Binger, "The Dreams of Benjamin Rush" 1653–1659; Butterfield, "The Dream of Benjamin Rush" 297–319.

7. I found Stephen Greenblatt's succinct formulation of the theory of oppositional self-creation of great value in evaluating the narratives written by early Americans, and his most nuanced application of this theory set high goals. Greenblatt, *Renaissance Self-Fashioning*, 9. See also Gregg, *Self-Representation*, 46–47, 119, 121, 161; James, *The Principles of Psychology*, 289; and M. Douglas, *Natural Symbols*, 93–112. For a study of self-fashioning and the American experience see Smith-Rosenberg, "Domesticating 'Virtue': Coquettes and Revolutionaries in Young America," 160–184.

8. Alfred Young's rich biographical analysis of Boston shoemaker George Robert Twelves Hewes (born 1742) suggests how some of these changes could come about for a very poor white male: "[T]he experience of participating in the Boston Massacre, the Boston Tea Party, and countless other events of resistance enabled Hewes to cast off deference." Near the end of his long life Hewes defined himself as the equal of all patriots, whatever their class. Young, "Afterward: How Radical Was the American Revolution?" 324; Young, "George Robert Twelves Hewes," 623.

9. See Ricoeur, *Time and Narrative*, 159; Bruner, "Life As Narrative," 11–32; Bruner, *Acts of Meaning*; M. White, "Family Therapy," 80. On self change see J. Lyons, *The Invention of the Self*; Elbaz, *The Changing Nature of the Self*; Spacks, *Imagining a Self*; Cox, "The Stranger Within Thee"; Nussbaum, *The Autobiographical Subject*.

10. Hegel held that "An individual makes its appearance in antithesis to an individual." Gregg expands on this theory as well as on Adorno's ideas about authoritarian personalities and the other to apply to all personality development. Gregg, *Self-Representation*, 15–33.121, 200, 206, 207. For the Hegel citation, and for his discussion of "Lordship and Bondage" and their relationship to self-consciousness, see Hegel, *The Phenomenology of Mind*, 231, 228–240. Adorno, *The Authoritarian Personality*. Greenblatt, in *Renaissance Self-Fashioning*, 8–9, builds on postulates very close to these. See also Barker-Benfield, *The Horrors of the Half-Known Life*, 26.

11. See Beauvoir, *The Second Sex*, the classic study of women as other.

12. Lott, *Love and Theft*. See also Roediger, *Towards the Abolition of Whiteness*, 66; Volkan, *The Need to Have Enemies and Allies*.

13. Occum (1723–1792), "A Short Narrative of My Life," 12–18; Peyer, "Samson Occom," 208–217. Other narratives by Indians, especially those of whites who became Indians such as Mary Jemison (born 1742 or 1743), John Dunn Hunter (born 1798?), and John Tanner (born 1780?), reveal the often convoluted complications of self-image and other internalized by these people, who crossed and recrossed white/Indian boundaries. Jemison's narrative reveals that although she was "taken by the Indians" when about fifteen, she maintained positive yet painful ties to her natural parents (murdered by the Indians who took her) and to white culture throughout her life. At the age of eighty she noted, "I frequently dream of those happy days [of child-

hood]." While she chose to remain an Indian, married a Delaware and a Seneca, and raised her children as Indians, she named them Thomas, Jane, Nancy, Betsey, Polly, John, and Jesse, after her parents and siblings, symbolically passing her bifurcation to the next generation. When she contemplated returning to white society she reminded herself that the whites "would despise them, if not myself." The history of the Jemison family may well suggest the difficulties the second generation experienced as well. Mary's son John murdered his brothers, Thomas and Jesse, and was himself murdered by two other Indians. Mary was suspected of being a witch. See Seaver, *A Narrative of the Life of Mrs. Mary Jemison*, 63, 77, 119–120, 141, 149, 160; Hunter, *Memoirs*; Tanner, *A Narrative*.

Okah Tubbee, while enslaved as an African, insisted that he was an Indian and that the black woman who claimed she was his mother was lying. Based on a dream vision, he developed new musical instruments and envisioned "that the harmony [of his music] might melt the savage heart, and unite the broken and wasting tribes." He and his Indian wife developed stage presentations of Indian culture featuring his new music. Tubbee, *A Sketch of the Life*, 75. See also Littlefield, "Introduction," *The Life of Okah Tubbee*.

14. See Butler, *Awash in a Sea of Faith*; Hoffman and Albert, *Religion in a Revolutionary Age*. There is a serious debate over the numbers who were affiliated with churches in the greater Revolutionary period. See Finke and Stark, *The Churching of America*, 55–59, 113; and Heyrman, *Southern Cross*, 13, 261–266, who disputes their figures. She holds that only "a negligible percentage of African Americans" were evangelicals in 1776 and that no more that 10 percent of all adults were. While formally enrolled black Baptists were not yet a large group, there were African American members in virtually every Southern Baptist church, and the enslaved responded widely to the Baptist faith. See Sobel, *Trabelin' On*.

15. For a fine survey see Wright, *African Americans in the Colonial Era*. It is estimated that there were some 500,000 African Americans out of a total population of 2,600,000 in 1774. On African American participation in the war see Quarles, "The Revolutionary War as a Black Declaration of Independence," 285.

16. See Nash, *The Urban Crucible*; Kulikoff, "The American Revolution, Capitalism, and the Formation of the Yeoman Classes," 80–119; Kulikoff, "Was the American Revolution a Bourgeois Revolution?" 58–89; Davis and Engerman, "The Economy of British North America," 21.

17. On "profound social upheaval" see Nash, cited by Young, "American Historians Confront 'The Transforming Hand of Revolution,'" 477–478. On changing gender roles see Norton, *Liberty's Daughters*; Kerber, *Women of the Republic*; Bloch, "The Construction of Gender in a Republican World," 601–606. Branson, "Women and the Family Economy in the Early Republic," 47–71 presents a case study of the economic activities of two generations of women. In the first generation Elizabeth Meridith (born 1742) was very active in the family tanning business, keeping records, borrowing money, collecting debts, and planning for the future. In the next generation

her daughter-in-law became active in social and cultural affairs but did not take any part in the family business. For a discussion of these changes, and the courts, see Dayton, *Women Before the Bar*, 9.

18. On the co-opting of the lower classes into the Revolutionary movement see Egnal and Ernst, "An Economic Interpretation of the American Revolution," 10. On the co-option of the Baptists in Virginia, see R. Isaac, "Evangelical Revolt," 345–368. For the South in general, see Hoffman, "The 'Disaffected' in the Revolutionary South," 273–316. For Baptists in Massachusetts see Juster, *Disorderly Women*. On "fantasy wish-fulfillment" see Weinstein and Platt, *The Wish to be Free*, 7.

19. See Meranze, "Introduction," *Benjamin Rush*, xvi, for a discussion of the use of education for purposes of control.

20. See Stearns and Stearns, eds., *The Struggle*; Stearns and Stearns, eds., *Emotion and Social Change*.

21. Individual Indians' dreams have been widely reported and analyzed by psychologists, anthropologists, and historians. See Wallace, "Dreams and Wishes of the Soul," 234–248; Richling, " 'Very Serious Reflections,' " 148–169; Irwin, "Contesting World Views," 259–269; Merritt, "Dreaming of the Savior's Blood," 723–746; D'Andrade, "Anthropological Studies of Dreams," 296–332; Tedlock, *Dreaming*; Kluckhohn and Morgan, "Some Notes on Navaho Dreams," 120–131; Devereux, *Reality and Dream*, 171–198. For a description of Lakota dream beliefs and practices see St. Pierre and Long Soldier, *Walking in the Sacred Manner*.

22. Donald Jackson suggests that this may well be a report of Champlain. *Black Hawk*, ed. Jackson, 41–43.

23. See Jedrej and Shaw, *Dreaming*.

24. See chapters 2 and 4 of this book. John Leland (born 1754) dreamt that God would instruct him. Leland, *Some Events*, 14. Lucy Richards (born 1792) wrote that "even in dreams and visions of the night God opens the ears of man, and sendeth to him instruction." She begged God to speak in a way that she could understand. Richards, *Memoirs*, 239.

25. Two important collections of essays on the dream and culture are Von Grunebaum and Callois, *The Dream*, and Tedlock, *Dreaming*. See also the work of the "culturalist school" on the influence of social life on the dream: Bonime, "A Culturist View," 79–99; Ullman, "Social Roots of the Dream," 160–196; O'Nell, *Dreams, Culture and the Individual*; Lee, "Social Influences in Zulu Dreaming," 265–283; LeVine, *Dreams and Deeds*.

26. At present, "North Americans are generally enculturated to disattend their dream life, even to cognize dream life as being associated with 'evil,' 'death,' and 'madness,' hence something to fear . . ." Laughlin et al., "The Ritual Transformation of Experience," 125.

27. On modern cultures "derogatory attitude towards dreams," see Bastide, "The Sociology of the Dream," 199–211.

28. Ullman, "Dreams and Society," 290–291; Ullman, "Societal Factors in Dreaming," 282–293.

29. Beradt, *The Third Reich of Dreams*, 5, 9, 95–108, 111–120. See Rupprecht, *The Dream and the Text*, for an excellent introduction to issues in

contemporary dream interpretation, particularly with regard to historical and cultural concerns. For surveys of recent works see Sobel, "The Revolution in Selves," 204–205; Moffitt, Kramer, and Hoffman, *The Functions of Dreaming*; Shafton, *Dream Reader*.

30. Kohut, *The Restoration of the Self*, 109; Kohut, *The Search for the Self*, 3:138–140, 147–148.

31. Ibid., 139.

32. See R. Greenberg, "Self-Psychology and Dreams."

33. Fiss, "The 'Royal Road to the Unconscious,' " 403; Fosshage, "Dream Interpretation Revisited," 161–175; Sand and Levin, "Music and Its Relationship to Dreams and the Self," 184. For the view that virtually all dreams relate to the self, see Atwood and Stolorow, *Structures of Subjectivity*; Fiss, "An Empirical Foundation for a Self Psychology of Dreaming," 161–192; Fosshage, "The Psychological Function of Dreams," 641–669; Gabel, "Monitoring the State of the Self in Dreams," 425–451; R. Greenberg, "Self-Psychology and Dreams," 98–102; R. Greenberg and Pearlman, "A Psychoanalytic-Dream Continuum," 441–448; Ornstein, "On Self-State Dreams in the Psychoanalytic Treatment Process," 87–104; Tolpin, "Self Psychology and the Interpretation of Dreams," 255–271. It has been suggested that Kohut's ideas are too positive. Alford, for example, who relied on Kohut's theory in his analyses of the construction of self in thinkers from Plato to Rawls, felt a strong need to balance Kohut's concepts with insights from Jacques Lacan in order to show "the self to be less whole and integrated than Kohut's idealistic account sometimes suggests." Alford, *The Self*, 19–20. For other criticism see Slap and Trunnell, "Reflections on the Self State Dream," 251–262.

34. Gabel, "Monitoring the State of the Self," 438–449; Ullman and Zimmerman, *Working with Dreams*; Bollas, *The Shadow of the Object*.

35. Foucault, *Technologies of the Self*.

36. Rossi, *The Psychobiology of Mind-Body Healing*, 34; Rossi, *Dreams and the Growth of Personality*. See chapter 1 of this book for further consideration of Rossi's continuum.

37. Bollas, *Forces of Destiny*, 47.

38. Bollas, *The Shadow of the Object*, 157–158, 165–169. Bollas holds that in extreme cases of extractive introjection mental structure and "loss of one's sense of one's own person" can be brought about. For a working definition of introjection and projection, and for a discussion of male-female and slave-master exchanges, see Scharff, *Projective and Introjective Identification*, 87–92, 205–209. See Lott, *Love and Theft*, 19; Roediger, *Towards the Abolition of Whiteness*, 66.

39. Leland, *Some Events*; Watters, *A Short Account*. On Sherman, see chapter 4 of this book.

40. On "anticipatory socialization," see J. Douglas, "The Emergence, Security and Growth of the Sense of Self," 77. On socialization through storytelling see P. J. Miller, "Narrative Practices," 158–179.

41. Gronniosaw, *A Narrative*, 22. Peck, *The Life and Times*, 51; E. Thomas, *Reminiscences*, 31. See also the apparently fictive Eliza Webb or Lucy Brewer, *The Female Marine*, 27. Elias Cornelius, a student at Yale, felt

his life was deeply affected when, in 1813, he read the life of the ascetic mystic Susanna Anthony. See Rubin, *Religious Melancholy*, 112–113. In 1830 a woman reported to Eleazar Sherman that her awakening had occurred as a direct result of reading his autobiography. Sherman, *The Narrative*, 2:55.

Many narrators, among them Franklin, J. Lathrop, and Glendinning, reported being impressed with reading John Bunyan. While traveling in America Tocqueville and Beaumont were given a life narrative by the white Indian John Tanner (born about 1780), and it is likely that it altered their understanding of American racism. Tanner's gift is noted in Beaumont, *Marie*, xiii.

42. In the second edition of her autobiography, Eldridge notes that she sold "about nineteen hundred" copies of the first edition. Eldridge, *Elleanor's Second Book*, 14. Truth used the money she gained from book sales to purchase a home and to support herself. Mabee, *Sojourner Truth*, 52–59, 94–95, 211–212, 215–216. Many ex-slave narratives were expressly written to raise money to purchase the author's enslaved family. See, for example, Grandy, *Narrative*, which was "sold for the benefit of his relations still in slavery." Authors were widely given 10 percent of the price of the book by publishers, but many of the narratives were printed for the authors, who paid costs and then sold the books themselves. See D. Hall, "The Uses of Literacy in New England," 9.

Inasmuch as a key issue in this study is the promotion of self change and the self-promotion that was undertaken in this period, self-narratives published in this same period were chosen for analysis. Rare exceptions were made in several cases of rich self-narratives of those who grew up and wrote in this period but were published later, such as that of Rebecca Jackson (born in 1795), *Gifts of Power*, which was not published until 1981. A number of the published narratives were transcriptions of oral testimonies, often changed by the editors, or edited versions of materials published after the deaths of the authors. In her analysis of both the difficulties and the value of using "mediated" narratives, Jean M. Humez views both the writer and the narrator as participants. Humez, "In Search of Harriet Tubman's Spiritual Autobiography,"175; Humez, "Reading *The Narrative of Sojourner Truth* as a Collaborative Text," 29–52.

43. Foucault, *Technologies of the Self*.

44. Bollas, *The Shadow of the Object*, 157–169. See also Volkan, "The Need to Have Enemies and Allies," 219–247; Volkan, *The Need to Have Enemies and Allies*. Another interpretation suggests that the parts attacked in the other were projected by the self onto the other, but were always in the self and could be reclaimed. See Scharff, *Projective and Introjective Identification*, 87–92, 205, 209; Godwin, "On the Function of Enemies," 79–102; Heideking, "The Image of an English Enemy During the American Revolution," 91–108; Lott, *Love and Theft*, 19.

45. "To reframe . . . means to change the conceptual and/or emotional setting or viewpoint in relation to which a situation is experienced and to place it in another frame which fits the 'facts' of the same concrete situation equally well or even better, and thereby changes its entire meaning." Wat-

zlawick, Weakland, and Fisch, *Change*, 134, 95. Change can also come about through a "corrective emotional experience." Alexander and French, *Psychoanalytic Therapy*, 67. Modern psychoanalysis can be seen as based on the acceptance of its ideology and submission to its practitioner. It often involves participation in an ordeal and leads to a reframing of past reality that enables the individual to create a new future. Watzlawick, *The Language of Change*, 131. Milton Erickson shared this view. See Hanley, "Erickson's Contribution to Change in Psychotherapy," 36. Arthur Burton, reviewing fourteen psychotherapies, concludes, "Regardless of the healing system which is proffered, in order to be healed the patient must accept—yes, have a readiness to believe in—the values, circumstances, and efficacy of that particular system." Burton, *What Makes Behavior Change Possible?* 323. See also the theory of a need for an authority in relation to ending an addiction in Bateson, "The Cybernetics of 'Self': A Theory of Alcoholism," 309–313.

46. Coser, "Greedy Organizations," 196–215. On psychosocial development and the Revolution, see Fliegelman, *Prodigals and Pilgrims*; Burrows and Wallace, "The American Revolution," 266–303.

47. See P. J. Miller, "Narrative Practices," 158–179.

48. While I have chosen *not* to consider these narratives by their common genre categorizations (Indian captivity narratives, slave narratives, soldiers' narratives, and so forth), virtually all these types were included.

49. Jane Flax, in a fairly positive consideration of postmodernist arguments for deconstruction of self, does note that they are both "intriguing and disappointing." See Flax, *Thinking Fragments*, 230–231; and Flax, *Disputed Subjects*, 106.

50. Alan Roland, who worked as an analyst in the United States as well as in India and Japan, emphasizes "that the kinds of potentialities persons actually develop, how they function and communicate in society, what their mode of being and experience is in the world and within themselves, and what their ideals and actualities of individuation are depend overwhelmingly on the given culture and society to which they belong." Roland, *In Search of Self in India and Japan*, 324. See Gardner, *Frames of Mind*, 242; Geerts, " 'From the Native's Point of View' " 123–136.

51. On "ontological security" see Laing, *The Divided Self*, 41–42; Molino, "Christopher Bollas," 13. For an impassioned defense of the need for a unified sense of self, see Glass, *Shattered Selves*, xi–xii, 14–15, 24, 98.

52. *Prayers for the New Year*, 288. In the postbiblical period there were, as well, accepted methods for undertaking repair involving consultation with three recognized dream interpreters. On the views of postbiblical interpreters see Frieden, *Freud's Dream of Interpretation*, 93; Frieden, "Talmudic Dream Interpretation," 103–111; Covitz, *Visions of the Night*, 2; Bilu, "Sigmund Freud and Rabbi Yehuda Halevy," 443–463; Bakan, *Sigmund Freud and the Jewish Mystical Tradition*.

53. Havens, *A Safe Place*, 153. Havens is referring to his goals in working with (living) patients, while my own goals clearly refer to repairing our memory of these narrators and to the use we make of the past.

249

CHAPTER 1

1. Letter to Elizabeth Lamb Pinckney, the first Mrs. Charles Pinckney, in Pinckney, *The Letterbook*, 19.

2. Spacks, *Imagining a Self*, 8–9. See C. Stearns, " 'Lord, Help Me Walk Humbly,' " 52; C. Taylor, *Sources of the Self*, 159–176. For important considerations of personal development in early America see P. Brown, *Modernization*, 94–121; and Greven, *The Protestant Temperament*.

3. Fox holds that, actually, "Locke had severed substance from selfhood and had paved the way for the ultimate denial of the abiding self." Fox, "Locke and the Scriblerians," 5; Fox, *Locke and the Scriblerians*.

4. Pinckney, *The Letterbook*, c. June 1742, 47. Richardson's *Pamela*, published in November 1740, was ostensibly based on a true story. The claim was made that the autobiographical letters were written by the heroine and edited by Richardson. Pamela's values were severely criticized by many contemporaries, beginning with Henry Fielding in *An Apology for The Life of Mrs. Shamela Andrews In which the many notorious Falsehoods and Misrepresentation of a Book called Pamela are exposed and refuted . . .*, "by Conny Keyber" [pseud.] (1741). See Kreissman, *Pamela-Shamela*. On Richardson's view of the self, see Cox, " 'The Stranger Within Thee,' " 61–65. Many other early novels, such as Daniel Defoe's *The Life and Surprising Adventures of Robinson Crusoe* (London, 1719), were written in the form of "true" life narratives; some were based on actual lives, others purported to be.

5. Scott notes that three years before the first Mrs. Charles Pinckney died, Eliza Lucas "absentmindedly signed a letter to him 'Eliza Pinckney.' " It seems much more likely that this was a "Freudian error" and that Eliza Lucas unconsciously hoped and at some point more consciously planned to replace his ailing wife after her death. J. Scott, "Self-Portraits," 65. This letter, of February 6, 1741, can be found in Pinckney, *The Letterbook*, 12. Eliza Lucas and Charles Pinckney were married in May 1744.

6. Pinckney's resolves, which indicate her commitment and sense of self, are reprinted in Ravenel, *Eliza Pinckney*, 115–118.

7. Mary Cooper, a farm wife near Oyster Bay, Long Island, in whose diary of 1763–1773 this use of "we" is found, as cited by Boydston, *Home and Work*, 13.

8. J. Young, *Autobiography of a Pioneer*, 126.

9. Lowenthal suggests, "Well into the eighteenth century even reflective men took life to be 'a discontinuous succession of sensory enjoyments' interspersed with abstract reflection in Starobinski's phrase, with 'chance events and momentary excesses' featuring successive unrelated episodes." Lowenthal, *The Past Is a Foreign Country*, 198. On the concept of a communal or we-self in Eastern cultures see Roland, *In Search of Self*, 8, 225.

10. Gillis, "From Ritual to Romance," 95–96.

11. Sabean, *Power in the Blood*, 35, referring to German men.

12. Misch and Snell believe that self-fashioning was described in personal narratives from post-Homeric Greece. Although there were other periods in which some people apparently had both a far stronger sense that they could

fashion themselves, narrative reports of such perception, such as that of Augustine (353–430) in his *Confessions*, are very rare before the second half of the eighteenth century. (Augustine also made significant use of his dreams in changing himself.) Misch, *A History of Autobiography in Antiquity*, 2:543, 558. Snell, *The Discovery of the Mind*, 1–22, 42–70.

13. Brumble, *American Indian Autobiography*.

14. Ibid., 135.

15. Hammon, *A Narrative*.

16. O. Clarke, *Things That I Remember*, 12.

17. Shaw, *A Narrative*, 130, 131, 133.

18. Rossi. *Dreams*, 131–138. The bracketed comments are from the table expanding on Rossi's categories in Purcell, Moffitt, and Hoffman, "Waking, Dreaming, and Self-Regulation," 212. Purcell et al. provide important evidence of the influence of dreams on the waking life of the dreamer. See also Greenberg et al., "A Research-Based Reconsideration," 531–550. Loehrich, *Thought Operations*, also holds that "the different levels of awareness" within a dream are of key significance. See Stockholder, "World in Dream and Drama," 379.

19. Shaw, *A Narrative*, 9, 15, 18, 20, 43, 74, 109, 111.

20. At the close of his narrative the devil was seen approaching again. Ibid., 159.

21. Ibid., 7, 108, 117, 118, 149–153.

22. W. Lee, *The True and Interesting Travels*, 19, 30. Redfield, *A Succinct Account*, 12. J. Thomas, *The Life of the Pilgrim*, 111. J. Green, *The Life*, 6. Many of those narrators who came to see their lives as patterned and themselves as dramatic actors continued to count up their accomplishments: John Churchman, a Public Friend, noted that he had traveled ninety-one hundred miles and attended one hundred meetings in four years and twelve days. Churchman, *An Account*, 166. Eleazer Sherman held one thousand meetings between 1829 and 1831. Sherman, *The Narrative*, 3:97. John Leland, a Baptist preacher, counted those he had baptized: 1,352 by 1824. Leland, *The Writings*, 34–35. On concern with and use of numbers, see Cohen, *A Calculating People*.

23. See Willey, *A Short Account*.

24. See A. Taylor, "Rediscovering the Context of Joseph Smith's Treasure Seeking," 18–28; A. Taylor, "The Early Republic's Supernatural Economy," 6–34; Quinn, *Early Mormonism*, 16, 114; Fabian, *Card Sharps, Dream Books, and Bucket Shops*. For valuable early Indian dream reports see Black Hawk, *Life*, 41–43, 129.

25. For an example see Fry, *The Autobiography*.

26. Hathaway, *Narrative*, 20–21; Coleman, *Memoir*, 43; McCorkle, "Religious Experience," 90.

27. James Dalton, Edward Donnelly, Samuel Godfrey, Samuel Green, George Lathrop, Michael Martin, and Thomas Powers all wrote of being fated to be criminals. Herman Rosencrantz and James Pearse were unusual in that they believed they had been good men who turned bad in their lust for money. See Dalton, *Life and Action*, 1, 9, 32; Donnelly, *Confession, 1*;

Godfrey, *Sketch of the Life*, 3; S. Green, *Life*, 3, 5; Lathrop, *Dark and Terrible Deeds*, 9; M. Martin, *Life*, 5–6; Powers, *Narrative and Confession*, 3–5; Rosencrantz, *Life and Confession*, 9–10; Pearse, *Narrative*, 11–12, 36–37.

28. William G. Brownlow (1805–1877), although he was writing a life narrative, was determined not to be "egotistical" and gave this as the reason he would not tell stories of his youth. Brownlow, "A Narrative," 263. Edward Willett (1701–1794) wrote his entire narrative about his wife and their marriage and never mentioned her name. (He gave no explanation.) Willett, *The Matrimonial Life*. Seth Coleman only mentioned the existence of his children when they died. Coleman, *Memoir*, 102. Both Joseph Lathrop (born 1731) and Lemuel Sawyer (born 1777) were strangely distanced from their own selves and wrote of themselves in the third person. Lathrop, *Dark and Terrible Deeds*; Sawyer, *Auto-biography*. For a discussion of the concern with pain in this period, see Halttunen, "Humanitarianism," 303–334.

29. In 1674 the English poet Thomas Traherne wrote, "A secret self I had enclos'd within,/That was not bounded with my clothes or skin." Traherne, *The Poetical Works*, 34. See also Payne, The Self and the Sacred, 33–49.

30. "Our sense of personal inviolability is a violable social gift, the product of what *others* are willing to respect and protect us from, the product of the way we are handled and reacted to, the product of the rights and privileges we are granted by others in numerous 'territories of the self.' " Shweder and Bourne, "Concept of the Person," 194.

31. For published American autobiographies written in this period see L. Kaplan, *Bibliography*. Imhof, "Life-Course Patterns," 247–270, notes that two hundred thousand early German funeral orations, consisting of several pages each, are extant. These are biographies, but some were based on self-reports such as the late-eighteenth-century collection of autobiographies edited by Karl Philipp Mortiz in *Magazin zur Erfahrungsseelenkunde*, noted by Kohli in "The World We Forgot," 285. Early Quaker autobiographies and British working-class autobiographies have been collected and republished on microfiche. See, for example, *The People's History*. The Society of Friends Archive in Haverford, Pennsylvania, has extensive autobiographical holdings from the early modern period, as do the Moravian Archives in Bethlehem, Pennsylvania, Winston-Salem, North Carolina, and the Archiv der Brüder-Unität, Herrenhut, Germany. Thirty Moravian women's autobiographies, 1750–1820, are in Faull, *Moravian Women's Memoirs*.

32. Habermas, *The Structural Transformation*, 54, 56, 49, 50; C. Taylor, *Sources of the Self*, 319, 201–207,305–318.

33. Sabean, *Power in the Blood*, 30–36, 48–49.

34. See Elias, *The Society of Individuals*, 169, 182–183.

35. J. Jordan, "A Relational Perspective," 21.

36. Spacks, *Imagining a Self*, 8–9; Cox, *"Stranger within Thee"*, 7.

37. Hegel, *Phenomenology*, 231, 228–240; Greenblatt, *Renaissance Self-Fashioning*, 9–10. See also Gregg, *Self-Representation*, 46–47, 119, 121, 161; James, *The Principles of Psychology*, 289; Douglas, *Natural Symbols*, 93–112; Smith-Rosenberg, "Domesticating "Virtue,' " 160–184.

38. Erikson's view of vectoral development, tied to age-linked tasks, is a description of the changes in self that were expected after the patterning of the life cycle became essentially uniform. This process (discussed in chapter 6 of this book) was under way in the period under discussion, but developmental changes were then far more likely to occur at random times in the life cycle than they are today. Erikson, *Childhood and Society*, 247–275; Kohli, "The World We Forgot," 271–303; and Kett, *Rites of Passage*.

39. Augé, *Non-Places*, 19–20.

40. Gregg, *Self-Representation*, 47. From Heraclitus to the modern period, many have held the view that human beings divide everything into a me and not-me. See James, *Principles of Psychology*, 289; Watzlawick, Weakland, and Fisch, *Change*, 18; Jung, *Symbols of Transformation*, 375. Edelman suggests that "a self/not self discrimination is structurally inherent in the central nervous system." Edelman, *The Remembered Present*, 98. It is also fairly widely held that "unwanted portions of the self are projected on the object." Modell, *The Private Self*, 56–59; Volkan, "The Need to Have Enemies and Allies," 219–247.

41. See Volkan, *The Need To Have Enemies and Allies*; Gregg, *Self-Representation*, 47; Godwin, "On the Function of Enemies," 79–102.

42. The narratives of James Hudson, *The Life and Confession*, and Jackson Johonnet, *The Remarkable Adventures*, do present the Indian as an alien other.

43. See Barker-Benfield, *The Horrors of the Half-Known Life*, 26.

44. See Gregg, *Self-Representation*, 47; Scharff, *Projective and Introjective Identification*, 87–92, 205, 209; Lott, *Love and Theft*, 19; Bollas, *The Shadow of the Object*, 157–169; Volkan, "The Need to Have Enemies and Allies," 219–247; Godwin, "On the Function of Enemies," 79–102.

45. Bollas, *The Shadow of the Object*, 158, 165–166. Bollas holds that in more extreme cases mental structure and "loss of one's sense of one's own person" can be brought about. See Scharff, *Projective and Introjective Identification*, 87–92, for working definitions of introjection and projection, and 205–209 ,for discussions of male-female and slave-master exchanges. See Lott, *Love and Theft*, 19; Roediger, *Toward the Abolition of Whiteness*, 66.

46. "[A] rule for the change of . . . rules . . . must be introduced from the outside." Watzlawick, *The Language of Change*, 134. "To reframe . . . means to change the conceptual and/or emotional setting or viewpoint in relation to which a situation is experienced and to place it in another frame which fits the 'facts' of the same concrete situation equally well or even better, and thereby changes its entire meaning." Watzlawick, Weakland, and Fisch, *Change*, 95. Alexander and French hold that change can come about due to a "corrective emotional experience." Alexander and French, *Psychoanalytic Therapy*, 67. Burton, reviewing fourteen therapies, concludes, "Regardless of the healing system which is proffered, in order to be healed the patient must accept—yes, have a readiness to believe in —the values, circumstances, and efficacy of that particular system." Burton, *What Makes Behavior Change Possible?* 323. See the discussion of the need for an authority in the process of change in Bateson, "The Cybernetics of 'Self,' " 309–313.

Modern psychoanalysis can be held to work only if there is an acceptance of its ideology and submission to its practitioner. It often involves participation in an ordeal and leads to a reframing of past reality that enables the individual to create a new future. Watzlawick, *The Language of Change*, 131. Milton Erickson shared this view. See Hanley, "Erickson's Contribution to Change in Psychotherapy," 36.

47. See Young, "Afterward," 324; Young, "George Robert Twelves Hewes," 561–623; F. Weinstein and Platt, *The Wish to Be Free*, 7, 20.

48. For the idea of self as narrative see Bruner, *Acts of Meaning*, 111–116; Schafer, *Retelling a Life*, 5, 94. On Moravian *Lebensläufe* see Sensbach, *A Separate Canaan*, xxii–xxiii; Faull, "Introduction," *Moravian Women's Memoirs*, xvii–xl. For the translated *Lebensläufe* of Andrew or Ofodofendo Wooma, 1729–1779, an enslaved Igbo Moravian, see Thorp, "Chattel With A Soul," 433–451.

49. See Bercovitch, *The Puritan Origins*, 17. Thomas Shepard adjured Puritans: "Fear not enemies without, but your selves at home." Shepard, *Parable*, 6.

50. Hopkins, *Sketches*, 87. Benezet is quoted by Rush, May 15, 1784, as cited by Woods, "The Correspondence of Rush and Sharp," 24. For additional evidence of the desire to reduce or go out of self, see Hathaway, *The Narrative*, 15, 20, 22, 34; E. Collins, *Memoirs*, 38.

51. "I think I can with honesty say, that at the age of almost fifty years, if God were to leave me to choose for myself . . . I would be very unhappy in the thought. If I know myself, my petition would be, Lord choose my changes." McCorkle, "Religious Experience," 90, 89. Byrd, *Narratives*, 97.

52. Coleman, *Memoir*, 41–43, 102–103. A few years later Coleman bowed "the neck of my soul under the feet" of God. Coleman had just finished his studies at Yale and was preparing to become a doctor. His marriage to Christ and his continuing self-subjugation did not signal any intention to withdraw from the world. He soon went into practice, married, and fathered a large family, but he retained his commitment to take Christ as his husband, which meant that he longed to follow Christ's will and to lose his own.

53. Susanna Anthony and Sarah Osborn were founding members of a Religious Female Society that introduced a large group of New Haven women to their values. See Hopkins, *The Works*, 1: 98–99; Anthony, *The Life*, 7–8; Osborn, *Memoirs of the Life*, 53; Osborn was accused of having self-pride and wrote that indeed, while she had been fighting self for thirty-two years, "the Traitor is there still." Osborn and Anthony, *Familiar Letters*, 11, 61; Hambrick-Stowe, "The Spiritual Pilgrimage of Sarah Osborn," 408–421; Norton, " 'My Resting, Reaping Times,' " 515–529.

54. "I sealed to be the Lord's; and here God sealed to be mine, my Father, my Redeemer, and my Sanctifier; my only, everlasting refuge and hope." Anthony, in Osborn and Anthony, *Familiar Letters*, 19. Anthony, *The Life*, 8, 33, 38.

55. See Lovejoy, "Shun Thy Father and All That," 71–85.

56. Garrettson, *The Experience*, 27–31.

57. A. Weinstein, *Fictions of the Self*, 3–18, discusses self in twelve fictive autobiographies from the early modern period; Spacks, *Imagining a Self*, parallels fictive and "true" English autobiographies of the eighteenth century. Marie-Paul Laden maintains, "Most novels written in the first half of the eighteenth century in France and England were fictive autobiographies." Laden, *Self-Imitation*, 9.

58. Matty was an enslaved child, hired by the Smiths from her owner. See *American Mother*, identified by Fredrika J. Teute as written by Margaret Bayard Smith (1778–1844), and M. Smith, *The Diversions of Sydney*. I am indebted to Fredrika Teute for bringing these texts to my attention. Smith and her works are discussed by Teute in "In 'the gloom of evening,' " 37–58; and in " 'A Wild, Desolate Place,' " 47–68. See also Miller, "Narrative Practices," 158–179.

59. See Starobinski, *The Invention of Liberty*, 207.

60. On Benjamin Franklin as a "self-actualizer," see P. Franklin, *Show Thyself a Man*; Seavey, *Becoming Benjamin Franklin*. On the history of autobiographies see Weintraub, *The Value of the Individual*, 228–260.

61. Rush, *The Autobiography*, 30, 40–41, 85–86, 167, 187, 222, 276, 288–291. Rush recorded this dream as an explanation of why he was no longer politically active in a March 23, 1805, letter to John Adams. Rush, *Letters*, 2:893–894. Binger, "The Dreams of Benjamin Rush," 1657. The quote of Rush's intentions "to prepare . . . morals," is from July 4, 1787, and is cited in D'Elia, "Benjamin Rush," 8. On Rush's scientific evaluation of dreams see Rush, "The Influence of Physical Causes Upon the Moral Faculty," 188. On Rush's dreams see also Butterfield, "The Dream of Benjamin Rush," 297–319; Edel, *Stuff of Sleep and Dreams*, 119–121. On Rush's dream of blacks in heaven, see Nash, *Forging Freedom*, 104. On Rush's religious development from membership in the Episcopal Church, which he had left by 1789, to Universalist (1791), and on to believing in voluntary moral associations, see Kloos, *A Sense of Deity*. For a discussion of Rush's need for control see Meranze, "Introduction." On November 19, 1775, Rush wrote to Julia Stockton, his sixteen-year-old fiancé, that if she would write him with total "unconstrained, & undisguised freedom, you will think you are only communing with your *other self*," Rush, *My Dearest Julia*, 22, emphasis added.

62. For a definition of the "signifying universe" or the "*mundus significans*" see Greene, *The Light in Troy*, 20.

63. See Stiles (1727–1795), *Literary Diary*, 1:132. Although Stiles maintained, "I am perhaps least subject to Dreams of any man in Life," he occasionally reported his own dreams. See 3:431 and 3:176 for examples. Samuel King's "Portrait of Ezra Stiles," 1771, is discussed in Dillenberger, *The Visual Arts*, 18, 40.

64. On culture pattern dreams, archetypal dreams that have assumed central importance in a particular culture, see Lincoln, *The Dream*, 22; and Dodds, *The Greeks and the Irrational*, 102–134. The only study I know of that has considered the historical change in dreams over time is that of Jacques Bousquet, *Les Themes du Rêve dans la Litarature Romantique* (Paris, 1964), summarized by Bastide, "Dreams and Culture," 42. Bousquet

analyzed changes in dreams from 1780 to 1900 and maintained that visions of the sky and garden came into dreams as the secularization of heaven, while the city became the symbol of punishment in place of hell. Bousquet maintained that it was only after 1870 that the bizarre became dominant in dreams. See also Bastide, "The Sociology of the Dream," 199–211.

65. Bunyan, *The Complete Works*, 1:1–42; 2:9–135; 4:445–458. See M. Schneider, "John Bunyan's *The Pilgrim's Progress.*" For a report of an enslaved African reading Bunyan and taking him to heart see Gronnoissaw, *A Narrative*, 22. On English dream interpretation in this period see Armstrong and Tennenhouse, "The Interior Difference," 458–478.

66. Joshua Comstock, John Barr, John Benson, William Keith, Christian Newcomer, Ephraim Stinchfield, Frederic Swan, and George White all dreamt of visiting hell. Robert Bailey, William Glendinning, James Jenkins, and Benjamin Banneker were visited by the Devil, while Frederic Swan, Jacob Ritter, Sarah Hamilton, Rachel Lucas, and Rebecca Jackson all described dreams of journeys to heaven.

67. Barr, *History*, 19. Barr, a farmer, became a ruling elder in a Presbyterian church in Rowan City, North Carolina, where he lived from the age of fifteen until his death at eighty-two. He wrote this narrative in 1814.

68. See Bath, *Speaking Pictures*; Ashworth, "Natural History," 303–332. The Bible was printed in illustrated or hieroglyphic form, with the Holy Ghost depicted as a dove flying downward, and life as "a child, or youth, with a flaming torch . . . blowing bubbles from . . . a common tobacco-pipe." See Clouston, *Hieroglyphic Bibles*. The first picture Bible was published by J. A. Comenius in Nuremberg in 1657, and the first English version, by Charles Hoole, appeared in 1658 in London. Clouston cites a New England edition of 1794, in which hope, peace, and righteousness were pictured as women, each with different symbols: an anchor, an olive branch and a dove, and a sword and a balance. *The Hieroglyphic Bible*, 66–69, included all these images, which were taken from a pool of commonly shared visual symbols, part of the signifying universe. See Reilly, *A Dictionary*, for a very important compilation of Colonial visual images, including a large number of Africans. These images did change over time, but they seem to have had a long life. The dove, for example, was apparently once the symbol of the sexuality of the goddess Venus. Walker, *The Woman's Dictionary*, 100. Perhaps it was due to the femininity of the soul in biblical Hebrew that early Christians adopted the dove as the symbol of the Holy Spirit. See Matthew 3:16. See also Fischer, *The Complete Medieval Dreambook*, 60; Walker, The Woman's Dictionary, 206, 3671, 399, 400. The dove also symbolized sadness in both the pre-Christian and early modern periods. Frederick Douglass suggested that "moans of the dove" symbolize sorrow and "the grave at the door." See Douglass, *Narrative*, 78. Garrettson compared the church to a dove, and Rebecca Jackson saw God's city as a dove. Garrettson, *The Experience*, 266; Jackson, *Gifts of Power*, 247. Elizabeth "mourned sore like a dove." Elizabeth, *Memoir*, 4.

69. Bruce notes that in two cases containing detailed evidence about the wares carried by itinerant book peddlers, that of a Frenchman in 1825, and a German in 1812, both had dreambooks in their backpacks. Burke, *Popular*

Culture, 254, 257. Ashton, *Chapbooks*; and Spufford, *Small Books*, discuss, among others, the chapbooks *Dreams and Moles, with their Interpretation and Signification*; *The Old Egyptian Fortune Teller's Last Legacy*; and *The History of Joseph and His Brethren*.

70. *The New Book of Knowledge*. See Weiss, *Oneirocritica Americana*, 9–10; Artemidorus, *The Interpretation of Dreams*, 58, 188, 189. This work was translated into English in 1606, and by 1800 was in its thirty-third English edition. On the history of dream manuals see Bitel, "*In Visu Noctis*," 39–59; Thorndike, "Ancient and Medieval Dream-Books." Christian dream books used material from Artemidorus but widely ascribed it to Daniel. The earliest volume with the title *Somnia Danielis* was apparently a Greek work from the fourth century. Many variants were written between the seventh and fifteenth centuries, with English translations appearing in 1481 and 1500. Fischer suggests that the *Somnia Danielis* was "but a collection of self-perpetuating topics stemming from the ancient tradition." Fischer, *The Dream*, 31. See also Fischer, *The Complete Medieval Dreambook*, 8, 9; Fischer, "Dreambooks," 1–20. See Kruger, *Dreaming*; LeGoff, *Time, Work and Culture*, 201–351; Sobel, "The Revolution in Selves," 163–205.

71. Breckinridge, *Lucy Breckinridge*, 52, 98. Artemidorus, *Dreams*, 25. Breckinridge is discussed in Graff, *Conflicting Paths*, 218–221, 228. This story of peaches and death may relate to an earlier folk belief relating peach trees to burial sites, inasmuch as another story tells of a soldier killed in the Revolutionary War claiming that he was buried with a peach in his pocket, and that as a result a peach tree grew from his grave; cited by Lyman C. Draper, *Kings Mountain and its Heroes* (Cincinnati, [1881] 1954), 93. I am indebted to Sharon Halevi for this reference.

72. For a sensitive analysis of Artemidorus's work, see P. Miller, *Dreams in Late Antiquity*, 29–31, 77–91.

73. Breckinridge, *Lucy Breckinridge*, 52, 98.

74. Handler, "Masonic Symbols," 45–55; Guralnick, "The All-Seeing Eye." Hall warns "against the presumption that ordinary people think in different ways, or possess a separate culture, from the modes of an 'elite.' " D. Hall, "The World of Print and Collective Mentality," 177.

75. Dutton, *The Politics of Dreaming*, 258. Dutton discusses the tenth-century introduction of a new symbolic language, "crowded" with wild animals. Some of these were still in eighteenth and nineteenth century writings, where a roaring lion was occasionally the symbol of the devil. See Jackson, *Gifts of Power*, 246. Palmer, "The Inhabitants of Hell," 20–41. In the early pictures of the devil as a black man, he was not shown as having Negroid features. See collected illustrations in Guiley, *The Encyclopedia of Witches*, 97–98, and the discussion of the blackening of the devil in W. Jordan, *White over Black*, 7, 24, 39n, 41, 258–259. Irving, "The Devil and Tom Walker,", 443–444. For a color print of the Deas painting see McElroy, *Facing History*, 26. (I was able to obtain permission to reprint this.)

See chapter 2 of this book for a discussion of images of the devil in the narratives. Although it was not a ruling idea, individuals had taken visions of the African to betoken the devil in earlier periods: When the twenty-two-year-old Vivia Perpetua was condemned to die for her Christian faith in 202 and was to be put into the arena with wild beasts, she dreamt that she would fight and overcome a violent Ethiopian. She interpreted this dream to mean that her opponents in the arena represented the Devil. Misch, *A History of Autobiography*, 2:511. (Others have translated the term Perpetua used to mean an Egyptian. See P. Miller, *Dreams in Late Antiquity*, 162.)

76. The Pythagorean Table of Opposites, as posited by Aristotle, placed right, male, and light on the good side and left, female, and dark on the side of evil. (The other pairs in the Pythagorean Table of Opposites are limit/unlimited; odd/even; one/plurality; rest/moving; straight/curved; square/oblong.) Lloyd, *Polarity and Analogy*, 48–49, 33; Lloyd, "Right and Left in Greek Philosophy," 167–186; See Aristotle, *The Categories of Interpretation*, 2–112. In the Bible, Psalms 16:11, it is written that at God's "right hand there are pleasures for evermore." Patsy Moses, born in Texas before the end of slavery, held that "To dream of clear water lets you know you is on the right side of God." Moses, in Rawick, *The American Slave*, 5:142. The Meru are divided into superior and inferior clans and denote the superior clans as the "white clans," indicating that colors are symbolic of ascribed value, and not of skin color; it has been suggested, however, that the Meru also hold that the white man is to be correlated with right and superior, while the black man is left and inferior. Needham, "The Left Hand of the Mugwe," 25–26. Manichaeanism, which developed in Chaldea, c. 250 A.D., was also based on the belief in a polarity of good (the light) versus evil (darkness) as the forces that brought the world into existence. Evidence that this still plays a role in Greek culture can be found in the comments of Chantiles, who notes that Greeks "use *mavro* (black) for the undesirable, as in 'black fate,' and 'black luck.'. . . For the two-faced person, Greeks use the expression 'Black man, white words.' Racial types, however, are not described as 'black and 'white.' " White is used to refer to the very best of anything, including knowledge, weather, and foods. Chantiles, *The Food of Greece*, 33. Such a polarity was very significant in ancient Greek thought, and in the western tradition that grew out of it, as well as in traditional African cultures.

77. Earle, *Child Life*, 166–167; Stinchfield, *Some Memoirs* 6.

78. Shaw, "Dreaming as Accomplishment," 45. See Sobel, *Trabelin' On*, 115; Mbiti, *African Religions*, 212; S. Drake, *Black Folk*, 1:73, 107, 335 n. 12, 350 n. 3.

79. The first known American publication of a dream manual was that of *The New Book of Knowledge* (Boston, 1767). This was a motley collection taken from English dream books, as was the far more extensive *The Universal Interpreter of Dreams and Visions*, 2 parts (Baltimore, 1795). The first part was an edited copy of an interesting English volume, Thomas Tryon, *Pythagoras* (London, 1691). The second part, titled *The Universal Dream-Dictionary*, was a 113-page alphabetical dictionary of dream imagery, also based on English sources. It was reprinted separately by print shops in Philadelphia, Baltimore, Wilmington (Delaware), and New York at least five times between 1797 and 1821. See the excellent bibliography in Weiss, "Oneirocritica Americana."

80. *The Universal Interpreter*, 132, 138, 189.

81. *The Universal Dream-Dictionary*, 103, 107, 109. This volume was part of *The Universal Interpreter of Dreams and Visions* (1795).

82. Hilmer holds that Sewall "recognized the right of the body to be itself" and that it was not an emblem for him. I think that the striking evidence cited by Hilmer provides the basis for the contrary conclusion as well. Hilmer, "The Other Diary of Samuel Sewall," 358, 361.

83. Traditional Fon appliquéd cloths depict separate heads as well as hands and feet. See M. Adams, "Fon Appliquéd Cloths," 28–41. Clarke and Clarke, *Narratives of the Sufferings*, 40. Malin's recording of the dream of the Universal Friend dated "10th of the 9th Month, 1815," in the mss. Rachel Malin's Dream and Date Book. In *The Universal Dream Dictionary*, 149, it is noted that "To dream you have a great head, or a head bigger than ordinary, and very highly raised, that signifies dignity or prelateship, or at least some charge or office, where he shall be obeyed and esteemed." For a psychological interpretation of separate heads in dreams see Lewin, *The Image and the Past*, 37–39, 55, 59–60, 62, 107, 111–113.

84. *Universal Dream-Dictionary*, 126, 143.

85. For an extensive discussion of sexuality in Artimedorus, see Foucault, *The Care of the Self*, 4–68.

86. Russell, *The Complete Fortune Teller*, 10. I am indebted to Dick Newman, who was at the New York Public Library, and to Jan Malcheski of the Library of the Boston Athenaeum, for a copy of this chapbook. No Chloe Russell is listed in the Boston Directory for 1789 or 1800, and I have not found any Massachusetts census record for a Chloe Russell. Over half of the symbols explicated in the Russell dream book, some sixty-eight, betokened adversity and troubles, including anger, sickness, and economic decline, suggesting that dreamers were somewhat more apt to be punished than rewarded, as sixty entrees suggested prosperity, satisfaction, success, and respect. While seven symbols were held to presage disappointment in courtship, none of these made overt sexual reference. For example, it was held that if you dream of "ghosts, apparitions, specters, and such things," you should expect that "the person you love, hates you."

87. *Universal Dream-Dictionary*, 101, 106, 164, 174, 113,145, 166, 167. When the Puritan Samuel Sewall dreamt of sexual union with his own wife, he wrote of it only in Greek, calling it a "sweet Dream." Sewall, August, 1785, *The Diary*, 1:176.

88. Indians' dreams have been reported and analyzed, and their roles in differing Indian societies have been considered by psychologists, anthropologists, and historians. See, for example, Wallace, "Dreams and Wishes of the Soul," 234–248; Richling, " 'Very Serious Reflections' " 148–169; Irwin, "Contesting World Views," 259–269; Merritt, "Dreaming of the Savior's Blood," 723–746; D'Andrade, "Anthropological Studies of Dreams," 296–332; Tedlock, *Dreaming*; Kluckhohn and Morgan, "Some Notes on Navaho Dreams," 120–131; Devereux, *Reality and Dream*; Eggan, "The Significance of Dreams," 171–198. For a description of Lakota dream beliefs and practices see St. Pierre and Long Soldier, *Walking in the Sacred Manner*.

89. Father Ragueneau, in "Indian Relations," cited by Wallace, *The Death and Rebirth of the Seneca*, 61. Wallace, an anthropologist and a psychiatric researcher, was convinced that the Iroquois "knew the great force of unconscious desires, were aware that the frustration of these desires could cause mental and physical (psychosomatic) illness. They understand that these desires were expressed in symbolic form, by dreams, but that the individual could not always properly interpret these dreams himself." Ibid., 63. See Axtell, *The Invasion Within*, 15–17.

90. Richling suggests that Inuit dreams showed fear of "loss of family and fellows," due to "the abandonment of the customs and ethos that insured survival in the past." Richling, " 'Very Serious Reflections' " 164.

91. John Eliot (1604–1690), who was a preacher to Indians in Massachusetts, believed that many of the events predicted in his dreams came true. While many Europeans who did not work with Indians believed this, it is likely that Eliot's belief was reinforced through his extensive contact with Indians. Eliot's belief in the predictive value of dreams was reported by Cotton Mather in his *Magnalia Christi Americana* (1702), as is noted in D. Hall, *Worlds of Wonder*, 109.

92. The contemporary Zulu Shaman Mutwa states, "We believe in Africa that if you dream of something . . . that you should try to do the thing of which you have dreamt." Mutwa, *Song of the Stars*, 173, 174.

93. R. Shaw, "Dreaming as Accomplishment," 37.

94. Communication to the author, Shalem, Tel Aviv, November 29, 1998.

95. In Jedrej and Shaw, *Dreaming, Religion and Society in Africa*, eleven contemporary historians and anthropologists have analyzed the function of dreams in African cultures. Citations are from Ray, "Dreams of Grandeur," 68–69; Mpier, "Dreams Among the Yansi," 103, 107–108. See also Field, *Search for Security*, 190–191, 285–286, 312–313; Shorter, *Jesus and the Witchdoctor*, 153–159; Berglund, *Zulu Thought-Patterns*, 97, 119, 136, 286, 294; Parrinder, *West African Psychology*, 185–197; LeVine, *Dreams and Deeds*, which is based on a study of dream reports from Ibo, Yoruba, and Hausa students, finds that the frequency of achievement and social compliance imagery in their dream reports can be correlated with the differing concerns of the three societies.

96. Rattray, *Religion and Art in Ashanti*, 192–196; Seligman, "Appendix to Chapter XXI," 197–204.

97. See H. Fisher, "Dreams and Conversion," 217–235. There is an account of an Ijaye captive in 1862 who knew little of Christianity and whose attachment to his traditional religion was strong. He dreamt that he and his *orisa*, Osun, Ibeji, and Ifa (wooden deity figures), were to be burned, but the following night only his *orisa* were burnt in a dreadful fire, while he was set free and told "never again fall down before these *orisa*." He believed this dream mandated his conversion to Christianity. McKenzie, "Dreams and Visions from Nineteenth Century Yoruba Religion," 129. Omoyajowo reports that 95 percent of the candidates for the Lutheran ministry that he interviewed in Nigeria claimed they were called to the ministry in their dreams. Omoyajowo, *Your Dreams*, 15. In 1954 R. Jolla sang a dream song

very much in the old tradition. Jolla, recorded on *Music From The South; Elder Songsters*, Folkways Record FP 656, Vol. 7, side 2, band 7. See also Watson and Johnson, eds., *God Struck Me Dead*.

98. Russell, *The Complete Fortune Teller*. On nineteenth-century dream books ostensibly written by African Americans, see Fabian, *Card Sharps*, 142–150.

99. R. Jackson, *Gifts of Power*. Although her narrative was not published in the greater Revolutionary era, it is included because it reveals a women who did lead a public life, and it provides a rich illustration of her perception of change in her own and others' lives. Her narrative was known and read by other Shakers in the period.

100. In the mid-1930s a very revealing study was made of Sea Island beliefs and practices by Samuel Miller Lawton, who lived on Port Royal Island for over a year. Lawton interviewed fifty-five adult believers, "28 of whom were ex-slaves." Eight-six percent of all the adults were "directed by the Spirit in a dream or vision" to choose their particular guide. Fifty-four out of the fifty-five had a vision during the period that they were "seekin' " salvation. Lawton, "The Religious Life of South Carolina Coastal and Sea Island Negroes," 131–150, 160. I am deeply indebted to Grey Gundaker for bringing this work to my attention. See also Creel, "*A Peculiar People*," 284–302.

101. Lawton, "The Religious Life of South Carolina Coastal and Sea Island Negroes", 138–139, 164, 166. In the contemporary African conversion dreams reported by Curley, "Dreams of Power," 28–29, bright light often signifies conversion, and preachers play a significant role in suggesting interpretations.

102. For evidence of the practice of seeking in other locales, see Raymond, "The Religious Life of the Negro Slave," 680–682.

103. Bradford, *Scenes*, 56, 79–80, 82–83.

104. See Sobel, '*Trabelin' On*, 108–128, 246–247. In many ancient traditions the color white is "accepted as the symbol of innocence of soul, purity of thought, [and] holiness of life." Bayley, *The Lost Language of Symbolism*, 2:38.

105. Johnson, *God Struck Me Dead*, 13, 63, 148; Sobel, *Trabelin' On*, 108–109, 112, 229.

106. Parrinder, *West African Psychology*, 17–18, emphasis added.

107. R. Shaw, "Dreaming as Accomplishment," 45, emphasis added. See Sobel, *Trabelin' On*, 115; Mbiti, *African Religions*, 212; S. Drake, *Black Folk*, 1:73, 107, 335 n. 12, 350 n. 3. Examples from the narratives are discussed in chapter 3 of this book.

108. It has been suggested that in the modern period the Meru also hold that the white man is to be correlated with right and superior, while the black man is left and inferior. See Needham, "The Left Hand of the Mugwe," 25–26.

109. Swan, *Remarkable Visionary Dreams*, 5. I would like to thank John Saillant for transcribing this document onto the Internet, and Sharon Halevi for bringing it to my attention.

110. It should be noted, especially as Swan was ill and close to death, that white also signifies death in many African cultures.

111. Ireland, *The Life*, 192.

112. See Gregg, *Self-Representation*, 47; Watzlawick, Weakland, and Fisch, *Change*, 18. Scharff, *Projective and Introjective Identification*, 89–95, 205, 209.

113. Jackson's dreams are discussed in chapter 3 of this book.

114. Edwards, *The Works*, 1:91. David Hume, 1739, and William Smellie, 1799, held similar views. Smellie, *The Philosophy of Natural History* (Edinburgh, 1799), 2:375–377. Josselin, an English clergyman, reported in his diary that in one dream he had committed very aggressive acts. This dream convinced him that "my passions are too strong for me." Josselin, *The Diary*, September 12, 1644, 20.

115. Ritter, *Memoirs*, 9, 11.

116. Ibid., 24, 38–40.

117. Glendinning, *The Life*, 3–5, 7, 12, 17, 30. Glendinning was an original member of the Methodist Committee of Assistants, a five-member administrative board chosen by the twenty preachers at the conference of 1777. Baker, *From Wesley to Asbury*, 100. Boehm records that Glendinning "was remarkably eccentric, if not a little 'cracked,' " and that he became a "Republican Methodist" and then a Unitarian. Boehm, *The Patriarch*, 337. There is an extended discussion of Glendinning in Heyrman, *Southern Cross* 28–33, 58–66, 274 n.1. Heyrman views Glendinning's persona as "informed by a variety of seventeenth-century evangelicals." She seems to view him and most other religious men as fairly consciously adopting persona. See also Asbury, *Journal and Letters*, November 6, 1780, 3:105–106, 111–112.

118. Glendinning, *The Life*, 30, 32, 33, 35.

119. By 1791 Glendinning was barred from preaching in Methodist churches. He took to preaching in the streets or at frolics.

120. Kohut, *The Restoration of the Self*, 109.

121. Bollas, *Forces of Destiny*, 47.

122. Dreams and visions were shared in most sects and new churches. See the dreams in the collection of writings by the followers of the Universal Friend, Jemima Wilkinson, recorded in Malin, Dream and Date Book. Baptist and Methodists very often reported dreamed-of soul travels in their sermons and testimonies. Almost every Baptist and Methodist narrative from the period 1740–1840 includes a dream report that was shared with a congregation. See, for a Baptist example, Leland, *Some Events*, 10, 14, 15; for a Methodist, Jenkins, *The Experience*, 9, 11, 34, 39, 47, 97, 159. Early Quaker narratives, prior to committee editing, were full of dreams. See, for example, Richardson, *An Account*, 33, 48, 53, 62. A newly married Moravian couple, whose marriage had been by church arrangement, exchanged dream reports as a way of establishing intimacy between themselves. See Fries, *The Road to Salem*, whose data is taken from the autobiography of Anna Catharina [Antes], 1726–1816, which is housed in the Moravian Archives, Winston-Salem, North Carolina.

123. Drinker, *The Diary of Elizabeth Drinker*, July 23, 1799, 2:1192. For a selection of dreams in the various types of sources—legal documents, newspapers, diaries, and literature—see the following: Accomack, Virginia, Wills, 1682–1697, 94a, for the record of the dream report of Eleanor Hues. (I want to thank Douglas Deal for this and other dream reports.) A dream report of a man who turned into a "Beast with a pair of Horns" was printed in *The New York Gazette*, April 3, 1738, 529–530. Walcot, *The New Pilgrim's Progress*, 74 ff.; Thomas Chalkley reported a dream he heard from a ship's doctor in January 1698/9, which he interpreted as foretelling that the doctor would soon die if he did not give up drink. The doctor indeed died at sea during the journey. Chalkley, *A Journal*, 25–28. Grace Galloway reported that she had a discussion about keeping slaves and was troubled about the legitimacy of this, and that night "dream'd of our Negroes & cou'd not get them out of my Mind am uneasy about them." Galloway, "Diary of Grace Gowden Galloway," 63. I am indebted to Laurie Wohlberg for this citation. Vandeleuer (pseud.), *A History*, 34 ff., presents what is claimed to be the lengthy dream of his Native American mother-in-law. See William Widger's dream, which can be understood to relate to the Revolution as an illegitimate child—not the one that he had fought for—as well as the fear that his wife was unfaithful while he was in a British prison, in Lemisch, "Listening to the Inarticulate," 1–29. For concern with dreams in Revolutionary-era journals, see "An Extraordinary Dream," *Pennsylvania Magazine*, January, 1775, 16; Benjamin Rush's "Paradise of Negro Slaves" appeared unsigned in the *Columbian Magazine*, 1 (1788); 235 as did "The Benefits of Charity—A Dream," 578; Dr. James Beattie (1735–1803), "On Dreaming," reprinted from *Dissertations, Moral and Critical* (London: 1783): 329–335, 359–363, 416–420; "The Dreamer . . . , A Politico-Philosophical Tale," 2 (1789): 190–195, 247–251; "Authors turned Traders: A Dream," 202–206. Zuriel Waterman recorded a six-page dream in the Memorandum Book for the Sloop Retaliation, May 1780. I am indebted to Manfred Wasserman for bringing this work to my attention. William Jenks (1778–1866) recorded his dreams of 1798 in a notebook he titled Somnia. I am indebted to Robert Gross for bringing Jenks's dreams to my notice. Louisa Adams Park, Diary for 1800, includes dreams of her absent husband. *The Orleans Gazette* (New Orleans) of February 9, 1805, featured a long letter to the editor signed by Gilbert Hurlstone, which was centered on a dream that seemed to suggest that the new American government would bring about freedom and justice, but a Mr. Shylock (a Jew) rendered an opposite interpretation of the dream. I want to thank David Walstreicher for bringing this dream report to my attention. Charles Brockden Brown used dreams in his novel *Wieland*, 99. See also "A Dream," [1831] by Edgar Allen Poe, in *The Unknown Poe*, 55–57, which reports a dream in which the dreamer participated in the crucifixion of Christ, "driving the sharpest nails through the palms." This was "A Dream" published over the initial P in the Philadelphia *Saturday Evening Post* on August 13, 1831. Kenneth Silverman notes that Poe loved the dream state and saw dreams "as a path for memory." Silverman, *Edgar A. Poe*, 77, 227. See the discussion of Poe in chapter 6 of this book. For a collection of brief

dream reports from slave narratives, see M. Jackson, *The Struggle For Freedom*, 219–224; for a similar collection from white Methodist sources see Byrne, *No Foot of Land*, 55–82.

124. *The Prodigal Daughter* is set in Bristol and may well have been written there, but the only edition from outside North America I have found is from Glasgow and is undated. (A copy is in Harvard University Library.) Between 1758(?) and 1819 this chapbook was repeatedly printed in Boston as well as in Worcester, Providence, Newport, Hartford, New York City, and Philadelphia. Alice Earle reported on the popularity of this book in *Child Life in Colonial Days*, 256. Illustrations from this text have been reprinted in Reilly, *A Dictionary*, 331–337.

125. *A Dream To All Friends of Zion*, 5, 8; At least one Revolutionary soldier, David Perry, later claimed to have been given a dream vision of the war twelve years before it actually began. Perry, *Recollections of an Old Soldier*, 40–41.

126. "The History of Dream Interpretation," 119–122, emphasis in original. For other criticism of belief in dreams, see Paine, "An Essay on Dream" (1803). Benjamin Rush held that dreams negatively "affect the memory, the imagination, and . . . judgment. . . . In some cases the imagination only is deranged in dreams, in others the memory is affected, and in others the judgment." Rush, "The Influence of Physical Causes upon the Moral Faculty," 188. A further discussion of Rush and dreams is in the following chapter.

127. Grimes, *Life*, 125. Grimes, numbers and dream books are discussed further in chapter 4 of this book.

128. For his collection of predictive death dreams see Rush, *The Autobiography*, 187.

129. Asbury, *Journal and Letters*, July 13, 1783, 1:443.

130. Newell, *Memoirs*, 103–105. Newell foretold other deaths as well. I am indebted to Jon Butler for this reference.

131. A. Taylor, "The Early Republic's Supernatural Economy," 10, citing the journal of Silas Hamilton. On the role of dreams in the widespread hunts for treasure see also Brooke, *The Refiner's Fire*, 30–33, 40, 50–54, 57–58; A. Taylor, "Rediscovering the Context of Joseph Smith's Treasure Seeking," 18–28; and A. Taylor, "The Early Republic's Supernatural Economy," 38. For betting on dream numbers see Grimes, *The Life*, 125. Betting on dream numbers is a practice well documented in contemporary Africa, and it may well be a long-standing tradition. There is evidence that dreamed-of numbers were being bet on earlier, as noted in Grimes, but Harry B. Weiss has found that the practice of publishing lucky numbers began in America in 1862 with *The Golden Wheel Dream Book*, whose full title claimed it was the "most complete work on . . . interpreting dreams ever printed, containing an alphabetical list of dreams, with their interpretations and the lucky number they signify." This signaled a rare rapid change in the tradition: Almost immediately, virtually all American dream manuals added similar numerical significations. Weiss, *Oneirocritica Americana*, 15. On the subsequent use of dreamed numbers, or of the assigned numerical equivalents of dreamed objects, in the African American community, see *Aunt*

Sally's Policy Players' Dream Book; Genuine Afro Dream Book. The Right Numbers from Dreams. See also Fabian, *Card Sharps,* 142–150. I want to thank Bernard Bierlich for allowing me to read his manuscript, "The Head and the Heart: Luck, Divination and Lotto Playing in Northern Ghana," 1996. During Bierlich's stay in Ghana he found that dreams were often used to determine numbers bet upon. As the only white person living in the area, numbers associated with him, such as his car's license plate, were also regarded as being of special significance and were often used in betting, sometimes in reverse.

132. Swann, *The Evangelist,* 50–51.

133. Breckinridge, *Lucy Breckenridge,* 161.

CHAPTER 2

1. Robert Pyle, "Robert Pyle's Testimony," in "An Early Quaker Anti-Slavery Statement," 104.

2. Robert Pyle's surname has been alternatively written as Piles: See ibid. and Robert Piles, "Paper About Negroes" (1698)

3. Bollas holds that in extreme cases of introjection mental structure and "loss of one's sense of one's own person" can be brought about. Bollas, *The Shadow of the Object,* 158, 165–166. For working definitions of introjection and projection, and for discussions of male/female and slave/master exchanges, see Scharff, *Projective and Introjective Identification,* 87–92, 205–209.

4. Benson, *A Short Account,* 60, 85, 88, 95.

5. J. Collins, *A Revolutionary Soldier,* 141–153.

6. Glendinning, *The Life.* Heyrman, *Southern Cross,* 28–33-, 58–66, 274 n.1.

7. Donnelly, *Confession,* 1.

8. Indeed, York did not remain in the fields: He eventually became a professor of logic in Rutherford, North Carolina. York, *The Autobiography,* 16.

9. S. Green, *Life.*

10. Oehler, *The Life,* 90. Oehler, born in Alstadt, Germany, in 1781, arrived in the United States in 1799 as a redemptioner but bought out his sixty-five-dollar passage in six months. Although he had been trained as a tailor in Germany, he worked as a dancing and fencing teacher in Alexandria and nearby towns, and only later returned to tailoring. He claimed that in the interim, while on a sea journey, he had been captured by the forces of Toussaint L'Ouverture and that they gave him the choice of joining the revolution to liberate Haiti or death and that after he joined the army he rose to lead fifteen hundred men but chose to escape to a British ship when he was able to. His tall tale of his travels on this British ship, however, puts his truthfulness into question: Oehler claimed that he saw Arab women in Alexandria walking around in public with their left breasts exposed.

11. Pearse, *A Narrative,* 35–37. 75.

12. Arms, *Incidents,* 140–141. When she married, Mary's mother was given ownership of Aunt Patty, a family slave. When her husband took the family from Maryland to the old Northwest she was "obliged" to leave Aunt

Patty behind. Many years later, after Mary's mother's death, and after Mary had been abandoned by her father and had become blind, she found Patty, apparently free, living with her daughter in Chicago. Patty cried over Mary, told her many stories of her mother's life, and showed her many things her mother had given to her, including the Bible that she promised to leave for Mary at her own death.

13. Rachel O'Connor (born 1774), who was running a slave plantation in Louisiana in the 1830s, suffered "uneasy dreams" when a slave on a neighboring plantation poisoned the white family. On August 3, 1835, in fear of a slave revolt, she recorded, "In my dreams I call out for my mother to come to me." Nevertheless, she also recorded her deep emotional attachment to her enslaved "family." O'Connor, *Mistress of Evergreen Plantation*, 173, 247, 268. See also Craven, *Rachel of Old Louisiana*.

14. H. milton, *A Narrative*; Andrews, *Memoir of Mrs. Ann R. Page*, 17–18; W. Williams, *The Garden of American Methodism*, 100. See also G. Brown, *Recollections*, 61.

15. Byrd, Commonplace Book, 27; Byrd, *Another Secret Diary*, 166. See the discussion of his Commonplace Book and attitude toward women in Lockridge, *On the Sources of Patriarchal Rage*. Thomas Jefferson understood the law to be that if a person could prove that in each of three generations there had been one white parent, the person in the third generation was legally white. (This would have made Sally Hemings' children legally white but not free.) See Jefferson, letter to Frances Grey, March 4, 1815, cited by Stanton, " 'Those Who Labor for My Happiness,' " 152, 174 n. 21.

16. While a majority of the documented interracial couples were white men and black women, a significant minority were white women cohabiting with black men. See, for examples, Johnston, *Race Relations*, 250–257; Woodson, "The Beginnings of Miscegenation," 335–353; Williamson, *New People*; Aptheker, *Anti-Racism in U.S. History*, 25–36, with bibliography on 202 n. 22; and Hodes, *White Women, Black Men*.

17. Hemings, "The Memoirs of Madison Hemings." Jefferson's statements can be found in W. Adams, *Jefferson's Monticello*, 188, and in an interview he gave to William W. Whitcomb, an itinerant bookseller on May 31, 1824.

Rumors of Jefferson's paternity of the children born to Sally Hemings had become a political issue by 1802. While Jefferson's actions in relation to Hemings' children seemed to suggest a special relationship (he allowed the older two to leave the plantation and become free, and he freed the youngest two in his will), Jefferson never acknowledged his paternity in any public or known written statement. Based on what they believed to be his morality and sense of responsibility as a father, most white scholars, including Dumas Malone, Erik Erikson, and Joseph J. Ellis, could not accept that it was possible for Jefferson to have fathered Hemings' children, as he had not acknowledged them. When, in 1974, Fawn Brodie published a psychohistorical analysis of Jefferson's writings and actions that argued strongly for his long-term sexual and emotional involvement with Sally Hemings, it was attacked as imaginative fiction by many scholars and denigrated by those who sought to uphold Jefferson's honor, such as Virginius Dabney. In 1998 Annette Gordon-Reed presented a very strong case for Jefferson's paternity. Much as if she were arguing it in a court of law, Reed based her arguments on a wide range of evidence and emphasized the black narratives that attest to Jefferson's paternity. DNA tests of living family members provided scientific evidence that strongly supports Jefferson's paternity in 1998. See Malone and Hochman, "A Note on Evidence," 523–528; Erikson, *Dimensions of a New Identity*; Brodie, *Thomas Jefferson*; Dabney, *The Jefferson Scandals*; Ellis, *American Sphinx*; Gordon-Reed, *Thomas Jefferson and Sally.* On the DNA evidence see Foster et al., "Jefferson Fathered Slave's Last Child." For the complete reversal in Ellis's views see Lander and Ellis, "Founding Father."

18. Jacobs, *Incidents*, 28. Evidence uncovered by Yellin shows that this work is closely autobiographical, and that it was Dr. James Norcom who was called Dr. Flint in Jacob's work. See the discussion of the likelihood that Jacobs was actually raped by Norcom in Fox-Genovese, *Within the Plantation Household*, 392, and in Davie, " 'Reader, my story ends with freedom,' " 86–109.

19. Busey, *A Souvenir*, 54–55. Busey's life is discussed in Graff, *Conflicting Paths*, 94–95.

20. Clay, *The Life*, 30.

21. "Register of Inhabitants of Nazareth," as cited by Merritt, "Dreaming of the Savior's Blood," 739.

22. Bailey, *The Life and Adventures*, 13.

23. This dream report is from the daughter of Methodist George Lewis, who told it to the circuit rider Nelson Reed, April 19, 1781, as cited in Heyrman, *Southern Cross*, 55.

24. Gates, *The Trials*, 11, 30.

25. Ann Page manumitted her slaves in 1832 and sent many of them to Africa. See Andrews, *Memoir of Mrs. Ann R. Page*, 17–18. Samuel Green beat a black to death and was hanged for his murder in 1822. S. Green, *Life*, 44.

26. See Sedgwick, *Between Men*.

27. Marietta, *The Reformation of American Quakerism*.

28. In his "Gospel Family Order . . . of Whites, Blacks and Indians" (London, 1676), George Fox expressed deep concern for the proper treatment of the enslaved, as well as alarm at the "Sodom and Gomorra" sexual behavior of owners that he observed, but he did not call for the immediate end of slavery. He seemed to regard the conversion of Africans as a herald of the last days, and thus while he saw man stealing as a sin, and the conditions under which the enslaved were forced to live as evil, he apparently regarded this evil as part of the plan leading to a greater good. Fox, *Journal*, 32, 40, 601–609; The reactions to the enslavement of Africans of Nicolaus Zinzendorf, Charles and John Wesley, and George Whitefield (all of whom experienced life in a New World slave society, and each of whom developed a significant relationship with at least one African) were similar to that of George Fox. See, for example, on Nicolaus Zinzendorf's relationship with Anthony

(born c. 1715 in St. Thomas), whose testimony led Zinzendorf to reframe the Morvarians' mission and to make a major outreach to the enslaved, Sensbach, *A Separate Canaan*, 29–43.

29. Marietta, *The Reformation of American Quakerism*, 115–120; Soderlund, *Quakers and Slavery*, 26–31; T. Drake, *Quakers and Slavery*, 51–64, 68–71.

30. Sandiford, *The Mystery of Iniquity*. Sandiford, born in 1693, became very depressed and ill after his expulsion from the Society in 1729 and died in March of 1733. Vaux, *Memoirs*, 59–70.

31. Lay, *All Slave Keepers*. Vaux, *Memoirs*. Lay may have been expelled earlier.

32. For alternative readings of Woolman's development see M. Stewart, "John Woolman's 'Kindness Beyond Expression.' "; Shea, "The *Journal* of John Woolman."

33. Mifflin also convinced his father to free his one hundred slaves and began a public project to end slavery. Mifflin, who was attacked for his refusal to fight the British, defended freeing the enslaved as befitting revolutionary ideology. Mifflin, *The Defense*, 4, 5, 9. "Truth" in contemporary Quaker usage was defined as "ultimate spiritual reality." Woolman, *The Journal*, ed. Moulton, 314.

34. Woolman, *The Journal*, ed. Moulton, 33, 46 , 50–51. Woolman never mentioned that there were any black servants in his own home or that of his parents, but "Negro Maria," an African American women, worked for his sister Elizabeth Woolman and was paid by her estate in 1747. When Negro Maria died in 1760, John Woolman administered her estate of eleven pounds and eight shillings, raising the possibility that she had some long-term relationship with his family. "To cash paid Negro Maria," in the records of the estate of Elizabeth Woolman, 1746/7; "Negro Maria her Estate, 1760." Woolman, Book of Executorship, 1, 14.

35. Many historians have assumed that this was the case. See, for example, Levenduski, *Peculiar Power*, 102.

36. Woolman, *Journal*, ed. Moulton, 152.

37. Woolman also recorded that "one hundred pounds to be reserved for the negroes is in Henry's hands." Woolman, Book of Executorship, 3.

38. John Demos suggests that the first period of childhood was then regarded as lasting from birth to about seven, followed by youth from about age seven to about age thirty. Demos, "Historical Treatment of the Age Group," 74. See also Kamen, "Changing Perceptions of the Life Cycle, 180–221.

39. Woolman, *Some Considerations on the Keeping of Negroes*; Woolman, *The Journal*, ed. Moulton, 153.

40. Ibid., 152 n. 57. Woolman edited this note out and then reinserted it. If this person was twenty-three in 1769, he was born in 1745, was thirteen when indentured by Woolman in 1753, and was bound out until 1775.

41. Ibid., 150 (June 1769).

42. Ibid., 153; "Plea for the Poor," in ibid., 272.

268

43. Woolman, *Journal*, ed. Gummere, 271. Woolman, *Considerations on Keeping Negroes, Part Second*; Woolman, "On the Slave Trade," (1772): Woolman, *Remarks on Sundry Subjects* (1773); all can be found in *The Works of John Woolman*. "The Plea for the Poor" contained within it what might be a history of the family of the young man he had wronged, and an unacknowledged condemnation of himself. Woolman wrote, "Suppose an inoffensive youth, forty years ago, was violently taken from Guinea, sold here as a slave, laboured hard till old age, and hath children who are now living." Woolman estimated that 141 pounds would be due the family. He made no note of the relevance of the facts to himself when he stated, "To keep Negroes as servants till they are thirty years of age and hold the profits of the last nine years of their labour as our own, on a supposition that they may sometime be an expense to our estate, is a way of proceeding which appears to admit of improvement." Woolman, "Plea for the Poor," 268, circa 1763–1764.

44. Philip J. Schwarz recounts a case in which the silence of Quaker elders visiting a Quaker slaveholder had the effect of bringing about a dream of African control of the gates to heaven and resulted in the manumission of this Quaker's slaves. Schwarz, "Clark T. Moorman, Quaker Emancipator." See also Bauman, *Let Your Words Be Few*.

45. Woolman, *Journal*, ed. Moulton, 24, 46–47, 161–162, 184–186, 297–298, 304. In 1774, in preparing Woolman's manuscript journal for publication, a Friends editorial committee edited out the dreams, and subsequent published versions apparently did not include them until the Moulton edition. See, for example, the first and dreamless edition of *The Journal* (1774), in *The Works*, part one. This version did include Woolman's visionary experiences.

46. Laughlin, McManus, Rubinstein and Shearer, "The Ritual Transformation of Experience," 110.

47. Woolman observed a cloud, which had come out of the fast moving moon, transformed into a "beautiful green tree." The verdant tree soon withered, however, due to the intense heat of the sun. "There then appeared a being, small of size, full of strength and resolution, moving swift from the north, southward, called a sun worm." This dream suggests a family constellation: the feminine moon gave birth to the cloud that was transposed into the beautiful tree. The sun, ostensibly male, brought death to the tree, but that was when the sun worm or son appeared, "full of strength and resolution." The entries that Woolman wrote immediately after this dream report can be regarded as associations, and they strengthen the likelihood that this was a rendering of the family romance. Woolman wrote of an evil act that he committed as a child, in which he killed a robin by throwing stones at her, and then, realizing that her brood would die a slow and painful death, he chose to kill them as well. This memory in turn led him to think of an "undutiful" comment he had made to his mother, which his father had rebuked him for. This rebuke had "awakened [me] to a sense of my wickedness." Woolman did not comment directly on the meaning he found in this dream, but he made it clear that "[t]hough I was a child, this dream was instructive to me." The juxtaposition of these tales to the dream suggests

269

several readings. Perhaps Woolman saw his mother as vulnerable, as open to harm from him much as he had harmed the mother bird. She, however, had informed his father of his transgressions, and perhaps he felt that she had betrayed him and that he had been made vulnerable much as the baby birds were. He may also have felt that his father was like the sun in his dream, and that his power was dangerous. He may have taken it as a warning that he himself could be burned out, but could choose to take a different path of "strength and resolution."

48. Rossi holds "that inter-modal shifts between sensations, perceptions, emotion, imagery, cognition, identity, and behavior were characteristic of the process of psychological growth and change." Rossi, *The Psychobiology of Mind-Body Healing*, 34; Rossi, *Dreams*.

49. There are many images and emotions in this second dream parallel to those Woolman felt in his first recorded dream, but there are also many opposites. Here again there are two heavenly orbs, now two suns, as in African and African American stories, but both are "dull and gloomy." Woolman is again an observer, but he moves from a field outside (where a fire storm approaches) to the inside of a house with shaky floors. He envisions many more people than in his earlier dream: one group (of passive observers) was within the house, and the second (training for violent activity in the army) was outside. He was alienated from both. See Marietta, *The Reformation of American Quakerism*, 95.

50. Manuscript of Woolman's Journal, 30.

51. Woolman, *The Journal*, ed. Moulton, 46–47.

52. Ibid., 175–176,191.

53. Churchman, *An Account*, 186. A dream of interracial harmony was reported by an Indian in 1749, when Keposch, a Delaware who had been converted by the Moravians, reported that many years earlier he had dreamt that "he was lifted up . . . in the air, and saw the world under him as a small ball in a child's play yard, in which white, brown, and black people' lived together." Bethlehem Register, "Nethlehisches Kirchen-Buch," 105–106, January 13/24. 1749, as cited by Merritt, "Dreaming of the Savior's Blood, 739.

Osborn and Hopkins also saw the Revolutionary War as a punishment for participation in the slave trade; they wrote that "God would frown upon Newport," for its role in the slave trade and felt that the shelling of the Rhode Island city was proper punishment. Hopkins came to see the Revolution's success as due to the Continental Congress cutting off the slave trade. Hopkins, "A Dialogue Concerning the Slavery of Africans." Hopkins, *The Works*, 1:129 note. Osborn and Hopkins are discussed later in this chapter.

54. Woolman, *The Journal*, ed. Moulton, 161.

55. *The Universal Dream-Dictionary*, 114, 141.

56. "Register of Free Negroes," York County, Virginia, Guardian Account Books, 1780–1823, i-xv, 417–428; 1823–1846, 1–11. I am indebted to Lou Powers, who brought this source to my attention. Saffin, *A Brief and Candid Answer*, 5; Towner, "The Sewall-Saffin Dialogue on Slavery," 40–52. Still's dream is reported in Peck, *The Life*, 97–98. I am indebted to Jon Butler for this last reference.

57. See P. C. Miller, *Dreams in Late Antiquity*, 103, for a survey of early commentaries. Freud, *The Interpretation of Dreams*, 355 n. 2. Otto Rank's "A Staircase Dream" (1911) was included in the Freud volume in the fourth through seventh editions, 1914–1922, 369–372. Fernandez, *Persuasions and Performances*, 225; "The Ladder was a favorite emblem of the roadway of the Gods, because it predicted a gradual ascent in goodness, a progress step by step and line upon line towards Perfection." Bayley, *The Lost Language of Symbolism*, 1:32. Reilly, *A Dictionary*, 277–280. For the Akan in Africa, "The ladder of death expresses the equality of all men in the presence of death." P. Appiah, "Akan Symbolism," 67. On the Akan see also K. Appiah, *In My Father's House*, 67. See the Jacob's ladder in the *Bible Quilt* by Harriet Powers (1837–1911), ca. 1886, reproduced in Vlach, *Afro-American Tradition*, 46.

58. See Pyle, "Robert Pyle's Testimony."

59. Woolman, *Journal*, ed. Moulton, 152 n. 57.

60. Ibid., 161–162. See also A. Sampson, *The Wonderful Adventure*, 32. Sampson, describing his trip as a sailor on a ship that went to Africa to procure slaves, claimed that he witnessed white slavers chop up old people and children to feed the others they had enslaved.

61. Daniel Smith, "Explaining his act of going naked at an Independents' church in Hull, June 24, 1673 . . . ," cited by Bauman, *Let Your Words Be Few*, 89. On "The Performance of Metaphors," see ibid., 84–94.

62. I Samuel 12:3; Woolman, *The Journal*, ed. Moulton, 272.

63. Artemidorus, *The Interpretation of Dreams*, 52–53.

64. Woolman recorded this dream in October 1772, but noted he had dreamed it two and a half years earlier. Woolman, *The Journal*, ed. Moulton, 185–186.

65. Woolman interacted with other individuals in only one dream, that of a peace mission to Indians, discussed later in this chapter.

66. Ibid., 161, 272.

67. Ibid., 187.

68. See the discussion of the "little me" in chapter 1 of this book.

69. J. Thomas, *The Life*, 20.

70. Woolman, *The Journal*, ed. Moulton, 160 n. 6.

71. Reported by an unnamed English Friend after the death of Woolman, *ibid.*, 304.

72. On Woolman's journey to Wyalusing in western Pennsylvania see M. Stewart, "John Woolman's 'Kindness Beyond Expression,' " 263–266. On eating together as the most basic of human events that distinguishes man from the apes, see G. Isaac, "The Food-Sharing Behavior of Protohuman Hominids," 90–108.

73. Woolman, "Plea to the Poor," 272.

74. D. Davis, *The Problem of Slavery*, 518–528; Aptheker, "The Quakers and Negro Slavery," 331–362.

75. Evans, *Joshua Evan's Journal*, 17, 18, 139, 188.

76. On the exclusion of Isaac T. Hopper, an abolitionist activist, by the New York Quakers in 1838, see Meaders, *Kidnappers in Philadelphia*, 24–26; Child, *Isaac T. Hopper*, 386–399.

77. See Wood, " 'Liberty Is Sweet,' " 149–184.

78. Bartlett, *Census of Rhode Island of 1774*, 24. A memorial to Hopkins refers to an article in the *Albany Weekly Patriot* and in *The Christian World* of October 1843 (not located), which reportedly emphasized Hopkins's deep feelings of guilt over his own slave owning. Osborn and Hopkins, and through their influence Joseph Fish and Ezra Stiles, became very involved in the lives of Quamine and Yama, who were sent to study for the purpose of becoming missionaries in Africa. Quamine's account of his religious experience, dictated to a black woman, was passed among them and convinced them of his God-given faith. Hopkins, who had worked for manumission, later became convinced that Americans would not change sufficiently to allow blacks true freedom, and that the colonization of ex-slaves in Africa was the only solution. Hopkins, *Works*, 1:129 n. 130; 2:618–619. See Rubin, *Religious Melancholy*, 103–110; Lovejoy, "Samuel Hopkins," 227–243.

79. Carter, *The Diary*, July 25, 1776, 2:1064,.

80. Garrettson, *The Experience*, 9, 22, 27, 30,31. Payne maintains that "the idea of submission is absent from" Garrisons journal. Payne, "Metaphors of the Self and the Sacred," 31–47, See also Sobel, *Trabelin' On*, 108–109, 112, 229. For a discussion of early Methodist reliance on dreams see Wigger, "Taking Heaven by Storm," 167–194.

81. Garrettson, *The Experience*, 160.

82. Ibid., 205, 207.

83. Ibid., 31, 36, 40, 42, 45, 50. On Garrettson's role in the church see Williams, *The Garden of American Methodism*, 41, 47, 112. Methodist women are discussed in chapter 5 of this book.

84. Garrettson, *The Experience*, 76–77, 156, 245. Garrettson's manuscript Journal, reprinted in full in the volume edited by Simpson, reveals that Garrettson preached to and spent far more time with the enslaved than does the originally published edited version. See Garrettson, *American Methodist Pioneer*, 147, 158, 190, 198, 218, 227, 241, 242, 257, and 389. Garrettson's major essay on slavery is *A Dialogue Between Do-Justice and Professing Christian* .

85. See chapter 5 of this book for a discussion of Catherine Livingston, and chapter 6 for her portrait. A "person" often meant a women in the eighteenth and early nineteenth centuries, as it still does today. See the letter of the Reverend Mr. Cotton to the Reverend Mr. Prince of July 26, 1743, reprinted in *The Christian Century*, 1743, 261, in which Cotton wrote that at a revival in a town south of Boston, in the summer of 1741, a "person . . . cried out" at an evening church service although "she" had not approved of such behavior prior to this time. Ralph Waldo Emerson, writing of his wife, noted, "Persons are fine things, but they cost so much." See Newfield, "Loving Bondage," 183–193.

86. Hamilton, *A Narrative*, 7. The title page states, "Taken from her own Mouth."

87. Ibid., 1–5. Contemporary Quaker converts told of the pain of adopting Quaker dress. Throwing evil goods into a fire also had a long history that continued into the period under discussion. Extremists, such as James Davenport burned books in the First Great Awakening, and later children at the Oneida Community were adjured to throw their most beloved toys into a fire.

88. This is reminiscent of the ball of thread given to Theseus by Ariadne. See Lifshin, *Ariadne's Thread*.

89. Hamilton, *A Narrative*, 4.

90. Ibid., 12

91. Ibid., 4.

92. Hamilton's father encouraged a rowdy mob to hold her, and she was almost caught. She escaped with the aid of a Presbyterian minister who raised money for her getaway trip to Vermont. She had earlier been supported in North Carolina by the unnamed Baptist minister who converted her.

93. Rush, *An Address*, (1773), 3–18.

94. Davies, *Sermons*, 2:24

95. While Rush published his antislavery essay in 1773 and joined the Pennsylvania Abolitionist Society in 1787, it was not until July of 1788 that he wrote out a formal statement promising William Grubber freedom; that freedom was not to be awarded until February of 1794, some six years later. See Hawke, *Benjamin Rush*, 36, 362.

96. Rush, "Commonplace Book," June 17, 1799, in *The Autobiography*, 246. Rush also noted that Grubber secretly made a ring of some strands of Rush's hair, marking his emotional attachment to Rush.

97. Rush to Jeremy Belknap, August 19, 1788, in Rush, *Letters*, 1:482. On Derham see Rush, writing to the Pennsylvania Abolition Society on November 14, 1788, ibid., 1:497.

98. Rush, "Paradise of Negro Slaves", 235–238. See also Nash, *Forging Freedom*, 104; Hawke, *Benjamin Rush*, 11, 84, 107, 354, 361. Rush was aware that he had altered his concern with the poor, as well as his own ambitions, as a result of dreams. See Binger, "The Dreams of Benjamin Rush," 1653–1659; Butterfield, "The Dream of Benjamin Rush," 297–319; Rush, *The Autobiography*, 187, 198, 357–360, 259; Rush, *Letters*, 2:994, 1021.

99. Rush wrote more about the meaning of dreams than anyone else in this study. As a doctor particularly concerned with mental illness, he recognized the effect of such illnesses on dreams. He also knew that the instincts and emotions played out a drama in them. Rush, "The Influence of Physical Causes on the Moral Faculty," 188; Rush, *Medical Inquiries*, 300; Rush, *Lectures on the Mind*, 385–402. See Kindermann, *Man Unknown to Himself*, 114–116.

100. See Sobel, *Trabelin' On*; Sobel, *The World They Made Together*; Boles, *Masters and Slaves*.

101. Taylor, *A History*. See also Fristoe, *A Concise History*; Semple, *A History*; L. Jackson, "Religious Development of the Negroes," 68–239.

102. Taylor, *A History*, 13, 258. 289.

103. Ibid., 297, 6, 43, 177, 33–34, 62, 149, 153–154.

104. Ibid., 156.

105. Ibid., 119. For use of the term "white negroe" see Malvin, *Autobiography*, 72.

106. Taylor's limited self-view is reflected in the title he gave his narrative. He called it "A history of the ten churches" he had served and only appended as a subtitle the fact that in this history "will be seen something of a journal of the author's life."

107. Boehm, *The Patriarch*, 69, 70. Boehm's father was a Mennonite who became one of the founders of the Brethren, together with Christian Newcomer and Philip Otterbein. Their beliefs and practices had been deeply influenced by Wesleyanism. Wittlinger, *Quest for Piety*, 10–11, 20–24.

108. Boehm, *The Patriarch*, 141. One of Jenkins's critics felt constrained to write him many years later to confess that he too now shouted. Jenkins, *Experience*, 44, 47, 50, 205: Capers, "Recollections," 11–228. On Richard Whatcoat see Baker, *From Wesley to Asbury*, 103–104, 159–160.

109. Jenkins, *Experience*, 121.

110. Garrettson, *American Methodist Pioneer*, 270. Eleazer Sherman, in Darien, Georgia, in 1818, heard a slave owner tell of his conversion by one of his slaves, whose prayers had convinced the owner that God spoke to him directly. Sherman, *The Narrative*, 50–51.

111. Boehm, *The Patriarch*, 90–94, 141–144. See Leland, *Some Events*, 23–25, for a white preacher awakening congregants at an ecstatic (delayed) funeral.

112. Garrettson, *American Methodist Pioneer*, 237, 238, 251, 266–270. Harry Hosier, born in North Carolina, was a traveling preacher from 1781 until 1805, but he apparently became an alcoholic and gave up preaching for a period. He had stopped drinking and was preaching again at some time before his death in 1810. Some white Methodists suggested that he, and other blacks, could not cope with elevation in status. See Boehm, *The Patriarch*, 92; Williams, *The Garden of American Methodism*, 143. Henry Evans, a free black Methodist preacher, also came to have a very large white following. Evans founded the first Methodist church in Fayetteville, North Carolina, and his first congregants were primarily black, but over the years many white people joined his church. In 1808 a white preacher was sent to take over his pulpit, and Evans was forced to accept a secondary role. William Capers compared his character to that of St. Paul. See Capers, "Recollections," 129–130; Travis, *Autobiography*, 101; Jenkins, *Experience*, 120,199. In 1754 Woolman dreamed that he "saw two lights in the east resembling two suns, but of a dull and gloomy aspect." Woolman, *Journal*, ed. Moulton, 46.

113. Boehm, *The Patriarch*, 213.

114. Hayden, *The Narrative*, 4, 16. A drawing of the two suns, as Hayden saw them, is opposite page 24. Maude Southwell Wahlman notes that Harriet Powers embroidery included "an appliquéd light sun for life, as well as a dark "midnight" sun for the undersea world of the ancestors." Wahlman, Introduction, in Tobin and Dobard, *Hidden in Plain View*, 11.

115. Clarke and Clarke, *Narratives*, 40.

116. Vusamazulu Credo Mutwa discusses ancient African rock carvings depicting two suns. Mutwa, *Song of the Stars*, chapter four, n. 2, n.p.; 193.

117. "The colored people are fond of figures." Boehm, *The Patriarch*, 212.

118. Thompson, *Flash of the Spirit*, 11. Jenkins, *Experience*, 10, 31–32.

119. Jenkins also believed that turning an alligator on its back would bring rain. Ibid., 10, 13, 17, 32–34.

120. Boehm recorded that this child had been baptized by Asbury in 1809. Boehm, *The Patriarch*, 270.

121. Jenkins. *Experience*, 159. On the monetary contributions of slaves, see Capers, "Recollections," 161, 394.

122. Jenkins, *Experience*, 172, 176, 208, 214, 230.

123. Ibid., 41–42, 120,193, 199, 205, 209, 230, 123,

124. At ten, Jenkins had dreamed that he met the Savior, who gave him a beautiful New Testament. Ibid., 11, 142, citing Asbury at the 1804 General Conference. Boehm felt that Asbury "was a great friend of the colored race, whom he called his 'black sheep.' " Boehm, *The Patriarch*, 270.

125. Jenkins was writing in 1842, when he was seventy-eight. Jenkins, *Experience*, 39, 42, 11, 214, 105, 232.

126. Smith, and Dailey, in T. Smith, *The Experience*, 83,196.

127. As a young man Gates thought he saw a "coloured man" wafting through the air, who came to warn him to stay away from frivolous parties. Gates, *The Trials*, 11, 30, 109–110, 167. Moorman's experience is analyzed by Schwarz, "Clark T. Moorman, Quaker Emancipator," 27–35.

128. "The introjector takes in a feeling, an idea, or a part of the self or object of another person. . . ." Bollas, *The Shadow of the Object*, 163. Scharff, *Projective and Introjective Identification*, 87.

129. Lhamon, *Raising Cain*, 42, 44.

130. Lott, *Love and Theft*, 71, 52. See Roediger, *The Wages of Whiteness*, 96, 100.

131. William Otter's narrative gives his birth date as 1789, but Stott has located a record of his baptism in 1787. Otter, *History of My Own Times*, 5.

132. Roediger, *The Wages of Whiteness*, 13.

133. For discussions of projection of instinctual life on black people see Jordan, *White over Black*, 40–43, 579–582; Slotkin, *Regeneration Through Violence*, 551–558.

134. Stott, editor of a 1995 edition of Otter's narrative, believes that the primary title, *History of My Own Times*, was given in reaction to a book of the same title written by Rev. Daniel Barber, a Catholic convert who had been an Episcopal minister, whose pious narrative dealt with his conversion and other spiritual matters. Certainly, Otter's worldview was antithetical to Barber's. Otter's full title for his narrative was *The History of My Own Times; or, The Life and Adventures of William Otter, Senior, Comprising A Series of Events and Musical Incidents Altogether Original*, but the events that he narrated as the history of his times were only the events that he caused, not those of national importance. He saw himself as being at the center of his own life and at the center of many lives around him. Otter, *History of My Own Times*, ed. Stott, 163, 181–183.

135. Lott, *Love and Theft*, 234. For a survey of the violent and crude humor of a number of writers in this period, who often pictured blacks as suffering, see Otter, *History of My Own Times*, ed. Stott, 205–206.

136. Otter, *History of My Own Times*, 5, 53, 69, 71, 82–83. Stott notes that these "dance houses" were actually houses of prostitution. The fact that Otter paid for sexual encounters clearly would not have fit the image he was trying to project, and he therefore hid their true nature. See Otter, *History of My Own Times*, ed. Stott, 44, n.49. On gangs of young men and their violent actions, see Gilje, *The Road to Mobocracy*, 15, 153–170, 258–264; and Wilentz, *Chants Democratic*, 55–56, 256, 262, 264, 269–70,300, 394; Otter, *History of My Own Times*, 99, 105.

137. Otter, *History of My Own Times*, 114–116. Gilje points out that attacks on African American churches were common, and he suggests that white people chose these as targets as they were recognized as a source of emotional support for blacks. Gilje, *The Road to Mobocracy*, table 3, "Rioters Harassing Black Churches, 1808–1830," 155. An eighteenth-century gang of white Philadelphia youths that often harassed blacks was called "White Boys." On gang activity see Laurie, *Working People of Philadelphia*, 61–66, 151.

138. Otter, *History of My Own Times*, 126.

139. Ibid., 220–221, 226, 227, 230–233.

140. Otter sought out and found someone who claimed this man as a runaway, and he was paid for his double trick. However, the owner sought to trick Otter out of half of his payment. Otter took him to court and was proud of his success there as well. Ibid., 342–348,

141. Otter, *History of My Own Times*, ed. Stott, 203.

142. Otter, *History of My Own Times*, 128.

143. Otter repeated this pattern of causing blacks pain and relieving the pain he had caused. To trick a black man who had taken drinks from his whiskey bottle, he put turpentine into the whiskey. When it caused the black man to have "such dreadful burning in his belly, . . . he said he was burning up alive," Otter came to his rescue him with a bottle of oil, which caused him other complications and brought Otter and his friends more amusement. Ibid., 290.

144. Ibid., 306. Stott, while recognizing that this was a violent culture and "a rough, raw and rowdy society," suggests that Otter was a sadist. Otter, *History of My Own Times*, ed. Stott, 213, 221. I believe his acts were not outside of the acceptable in this time and place. The phrase "dance to me Miss Betsy" may well come from a popular black song. Robert Hayden uses the refrain "Pretty Malinda, dance with me" and "Pretty Malinda, come to me" in a poem on African American flying, reprinted in Walters, " 'One of dese mornings,' " 3.

145. Otter, *History of My Own Times*, 137.

146. Stott holds that Otter's world of violence was "becoming marginalized" even as he wrote, and that he wrote, in part, to defend it. Otter, *History of My Own Times*, ed. Stott, 221.

147. Holt, "Marking," 10.

148. Laurie, *Working People of Philadelphia*, 62–64; Runcie, " 'Hunting the Nigs' in Philadelphia," 187–218.

149. *Niles Register*, 49, no. 1, September 5, 1835, cited by Nash et al., eds. *The American People*, 260. See D. Grimsted, *American Mobbing*, 3–32; Laurie, *Working People of Philadelphia*, 61–66; Laurie, *Artisans into Workers*, 52–73; Wilentz, *Chants Democratic*, 264–271.

150. Otter, *History of My Own Times*, 357.

151. Ibid., 356, Otter had become a tavern owner, but his tavern in Emmitsburg, Maryland, was destroyed by fire in 1845. He resumed dealing in liquor in Baltimore, where he was living by 1849. He died there in April 1856. See Otter, *History of My Own Times*, ed. Stott, 179.

152. Lott, *Love and Theft*, 234.

153. Pertinex Placid, "A Tale of a Nose," 445–448. I was alerted to this dream report by the reference to it and the citation of the song in K. Greenberg's cogent analysis of Southern folkways and mores, "The Nose, the Lie, and the Duel in the Antebellum South," 74. David Waldstreicher suggested to me that he felt that this tale might well have been by Edgar Allan Poe, and indeed there is much to suggest that it was. Poe was contributing material to this journal at this time (in fact the article following "The Tale of the Nose" was written by Poe, and this was followed by another by Pertinex Placid. Perhaps Poe used the pen name to hide the fact that he had contributed so many pieces to this one edition. (Poe took on the role of editor of this journal in the next edition.) The tale opens with a statement of its moral purpose, which fit Edgar Allan Poe's aims, and includes a reference to the author as "E." Poe's situation parallels that of the writer: he was then in extreme economic need, and indeed was warned by his foster father, and no doubt others, that he was headed for ruin. An analyst of Poe's contributions to this journal nevertheless sees this piece as one that Poe learned from rather than wrote. See Whitty, *Poe and the Southern Literary Messenger*, 86. Poe did see dreams "as a path for memory" arousal, and his first published tale may have been "A Dream," which was published with the signature P. in the *Saturday Evening Post* of August 13, 1831. In this tale the narrator sees himself as one of those who was nailing Jesus to the cross. See Silverman, *Edgar A. Poe*, 87, 227. Contemporary dream books did suggest that the nose was a phallic symbol. See *The Universal Dream-Dictionary*, 173–174.

CHAPTER 3

1. Sojourner Truth, Boston speech, January 1, 1871, on the occasion of the eighth anniversary of the Emancipation Proclamation, in Loewenberg and Bogin, *Black Women in Nineteenth-Century Life*, 240–242; the editors have "dropped" the "patois rendition."

2. Douglass, *Narrative*, 59.

3. Douglass thought he was born in 1817, but Dickson Preston has established that he was born in February 1818 and may have been seven when this event occurred. Preston, *Young Frederick Douglass*, 32–34.

4. For varying views on the issue of black and white cultural interaction see Wright, *African Americans in the Colonial Era*; Joyner, *Down by the Riverside*; Joyner, "Believer I Know"; Berlin, "Time, Space and the Evolution of Afro-American Society"; Berlin, *Many Thousands Gone*; 44–78; Morgan, *Slave Counterpoint*, 441–497; and Gomez, *Exchanging our Country Marks*.

5. Estimates of those who took their freedom vary. See Frey, *Water from the Rock*, 211.

6. Berlin and Hoffman, eds., *Slavery and Freedom*; Berlin, *Many Thousands Gone*, 228–255.

7. S. White, *Somewhat More Independent*, 24–55; Wright, *African Americans in the Early Republic*, 129.

8. Jeremiah Asher wrote of his father's attempts to persuade him to accept white children's' insults passively, and his own need to stand up for himself and his rights. Asher, *Incidents*, 6.

9. On the decline in white indentures see Rorabaugh, " 'I Thought I Should Liberate Myself from the Thraldom of Others,' " 185–220.

10. Beattie, "Representations of the Self in Traditional Africa," 313–320. Beattie's essay surveys and responds to thirty-two essays on self in Africa collected in *La notion de personne en Afrique noire* (Paris, 1973). See also LeVine, "The Self and Its Development in an African Society," 43–65; LeVine, "The Self in an African Culture," 37–47; Morris, *Anthropology of the Self*, 118–147; Lienhardt, "Self: Public, Private," 141–155. In some African cultures women and slaves were seen as unable to achieve the full development that free males might attain, but African cultures generally recognized aspects of individual character and inwardness in both males and females, although these traits were by and large to be kept private. Morris, "African Philosophy and Conceptions of the Person," 147; Ottenberg, *Boyhood Rituals in an African Society*, 28–29.

11. "A Louisiana planter humiliated disobedient male field-hands by giving them 'women's work' such as washing clothes, by dressing them in women's clothing, and by exhibiting them on a scaffold wearing a red flannel cap." Stampp, *The Peculiar Institution*, 172, citing the diary of Bennet H. Barrow.

12. Fortes, *Religion, Morality and the Person*, 193.

13. Greenblatt, *Renaissance Self-Fashioning*, 176.

14. Davies, *Letters*, 30.

15. On contemplating suicide see the narrative of Ofodobenda Wooma, an Igbo, who became York and then Andrew (1729–1779), in Thorp, "Chattel with a Soul," 450.

16. See Sobel, *Trabelin' On*; and Sobel, *The World They Made Together*.

17. See R. Allen, *The Life*. On the organization of "the AME Zion (1800), Abyssinian Baptist (1804), and St. Philip's Episcopal (1820) in New York; the African Baptist (later the First Independent Baptist Church of People of Color) (1805) and AME (1818) in Boston; the Bethel AME (1797) and Sharp Street AME Church (1799) in Baltimore," see Wright, *African Americans in the Early Republic*, 156; Gravely, "The Rise of African Churches in

America," 58–73; Curry, *The Free Black in Urban America*; Nash, *Race and Revolution*, 67–73; E. Smith, *Climbing Jacob's Ladder*, 29–57, 75–87.

18. V. Smith, *A Narrative*; Desrochers, " Not Fade Away.' " On the honor of the enslaved see also Bruce, *The New Man*, iii.

19. V. Smith, *A Narrative*, 11, 12, 14, 16, 24. See also Watson, *Narrative*, 26, for white theft from blacks.

20. Smith was buried in the churchyard of the First Congregational Church in East Haddam, Connecticut, in 1805, but he did not mention church membership in his narrative.

21. On the white Methodist Church in this period, see Richey, *Early American Methodism*. The white Methodist church was actually a mixed-race church: In New York City, for example, approximately one third of the members were African Americans.

22. White did not mention his father until he noted that his father was dead when he sought out his parents after he was free. White states that he was manumitted by will after the death of his last owner. G. White, *A Brief Account of the Life*, 5, 6, 8. Graham Russell Hodges has located an advertisement placed by a Trenton, New Jersey, jailer in 1787, noting that he was holding a "NEGRO . . . who calls himself GEORGE WHITE, and says he is a free man, . . . and has lived the greatest part of his time with Colonel William Johnson." Hodges believes this George White was the narrator and that his last owner was still alive when he manumitted him. Hodges, *Black Itinerants of the Gospel*, 11. The years of enslavement that White noted in his narrative would place his manumission in 1790. However, he also says he arrived in New York City in 1791 and that he had taken three years to work his way from Maryland to New York. On manumission in Maryland see Fields, *Slavery and Freedom*, 1, 5; and Quarles, " 'Freedom Fettered,' " 299–304.

23. G. White, *A Brief Account*, 7–10, emphasis added.

24. Ibid., 14, 22, 28. Doves were often assumed to betoken peace, as they had for Noah in the Ark; others made the association to the Holy Ghost. For Frederick Douglass the moans of a dove symbolized sorrow and "the grave at the door," as they had for Elizabeth, who wrote of mourning "sore like a dove." Rebecca Cox Jackson wrote that God's City "was like a dove." Freeborn Garrettson also compared the church to doves, "which are in the cleft of the rocks." Douglass, *Narrative*, 78; Jackson, *Gifts of Power*, 247; Garrettson, *American Methodist Pioneer*, 266; Elizabeth, *Memoir of Old Elizabeth*, 4. Puckett, *Folk Beliefs*, 77, 120, 268, 326, 354, 434, 488, 510.

25. Using Rossi's ladder of self-concern, this transformation in a dream indicates a significant change in self. See Rossi's table, given in chapter 1 of this book. In the seventeen dreams reported by Frederic W. Swan, the color white is consistently noted in relation to men, angels, and objects. Swan, *Remarkable Visionary Dreams*, 3–16. I am indebted to John Salliant for putting a copy of this document on the Internet, and to Sharon Halevi for bringing it to my attention.

26. G. White, *A Brief Account*, 24.

27. On New York City blacks see S. White, *Somewhat More Independent*; and Wilentz, *Chants Democratic*.

28. G. White, *A Brief Account*, 34; D. Payne, *History*, 37. White joined the New York African Methodist Church and was ordained a deacon in 1822 but aroused opposition and was expelled in 1829. Hodges, *Black Itinerants of the Gospel*, 16–18. Many of New York City's Africans were moving from mixed churches to all-black churches. See Grossi, " 'It Is Worth That Makes the Man.' "

29. Rush, "Commonplace Book", January 25, 1801, *The Autobiography*, 165.

30. Alpers, "The Story of Swema," 198. Swema was born in Yaoland in east central Africa, about 1855. See also Fisher, "Dreams and Conversion in Black Africa."

31. There were black women in Catholic convents in America, and black members of the Shaker communities, especially in Pennsylvania and in Kentucky, where they were in a segregated family. A few African American individuals such as Sojourner Truth were attracted to and joined other communities. See Pease and Pease, *Black Utopia*. On African Moravians see Sensbach, *Separate Canaan*.

32. Swan, *Remarkable Visionary Dreams*, 13.

33. Banneker, Almanac, December 13, 1797. Banneker's dream reports were published in Bedini, *The Life*, 334–335. My reading of the manuscript differs somewhat from Bedini's. See Hurry, "An Archeological and Historical Perspective," 361–369.

34. Aptheker, *American Negro Slave Revolts*, 101–102, 224.

35. Ball, *Slavery*, 221, 220. It is significant that it was through a dream that Benjamin Rush came to realize that this was the pervasive black view. See chapter 2 of this book.

36. W. Brown, *Narrative*, 95–96, emphasis added.

37. Ibid., 98, 103, 104.

38. See Adorno, *The Authoritarian Personality*; Bettelheim and Janowitz, *Social Change and Prejudice*.

39. Truth, Boston speech, January 1, 1871, in Loewenberg and Bogin, *Black Women in Nineteenth-Century Life*, 240–242, the editors have "dropped" the "patois rendition."

40. Wilson, in her preface, openly noted, "I have purposely omitted what would most provoke shame in our good anti-slavery friends at home." Wilson, *Our Nig*, 3.

41. Anderson, *Life*, 5, 11–12.

42. See Wright, *African Americans in the Early Republic*, 8–42; Tadman, *Speculators and Slaves*.

43. Anderson, *Life*, 18, 26, 29, 30.

44. For a celebration of July 4, 1836, by the enslaved, see Sensbach, *A Separate Canaan*, 572 n.41. After the emancipation of West Indian slaves, free blacks in the North celebrated August 1. See Grandy, *Narrative*, 45. See also Waldstreicher, *In the Midst of Perpetual Fetes*, 315; 324, 328, 339, 341.

45. Anderson, *Life*, 35. See Larison, *Sylvia Dubois*, 69.

46. Anderson, *Life*, title page, 30, 35. When Lunsford Lane bought his own freedom, "it seemed as though I was in heaven." and when he was rescued from a mob, he "had deep and strange communion with my own soul." See Lane, *The Narrative*, 15, 52.

47. W. Brown, *Narrative*, 104.

48. Josiah Henson recalled that the moment he reached freedom in 1830, "I threw myself on the ground, rolled in the sand, seized handfuls of it and kissed them, and danced round till, in the eyes of several who were present, I passed for a madman." Henson countered, " 'O, no, master! don't you know? I'm free!' " Henson, *Father Henson's Story*, 126–127.

49. Anderson, *Life*, 43, 44, 49.

50. Ibid., 36, 37, 40.

51. Clarke and Clarke, *Narratives*, 26.

52. Anderson, *Life*, 59, 78, 80.

53. The Hebrew word for this curse is usually translated as "leprosy," in as much as the skin was described "as white as snow." The same punishment was given to Miriam, and it was also a temporary warning punishment given to Moses (Exodus 4:6 and Numbers 12:10). Gehazi's punishment was, however, marked by being "for ever"—apparently for all his descendants as well. See Anderson, *Life*, 61. 47, 50, 78–79. I want to thank Hagai Doron for researching Talmudic, Midrashic, and medieval commentaries on this issue for me. One of the key problems dealt with in many of these texts was the seeming disproportion between the crime and the punishment. Anderson did not see this as a problem, as he felt that the crime of slave buying merited such a permanent punishment.

54. Henson, *Father Henson's Story*, 53.

55. Henson arrived in Canada on October 28, 1830. Ibid., 126.

56. Grandy, *Narrative*, 11, 21. Grandy's narrative presents his meeting with Minner as fortuitous, as if he himself had not planned it, but he reveals that Minner had earlier told him that he would help him buy himself at any time.

57. Ibid., title page, 25, 26. Grandy purchased his wife for three hundred dollars; one of his daughters had already purchased both herself and one sister. He sought to buy four other children and four grandchildren. Grandy had been raised together with the white children of the Billy Grandy family. It was one of these white children, James Grandy, who took the first six hundred dollars as the self-purchase price from Moses Grandy and then sold him. Moses Grandy recounts that James's sister and her husband (the Grices) worked very hard to get James to honor his agreement, and even turned to the courts, but failed. Other whites responded by disgracing James Grandy: "They would not suffer him to remain in the boarding house, but turned him out, there and then, with all his trunks and boxes." This white reaction of feeling collectively dishonored by the immoral behavior of Moses Grandy's owners eventually helped Grandy. Apparently shamed by the second case of white trickery that Grandy suffered, a Mr. Brooks, described as one of the most brutal of white overseers in his neighborhood, convinced the man who had purchased Grandy to sell him to Minner so that he might

purchase himself. Grandy described in detail the barbaric cruelty of this overseer Brooks, for which he was never punished, at the same time that he felt constrained to acknowledge that "it was the word of this man which gained my freedom." Ibid., iii, 41.

58. Ibid., 25.

59. Reynolds, writing of the ZeZuru in "Dreams and the Constitution of Self among the ZeZuru," 22; and Shaw, "Dreaming as Accomplishment," 45.

60. Phillis Cogswell, Conversion Narrative, April 22, 1764, reprinted in Seeman, " 'Justise Must Take Place,' " 413.

61. Elizabeth, *Memoir*, 8. See Humez, " 'My Spirit Eye,' " 129–143; D. Williams, "Visions," 87–88.

62. Jackson, *Gifts of Power*, 111 (1831), 188 (1841). For a further discussion of flying, see chapter 6 of this book.

63. Braxton finds Jackson's use of blackness (as sin) and whiteness (as purity) "perplexing and confusing" and fears it was due to a loss of racial identity. In this case Braxton, whose analyses are generally very encompassing, does not take into account African attitudes to the symbolic valence of these colors. See Braxton, *Black Women Writing Autobiography*, 62, and chapter 6 of this book.

64. Swan, *Remarkable Visionary Dreams*. For Frederick Douglass, sailing ships "robed in purest white" symbolized freedom. Douglass, *Narrative*, 95.

65. Benjamin Rush dreamed that a black man in heaven said, "That colour [white] which is the emblem of innocence in every other creature of God, is to us a sign of guilt in man." Rush, "Paradise of Negro Slaves," 187. However, African American John Marrant, praying for blacks' salvation, prayed for blacks to be made "white in the blood of the lamb." Marrant, *A Narrative*, 22 (July 18, 1786) .

A story told by the Igbo Ofodobenda Wooma (given the name Andrew in America) indeed suggests that Africans may have regarded white skin differently. Andrew (born 1729) recorded that he was taken captive and enslaved by Africans, and that in 1740, when he was taken to the coast to be sold into the Atlantic trade, he and a friend "were terribly frightened because we saw 2 white people coming toward us. We thought sure they were devils who wanted to take us, because we had never before seen a white man and never in our lives heard that such men existed." Andrew, in Thorp, "Chattel with A Soul," 450.

66. Jackson, *Gifts of Power*, 95, 236. Jones suggests that the color of God was not a question in Africa before the coming of white Christians but that since that time "the tendency to color God black recurs in a broad base of Christian Black religious thought." He cites a Congolese woman, Kimpa Vita/Beatrice, who in San Salvador in 1700 saw Christ and the apostles as black. Jones, *The Color of God*, 38, 39.

67. Contemporary analysts might well see this dream action, just as clearly, as symbolic of sexual union. Jackson was in conflict with her husband over sexual relations until the fall of 1836, when he apparently attempted to kill her. She then had a vision of her God-given role. Jackson, *Gifts of Power*, 92, 133, 135 n.15, 148, 146–147. On the significance of chairs,

see Gundaker, "Tradition and Innovation in African-American Yards," 58–96. See also Hampton, "The Throne of the Third Heaven of the Nations Millennium General Assembly," (1950–1964), National Museum of American Art, Smithsonian, Washington D.C. See Samuel King's "Portrait of Ezra Stiles," reprinted in chapter 1 of this book, for the use of black specks to betoken evil.

68. Jackson, *Gifts of Power*, 191.

69. Watzlawick, Weakland, and Fisch, *Change*, 42.

70. Ibid.

71. Jackson, *Gifts of Power*, 98.

72. Ibid., 147, 282. Jackson stands in stark contrast to Banneker, who did not have such spiritual guidance, and whose inner devils continued to haunt him, but he too may have dreamt of a cosmogram. See his dream of December, 1791, referring to a "Quincunx," which is further discussed in chapter 6 of this book. On the cosmogram, see Thompson, *Flash of the Spirit*, 108–115. The spiritual narratives collected from former slaves refer to this correlation of directions and spiritual powers. See, for example "You Must Die This Day," a vision in which the narrator traveling on a white path, goes east and then views a savior coming from the northeast. Watson, *God Struck Me Dead*, 63–64.

73. Turner, *The Confessions*. While Turner's men did not kill a few of the whites they encountered, their decisions were based on previous private interaction, not on an ideological stance: they spared "Giles Reese, on whose farm Turner's wife resided, the family of John Clark Turner, Turner's childhood playmate, and a poor white family who, Turner believed, 'thought no better of themselves than they did of Negroes.' " Wright, *African Americans in the Early Republic*, 111.

74. Walker, *Walker's Appeal*, 29. See Aptheker, *"One Continual Cry."*

75. See Werner, *"Reaping the Bloody Harvest,"* 298.

76. See Pease and Pease, "Black Power—the Debate in 1840," 26; Pease and Pease, *They Who Would Be Free*, which deals with the factions and divisions in the black community circa 1840.

77. Stewart, *Maria W. Stewart*, 63. After she delivered this radical address in 1833 Stewart apparently came under attack from blacks in Boston and felt that she had to leave the community. Stewart, who knew Walker well and was deeply influenced by him, had become a " 'warrior' " for " 'the cause of oppressed Africa' " after Walker's suspicious death in 1830, but she was not yet ready to call on black people to kill whites. On the contrary, in 1832 she had asked Africans to "sheath your swords, and calm your angry passions. Stand still and know that the Lord he is God. Vengeance is his, and he will repay." Ibid., 39.

78. Garnet, "An Address To The Slaves of the United States of America, Buffalo, N.Y., 1843," reprinted in Ofari, *"Let Your Motto Be Resistance,"* 144–153.

79. Garnet had escaped to the North and relative freedom with his family in 1824. In New York his family was broken apart when slave catchers were searching for them. In 1835 he and other black students were violently

hounded out of the Noyes Academy in New Hampshire. This violence led them to pledge "that when they . . . completed their education they would go to the South and foment slave rebellions." Garnet, who became a Presbyterian minister, a teacher, a writer and newspaper publisher, an abolitionist, and a Liberty Party organizer, did his utmost from the North to arm himself and resist attackers and to shame southern slaves into rebellion. He accused the enslaved of willingly serving the vilest needs of slave owners. Later, Garnet did support John Brown, helping him find backers in the black community, and he apparently committed himself to fight with Brown, but when the call came to join Brown in 1859, he did not respond. Perhaps it was too late, both for Garnet and for such acts of violence. Earl Ofari, in his study of Garnet, simply notes that "Garnet became somewhat disillusioned with Brown when he was forced to cancel his plan of attack" in 1858. Ofari, *"Let Your Motto Be Resistance,"* 7, 106.

80. Hazlip, *The Sweeter the Juice*, 177. The African American minister Daniel H. Peterson provides further evidence from this period of black hatred of whites. Peterson, *The Looking-glass*, 18.

CHAPTER 4

1. Walker, *Appeal*, 19.
2. See P. Stearns, *Be a Man*, 51, 56, 57, 69–76, 86. Stearns views the Industrial Revolution as the key factor undermining patriarchy.
3. Eight of the narratives in this study were written by people who served in the armed forces. The soldiers were: Frances T. Brooke, James P. Collins, Jackson Johonnet, Joseph Martin, Levi Redfield, Jacob Ritter, Deborah Samson, and John R. Shaw. In addition, John Gano was a chaplain in the American army. See Brooke, *A Narrative*; J. Collins, *Autobiography*; Johonnet, *The Remarkable Adventures*; J. Martin, *A Narrative*; Redfield, *A Succinct Account*; Ritter, *Memoirs*; Mann, *The Female Review*; Shaw, *A Narrative*; Gano, *Biographical Memoirs*.
4. Ritter, *Memoirs*, 13–14.
5. J. Collins, *Autobiography*, 52.
6. See Martin, *Private Yankee Doodle*, 35, 48–49, 51, 52, 55, 58, 76, 84, 118, 119, 122, 168.
7. Ibid., 234.
8. Osborn and Anthony, *Familiar Letters*, 135. For a further discussion of these black and white memories of the war, see chapter 6 of this book.
9. For a rare and perceptive discussion of eighteenth-century American male "fury against women" see Lockridge, *On the Sources of Patriarchal Rage*.

Three of the narratives written by men in this study, Isaac Martin, Edward Willett, and James Patton, stand out as unusually positive in relation to women. Patton, who might well be termed a proto-feminist, held "that women have never been allowed their just weight in society; were they permitted to use their influence in society to which I consider them entitled, they would contribute much more to the success of business through life, than is generally imagined." I. Martin, *Journal*, 12, 21–22, 45, 63; Willett, *The Matrimonial Life*, 26, 32–34; Patton, *Biography*, 15–16. See also the narrative of Henry Ware, which emphasizes the role that his mother played in his life but also reveals his ambivalence about her. Ware, *The Recollections of Jotham Anderson* [pseudonym].

10. Dayton's study of law and society in eighteenth-century Connecticut details the process whereby "legislators, judges, jurors, lawyers, [and] testators . . . collectively manifested an impulse to reassert legal rules and approaches that buttressed male authority and male property rights. Dayton, *Women Before the Bar*, 67, 226.

11. Smith-Rosenberg, "Domesticating 'Virtue,' " 166.

12. *The Huntington Letters*, 81, 127. Helen K. Brasher noted in her diary that during the Revolution her husband, Abraham Brasher, put the country before family. See "The Narrative of Mrs. Abraham Brasher, giving her account of her experiences during the Revolutionary War," New York Historical Society, 23–46. I am indebted to Laurie Wohlberg for this reference.

13. Shaw, *A Narrative*, 51; Sampson, *The Experiences*, 130; W. Lee, *The True and Interesting Travels*, 30; S. Green, *Life*, 13. Green confessed that he had always been evil, but according to his report his criminal acts grew significantly during the war. Jenkins, *Experience*, 16.

14. Griffith accused himself of indulging in "worldly pleasures" and "fleshly gratifications." Griffith, *A Journal*, 10, 17. Daniel Stanton feared the lack of morality and looked to the church as a controlling and guiding mother, whom he had envisioned in a dream. Stanton, *A Journal*, 13. See Gilbert in *Winding Down*, 65, 86, 87. Gadlin suggests that "[p]eople must have panicked at the flood of unchecked impulse that suddenly became their own responsibility." Gadlin, "Private Lives and Public Order," 43.

15. Volkan, "The Need to Have Enemies and Allies," 219–247; Volkan, *The Need to Have Enemies and Allies*; Godwin, "On the Function of Enemies," 79–102; Stansell, *City of Women*, 23.

16. Smith cites the wills of the poor in Philadelphia as indicative of the "more companionate" marriage that was developing among the poor. B. Smith, *The 'Lower Sort'*, 184–188; Wilentz, *Chants Democratic*, 249; Laurie, *Working People of Philadelphia*, 94–95; Stansell, *City of Women*, 30.

17. Walker, *Appeal*, 19.

18. Goodell, "John Saffin and His Slave Adam," 112; Starling, *The Slave Narrative*, 50–52.

19. After his conversion, Offley claimed, "I have been enabled to see things in a different light, and believe the man is greater who can overcome his foes by his Christlike example," but he still voiced his original view of manliness and self-protection and clearly did not give it up. Offley, *A Narrative*, in Bontemps, *Five Black Lives*, 136.

20. "[I]f anybody meddled with Grimes, he was sure to be punished, if he wasn't stronger and a better man than I was. I did no more than any one would do when abused. . . ." Grimes, *The Life* , 122.

21. Douglass, *Life*, 143. For an earlier description of his feelings, which differs slightly, see Douglass, *Narrative*, 104–105.

22. Douglass, *Narrative*, 7. "Black assertiveness in the market place and in the creation of their own institutions antagonized lower-class whites, and black willingness to riot in 1801, 1819, 1826, and 1832 fulfilled the negative expectations of the white elite." Gilje, *The Road to Mobocracy*, 158.

23. On African Americans response to the war see Quarles, "The Revolutionary War as a Black Declaration of Independence," 283–384.

24. David George was serving the Silver Bluff Church in Aiken County, Georgia, by 1773. During the war, he and forty-nine other enslaved people fled to Savannah, where most took their own freedom. George is quoted in a letter from the Reverend Joseph Cook of Euhaw, South Carolina, September 15, 1790, and in George, "An Account of the Life of Mr. David George." See also Sobel, *Trabelin' On*, 105–106, 189, 311; Frey, *Water from the Rock*, 38–39, 196, 200, 324.

25. Bloch, "The Gendered Meanings of Virtue," 37–58.

26. See Gillis, "From Ritual to Romance," 87–121. Men are cited as crying throughout the narratives; see chapter 6 of this book.

27. Brunt, *The Little Medley*, 5, 6, 10, 15, 16.

28. Powers, *The Narrative*, 4, 5. Dayton holds that the courts "were backing off from convicting and hanging white men for rape" and believes that by "the 1760s it was clear that rape stories were being elevated to a form of entertainment." Dayton, *Women Before the Bar*, 184–231, 283. See also Breen, "Making History," 77–92.

29. Gross, *The Last Words*, 10.

30. Manuel, "Toward a Psychological History of Utopias," 293–322.

31. See Bordin, "The Sect to Denomination Process in America," 77–94; Hatch, *The Democratization of American Christianity*, 193–209.

32. Churchman, *An Account*, 24. See Mack, "Gender and Spirituality in Early English Quakerism," 43, 48. "Truth" was seen as the "ultimate spiritual reality." Woolman, *The Journal*, ed. Moulton, 314.

33. Churchman, *An Account*, 24.

34. Ibid., 128, 217.

35. Ibid., 14, 25, 26, 226. Catherine [Payton] Phillips (born 1727) traveled with Margaret Churchman and met with John Churchman. Phillips, *Memoirs*, 131, 135.

36. Churchman, *An Account*, 132–133.

37. Wesley did have a romantic attachment while in America. On this and on Sally Kirkham's influence see Pollock, John Wesley, 34–70; on other women who influenced Wesley see E. Brown, *Women of Mr. Wesley's Methodism*, 32–34. On English Methodists and sexuality see Barker-Benfield, *The Culture of Sensibility*, 76, 82–83; Chilcote, *She Offered Them Christ*, 21.

38. Bishop Francis Asbury, cited by Boehm, *The Patriarch*, 221. Asbury, *The Journal*, 2:474.

39. On the Methodist congregation as a fictive family see A. Schneider, *The Way of the Cross Leads Home*, 123–124.

40. Garrettson, *Experience*, 10, 11.

41. Ibid., 41.

42. Ibid., 45.

43. Feathers have been associated with males acting in nonaggressive ways in other circumstances. For example, women handed out white feathers to men who were not in uniform in London during World War I. See Gilbar, "Soldier's Heart," 433.

44. See also Garrettson's behavior at the siege of Yorktown. Garrettson, *Experience*, 165, 170, 207–208. Hall, in a comparative study of dreams of men and women in different twentieth-century cultures, has found that for men most dream interactions are aggressive. See C. Hall, " 'A Ubiquitous Sex Difference in Dreams' Revisited," 1109–1117; Hall, Domhoff, Blick, and Weesner, "The Dreams of College Men and Women," 188–194.

45. Garrettson, *Experience*, 171–175.

46. "It is . . . difficult to tell when the belief in Mother Ann as the female incarnation of Christ began." It can be found in Shaker literature by 1801, but Mother Ann Lee was also seen as Jesus's wife and the second Eve. See Kitch, *Chaste Liberation*, 125–130, 159 n. 4.

47. Catherine Livingston to Catherine Rutsen, December 3, 1791, in Ruether and Keller, *Women and Religion in America*, 2:363; Lobody, "Lost in the Ocean of Love," 130–133, 277; Lobody, " 'A Wren Just Bursting Its Shell,' " 19–38; Simpson, "Introductory Biographical Essay," in Garrettson, *American Methodist Pioneer*, 10–11.

48. Hathaway, *Narrative*, 3, 55, 56.

49. Boehm, *Patriarch*, 414, 431, 193.

50. Leverenz, *The Language of Puritan Feeling*, 132.

51. Asbury, *The Journal*, 3:428, March 24, 1810.

52. Ibid., 425, January 26, 1810; 450, May 12, 1811.

53. Boehm married Sarah Hill in 1818, when he was forty-three, and noted that 1818 was "the most memorable year of my life." Boehm, *Patriarch*, 470.

54. Capers, "Recollections," 143.

55. Garrettson, *Experience*, 45.

56. Boehm, *Patriarch*, 452, 234, 239, 435. In his Last Will and Testament, June 6, 1813, Asbury left "To all my nominal Children a Bible." Asbury, *Journal*, 3:472–473. Boehm distributed more than four hundred Bibles to Asbury's namesakes. For letters Asbury wrote to his "children," see Asbury, *Journal*, 3:425, 427, 437, 505. James Jenkins named his daughter Elizabeth Asbury Jenkins after Asbury's mother.

57. Kelly, "Family and Society," 117.

58. For Mothers in Israel, see Jenkins, *Experience*, 62, 66; Hopkins, *Sketches*, 40–41; Boehm, *Patriarch*, 61; and John McCorkle, in Barr, *History of John Barr*, 76.

59. Godbeer, " 'The Cry of Sodom,' " 272; Katz, *Gay American History*, 24–27; D. Greenberg, *The Construction of Homosexuality*, 344.

60. Nissenbaum, *Sex, Diet and Debility*, x, 26–36, 115–116. Barker-Benfield, *The Horrors*, 167; Gadlin, "Private Lives and Public Order," 51–52. There was, as well, a decline in premarital conception, and a continuing reduction in the size of families. See D. Smith, "The Long Cycle in American Illegitimacy and Prenuptial Pregnancy," 375; MacDonald, "The Frightful Consequences of Onanism," 423–424. At his trial, Sherman broke down and

asked his judges what they thought he should do with his life. He was advised not to continue as a preacher and seemed inclined to accept this advice, but he later rejected the conclusions of the panel. He did publish a fourth volume of his narrative, as he had intended to before his trial, and he clearly resumed his career, as in 1843 he published a sermon. See below, note 66.

61. Sherman, *The Narrative*, 1:16.

62. Ibid., 1:18, 65, 68; 2:19–20, 45, 65, 66.

63. Ibid., 1:78.

64. Sherman mentions preaching at seven different factories and mills. He also visited Georgia, and preached to the enslaved. Ibid., 1:42–51; 3:39, 40.

65. Ibid., 3:23

66. The charges were originally aired in *The Light or Two-Edged Sword*. See H. Brown, *Trial of Elder Eleazer Sherman*; Sherman, *Reply of Elder Eleazer Sherman*, 8, 12. Although the council decided that Sherman should give up all preaching, in his *Narrative* of 1835 he declared that Christ judged him and not his fellow men. A talk published in 1843 refuting William Miller's ideas about the imminent end of the world in 1844 identified Sherman as an elder in Taunton, Massachusetts, although the name of his church was not given. Sherman, *The Narrative*, 4:47–49; Sherman, *A Lecture*.

67. Shaw was proud of his overnight temporary marriages, and of breaking his promises. Shaw printed a poem to "Hymen" when he wrote of his marriage. Shaw, *Narrative*, 74, 108–111, 57.

68. Bailey, *Life*, 49. See Fabian, *Card Sharps*, 14–23.

69. Bailey, *Life*, 51. 55. 65.

70. Ibid., 66–67, 162, 148, 207.

71. Ibid., 38–39, 334, 344.

72. See Sedgwick, *Between Men*.

73. H. Brown, *Trial of Elder Eleazer Sherman*, i.

74. Grimes also played the white man, or passed, while he was a slave. Grimes, *The Life*, 64, 71, 95–96.

75. Ibid., 66, 80.

76. Ibid., 113, 116, 122.

77. On use of dreamed numbers, or of the assigned numerical equivalents of dreamed objects in the African American community, see Fabian, *Card Sharps*, 142–150; and *Old Aunt Dinah's Policy Player's Guide*; *Aunt Sally's Policy Players' Dream Book*; *Genuine Afro Dream Book*. I want to thank Bernard Bierlich for allowing me to read his manuscript, "The Head and the Heart." In Bierlich's research in Ghana he found that dreams were often used to determine numbers bet upon, as was his car's license plate. Grimes, *The Life*, 125, 77, 83, 91, emphasis added.

78. Ibid., 120, 125, 127.

79. Starling holds that "the slave narrator's concept of the world as a stage and of his role as the 'bad part' assigned him to play is the most distinct, single impression left upon the reader by the slave narratives before 1836." Starling, *The Slave Narrative*, 105.

80. Ibid.

81. Ibid.

82. Laurie, *Artisans into Workers*, 132.

83. Cashin, *A Family Venture*, 86; Kimmel, *Manhood in America*, 13–42; Wilentz, *Chants Democratic*, 185; Laurie, *Working People of Philadelphia*, 19, 28, 34, 38, 97, 103–104, 107, 117–120, 133.

84. See Roediger, *The Wages of Whiteness*; Laurie, *Artisans into Workers*, 87–88, 102; Laurie, *Working People of Philadelphia*, 94–95; Kessler-Harris, *Out to Work*, 47, 69; Kimmel, *Manhood in America*, 32.

85. As the study of early modern masculinity expands, more doubts about its stability are raised. See B. Smith, "The Material Lives of Laboring Philadelphians," 163–202; B. Smith, "Poverty and Economic Marginality in Eighteenth-Century America," 85–118; Calvert, *Children in the House*; Smith-Rosenberg, "Domesticating 'Virtue,' " 160–184; Gillis, "From Ritual to Romance," 87–121; Cott, "Passionless." 210–236; Mintz and Kellogg, *Domestic Revolutions*, 43–66; Schultz, "God and Workingmen," 129.

86. Tocqueville, *Democracy in America*, 2:201, 211, 214. For a superb critique of Tocqueville see Kerber, "Separate Spheres." See the description of the separation of men and women at social events in M. Hall, *The Aristocratic Journey*, 125, 209, 162, 209, 212. Carnes, *Secret Ritual and Manhood*, 149. Cashin, *A Family Venture*, 32. On masculinity, see Rotundo, *American Manhood*, 3–5, 10–31; and P. Stearns, *Be a Man*, 44, 45.

CHAPTER FIVE

1. Clarke, *Things That I Remember*, 6, 13.

2. This evidence led Laurel Thatcher Ulrich to conclude that "[m]ost models of the 'patriarchal family economy' ill fit the evidence of eighteenth-century diaries." Ulrich, "Housewife and Gadder," 33. Hannah Adams (born 1755) was a New England woman who felt she "was educated in all the habits of debilitating softness," but she nevertheless was able to become an historian. See Adams, *A Memoir*, 2. Elizabeth Allen was "persecuted" for reading, writing, and spending time alone, not proper activities for a girl, and felt that this persecution ruined her life. E. Allen, *Sketches of Green Mountain Life*, 7–8.

3. Dayton, *Women Before the Bar*, 13. For a suggestive study of the interconnections of race, gender and power see K. Brown, *Good Wives, Nasty Wenches, and Anxious Patriarchs*.

4. Juster, "Patriarchy Reborn,", 58–81; Juster, *Disorderly Women*, 41–43; Brekus, *Strangers and Pilgrims*.

5. See Cashin, "Introduction," 1–42. In the South there was a range of development, and generally women were doing more in areas where slaveholding was limited. See, for example, the analysis of women's roles in Halevi, "The Path Not Taken."

6. Lebsock, *The Free Women of Petersburg*, 87–111.

7. Ulrich, "Housewife and Gadder," 33. On changing gender roles see Norton, *Liberty's Daughters*; Kerber, *Women of the Republic*; Bloch, "The Construction of Gender in a Republican World," 601–606. See Branson, "Women and the Family Economy in the Early Republic," 47–71 for a case

study of two generations of women. The first Mrs. Meridith, Elizabeth Meridith (born 1742), was very active in the family tanning business, keeping records, borrowing money, collecting debts, and planning for the future. In the next generation her daughter-in-law became active in social and cultural affairs, but not in work. See also Dayton, *Women Before the Bar*, 9, for a discussion of the changes "in women's and men's relations to commercialization, to the public theater of the courtroom, and to religious attitudes toward sin and human culpability." The change in eighteenth-century black women's lives is more difficult to document, but see Lebsock, *The Free Women of Petersburg*.

8. Garber, *Vested Interests*, 16–17. See J. Scott, "Gender,", 1059.

9. Abigail Adams to John Adams, March 31, 1776, in *Adams Family Correspondence*, 1:370.

10. John Adams to Abigail Adams, April 14, 1776, in ibid., 1:382.

11. Abigail Adams, May 7, 1776, in Adams and Adams, *The Book of Abigail and John*, 127. Heilbrun, *Writing a Woman's Life*, 15. Greenblatt, *Renaissance Self-Fashioning*, 9. On the increasingly male orientation of the law in New England, see Dayton, *Women Before the Bar*, 13, 67. For a study of change in personality and the empowerment of women during the Revolution, see Wohlberg, "Women and the Making of American History."

12. Poor cited by Rotundo, *American Manhood*, 4.

13. Carr, April 8, 1829, cited by Cashin, *A Family Venture*, 49.

14. The churches became more feminized as men faced the outer world and women found themselves, by and large, limited to a communal context. See Bloch, "The Gendered Meanings of Virtue," 37–58; Kerber, *Women of the Republic*.

15. While reactions outside the Quaker community were often ostensibly negative, those who attacked Quaker women were thereby forced to think about and deal with the role of women in public in a new way. Jay Fliegelman has noted, "In Latin, *publicus* signifies a public man or magistrate, *publica* a public woman or prostitute." Fliegelman, *Declaring Independence*, 130.

16. Woolman, *The Journal*, ed. Moulton, 314.

17. Phillips, *Memoirs*, 34, 97–101, 111, 113, 115. On Ranters and Quakers in America see Lovejoy, *Religious Enthusiasm*, 113–115, 141–144.

18. Phillips, *Memoirs*, 110, 122. See the relevant dream reported by Churchman at the time of their meeting in England, June 6, 1753, in Churchman, *An Account*, 132. Neale, *Some Account of the Life*, 107.

19. Phillips, *Memoirs*, 131, 139–141.

20. Ibid., 156–157.

21. Ibid., 13, 22, 208. 215. William Phillips had children from his first marriage, and Catherine Payton may well have thought that obligations to them would limit her work. By the time William and Catherine were married, William Phillips's children were adults, and as Catherine was forty-five, she was unlikely to have children.

22. Ibid., 1, 278.

23. Neale, *Some Account of the Life*, 108, 111, 112. Mary Peisley married Samuel Neale four months after returning from America and died two days later. Both Phillips and Peisley wrote of dreams: Phillips, *Memoirs*, 325 n,

wrote of her brother's dream of two women, "Virtue and Vanity, who each solicited his company." Neale, *Some Account of the Life*, 103, told of a dream foretelling her father's death.

24. Ashbridge, *Some Account*, 25.

25. Ibid., reprinted in Shea, *Journeys in New Worlds*, 148, 153–154. See Shea's excellent introductory essay, "Elizabeth Ashbridge and the Voice Within," 119–146. See also Levenduski, " 'Remarkable Experiences in the Life of Elizabeth Ashbridge',' " 271–281, and Levenduski, *Peculiar Power*, 83, for a perceptive discussion of the role Ashbridge played in her own entrapment.

26. Inasmuch as Elizabeth had lived with Quaker relatives in Ireland and left there planning to visit her relatives in Pennsylvania, it seems most likely that she would have been informed that they were Quakers, but she may well have "forgotten" this fact.

27. Jung, *Collected Works*, 12:6.

28. Ashbridge, *Some Account*, 11.

29. Daniel B. Shea, in his introduction to Ashbridge's narrative, notes that Aaron Ashbridge, after the death of his wife, drank to excess and was disowned by the Goshen Meeting they both had belonged to. Shea, "Elizabeth Ashbridge and the Voice Within," 141.

30. After serving as an indentured servant, Elizabeth had chosen not to return home because she would have appeared (and was) poor and without direction. Elizabeth Ashbridge died in Ireland in 1755 while on her preaching journey. Appended to her narrative was a memoir written by her husband and testimonies from meetings she had visited.

31. Judge, *Memoirs*, 10, 29, 371, 378, 396.

32. See Stearns and Stearns, *Anger*; Heilbrun, *Writing a Woman's Life*, 15.

33. Osborn, *Memoirs*, 11,12, 14, 15, 19.

34. Ibid., 30, 32, 36–39.

35. Ibid., 33, 49. Hopkins in ibid., 70–74. For a history of the society, incorporated in 1806 as the "Religious Female Society" (and renamed the "Osborn Society" in 1826), see the memoir by Park, in Hopkins, *The Works*, 1:99. See also Hambrick-Stowe, "The Spiritual Pilgrimage of Sarah Osborn," 408–421; Norton, " 'My Resting, Reaping Times,' ", 515–529.

36. Osborn and Anthony apparently had very serious disagreements. See Osborn, *Memoirs*, 197. Henry Osborn, who lived until 1778, is very briefly mentioned in the published narratives.

37. Osborn and Anthony, *Familiar Letters*, 17, 45.

38. Hopkins, in Osborn, *Memoirs*, 372. See Smith-Rosenberg, "The Female World of Love and Ritual," 1–30.

39. Osborn, Letters, May 4, 1747, punctuation added.

40. Kenneth P. Minkema suggests that Edwards may well have influenced Hopkins, his student, in this direction long before Osborn did. See Minkema, "Jonathan Edwards on Slavery and the Slave Trade," 823–834.

41. David A. Grimsted credits Osborn with writing an article on slavery for the *Newport Mercury*. D. A. Grimsted, "Anglo-American Racism," 379–381. See also Lacey, "The Bonds of Friendship," 130 n. 12, and Norton, *Liberty's Daughters*, 129–133. Hambrick-Stowe, "The Spiritual Pilgrimage of

Sarah Osborn," 410. Hopkins did not credit Osborn with this role in his autobiography. Hopkins, *Sketches of the Life*, 74, 100; L. Sweet, "Samuel Hopkins, Father of African Colonization," 23–34.

42. Sarah Osborn to Joseph Fish, as transcribed by Norton, " 'My Resting, Reaping Times,' " 519.

43. Bartlet, *The Census of Rhode Island of 1774*, 24, lists six blacks in the household of Henry Osborn. I did not find any acknowledgment of the ownership of blacks in the writings of Sarah Osborn.

44. African Americans were the last group to leave the revival at the Osborn home. Osborn reported that sixty to seventy black people were still attending the Sunday meeting at her house in April 1768. Norton, " 'My Resting, Reaping Times,' " 520–521.

45. Sarah Osborn to Joseph Fish, August 9,1766, April 21, 1765; June 17, 1766, February 28-March 7, 1767; all as cited in ibid., 519–521. By February 28,1767, Osborn was claiming that many had changed their opinions and supported her revival activities.

46. Juster, "Patriarchy Reborn," 75, 66.

47. Willey, *A Short Account*, 24, 29.

48. Davis, *The Female Preacher or Memoir of Salome Lincoln*, 47.

49. Chilcote, *She Offered Them Christ*, 182, 239.

50. Juster, *Disorderly Women*, 108–144, 150, 169–176. Men and women entered the Methodist churches through separate doors, sat separately, and were organized into separate classes for their spiritual discussions. On Barbara Ruckle Heck, who rented a meeting place in New York City in 1767 and then spearheaded the opening of a Methodist chapel in New York City in 1768, see Stevens, *The Women of Methodism*.

51. Lobody, " 'That language might be given me,' " 134; Hempton, *The Religion of the People*, 183; Brekus, *Strangers and Pilgrims*; Chilcote, *She Offered Them Christ*. Earl Kent Brown maintains that while Wesley was in control "women became preachers, group leaders, founders of schools, active visitors and callers, benefactresses, models of Christian life for male and female alike, and even itinerants." After Wesley's death the position of women in the Methodist Church was reversed. "By the mid 1830s, female preaching had all but been suppressed in the connection." E. Brown, *Women of Mr. Wesley's Methodism*, xii, xvi.

52. Newell, *Memoirs*, 42, 66. I want to thank Jon Butler for bringing this dream to my attention. Fanny Newell is discussed in Graff, *Conflicting Paths*, 124.

53. Catherine Livingston to Catherine Rutsen, December 1791, in Ruether and Keller, *Women and Religion*, 2:363.

54. Catherine Livingston, dream of walking on water of April 13, 1790, in "Exercise Book," in Lobody, "Lost in the Ocean of Love," 308–309. Livingston, brought up in the Anglican and Dutch Reformed traditions, was brought to Methodism, at the age of thirty-eight, under the influence of a housekeeper in her mother's home. (She did not record this women's name or any other facts about her.) See Lobody, " 'A Wren Just Bursting Its Shell,' " 19–40.

55. Catherine Livingston to Catherine Rutsen, December 3, 1791, in Ruether and Keller, *Women and Religion in America*, 2:363. See Lobody, "Lost in the Ocean of Love," 6, 58–60, 99.

56. Livingston, December 21, 1788, ibid., 247–248.

57. Travis believed Katy "became a rational and consistent member of the church." Travis, *Autobiography*, 71–72.

58. On Shaker theology, codified after the death of Ann Lee, see "A Guide and Wall of Protection," in Jackson, *Gifts of Power*, 328–335. A collection of the dreams of Jemima Wilkinson and her followers can be found in the Jemima Wilkinson papers, 1771–1849. For a discussion of Wilkinson and gender see Juster, "To Slay the Beast," 27–37; Brekus, *Strangers and Pilgrims*, 80–97.

59. After Rebecca Jackson made an initial submission to a Quaker Mother in 1831, she had a vision of the female aspect of God. She saw "the Mother of the New Heaven and Earth, the Queen of Zion, with Her face toward me, as if waiting." For Jackson this signaled that she was empowered by means of a female spirit to go back into the world and work with her "people." Jackson, *Gifts of Power*, 246, 274. See Madden, "Reading, Writing, and the Race of Mother Figures," 210–234; and Braxton, *Black Women Writing Autobiography*, 61–72.

60. Jackson, *Gifts of Power*, 94–95. Credo Vusamazulu Mutwa, a Zulu shaman, describes a vision that preceded his spiritual rebirth and in which he saw his own dismemberment. The editor of his autobiography, Stephen Larsen, comments that he too had a similar vision before his own spiritual rebirth. See Mutwa, *Song of the Stars*, 10.

61. Rossi's theory would suggest that this was an act that would have great significance. Rossi, *Dreams*, 131–138.

62. Elizabeth, *Memoir*, 6, 7.

63. See Painter, "Soul Murder and Slavery," 125–146.

64. J. Lee, *Religious Experience*, 10–11, 12, 13, 14, 21. See also Elaw, *Memoirs*; D. Williams, "Visions," 81–89; Foote, *A Brand Plucked from the Fire*.

65. Stansell, *City of Women*, 23, 36, 81. Although there were boom periods, as in 1792–1801 and 1822–1834, inflation generally wiped out their benefits for the working class, and there were sharp declines in 1825 and 1829. On changing attitudes toward marriage see Chambers-Schiller, *Liberty, A Better Husband*.

66. Fisher, *Memoirs*. See also the narrative of Ann Eliza Dow Alby (born 1790), who was a deviant: she had children with many lovers, putting them out to be raised, but unlike Fisher, she converted and married a deacon. Alby, *Life, Adventures*.

67. Ibid., 9.

68. Ibid., 28, 42. See also the narrative of Hannah Hanson Kinney, who was accused of poisoning her third husband, but acquitted. Her first husband abandoned her, and her second died under suspicious circumstances. She had been very independent, and supported herself and children by running businesses in Boston. See Kinney, *A Review of the Principal Events*. See also Arms, *Incidents in the Life of a Blind Girl*; E. Allen, *Sketches of Green*

Mountain Life; and Lucas, *Remarkable Account*. All these women seemed to feel they were chosen but did not know what they were chosen for. African American Lucy DeLaney had an overarching goal, her own freedom, but, having been virtually written out of existence by her own mother, seemed uncertain about the nature of her self and her alien other. DeLaney, *From the Darkness Cometh Light*. Mary Marshall had a strong male alien other personified in her (Shaker) husband, but she did not have the institutional support to fight successfully. Marshall, "The Life and Suffering of the Author."

69. Carson, *The Memoirs of the Celebrated and Beautiful Mrs. Ann Carson*, 20, 40, 59, 93, emphasis added.

70. Richards, *Memoirs*, 175, 203–204, 239–240, 258. For evidence of the strong defense of women's preaching by a woman from Richards' hometown (Paris, New York), see Ryan, "A Women's Awakening," 95. Ryan, however, describes women in Utica as allowing their Female Missionary Society, active in the 1820s, to be absorbed into the male society, while they went on to form a Maternal Association, while in contrast, the unmarried Richards went on to missionize actively. See also Welter, "She Hath Done What She Could," 111.

71. Katz, *Gay American History*; Garber, *Vested Interests*, 16–17; Wheelwright, *Amazons and Military Maids*, 76–77, 132–135; Jelinek, "Disguise Autobiographies," 53–62; De Pauw, "Women in Combat," 209–226. In Europe, a stronger tradition of cross-dressing had once existed: "Little remained in nineteenth-century Holland of what had been a flourishing tradition of female cross-dressing in the seventeenth and eighteenth centuries." Dekker and van de Pol, *The Tradition of Female Transvestism*, 99, which also makes note of "119 cases of female cross-dressing [in the Netherlands] between 1550 and 1839."

72. Garber, *Vested Interests*, 16, 17.

73. Alfred Fabian Young points out that Samson was the spelling used by her father as well as by Deborah when she signed her name in the minutes of a Baptist church in 1780. I want to thank Young for allowing me to read his work on Deborah Samson in manuscript form, and for providing me with much information on her life. See Young, *Masquerade: The Life and Time of Deborah Sampson Gannett, Continental Soldier* (New York, forthcoming).

74. Mann, *The Female Review*; Mann, *The Female Review*, ed. Vinton, 134. See also Jelinek, "Disguise Autobiographies," 53–62; De Pauw, "Women in Combat," 209–276; Gannet, *An Address*.

75. April 15–17, 1775. Mann, *The Female Review*, ed. Vinton, 79 n. 16.

76. Cooper, *An Illustrated Encyclopedia of Traditional Symbols*, 124, 148; Olderr, *Symbolism*, 119; *The Universal Dream-Dictionary*, 11, 14, 16, 95, 111, 185, 188, 191. Shaker Rebecca Jackson saw the serpent's head as emblematic of lust. Jackson, *Gifts of Power*, 284. Among the New York Public Library holdings of Shaker drawings is one titled "Cutting the Serpents." Young points out that the culture recognized the snake as having political significance, while chopped-up snakes could symbolize disunity or the dismantling of an enemy as well.

77. Mann, *The Female Review*, 79–84, emphasis added. This dream is discussed in Freeman and Bond, *America's First Woman Warrior*, 163–177. On the phrase "gird yourself," see discussion of Job 38:3 in regard to Elizabeth, note 79.

78. In a Freudian reading of the dream, Freeman and Bond have interpreted this "gelly" as betokening semen. Freeman and Bond, *America's First Woman Warrior*, 175. Hannah Heaton also dreamed of a snake, which she believed to represent Satan, and of a bull, both of which came to her door. She interpreted these figures to mean that "trouble is acoming." Heaton, "Experiences or Spiritual Exercises," 10–11, 200. See also Lacey, "The World of Hannah Heaton," 280–304. The Reverend Joseph Travis reported dreaming of a bull that he overcame without bloodshed: "I dreamed one night that a huge and raging bull made at me at my church door, forbidding my entrance. I thought that many were standing around me, and rather carelessly looking on. I thought I cried for help, but not a soul would come to my assistance. I at length exclaimed, 'In the name of God, I seize you!" I caught hold on his horns, and twisted his neck entirely round, at which he ran from me, and apparently crept under the church. I greatly rejoiced at the victory I had obtained. The dream impressed me, and I verily thought it ominous of success." Travis, *Autobiography*, 54.

79. Elizabeth, *Memoir*, 9. Job 38:3 reads, "Gird up thy loins like a man; for I will demand of thee, and answer thou me." This is likely to have been the Bible reading Elizabeth referred to, and also accounts for Deborah Samson's use of the word gird. Elizabeth's life is discussed in Humez, " 'My Spirit Eye,' " 129–143.

80. Mann, *The Female Review*, ed. Vinton, 190–193, 213–215.

81. See Shy, *Winding Down*.

82. Fausto-Sterling, "The Five Sexes." 20–24.

83. Ellis, February 4, 1837, cited in Mann, *The Female Review*, ed. Vinton, xxxii.

84. Bowen, *The Female Marine*, 26, 27. This work was printed some twenty-one times between 1815 and 1818, with varying titles and with additions and deletions, and was variously attributed to Bowen, Baker, or Brewer. A pamphlet was published, ostensibly by the madam the author worked for, alleging that the true name of the author was Eliza Webb. A fictive response to Baker was also published: Sperry, *A Brief Reply*. For the most complete rendition of all the *Female Marine* texts available, based primarily on a "10th ed." of 1816 with interpolations from others, and with an excellent introduction as well as related documentation (including the Sperry pamphlet), see Cohen, *The Female Marine*. Cohen is convinced that these were works of fiction, and were probably written for the publisher Nathaniel Coverly Jr. by Nathaniel Hill Wright, a man in his employ. See also Medlicott, "The Legend of Lucy Brewer," 461–473; Medlicott's research established that this was a work of fiction. The name Brewer is used in this text.

85. It is estimated that there were two thousand prostitutes in Boston in 1820. See Pease and Pease, *Ladies, Women and Wenches*, 148–159.

86. Prince, *A Narrative*, 9. One Boston brothel, just possibly the one in which Prince worked, was run by Maria Williams, who was "a 'very black' madam, [who] was convicted for 'entertain[ing] white gentry' in her establishment." Pease and Pease, *Ladies, Women and Wenches*, 151.

87. Webb [Brewer], *The Female Marine*, 29, 37, 45, 53.

88. Ibid., 54. Pease and Pease, *Ladies, Women and Wenches*, 150, 151.

89. Webb [Brewer], *The Female Marine*, 37, emphasis added.

90. Siddons, *The Female Warrior*, 6–7.

91. Paul, *The Surprising Adventures*, 14. Cohen suggests that the narrative of Almira Paul, also published by Nathaniel Coverly Jr., is "probably fictional." Cohen, *The Female Marine*, 34, n.27. Stephens, *The Cabin Boy Wife*, 8. The men's clothes that women wore were apparently considered tainted by men and rejected by them afterward.

92. Cole [Hanson], *The Life and Sufferings*, 23, 27, 29.

93. Paul, *The Surprising Adventures*, 13, 18.

94. K. White, *A Narrative*, 62–63, 22–25.

95. Ibid., 54, 57, 69, 79, 101–102, 109.

96. Ibid., 118. White, who had been jailed because of her husband's debts, located him in Canada where he was living with another women. She demanded money from him but did not want him to return.

CODA

The saying used for this chapter title is quoted by the poet William Butler Yeats in his 1914 volume titled *Responsibilities*, where it is attributed to " 'an Old Play.' " It is cited by the poet Delmore Schwartz, who altered the phrase and its meaning when he used it as the title of a wonderful story (and of the volume in which it was published: "In Dreams Begin Responsibilities." Schwartz, *In Dreams*, 11, 172 n. 1. See also Hartmann, *Dreams and Nightmares*, 248.

1. Banneker, 1731–1806. The dream can be found in Banneker's Almanac, jottings, facing February 1797, 61; reprinted in Bedini, *The Life of Benjamin Banneker*, 333. Spelling and date as in manuscript. See also Hurry, "An Archeological and Historical Perspective on Benjamin Banneker," 361–369.

2. Vernal also means spring-like, youthful, or fresh.

3. *Webster's New International Dictionary* (1945), 2042. In this dream context *quincunx* could also have betokened an African cosmogram, with its four points, and the fifth at the center or on the cross made by the lines joining the other points providing a place for a Christ-like spirit figure, the man Banneker journeyed three days to consult. The three may well suggest a traditional African spirit journey as well as the tripartite nature of the Christian God. This interpretation is not outside the realm of early modern thought. In 1658 Thomas Browne published *The Garden of Cyrus*, a book about the ubiquitous quincunx in every area of matter; near the close of his book Browne even links the quincunx with dreams. Banneker might have read this work, which includes the suggestion that nine points in three rows can signify "the Greek *chi* standing for Christ." See Huntley, "*The Garden*

of Cyrus As Prophecy," 141. For a description of a three-day spirit journey, based on a common African tradition, see Almeida, *Capoeira*, 133–140. I want to thank Maya Talmon Chveiser for bringing this reference to my attention.

4. Hyatt, *Hoodoo–Conjuration–Witchcraft–Rootwork*, 5:facing page 1; 4:3314–3315, 3332.

5. This report was reprinted in other papers, and as no copy of the Georgetown paper is extant, is cited by Bedini, *The Life of Benjamin Banneker*, 122, from a copy of *The Maryland Gazette*, March 18, 1791, indicating further the celebrity Banneker was attaining. See Bedini, "The Survey of the Federal Territory," 76–95, 137–128.

Eugene Leach, of Trinity College, Connecticut, in a response to a talk in which I analyzed Banneker's dream (February 1999), suggested that Banneker may well have seen his surveying of Washington as creating a quincunx: he marked the four corners and placed a marker for the Capitol at the center.

6. Benjamin Banneker to Thomas Jefferson, August 19, 1791; reply by Thomas Jefferson to Benjamin Banneker, August 30, 1791. These two letters were reprinted in Banneker's Almanac for 1793. See also Jefferson's letter to the Marquis de Condorcet, August 31, 1791, and Jefferson's letter to Joel Barlow of 1809, which openly acknowledges that Jefferson suspected one of the Ellicotts helped him in his writing and comments that Banneker's letter "shows him to have had a mind of very common stature indeed." This correspondence is reprinted in Kaplan, *The Black Presence*, 118–123.

7. Bedini, *The Life of Benjamin Banneker*, 122, 237, 267. Bedini emphasizes the roles played by Banneker's grandmother and mother.

8. Banneker, "A Remarkable Dream, 10th Mo. 1762," which is taken from "a four-page manuscript written in Banneker's hand but unsigned," and published in the appendix of ibid., 330–333. Banneker's other recorded dream reports deal with an encounter with the devil (December 13, 1797); setting a deer at liberty but wounding it in the process (December 25, 1797); and acting as a healer and comforter for a wounded child (April 24, 1802). All are extant in Banneker's handwriting written in his manuscript of almanac calculations, and reprinted in Bedini. Bedini regarded all Banneker's dream reports as "fantasies" or attempts to write "essays" and did not take them seriously. See ibid., 267–268, 334–335.

9. Byrd often saw herself as a Jacob: treacherously dealing with her brother but pleading for mercy and rewarded by hearing the voice of God. A. Byrd, *Narratives*, 69-74, 75, 77.

10. Ibid., 68. On white women's reform work in the 1830s see below, note 93.

11. Mack, *A Narrative*, 3–4. Mack was the maternal grandfather of Joseph Smith Jr., the founder of the Mormon faith, who relied on dreams and visions, as had his grandfather, and who fulfilled his grandfather's dreams of proving himself worthy of approbation. See Brooke, *The Refiner's Fire*, 79–81, 83–86, 150.

12. Kett, *Rites of Passage*; Kett, "The Stages of Life," 166–191. Franklin, who went to school for less than two years, began to teach himself additional languages when he was past forty.

13. Graff, considering 250 individuals in this same period, has drawn a table of average ages when key events occurred, but his many-storied account indicates that individuals varied widely. Graff analyzes lives in three streams, which he terms "traditional paths," "transitional paths," and "emergent paths." See Graff, *Conflicting Paths*, 350.

14. Notwithstanding the randomness of life events, prior to the modern era some people believed that life was divided into periods of seven or nine years, in each of which a different aspect of development was preordained. While rarely referred to in the course of retelling a life, a few narrators revealed their continued acceptance of this belief when they thought about the last period of their lives or what was supposed to be the "grand climacteric" of seven times nine or sixty-three years of age, after which they expected to decline precipitously. In 1760, Susanna Anthony was convinced that she had undergone a particular spiritual development in each nine-year period of her life: "in the first Nine she trusted she was brot Home to god—the second call'd to conflict with violent temptations—the 3rd with some sickness and weakness of body in all which she Had been [bound] and brought to triumph over Satan and Death the king of terrors and ever since she has entered Her fourth Nine Her conflicts Has been with the world." Sarah Osborn, describing Anthony's beliefs in an undated letter to the Reverend Mr. Fish, in the manuscript collection of Sarah Osborn's letters, American Antiquarian Society. Anthony died in 1791 in her sixty-fifth year, shortly after her "grand climacteric." Many more people seem to have accepted that life was divided into four periods, which may have been based on a combination of seven-year periods. John Demos suggests that the first period of childhood was then regarded as lasting from birth to about age seven, followed by youth from about age seven to about age thirty (which equaled approximately the next three seven-year periods). These periods also bore some relationship to physiological growth, as both menarche and full growth were reached later in the eighteenth century than they are at present (at about fifteen to sixteen, and perhaps twenty-one to twenty-five, respectively). Adulthood (after thirty) and old age (after sixty) completed the categorization of life following youth. Demos, "Historical Treatment of the Age Group," 74. Kamen, "Changing Perceptions of the Life Cycle in American Thought and Culture," in *Selvages and Biases*, 180–221.

15. Over the course of the modern period (before the plague of AIDS), death "almost disappeared from early and middle adulthood" and tended "to strike in old age only." Kohli, "The World We Forgot," 278. See Aries, *Death in America*; Wells, *Revolutions in Americans' Lives*, 29–31, 94, 126–127; Imhof, "Life-Course Patterns of Women and Their Husbands," 247–270.

16. T. Smith, *Experience*, 9–14. See also G. Brown, *Recollections*, 46.

17. T. Smith, *Experience*, 17, 22.

18. Anthony to Osborn, n.d., in Osborn, *Familiar Letters*, 13. Rubin regards both Anthony and Osborn as suffering from "evangelical anorexia Nervosa." Rubin, *Religious Melancholy*, 110–118.

19. Joshua Evans, born in West Jersey in 1731, had a vision of "the glory of the Lord" when he was very young. Evans, *Joshua Evans's Journal*, 5. Joseph Lathrop was eight when he was "much aroused" by a revival in Norwich, Connecticut. J. Lathrop, *Sermons*, xiii. Isaac Martin believed that the Lord had "visited him frequently" when he was nine. I. Martin, *Journal*, 4. William Keith early dreamed of being saved from the fires of hell by a "form" who "was like the Son of God," and when he was between the ages of eight and ten (1774–1776), he felt God to be "all around me." Keith, *The Experience*, 6, 7. Mary Marshall, of Northumberland, New Hampshire, was "brought to serious reflections on a future state" at the age of nine in 1789. Marshall, "The Life and Suffering," 156. Abner Jones, living on the Vermont frontier, prayed in secret when eight or nine (1780–1781) and had an awakening. Jones, *Memoirs*, 11–13. Elizabeth, an enslaved child, felt an "overshadowing of the Lord's spirit" when she was about five (in 1771). Elizabeth, *Memoir*, 3. James Jenkins was ten when he "received my first religious impressions." Jenkins, *The Experience*, 9. Freeborn Garrettson was nine when the deaths of his mother, sister, and several "servants" led to a conversion. Garrettson, *The Experience*, 10–11. For two conversions (and dreams) see also Comstock, *A Short History*, 5, 16. At least twenty-three of those in this study reported very early conversions.

20. "I was fond of pleasure and loved this world more than God. . . . I was careless and carnal." Comstock, *A Short History*, 13.

21. Gates, *The Trials*, 6,7,30. The same pattern can be found in the lives of Garrettson, Sherman, and many others in this study.

22. Leland, *The Writings*, 10. Leland heard this voice when he was eighteen, in 1772. Auditory experiences in dreams or visions occurred to at least seven other narrators in this study: Asher, *Incidents*, 52; A. Byrd, *Narratives*, 74; Collins, *Memoirs*, 29; Duncan, *Extraordinary Conversion*, 14; Gano, *Biographical Memoirs*, 31; Garrettson, *The Experience*, 27; and Shaw, *A Narrative*, 130.

23. Leland played a role in developing opposition to slavery, as did Gates, although neither man wrote of these accomplishments in his narrative. Gates, like many of the others, changed his class standing while changing his life.

24. Judge, *Memoirs*.

25. Sherman, *The Narrative*, 8, 11. See also Richards, *Memoirs*, 21.

26. Sobel, *Trabelin' On*, 13, 110. 142. 232, 389 n. 13.

27. Shakers took the opposite position, regarding sexually segregated dancing as proper preparation for religious ecstasy.

28. Ashbridge, *Some Account*.

29. On broken banjos see Lomax, *Folk Songs*, 328.

30. Jenkins, *The Experience*, 9,10, 20, 58, 61, 62, 66. See the account of Richardson, a Quaker on a mission to America in 1700, who was often in tears and whose congregation often joined him in crying. On one occasion

one woman's clothes and the floor around her were reported to have been thoroughly wet. J. Richardson, *An Account*, 82, 91–93. Leland saw his public crying as the source of his spiritual growth. Leland, *Some Events*, 20. Richards, *Memoirs*, 24–25, 51. On the history of emotion see Stearns and Lewis, *An Emotional History*, 33–108.

31. Royster refers to the arguments against crying presented by a soldier going to attend the funeral of Faith Huntington, his officer's wife, November 28, 1775. This soldier and three compatriots "debated . . . [crying] at great length." Royster also records the fact that George Washington cried at parting from his officers at war's end, but Washington was from an earlier generation. Royster, *A Revolutionary People at War*, 58, 353. On crying at Scottish revivals, both in the Old World and the New, see Schmidt, *Holy Fairs*, 55, 78–79, 138, 144–145, 162, 216.

32. John 3:3–7.

33. Richards, *Memoirs*, 29, 128.

34. Coleman, *Memoirs*; Eleazar Sherman recounted that he was converted on January 10, 1815, at eight in the evening. Sherman, *The Narrative*, 15. Elam Potter recorded his conversion in 1764 in *Author's Account of His Conversion*, 8; James Jenkins recorded his conversion of February 2, 1790, in *The Experience*, 42. John Wesley had an experience of rebirth on May 24, 1738, after his work in Georgia. Before that, he had not believed it was possible. Wesley, *The Works*, 1:103. See Sobel, *Trabelin' On*, 93–95.

35. Coleman, *Memoirs*, 43.

36. Hume, *An Exhortation*, 76.

37. Hamilton, *A Narrative*.

38. Leland, *Some Events*, 21.

39. It was on this occasion in 1788 that his wife, Sally Devin Leland, protected him, "like a female angel." Leland, *Some Events*, 27.

40. Jenkins, *The Experience*, 39, 232.

41. Sometimes an individual desired to make a break with family but found it hard to act. Mary Mitchel, born to a Baptist minister and his wife in Newport, Rhode Island, in 1731, was sixteen when her father died. She was put out to a Quaker family, and at the age of twenty decided she wanted to join their Society, but her mother strongly objected and she did not act. It was not until a decade later, when she was thirty, that a visionary experience enabled her to make the move she had so long desired. Mitchel, *A Short Account*, 26.

42. In 1741 Sarah Osborn and Susana Anthony were founders of a long-lived women's society that played a very significant role in the lives of a large number of Newport, Rhode Island, women. This closed and secretive group made judgments and punished members as well as supporting them; demanded abstinence and encouraged fasting and lengthy prayer sessions. See Osborn, *Memoirs*, 70–74. In Seth Coleman's case, the secret society he joined when he went to Yale apparently helped him break his attachment to his family and arrive at new goals in life. He left Yale with a determination to become a physician, went on to study with a Dr. Hubbard at New Haven, and then set up his own practice in Amherst, Massachusetts. Coleman, *Memoir*, 47–48. Joseph Croswell (born 1715) was also a member of a New England

religious group "connected by solemn covenant" that prayed for each other every Saturday night, together or apart. They fasted twice a week, prayed seven times daily, and each member was enjoined to examine his heart nightly. Croswell, *Sketches of the Life*, 9, 11, 12. Secret societies of women in Philadelphia and Boston and Newport are discussed in Kujawa, "Religion, Education and Gender in Eighteenth Century Rhode Island," 117–120.

43. M. Fisher, "Lott Carey"; Poe, "Lott Carey," 49–61.

44. See Sobel, *The World They Made Together*, 171–178.

45. See the very lengthy description of a deathbed scene and shout appended to G. White, *A Brief Account*, 40–53. Jenkins provides many examples of whites, including himself, learning to shout. Jenkins, *The Experience*, 44, 50, 184, 205.

46. Eldridge, *Memoirs*, 21. The narratives provide many other examples of early home leaving: Samuel Godfrey was a cabin boy at age nine, and James M'Lean went to sea at ten. Richard Lee began to work at age five, and William Gross was put out by age eight.

47. In addition to the Patriotic Ladies at Edenton, North Carolina, and the organization of women in Philadelphia, see information on forty-six spinning meetings held in New England between 1768 and 1769, in Ulrich, " 'Daughters of Liberty,' " 216–217. For a consideration of the seven thousand men who were elected to local committees see Ammerman, *In the Common Cause*; Conroy, "Development of a Revolutionary Organization," 223–230; Starr, "Political Mobilization, 1765–1776," 231–239; Meier, *From Resistance to Revolution*; Norton, *Liberty's Daughters*, 166–169.

48. Royster, *A Revolutionary People*, 145, 352. See also Nash, *Social Change*.

49. Eldridge's narrative was prepared for publication by a group of white women, who appended songs and stories of their own writing at the end. The poetry is from a poem entitled "The Supplication of Elleanor" written by F.H.W., who was apparently Frances Harriet Whipple. Eldridge, *Memoirs*, 119. Whipple's full name appears as a supporter in a revised edition, *Elleanor's Second Book*.

Not all first home leavings were accomplished in childhood. African American John Malvin (born 1795), son of a free woman and an enslaved man, lived with his parents on a plantation until he was thirty-two. Then, "[i]n the year 1827, a spirit of adventure, natural to most young men, took possession of me, and I concluded to leave Virginia and go to Ohio." In a later period, a man of thirty-two would not have described himself as a "young man" nor would his act have been seen as "natural." Trained as a carpenter, Malvin was able to support himself from the time he left home. Settling in Cleveland Ohio, he integrated the Baptist church there; played an important role in the Underground Railroad; and was instrumental in establishing a haven for ex-slaves in Wilberforce, Canada. His home leaving separated the time that he had spent living much like a slave from his free life, and it marked the beginning of his creative and important community role. It became a significant event in view of the life he later lived, and in the autobiography that he later wrote. Malvin, *Autobiography*.

50. Prince, *A Narrative*, 5.

51. Anderson, *Life*, 5. William John Anderson memorialized his father by retaining his name, John Anderson, in his own.

52. Asher, *Incidents in the Life*, 5.

53. Clarke and Clarke, *Narratives*.

54. Marshall, "Life and Suffering," 155–156; E. Thomas, *Reminiscences*, 5; memorial to Sally Leland in Leland, *Some Events*, 43. See also Wilmer, *Memoirs*, 12.

55. Anthony, in Osborn and Anthony, *Familiar Letters*, 17, 45, 135; Marshall, "Life and Suffering," 155–156; Hopkins, *Sketches*, 78; J. Thomas, *The Life*, 3; R. Lee, *A Short Narrative*, 12, 21. The traumas of the war remained a significant part of many people's lives long afterward. Elijah Brown was a Philadelphia Quaker imprisoned and sent to Virginia for eight months (September to April 1778) when he refused to "affirm" his allegiance to Revolutionary Pennsylvania. Charles Brockden Brown, Elijah's son, spent that same period in what he remembered as a nighttime nightmare jail. Many years later, when he was writing gothic tales of dreams, nightmares, and murders, Brown wrote to a friend describing his childhood torment:

> Suppose . . . I should tell you, that when eleven or twelve years of age I spent twelve hours in each day, that is, that I passed the night, for 8 months together in *Jail*. In an apartment in which my chambers were hourly awoken by the clanking of chains and iron doors. Where my ears were continually assailed by blasphemies and obscenities. Where there was a continual suspicion of Inhabitants, of various and opposite characters, associated by Calamity. Wouldst thou place any credit in the narrative! I assure thee, my friend it is literally true.

Brown to Joseph Bringhurst, n.d., cited by Kafer, "Charles Brockden Brown and Revolutionary Philadelphia," 486.

56. Families, for example those of Franklin and Garrettson, were separated by opposite loyalties of family members. Abner Sanger, a man "of low and poor make" who was a "war resister," has left us important evidence of how this worked out in his little remarked life. See the diary of Sanger, *Very Poor and of a Lo Make*. See also Calhoon, "Loyalism and Neutrality," 247–259.

Hugh Simm, (1737–1810), a Scottish teacher in America at the time of the war, became a Loyalist and a quartermaster in the Loyal American Regiment. Writing to his brother in Scotland to tell him of the death of his second child soon after birth, he quotes his wife as saying: "The Calamities of War and public Distresses are at present So great that we Women may truly say blessed is the Womb that beareth not and the Papes which give no suck." Reprinted in DeWolfe, *Discoveries of America*, 148.

57. Gregg, *Self-Representation*, 5.

58. Woolman's personal taboos on tea and sugar (because they were products of slavery) were symbolically complicated. They were personally chosen limits that directed his energies, but at the same time, both the food and clothing practices suggest his cravings for these items. By controlling his own body, Woolman sought to control the social system. See Gregg, *Self-Representation*, 91.

59. Gregg reminds us that we have to concern ourselves with the binary structure in the self of every individual, not only in pathological or tragic personalities. "The other is a discourse of the self." Ibid., 161, 30.

60. See Fliegelman, *Prodigals and Pilgrims.*

61. "[T]he net effect of [the Revolutionary] war was a sharp decline in individual income. . . . Revolutions carried a high price. Recovery, furthermore, was painfully slow." The per capita income levels of 1770 were not equaled until after 1800. McCusker and Menard, *The Economy of British America*, 366–367, 373–374. For cautious agreement with this assessment, see Price, "Reflections on the Economy of Revolutionary America," 320. On deaths in the Revolutionary War see Peckham, *The Toll of Independence.* On the closing of the courts in Virginia during the Revolution, see Martin, *Modern Gratitude*, 150.

62. Haskell, "Giambattista Vico and the Discovery of Metaphoric Cognition," 69.

63. Carter, *The Diary of Colonel Landon Carter*, 750–751, April 17, 1773; Andrews, *Memoir of Mrs. Ann R. Page*, 88; Anthony, *The Life*, 91, 93; Ashbridge, *Some Account*, 15; Heaton, "Experiences or Spiritual Exercises," 19; Jackson, *Gifts of Power*, 71–72. J. Still, *Early Recollections*, 66. Christian Newcomer repeatedly dreamed of thunder heralding "the last day of judgment." Newcomer, *The Life*, 4. Dorothy Arew, sick and troubled with feelings of guilt, heard thunder and reportedly said that "the Devil cald for her." Deposition of Mary Ayres, August 18, 1681, Accomack County, Virginia, Wills, Deed and Orders, 1678–1682, 258. (I am indebted to Douglas Deal for this reference.) See the picture by Charles Deas, "The Devil and Tom Walker" (1838), discussed in chapter 1, which pictures lightning (and thunder) when the devil appeared.

64. Abbott, *The Experience*, 117–118.

65. Franklin, *The Autobiography*, 150–155, 159.

66. Franklin, *Experiments and Observations on Electricity*. See Campbell, *Recovering Ben Franklin*, 153; Mitchell, "The Politics of Experiment in the Eighteenth Century," 307–332; Thomas, *Religion*, 78–112.

67. Hathaway, *The Narrative*, 15, 20, 22, 34. Moses W. Keene, who killed his wife in a "dream-like" fit, was very unusual in that just before his execution he openly expressed his doubts that a human being "hath any spirit." Keene, *The Life*, 18.

68. Duncan, *Extraordinary Conversion*, 15. Abner Jones (born 1772), Thomas Smith (born 1776), James Pearse (born 1786), and Eleazer Sherman (born 1795) gave up their concerns with economic success, all accepting that such a path had led them to immorality. Herman Rosencrantz (born 1716), a convicted counterfeiter, was a rare criminal in this period in that he saw himself as originally having been a moral man. (Almost every other criminal who left a narrative wrote that he believed he had been born with evil inclinations.) Although Rosencrantz noted that he had suffered economic setbacks and could not support his family, he attributed his evil behavior to a lust for money that he had not given up in time. He confessed and accepted responsibility for his actions. He was executed in Philadelphia in May of

1770. See Jones, *Memoirs*; Pearse, *A Narrative*; T. Smith, *Experience*; Sherman, *The Narrative*; Rosencrantz, *The Life*. See also How, *Life and Confession*; Quinby, *A Short History*.

69. James Yonge (1647–1721) reached his grand climacteric (6 x 9) in 1709. His wife had died the previous year, while his daughter and "only grandson" as well as three friends of over twenty years standing all died in 1709. Yonge himself was quite ill that year and stopped keeping his journal, as though he had died spiritually. He noted that he "[n]ever after could recover from that heaviness of heart which this sickness and the great troubles which befell me so thick this year occasioned." Yonge, *The Journal*, 229.

70. "As late as 1850, life expectancy at birth for most white Americans probably was between forty and forty-five years, much the same as in the late eighteenth century. Black Americans could expect to live eight to ten years less on average." Wells, *Revolutions in Americans' Lives*, 126. See Aries, *Western Attitudes Toward Death*; Stannard, *Death in America*.

71. Wells, *Revolutions in Americans' Lives*, 44, 92. For a discussion of theories that explain this change, see Wells, *Uncle Sam's Family*, 28–56.

72. Calvert, *Children in the House*; Mintz and Kellogg, *Domestic Revolutions*, 17–21. For reference to a pure and perfect infant who should be kept from the evil in the world, see Park, *Diary*.

73. Child, *Isaac T. Hopper*, 3–26. See also, Hopper, *Kidnappers in Philadelphia*.

74. Dayton, *Women Before the Bar*, 62, 226 n136. Cott, "Passionlessness," 162–181; D'Emilio and Freedman, *A History of Sexuality*, 39–54. See also Kerber, *Women of the Republic*.

75. See Gillis, "From Ritual to Romance," 87–121.

76. See Lewis, "Happiness," and Marienstras, "Liberty."

77. See these documents in Bruns, *Am I Not a Man*, 428, 452. See Genovese, *From Rebellion to Revolution*.

78. Sedgewick [or Sedgwick], "Slavery in New England," 421. Sedgwick spelled the name variously as Maumbet, Mumbet, and Mom-Bett, suggesting it was a contraction of Mother Betty or Elizabeth.

79. Elizabeth Freeman, cited by Sedgwick in her "Journal" entry of November 29, 1829, *The Power of Her Sympathy*, 125.

80. The August 1781 "Mumbet Case" against John Ashley of Sheffield, Massachusetts, is reprinted in Bruns, *Am I Not a Man*, 468–470. See Zilversmit, "Quok Walker, Mumbet, and the Abolition of Slavery in Massachusetts," 614–624; Sedgwick, "Slavery in New England," 417–424; Wood, " 'Liberty Is Sweet,' " 149–184; and Kaplan, *The Black Presence*, 217.

81. On the slave owners' names she took with her out of slavery, and her life, see Painter, *Sojourner Truth*; Painter, "Representing Truth," 461–492; Washington, " 'Where the Spirit of the Lord Is, There is Liberty' "; Truth, *Narrative of Sojourner Truth*, ed. Washington, 118: Stowe, "Sojourner Truth, the Libyan Sibyl," 473. On her Zion Hill experiences see Johnson and Wilentz, *The Kingdom of Matthais*. On the hate and love of whites, see Truth in Loewenberg and Bogen, *Black Women*, 240, 241.

82. Douglass, "What I Found at the Northampton Association," in *Narrative of Sojourner Truth*, ed. Washington, xi.

83. Tubman, in Drew, *The Refugee*, 20. See also Bradford, *Scenes in the Life*; Quarles, "Harriet Tubman's Unlikely Leadership," 43–57.

84. For additional dreams of flying see Grandy, *Narrative*, 25; Elizabeth, *Memoir*, 8; and Jackson, *Gifts of Power*, 224, 235. While dreams of flying were far more common among African Americans than among whites, a dream report of white Thomas Smith, born in Maryland in 1776, had a mixture of African flying and the Christian heaven:

> One night I dreamed I was standing in an open space, and saw a white dove hovering over my head, and then lighting by my side. It said to me, 'The end of all things is at hand, and I have come for you;' then rising, it caught me by the shoulder, and mounted through the trackless air with the speed of an arrow. We passed the starry heavens, above which was, as it were, the brightness of many suns. I waved my hand, and cried, 'Glory!' and when I expected to have entered into heaven, I found my conductor descending to the earth, where, placing me upon my feet, he said, 'You cannot go to heaven now; the Lord has work for you to do;' and then vanished out of my sight.

Smith, while skeptical of dreams as calls to the ministry, fasted for three days, also a significant African number, and became a Methodist preacher. T. Smith, *Experience*, 17–18. Another white person who experienced a dream of flying, including flying over land, was Chloe Willey, of Goshen, New Hampshire, who had a series of dreams in 1788 in which a guide brought her to heaven and hell, after which "I thought I went with him through the air, where I saw all the land, and had a view of the situation of the churches." Willey, *A Short Account*, 23. Flying dreams are also discussed in chapter 5 of this book. See Reynolds, "Dreams and the Constitution of the Self among the ZeZeru," 22; and Shaw, "Dreaming as Accomplishment," 45. Seligman maintained that many cultures, worldwide, share the view that "dreams of flying mean success." Seligman, "Appendix to Chapter XXI," 41.

85. See Walters, " 'One of dese mornings,' " 3–30, for a discussion of the long tradition of African and diasporic tales of flying. Walters surveys the twenty-seven flying tales in the WPA Georgia Writers' Project *Drums and Shadows* and other folklore, as well as in the literary works of Toni Morrison and Paule Marshall. A little-known tale by Ralph Ellison involves black flying (in planes as well as in spirit) and the little me. See Ellison, "Flying Home," 277–299.

86. Bradford, *Harriet Tubman*, 113–114, spelling corrected. See also Conrad, *Harriet Tubman*. Tubman had certainly hated her owner, had prayed for his death, and believed that her prayers were instrumental in bringing it about. See Humez, "In Search of Harriet Tubman's Spiritual Autobiography," 175. Humez presents a very important analysis of the difficulties in and the value of using "mediated" narratives in which the writer and the narrator both participated. See also Humez, "Reading *The Narrative of Sojourner Truth* as a Collaborative Text," 29–52.

87. Bradford, *Scenes in the Life*, 26, 31–32,56, 79–80, 82–83, 114–115.

88. Tubman "laid great stress on a dream she had just before she met Captain [John] Brown in Canada. She thought she was in 'a wilderness sort of place, all full of rocks, and bushes,' when she saw a serpent raise its head among the rocks, and as it did so, it became the head of an old man with a long white beard, gazing at her, 'wishful like, jes as if he war gwine to speak to me,' and then two other heads rose up beside him, younger than he,—and as she stood looking at them, and wondering what they could want with her, a great crowd of men rushed in and struck down the younger heads, and then the head of the old man, still looking at her so 'wishful.' This dream she had again and again, and could not interpret it; but when she met Captain Brown, shortly after, behold, he was the very image of the head she had seen. But still she could not make out what her dream signified, till the news came to her of the tragedy at Harper's Ferry, and then she knew the two other heads were his sons." Memoir of an interview with Harriet Tubman, by Franklin Sanborn, 1863, in Bradford, *Harriet Tubman*, 118–119. John Brown had asked Tubman to join him in his attempt to begin a massive slave revolt in Harper's Ferry, Virginia, and she had intended to go with him, but was ill when he went South. Tubman ostensibly "venerated" Brown, but this dream, with its unthought known graphically portraying their failure, suggests a more negative judgment of aspects of the Browns (as snakes) and may have subconsciously brought about her illness and protected her from taking part in what she apparently believed to be a futile rebellion that would lead to death. When she herself had made plans to go South, both before and after Brown's attempt, psychic illnesses did not hold her back. She had other empowering dreams that helped her with these journeys, which fulfilled her commitment to help her people flee for their lives.

While it is widely reported that Tubman was ill when Brown went to Harper's Ferry, Earl Conrad claims that she was determined to join him and had gone to New York City when she learned of his failure. Conrad, *Harriet Tubman*, 28.

89. Stewart, *Religion and the Pure Principles Of Morality*, 38, emphasis added. Yee, *Black Women Abolitionists*, 115–16. While black women in the South were rarely cited as leaders of rebellions, two black women preachers were among the leaders of a conspiracy in St. Bartholomew parish in 1776. See Frey, *Water from the Rock*, 61–62. Others led slaves from bondage, and quite a few were known for their physical strength and fighting abilities. Sylvia Dubois "became famed for her feats of strength and for the prizefights in which she engaged," clearly breaking white gender boundaries. " "Obituary," in Larison, *Sylvia Dubois*, following page 117.

90. Osborn, *Memoirs*, 20; Elizabeth, *Memoir*, 14; Willey, *A Short Account*, 15, 17; A. Byrd, *Narratives*, 37–38, 77; Jackson, *Gifts of Power*, 183.

91. For a discussion of the idea of female "masculinity of mind" in the antebellum period see Matthews, "Consciousness of Self and Consciousness of Sex in Antebellum Feminism," 61–78.

92. Larison, *Sylvia Dubois*, 69.

93. The crusade of the New York Female Moral Reform Society that began in the 1830s expressed women's anger at men and tried to put women in control of men's sexual behavior, while the female temperance movement

attempted to put women in control of men's drinking. Smith-Rosenberg, *Disorderly Conduct*, 110.

94. See Chambers-Schiller, *Liberty, A Better Husband*. For a far more sanguine view of female development see Gillespie, " 'The Clear Leadings of Providence,' " 219.

95. See Brekus, *Strangers and Pilgrims*.

96. See Cogan, *All-American Girl*.

97. As Nina Baym has noted, the fictive autobiographies of women written by women in the 1790s, such as Susanna Rowson's *Charlotte Temple* (1794) and Hannah Foster's *The Coquette* (1797), depicted pampered women "as man's inevitable dupe and prey." While white male novelists by and large continued to script passive women (although the presumed male author of *The Female Marine* was an important exception), by the 1820s women writers, in strong contrast, were picturing young women who overcame terrible injustices by means of their own character development. Baym, *Woman's Fiction*, 17, 19, 35, 61.

98. Sedgwick, *A New England Tale*, 83.

99. Morris, *Private Journal*, 36, May 26, 1777. Morris had previously coped with English soldiers invading her house and threatening to burn it. See the rich analysis of the personal change she underwent in Riordan, "Identity and Revolution," 77.

100. Sedgwick does provide Jane Elton with a personal motive for conversion as well: the man she decides to marry is a Quaker. However, Sedgwick makes it clear that Elton was convinced of the superiority of the Quaker way to that of the Congregationalists, who are painted as two-faced and un-Christian. Sedgwick, *A New England Tale*, 162.

101. Sedgwick, describing the unmarried heroine of her last novel, *Married or Single?*, 1:vi.

102. Sedgwick, in describing her own origins to her young niece, to whom she addressed her private autobiography, wrote:

> I believe, my dear Alice, that the people who surround us in our childhood, whose atmosphere infolds us, as it were, have more to do with the formation of our characters than all our didactic and preceptive education. Mumbet had a clear and nice perception of justice, and a stern love of it, an uncompromising honesty in word and deed, and conduct of high intelligence, that made her the unconscious moral teacher of the children she tenderly nursed. . . .
>
> . . . Truth was her nature—the offspring of courage—truth and loyalty. In my childhood I clung to her with instinctive love and faith, and the more I know and observe of human nature, the higher does she rise above others, whatever may have been their instruction or accomplishment. In her the image of her Maker was cast in material so hard and pure that circumstances could not alter its outline or cloud its lustre.
>
> Sedgwick, *The Power of Her Sympathy*, 69–70.

103. Sedgwick held that "injustice and oppression have confounded" the "moral sense" of slaves, and as free people "they retain the vices of a degraded and subjected people." She saw Mumbet as an extraordinary exception. The only criticism that Sedgwick ever made of Mumbet was that she

was "the victim of her affections, and was weakly indulgent to her riotous and ruinous descendants," who "like most of their race, were addicted to festive joys." Sedgwick praised another black servant, Agrippa, or Grippy, for his insightful and satiric critiques of whites, but accused him of being servile as a servant and "a tyrant" with his own family. Sedgwick, ibid., 69–70. Sedgwick, "Slavery in New England," 424.

104. Mary Kelley notes that Sedgwick wrote as if she were unaware that "racial difference privileged Sedgwick and made Mumbet her subordinate." Clearly this is so, but it is also very important to recognize that this is exactly what her memory and memorializing of Mumbet led her to do: Sedgwick remembered her not as her inferior but as her mother. She remembered her as "never servile" but rather strongly independent, even to the point of leaving the Sedgwicks when Theodore Sedgwick remarried in November 1808, a year after Catherine's mother died. (Catherine Sedgwick was then eighteen.) Freeman had been running the household and caring for the children for many years, inasmuch as Mrs. Sedgwick had been incapacitated by mental illness and Mr. Sedgwick was away in Washington much of the time. She recognized that she would have to turn over these responsibilities to the new Mrs. Sedgwick. She chose to retire to the small house she owned, although Catherine noted that she joined the family in its celebrations and sorrows. Sedgwick, *The Power of Her Sympathy*, 125, 158; Kelley, "Introduction," in ibid., 16, 69.

105. Ibid., 424. This article is almost entirely about Elizabeth Freeman, and it praises Freeman for her role in bringing about her own freedom and controlling her own life. It is written with an emotional distance from the grief Sedgwick expressed in her journal and repeats what was popularly known of Freeman as well as family tales. Ibid., 125

106. See Fries, *The Road To Salem*, 194.

107. Ibid., 29, 56, 76, 81–82, 102, 105, 106. This volume is a biography of Anna Catharina Antes Ernst (1726–1816), based on Ernst's manuscript autobiography housed in the Salem, North Carolina, Moravian Archives. Dreams figure prominently throughout the narrative, most importantly when Anna Catharina and her designated second husband exchange dreams as a primary method of establishing intimacy between them. For additional Moravian dream reports see Faull, *Moravian Women's Memoirs*, 59, 71–72, 102.

108. As Allan Kulikoff holds, "[T]he success of the yeomanry in influencing public policy during the war and postwar years led yeoman to believe that they, the majority of voters, could rule," but after the war, "[t]he gentry ruling class and its allies observed this growth of democracy with horror and set about reimposing discipline upon an unruly rural population." Kulikoff, "The American Revolution, Capitalism, and the Formation of the Yeoman Classes," 100. Overlapping groups of women, black people, the poor, and the young had also experienced new dreams during and after the Revolution and tried to change their selves and their lives. On this period of hope for blacks, see S. White, *Somewhat More Independent*. For women the negative change can be dated from the end of the period in which some women could vote in New Jersey (1807). See Klinghoffer and Elkis, " 'The Petticoat Elec-

tors,' " 159–193. See Young, "Afterward: How Radical Was the American Revolution?," 337. On others and othering see Beauvoir, *The Second Sex*, xxvii, 64.

109. See Kruger, *Dreaming in the Middle Ages*; LeGoff, *Time, Work, and Culture*, 201–351.

110. The one dream that Catherine Maria Sedgwick reported in her journal led to her breaking a commitment. In October of 1836, on hearing of the suicide of William Jarvis, she wrote that he had been "a lover of mine" at an early age when she did not know her own heart "as I now do." They had been moving toward marriage when she dreamed:

> that the wedding day was come, that I was filled with horror but thought it too late to recede. My family were assembled. We were standing up, and Dr. West had begun the ceremony when making a last effort, I begged him to stop and turning to Jarvis said, "I cannot marry you. I do not love you!" He looked at me far more in sorrow than in anger. I shall never forget the expression and said, "You should have told me this before."

After she had this dream, she immediately wrote to Jarvis and broke off their relationship. Her commitment was to remaining free. Sedgwick, *The Power of Her Sympathy*, 152.

111. T.T. "A Dream,"; T.T. "Another Dream." See the lengthy discussion of these dreams in J. Stewart, "The Emergence of Racial Modernity," 181–222. Both dreams are recounted and discussed in Abzug, *Cosmos Crumbling*, 7, 156. A letter to Theodore Dwight Weld written by a Mrs. Sturges recounts her 1835 dream in which the enslaved took part in a vast wave of violence that was covering America:

> Spreading like wild fire from plantation to plantation; from cane-brake to cane-brake, a mighty army of blacks, goaded to madness by inhuman taskmasters, and unheard of wrongs, . . . arose upon their oppressors . . . the land was . . . deluged with blood, and . . . the yell of the assassins, and the shrieks of his expiring victims, pierced my ear.

Sturges to Weld, Putnam, Ohio, March 19, 1835, cited in Abzug, *Passionate Liberator*, 131.

112. The Methodists were still anxious to have believers contribute "dreams from God" at meetings and hoped that their outdoor campsites at revivals would provide a good setting for dreaming. See Cooley, "Manna and the Manual," 131–159.

113. Cited by Von Mehren, *Minerva and the Muse*, 49, 112–113.

114. Emerson, "Demonology," 13–14. Richard O'Keefe points out that the published essay, from 1877, includes writings from 1837–1838 as well as from 1850–1860. O'Keefe's discussion of this essay, which emphasizes the similarity of Emerson's positions to many of Freud's, is an extraordinarily rich analysis of Emerson on dreams, emphasizing his concern with women, sex, animals, and man's animal nature; it does, however, rest on a belief that Freudianism is, as it were, a fixed set of "universal truths" that

were partially recognized by Emerson. O'Keefe, " 'Demonology': Emerson's Dreams," 5–16. For a discussion of Fuller's impact on Emerson's thought see Zwarg, *Feminist Conversations.* Zwarg, however, does not consider Fuller's influence in regard to dream interpretation. For Fuller's judgment of Emerson's self-concern, see Warren, *The American Narcissus,* 75.

115. Emerson, *The Journals,* 7:525.

116. Blumin, *The Emergence of the Middle Class,* xi.

117. Shmidt, writing of the spiritual state of Lucas, is cited in Sensbach, *A Separate Canaan,* 233. Lucas, pressured by Shmidt, did not continue to report visions. Ryland, "Reminiscences of the First African Church, Richmond, Virginia," 211, 262–265, 323–325, 356. See Sobel, *Trabelin' On,* 208–210, 304–305. James Jenkins, a white slave owner, born to a slave-owning family in South Carolina in 1764, was much influenced by Africans' ideas about dreaming, spirits, and salvation, but by the time he came to write the narrative of his life in 1842 he, like others, was determined to distance himself from these ideas. He noted, "My notion about conversion was very incorrect; I thought it was nothing more than a dream or some strange sight." Jenkins, *The Experience,* 10. For African American dream lore 1840–1865 see the dreams reported in the following narratives: P. Still, *The Kidnapped and the Ransomed,* 130, 294; H. B. Brown, *A Narrative of Henry Box Brown,* 59; Douglass, *My Bondage and My Freedom,* 284–285; Clarke and Clarke, *Narratives of the Suffering of Lewis Clarke,* 55, 107–108; J. Brown, *Slave Life in Georgia,* 97–98; and in Johnson, *God Struck Me Dead.* A widespread concern with dreams is noted in the African American community after the slave period by Puckett, *Folk Beliefs of the Southern Negro,* 109, 188, 220, 328, 469. Ferris takes note of African American artists who speak of images taken from their dreams in "Vision in Afro-American Folk Art," 115–131.

118. Ferguson, *The Lure of Dreams,* 1. John Barr (born 1749) recounted dreams that were very important in his life and raised the possibility that angels still spoke to people; nevertheless, he distanced himself from dreams and claimed they were not truly significant. Barr, *History,* 10, 16–19, 21–22.

119. See, for example, Woolman, *[The] Journal* (1774).

120. Several people apologized for writing about their dreams. Sarah Beckhouse Hamilton's narrative revolves around one portentous dream, but she comments, "Although some people may make light of all dreams, yet I would beg your pardon for inserting this, for it was particularly interesting to me however foolish it may look to others." Hamilton, *A Narrative,* 3 n. When in 1815 Abigail Bailey wrote of the dreams she had in 1788, dreams that had warned her of her husband's incest with their daughter and his planned violence against his wife and sons, she nevertheless reported, "I have no idea that dreams are generally much to be noticed." A. Bailey, *Memoirs,* 23. For doubts about the significance of all dreams, see T. Smith, *Experience,* 18, 22.

Joseph Smith was originally believed to have been given his esoteric knowledge in a dream, but this was later referred to as a vision. See Quinn, *Early Mormonism,* 114; and Brooke, *The Refiner's Fire,* 134, 151, 153, 156–157, 178, 180, 182, 186–187, 192, 280–281.

121. For reports of Lincoln's dreams see Sandburg, *Abraham Lincoln*, 243–245. Lincoln's dream of his own death is known to African dream interpreters today. See Omoyajowo, *Your Dreams*, 13. For the postwar use of dreams see Vande Kemp, "The Dream in Periodical Literature," 88–113.

122. O'Flaherty, *Dreams*, 304.

123. Montague Ullman and the many others who are now sponsoring dream-interpretation groups, open to the participation of any individual who chooses to join, can be seen as reinstituting lay dream interpretation in a tradition similar to that of the eighteenth century, but in a far more organized fashion that makes the ground rules clear and systematizes the method in order to protect the dreamer as far as possible. See Ullman, *Appreciating Dreams*.

124. Margaret Fuller had a utopian vision of the possibilities of an altered reality. She believed that

> Male and female represent the two sides of the great radical dualism. But, in fact, they are perpetually passing into one another.... There is no wholly masculine man, no purely feminine woman....
>
> Let us be wise, and not impede the soul. Let her work as she will. Let us have one creative energy, one incessant revelation. Let it take what form it will, and *let us not bind it by the past to man or woman, black or white....* So let it be.

Fuller, *Woman in the Nineteenth Century*, 103–105, emphasis added.

125. When Elizabeth Cady Stanton (1815–1902) gave a speech on "The Solitude of Self," she posited an imaginary female Crusoe "as an arbiter of her own destiny, ... with her woman Friday on a solitary island." She did not recognize her racism in this vision of a liberated white woman with a black female slave. Stanton, speech given February 20, 1892, cited by Kerber, "Can a Woman Be an Individual?" 201.

126. Paul Watzlawick regards such binary worldviews as resulting from the reasoning of the logical left hemisphere, and he suggests that it takes "the language of dreams, fairy tales and myths," the language of the right hemisphere, to therapeutically change an "illusionary frame" or fixed notion constructed within a binary system. Watzlawick notes that hypnosis and delusions can serve the same purpose. Watzlawick, *The Language of Change*, 51, 120. See also Watzlawick, Weakland, and Fisch, *Change*, 18, 90, 98.

Bibliography

PRIMARY SOURCES

Abbott, Benjamin. *The Experience and Gospel Labours of the Rev. Benjamin Abbott. . . .* New York, [1805] 1832.

Adams, Abigail, and John Adams. *The Book of Abigail and John: Selected Letters of the Adams Family.* Cambridge, Mass., 1975.

Adams Family. *Adams Family Correspondence.* Ed. L. H. Butterfield. 2 vols. New York, 1965.

Adams, Hannah. *A Memoir of Miss Hannah Adams, Written by Herself.* Boston, 1832.

Alby, Ann Eliza (Dow). *Life, Adventures.* N.p., n.d.

Allen, Elizabeth. *Sketches of Green Mountain Life, With an Autobiography of the Author.* Lowell, Mass., 1846.

Allen, Richard. *The Life Experiences and Gospel Labors of Rt. Rev. Richard Allen. . . .* Philadelphia, [1887] 1960.

Anderson, William J. *Life and Narrative of William J. Anderson, Twenty-four Years a Slave; Sold Eight Times! In Jail Sixty Times!! Whipped Three Hundred Times!!!.* Chicago, 1857.

Andrew [Ofodofendo Wooma]. "Lebenslauf." In "Chattel with a Soul: The Autobiography of a Moravian Slave," by Daniel B. Thorp. *The Pennsylvania Magazine of History & Biography* 112 (1988): 433–451.

Andrews, Charles Wesley. *Memoir of Mrs. Ann R. Page.* 2d ed. New York, [1844] 1856.

Anthony, Susanna. *The Life and Character of Miss Susanna Anthony.* Ed. Samuel Hopkins. Worcester, Mass., 1795.

Aristotle. *The Categories of Interpretation.* Ed. Harold P. Cooke. Cambridge, Mass., 1938.

Arms, Mary L. Day. *Incidents in the Life of a Blind Girl. Mary L. Day, a Graduate of the Maryland Institution for the Blind.* 4th ed. Baltimore, 1859.

Artemidorus, Daldianus. *The Interpretation of Dreams; Oneirocritica.* Trans. Robert J. White. Park Ridge, N.J., 1975.

Asbury, Francis. *The Journal and Letters of Francis Asbury.* Ed. Elmer E. Clark. 3 vols. London, 1858.

Ashbridge, Elizabeth. *Some Account of the Fore Part of the Life of Elizabeth Ashbridge. . . .* Concord, N.H., 1810. Reprint in *Journeys in New Worlds: Early American Women's Narratives.* Ed. William L. Andrews, 117–180. Madison, Wis., 1990.

Asher, Jeremiah. *Incidents in the Life of the Rev. J. Asher, pastor of the Shiloh (colored) Baptist Church, Philadelphia. . . .* London, 1850.

Ashton, J., ed. *Chapbooks of the Eighteenth Century.* London, 1882.

Augustine, Saint. *Saint Augustine's Confessions; With an English Translation by William Watts, 1631*, Cambridge, Mass., 1960–61.

Aunt Sally's Policy Players' Dream Book. New York, 1889.

"Authors Turned Traders: A Dream." *Columbian Magazine* 2 (1789): 202–206.

Bailey, Abigail Abbot. *Memoirs of Mrs. Abigail Bailey*. Boston, 1815.

Bailey, Robert. *The Life and Adventures of Robert Bailey, from his Infancy up to Dec., 1821. . . .* Richmond, 1822.

Ball, Charles. *Slavery in the United States: A Narrative of the Life and Adventures of Charles Ball, A Black Man. . . .* New York, 1837.

Banneker, Benjamin. Almanac. Maryland Historical Society, Annapolis, Md.

Barr, John. *History of John Barr. . . .* Philadelphia, 1833.

Bartlet, J. R. ed. *The Census of Rhode Island of 1774*. Baltimore, 1969.

Beattie, James. "On Dreaming." *Columbian Magazine* 1 (1788): 329–335, 359–363, 416–420.

Beaumont, Gustave de. *Marie; or Slavery in the United States*. Ed. Alvis L. Tinnin. Stanford, [1835] 1958.

"[The] Benefits of Charity—A Dream." *Columbian Magazine* 1 (1788): 578.

Benson, John. *A Short Account of the Voyages, Travels, and Adventures of John Benson. . . .* N.p., 182[?].

Black Hawk, *Life of Ma-Ka-Tai-Me-She-Kia-Kiak or Black Hawk. . . .* Cincinnati, 1833. Reprint, *Black Hawk: An Autobiography*. Ed. Donald Jackson. Urbana, [1955] 1964.

Boehm, Henry. *The Patriarch of One-Hundred Years*. New York, 1875.

Bowen, Eliza [pseudonym; also Louisa Baker, Lucy Brewer, Eliza Webb, and Lucy West]. *The Female Marine. . . .* Boston[?], 1816.

Bradford, Sarah H. *Scenes in the Life of Harriet Tubman*. Auburn, N.Y., 1869.

————. *Harriet Tubman: The Moses of Her People*. Secaucus, N.J., [1886] 1961.

Brasher, Helen K. The Narrative of Mrs. Abraham Brasher, giving her account of her experiences during the Revolutionary War. . . . New York Historical Society, New York City.

Breckinridge, Lucy. *Lucy Breckinridge of Grove Hall: The Journal of a Virginia Girl, 1862–1864*. Ed. Mary D. Robertson. Kent, Ohio, 1979.

Brooke, Francis T. *A Narrative of my Life. . . .* Richmond, 1849.

Brown, Charles Brockden. *Wieland: or, The Transformation: An American Tale*. New York, [1798] 1846.

Brown, George. *Recollections of Itinerant Life*. 2d ed. Cincinnati, 1866.

Brown, Henry Box. *A Narrative of Henry Box Brown. . . .* Boston, 1859.

[Brown, H. H.] *Trial of Elder Eleazer Sherman, Before an Ecclesiastical Council, Held at the Meeting-House of the Christian Society in Providence, July 20 and 21,1835*. 2d ed. Providence, R.I., 1835.

Brown, John. *Slave Life in Georgia. . . .* London, 1855.

Brown, William Wells. *Narrative of William W. Brown, A Fugitive Slave. Written by Himself*. Boston, 1847.

Browne, Thomas. *The Garden of Cyrus; or The Quincuncial Lozenge, or Network Plantations of the Ancients Artificially, Naturally, Mystically Consider'd.* London, 1658.

Brownlow, William G. "A Narrative of the Life, Travels, and Circumstances Incident Thereto of William G. Browlow." In *Helps to the Study of Presbyterianism,* by William G. Brownlow, 241–299. Knoxville, 1834.

Bruce, Henry Clay. *The New Man. Twenty-nine Years a Slave. Twenty-nine Years a Free Man.* York, Pa., 1895.

Bruns, Roger, ed. *Am I Not a Man and a Brother: The Antislavery Crusade of Revolutionary America. 1688–1788.* New York, 1977.

Brunt, Jonathon. *A Few Particulars of the Life of Jonathan Brunt. . . .* 3d ed. N.p., 1797.

———. *The Little Medley . . . .* Knoxville, 1809.

Bunyan, John. *The Complete Works of John Bunyan.* Ed. Henry Stebbing. 4 vols. London, 1859.

Busey, Samuel Clagett. *A Souvenir, with an Autobiographical Sketch of Early Life. . . .* Washington, D.C., 1896.

Byrd, Ann. *Narratives, Pious Meditations and Religious Exercises of Ann Byrd, Late of the City of New York. . . .* 2d ed. Byberry, Pa., 1844.

Byrd, William II. *Another Secret Diary of William Byrd of Westover, 1739–1741; With Letters and Literary Exercises, 1696–1726.* Ed. Maude A. Woodfin and Marion Tinling. Richmond, 1942.

———. Commonplace Book. Virginia Historical Society, Richmond, Virginia.

Capers, William. "Recollections." In *The Life of William Capers,* by William M. Wightman, 11–228. Nashville, 1858.

Carson, Ann Baker. *The Memoirs of the Celebrated and Beautiful Mrs. Ann Carson. . . whose Life was Terminated in the Philadelphia Prison.* 2d ed. Ed. M. Clarke. Philadelphia, [1822] 1838.

Carter, Landon. *The Diary of Colonel Landon Carter of Sabine Hall, 1752–1778.* Ed. Jack P. Greene. 2 vols. Charlottesville, 1965.

Chalkley, Thomas. *A Journal or Historical Account of the Life, Labours, Travels, and Christian Experiences . . . of Thomas Chalkley.* Philadelphia, [1749] 1754.

Child, Lydia Maria. *Isaac T, Hopper: A True Life.* Boston, 1853.

Churchman, John. *An Account of the Gospel Labours and Christian Experience of a Faithful Minister of Christ.* Philadelphia, 1779.

Clarke, Lewis, and Milton Clarke. *Narratives of the Sufferings of Lewis and Milton Clarke, Sons of a Soldier of the Revolution. . . .* Boston, 1845.

Clarke, Olive Cleaveland. *Things That I Remember at Ninety-Five.* N.p., 1881.

Clay, Cassius. *The Life of Cassius Marcellus Clay. . . .* Cincinnati, 1886.

Cohen, Daniel A., ed. *The Female Marine and Related Works.* Amherst, Mass., 1997.

Cole [Hanson], Emma. *The Life and Sufferings of Miss Emma Cole.* 2d. ed. Boston, 1844.

Coleman, Seth. *Memoir of Doctor Seth Coleman, A.M., of Amherst. . . .* New Haven, 1817.

Collins, Elizabeth. *Memoirs of Elizabeth Collins*. . . . Philadelphia, 1833.

Collins, James Potter. *Autobiography of a Revolutionary Soldier*. Ed. John M. Roberts. Clinton, La., 1859.

Comstock, Joshua. *A Short History*. Providence, R.I., 1822.

Croswell, Joseph. *Sketches of the Life, and Extracts for the Journals and Other Writings, of the Late Joseph Croswell*. . . . . Ed. Jacob Norton. Boston, 1809.

Dalton, James. *Life and Actions of James Dalton, a Noted Street Robber*. . . . London, 1730.

Davies, Samuel. *Letters From the Rev. Samuel Davies . . . Shewing the State of Religion in Virginia . . . Particularly Among the Negroes*. 2d ed. London, 1757.

———. *Sermons On Important Subjects*. 3 vols. 5th ed. New York, 1792.

Davis, Almond H. *The Female Preacher; or Memoir of Salome Lincoln*. Providence, R.I., 1843.

DeLaney, Lucy. *From the Darkness Cometh Light; or Struggles for Freedom*. St. Louis, [189?].

DeWolfe, Barbara, ed. *Discoveries of America: Personal Accounts of British Emigrants to North America during the Revolutionary Era*. Cambridge, England, 1997.

Donnelly, Edward. *Confession of Edward Donnelly*. . . . Baltimore, 1808.

Douglass, Frederick. *Life and Times of Frederick Douglass*. New York, [1892] 1962.

———. *My Bondage and My Freedom*. New York, 1855.

———. *Narrative of the Life of Frederick Douglass, an American Slave. Written by Himself*. Boston, [1845] 1960.

[A] Dream To All Friends of Zion. N.p., 1775.

"[The] Dreamer . . . , A Politico-Philosophical Tale." *Columbian Magazine* 2 (1789): 190–195, 247–251.

Drew, Benjamin. *The Refugee: A North-Side View of Slavery*. Reading, Mass., [1855] 1969.

Drinker, Elizabeth. *The Diary of Elizabeth Drinker*. Ed. Elaine Forman Crane. 3 vols. Boston, 1991.

Duncan, Nehemiah. *Extraordinary Conversion of Nechemiah Duncan*. . . . Philadelphia, [1801] 1806.

Edwards, Jonathan. *The Works of President Edwards*. 4 vols. 8th ed. New York, 1856.

Elaw, Zilpha. *Memoirs*. London, 1846.

Eldridge, Elleanor. *Elleanor's Second Book*. . . . Providence, R.I., 1839.

———. *Memoirs of Elleanor Eldridge*. Providence, R.I., 1838.

Elizabeth. *Memoir of Old Elizabeth, A Coloured Woman*. Philadelphia, 1863.

Emerson, Ralph Waldo. "Demonology." In *Lectures and Biographical Sketches*, 9–32. Boston, 1888.

———. *The Journals and Miscellaneous Notebooks*. Ed. William H. Gilman et al. 16 vols. Cambridge, Mass., 1960–1982.

Evans, Joshua. *Joshua Evans's Journal.* Ed. George Churchman. Philadelphia, 1837.

Faull, Katherine M., trans. and ed. *Moravian Women's Memoirs: Their Related Lives, 1750–1820.* Syracuse, 1997.

Fisher, Elizabeth Munro. *Memoirs of Mrs. Elizabeth Fisher, of the City of New York.* . . . New York, 1810.

Fontaine, Felix. *The Golden Wheel Dream Book.* . . . New York, 1862.

Foote, Julia A. *A Brand Plucked From the Fire.* . . . Cleveland, 1886.

Fox, George. *Journal of George Fox.* Ed. John L. Nickalls. Cambridge, England, 1952.

Franklin, Benjamin. *The Autobiography.* Ed. Leonard W. Labaree. New Haven, 1964.

Fristoe, William. *A Concise History of the Ketockton Baptist Association.* . . . Staunton, Va., 1808.

Fry, Henry. "The Autobiography." In *Memoir of Col. Joshua Fry*, by P. Slaughter. N.p., n.d.

Fuller, S. Margaret. *Woman in the Nineteenth Century.* Columbia, S.C., [1845] 1980.

Galloway, Grace G. "Diary of Grace Gowden Galloway . . . June 17th, 1778 to July 1st 1779." Ed. Raymond C. Werner. *Pennsylvania Magazine of History and Biography* 55 (1931): 32–69.

Gannet, Deborah [Sampson]. *An Address, Delivered with Applause, At the Federal-Street Theatre, Boston, . . . Beginning March 22, 1802.* . . . Dedham, Mass., 1802.

Gano, John. *Biographical Memoirs of the Late Rev. John Gano.* . . . New York, 1806.

Garnet, Henry Highland. "An Address To The Slaves of the United States of America, Buffalo, N.Y., 1843." In *"Let Your Motto Be Resistance": The Life and Thought of Henry Highland Garnet*, by Earl Ofari, 44–153. Boston, 1972.

Garrettson, Catherine Livingston. "Diary" and "Exercise Book." In "Lost in the Ocean of Love: The Mystical Writings of Catherine Livingston Garrettson," by Diane Helen Lobody, 138–309. Ph.D. dissertation, Drew University, 1990.

Garrettson, Freeborn. *American Methodist Pioneer: The Life and Journals of the Rev. Freeborn Garrettson.* Ed. Robert Drew Simpson. Rutland, Vt., 1984.

———. *A Dialogue Between Do-Justice and Professing Christian.* Wilmington, Del., 1820.

———. *The Experience and Travels of Freeborn Garrettson, Minister of the Methodist-Episcopal Church in North America.* . . . Philadelphia, 1791.

Gates, Theophilus Ransom. *The Trials, Experience, Exercises of Mind, and First Travels of Theophilus Ransom Gates.* Poughkeepsie, N.Y., 1810.

Genuine Afro Dream Book. The Right Numbers from Dreams. Youngstown, Ohio, 1939.

George, David. "An Account of the Life of Mr. David George, from Sierra Leone, in Africa; given by himself in a Conversation with Brother Rippon of London, and Brother Pearce of Birmingham." In *The Baptist Annual Register* I, (1790–1793): 336–337, 473–477. Reprint, "Letters Showing the Rise and Progress of the Early Negro Churches of Georgia and the West Indies." *Journal of Negro History* 1 (1916): 69–92.

Gilbert, Benjamin. *Winding Down: The Revolutionary War Letters of Lieutenant Benjamin Gilbert of Massachusettes, 1780–1783.* . . . Ed. John Shy. Ann Arbor, Mich., 1989.

Glendinning, William. *The Life of William Glendinning, Preacher of the Gospel.* Philadelphia, 1795.

Godfrey, Samuel E. *A Sketch of the Life of Samuel E. Godfrey.* . . . 3d ed. Windsor, Vt., 1818.

Grandy, Moses. *Narrative of the Life of Moses Grandy, Late a Slave in the United States of America.* 2d American ed. Boston, 1844.

Green, Johnson. *The Life and Confession of Johnson Green.* . . . Worcester, Mass., 1786.

Green, Samuel. *Life of Samuel Green, executed at Boston, April 25, 1822, for the murder of Billy Williams.* . . . Boston, 1822.

Griffith, John. *A Journal of the Life, Travels and Labours in the Work of the Ministry.* . . . 2nd ed. Philadelphia, [1700] 1780.

Grimes, William. *The Life of William Grimes . . . Written by Himself.* New Haven, [1824] 1855. Reprint, *Five Black Lives*, ed. Arna Bontemps, 59–128. Middletown, Conn., 1971.

Gronniosaw, James Albert Ukawsaw. *A Narrative of the Most Remarkable Particulars in the Life of James Albert Ukawsaw Gronniosaw, An African Prince, as Related by Himself.* Bath, England, 1770.

Gross, William. *The Last Words.* . . . Philadelphia, 1823.

Hall, Margaret Hunter. *The Aristocratic Journey: Being the Outspoken Letters of Mrs Basil Hall. Written during a Fourteen Months' Sojourn in America 1827–1828.* Ed. Una Pope-Hennessy. New York, 1931.

Hamilton, Sarah Beckhouse. *A Narrative of the Life of Mrs. Hamilton.* . . . Greenwich, Conn., 1806.

Hammon, Briton. *A Narrative of the Uncommon Sufferings, and Surprizing Deliverance of Briton Hammon, a Negro Man.* . . . Boston, 1760.

Hathaway, Levi. *The Narrative of Levi Hathaway.* . . . Providence, 1820.

Hayden, William. *The Narrative of William Hayden.* . . . Cincinnati, 1846.

Heaton, Hannah. "Experiences or Spiritual Exercises." Typescript, Connecticut Historical Society, Hartford, Conn.

Hemings, Madison. "The Memoirs of Madison Hemings." In "Life among the Lowly." *Pike County (Ohio) Republican*, March 13, 1873. Reprinted in *Thomas Jefferson*, by Annette Gordon-Reed, 245–248. Charlottesville, 1998.

Hensen, Josiah. *Father Henson's Story of His Own Life.* Boston, 1858.

[The] Hieroglyhick [Hieroglyphic] Bible or Select Passages . . . for the Amusement of Youth. . . . 2d ed. Boston, 1814.

"[The] History of Dream Interpretation." *Pennsylvania Magazine or American Monthly Magazine* 2 (March 1776): 119–122.

Hodges, Graham Russell, ed. *Black Itinerants of the Gospel: The Narratives of John Jea and George White*. Madison, Wis., 1993.

Hopkins, Samuel. "A Dialogue Concerning the Slavery of Africans . . . ," (1776). In *Am I Not a Man, and a Brother: The Antislavery Crusade of Revolutionary America. 1688–1788*, ed. Roger Bruns, 397–426. New York, 1977.

———. *Sketches of the Life of the Late Rev. Samuel Hopkins, Pastor of the First Congregational Church in Newport, Written by Himself*. . . . Hartford, Conn., 1805.

———. *The Works of Samuel Hopkins, with a Memoir of his Life and Character*. 3 vols. Boston, 1852–1854.

Hopper, Isaac T. *Kidnappers in Philadelphia: Isaac Hopper's Tales of Oppression, 1780–1843*. Compiled by Daniel E. Meaders. New York, 1994.

How, David D. *Life and Confession*. . . . Ed. Joseph Badger. New York[?], 1824.

Hudson, James. *The Life and Confession of James Hudson who was Executed . . . for the murder of Logan, an Indian Chief*. . . . Recorded by Samuel Woodworth. Indianapolis, 1825.

Hume, Sophia. *An Exhortation*. . . . Philadelphia, 1747.

Hunter, John Dunn. *Memoirs of a Captivity among the Indians of North America*. Ed. Richard Drinnon. New York, [1824] 1973.

[Huntington, Anne and Benjamin H. Huntington]. *The Huntington Letters, in the Possession of Julia Chester Wells*. Ed. William D. McCrackan. New York, 1897.

Ireland, James. *The Life of the Rev. James Ireland*. Winchester, Va., 1819.

Irving, Washington. "The Devil and Tom Walker." In *The Complete Tales of Washington Irving*, ed. Charles Neider, 437–448. Garden City, N.Y., 1975.

Jackson, Rebecca Cox. *Gifts of Power: The Writings of Rebecca Jackson, Black Visionary, Shaker Eldress*. Ed. Jean McMahon Humez. Amherst, Mass. 1981.

Jacobs, Harriet A. [Linda Brent.] *Incidents in the Life of a Slave Girl, Written by Herself*. Ed. Jean Fagin Yellin. Cambridge, Mass., [1861] 1987.

Jemison, Mary. *The Narrative of the Life of Mrs. Mary Jemison*. Redact. James E. Seaver. Ed. June Namias. Normon, Okla., [1824] 1992.

Jenkins, James. *The Experience, Labours and Suffering of the Rev. James Jenkins of the South Carolina Conference*. N.p., 1842.

Jenks, William. Somnia. William Jenks Papers. Massachusetts Historical Society, Boston, Mass.

Johonnet, Jackson. *The Remarkable Adventures of Jackson Johonnet . . . who Served as a Soldier*. . . . Lexington, Ky., 1791.

Jones, Abner. *Memoirs of the Life and Experience, Travels and Preaching of Abner Jones*. . . . Exeter, N.H., 1807.

Josselin, Ralph. *The Diary of Ralph Josselin, 1616–1683*. Ed. Alan Macfarlane. London, 1976.

Judge, Hugh. *Memoirs and Journal of Hugh Judge*. . . . Byberry, Pa., 1841.

Keene, Moses W. *The Life and Confession*. . . . Maysville, Ky., 1842.

Keith, William. *The Experience of William Keith*. Utica, N.Y., 1806.

Kinney, Hannah. *A Review of the Principal Events of the Last Ten Years*. Boston, 1841.

Lane, Lunsford. *The Narrative of Lunsford Lane, Embracing an Account of His Early Life, the Redemption by Purchase of Himself and Family from Slavery, and His Banishment from the Place of His Birth for the Crime of Wearing a Colored Skin*. Boston, 1842.

Larison, C. W. *Sylvia Dubois, A Biografy of the Slav who Whipt her Mistres and Gand Her Fredom*. Ed. Jared C. Lobdell. New York, 1988.

Lathrop, George. *Dark and Terrible Deeds. . . .* New Orleans, 1848.

Lathrop, Joseph. *Sermons . . . With a Memoir of the Author's Life Written by Himself*. Springfield, Mass., 1821.

Lay, Benjamin. *All Slave Keepers that Keep the Innocent in Bondage, Apostates . . .* , 1737. Reprinted in *Am I Not a Man, and a Brother: The Antislavery Crusade of Revolutionary America. 1688–1788*, ed. Roger Bruns, 52. New York, 1977.

Lee, Jarena. *Religious Experience and Journal of Mrs. Jarena Lee. . . .* Philadelphia, [1836] 1849.

Lee, Richard. *A Short Narrative of the Life of Mr. Richard Lee*. Kennebunk, Maine, 1804.

Lee, William. *The True and Interesting Travels of William Lee. . . .* London, 1808.

Leland, John. *Some Events in the Life of John Leland*. Pittsfield, Mass., 1838.
———. *The Writings of the Late Elder John Leland*. New York, 1845.

Lincoln, Salome. *The Female Preacher; or Memoir of Salome Lincoln, Afterwards the Wife of Elder Junia S. Mowry*. Ed. Almond H. Davis. Providence, R.I., 1843.

Loewenberg, Bert James, and Ruth Bogen, eds. *Black Women in Nineteenth-Century American Life*. University Park, Pa., 1976.

Lucas, Rachel. *Remarkable Account. . . .* Boston, 1811.

Mack, Solomon. *A Narrative of the Life of Solomon Mack, Containing an Account of the Many Severe Accidents He Met with During a Long Series of Years. . . .* Windsor, Vt., 1811[?].

Malin, Rachel. *Rachel Malin's Dream and Date Book*. Otter-Wilkinson Papers, 1768–1872. Cornell University Library, Ithaca, N.Y.

Malvin, John. *Autobiography of John Malvin*. Cleveland, Ohio, 1879. Reprint, *North into Freedom: The Autobiography of John Malvin, Free Negro, 1795–1880*. Ed. Allan Peskin. Cleveland, Ohio, 1966.

Mann, Herman. *The Female Review. Life of Deborah Sampson, the Female Soldier of the War of the Revolution*. Ed. John Adams Vinton. Boston: 1866.
———. *The Female Review; or Memoirs of an American Young Lady; whose life and character are peculiarly distinguished—being a continental soldier, for nearly three years, in the late war*. Dedham, Mass., 1797.

Marrant, John. *A Narrative of the Lord's Wonderful Dealings with John Marrant, a Black. . . .* 2nd ed. London, 1785.

Marshall, Mary. "The Life and Suffering of the Author." In *Rise and Progress of the Serpent from the Garden of Eden.* . . . Concord, 1847.

Martin, Isaac. *Journal of the Life, Travels, Labours, and Religious Exercises* . . . . Philadelphia, 1834.

Martin, Joseph Plumb. *A Narrative of Some of the Adventures, Dangers, and Sufferings of a Revolutionary Soldier.* . . . Hallowell, Me., 1830. Reprint, *Private Yankee Doodle: Being a Narrative of Some of the Adventures, Dangers and Sufferings of a Revolutionary Soldier.* Ed. George F. Scheer. Boston, 1962.

Martin, Luther. *Modern Gratitude.* Baltimore, 1802.

Martin, Michael. *Life of Michael Martin, Who was Executed for Highway Robbery.* . . . Trans. and ed. F. W. Waldo. Boston, 1821.

McCorkle, John. "Religious Experience." In *History of John Barr*, by John Barr, 69–91. Philadelphia, 1833.

Mifflin, Warner. *The Defense of Warner Mifflin Against Aspersions Cast on Him on Account of His Endeavors to Promote Righteousness, Mercy and Peace, Among Mankind.* Philadelphia, 1796.

Mitchel, Mary. *A Short Account of the Early Part of the Life of Mary Mitchell.* . . . New Bedford, Mass., 1812.

M'Lean, James. *Seventeen Years' History of the Life and Sufferings of James M'Lean, an impressed American Citizen and Seaman.* . . . Hartford, Conn., 1814.

Morris, Margaret. *Private Journal Kept During the Revolutionary War.* New York, [1836] 1969.

Neale, Mary Peisley. *Some Account of The Life and Religious Exercises of Mary Neale, formerly Mary Peisley.* Dublin, 1795.

[The] New Book of Knowledge . . . The Interpretation of Dreams. . . . Boston, 1767.

Newcomer, Christian. *The Life and Journal of the Rev. Christian Newcomer.* Hagerstown, Md., 1834.

Newell, Fanny. *Memoirs of Fanny Newell; Written by Herself.* . . . 3d ed. Springfield, Mass., [1824] 1833.

Occum, Samson. "A Short Narrative of My Life" [1768]. In *The Elders Wrote: An Anthology of Early Prose by North American Indians 1768–1931*, ed. Bernd Peyer, 12–18. Berlin, Germany, 1982.

O'Connor, Rachel Swayze. *Mistress of Evergreen Plantation: Rachel O'Connor's Legacy of Letters, 1823–1845.* Ed. Alie Webb. Albany, N.Y., 1983.

Oehler, Andrew. *The Life, Adventures, and Unparalled Sufferings of Andrew Oehler.* . . . Trenton, N.J., 1811.

Offley, G. W. *A Narrative of the Life and Labors of the Rev. G. W. Offley, A Colored Man, and Local Preacher.* . . . Hartford, Conn., 1860. Reprinted in *Five Black Lives*, ed. by Arna Bontemps, 129–137. Middletown, Conn., 1971.

Old Aunt Dinah's Policy Player's Sure Guide to Lucky Dreams and Lucky Numbers. New York, n.d. [c. 1851].

Osborn, Sarah. Letters, 1743–1770; 1779. American Antiquarian Society, Worcester, Mass.

Osborn, Sarah. *Memoirs of the Life of Mrs. Sarah Osborn.* Ed. Samuel Hopkins. Worcester, Mass., 1799.

———, and Susanna Anthony. *Familiar Letters, Written by Mrs. Sarah Osborn, and Miss Susanna Anthony, Late of Newport.* Newport, R.I., 1807.

Otter, William. *History of My Own Times; or, The Life and Adventures of William Otter, Senior, Comprising A Series of Events, and Musical Incidents Altogether Original.* Emmitsburg, Md., 1835. Reprinted as *History of My Own Times,* ed. Richard B. Stott. Ithaca, N.Y. 1995.

Paine, Thomas. "An Essay on Dream." (1803) In *Complete Writings of Thomas Paine,* ed. Philip S. Foner, 2:841–848. New York, 1969.

Park, Edward A. "Memoir." In *The Works of Samuel Hopkins, with a Memoir of his Life and Character,* 1:1–99. Boston, 1852.

Park, Louisa Adams. Diary for 1800. Park Family Papers. American Antiquarian Society, Worcester, Mass.

Patton, James. *Biography.* Asheville, N.C., 1850.

Paul, Almira. *The Surprising Adventures of Almira Paul.* . . . Boston, 1816.

Pearse, James. *A Narrative of the Life of James Pearse.* . . . Rutland, Vt., 1825.

Peck, George. *The Life and Times of Rev. George Peck.* . . . New York, 1874.

[The] People's History: Working Class Autobiographies. Woodbridge, England, 1986.

Perry, David. *Recollections of an Old Soldier.* . . . Windsor, Vt., 1822.

Peterson, Daniel H. *The Looking-glass, Bing a True Report of the Life, Travels, and Labors of the Reverend Daniel H. Peterson, a Colored Clergyman, . . .1812–1854.* . . . New York,1854.

Phillips, Catherine [Payton]. *Memoirs.* . . . London, 1797.

Pinckney, Eliza. *The Letterbook of Eliza Lucas Pinckney, 1739–1762.* Ed. Elise Pinckney. Columbia, S.C., [1972] 1997.

Placid, Pertinex [pseudonym]. "A Tale of a Nose." *Southern Literary Messenger* 1 (March, 1835): 445–448.

Poe, Edgar Allen. "A Dream [1831]." In *The Unknown Poe: An Anthology of Fugitive Writing,* ed. Raymond Foye, 55–57. San Francisco, 1980.

Potter, Elam. *Author's Account of His Conversion.* Boston, 1772.

Powers, Thomas. *The Narrative and Confession of Thomas Powers, a Negro.* . . . Norwich, Conn., 1796.

Prayers for the New Year. Trans. S. Singer. New York, 1931.

Prince, Nancy Gardener. *A Narrative.* . . . Boston, 1850.

[The] Prodigal Daughter. Boston, 1758.

Pyle, Robert. "Robert Pyle's Testimony." In "An Early Quaker Anti-Slavery Statement," ed. Henry J. Cadbury. *Journal of Negro History* 22 (1937): 492–493. Reprinted as Robert Piles, "Paper About Negroes" (1698). In *Am I Not a Man and a Brother: The Antislavery Crusade of Revolutionary America. 1688–1788,* ed. Roger Bruns, 9–10. New York, 1977.

Quinby, Josiah. *A Short History of a Long Journey.* New York, 1740.

Rawick, George P., ed. *The American Slave: A Composite Autobiography.* 19 vols. Westport, Conn., 1971–1977.

Ray, William. *Poems To Which Is Added a Brief Sketch of the Author's Life, and of His Captivity and Suffering Among the Turks. . . .* Auburn, N.Y., 1821.

Raymond, Charles A. "The Religious Life of the Negro Slave." *Harper's New Monthly Magazine* 27 (October, 1863): 680–682.

Reckitt, William. *Some account of the Life and Gospel Labours of William Reckitt. . . .* Philadelphia, 1783.

Redfield, Levi. *A Succinct Account of Some Memorable Events and Occurrences in the Life of Levi Redfield. . . .* Brattleboro, Vt., 1798.

Register of Free Negroes. York County, Virginia, Guardian Account Books, 1780–1823. Photocopy, Colonial Williamsburg Library, Williamsburg, Va.

Richards, Lucy. *Memoirs of the Late Miss Lucy Richards, of Paris, Oneida County, New York.* New York, 1842.

Richardson, Henry. *Pamela: or, Virtue Rewarded.* 2 vols. London, 1739.

Richardson, John. *An Account of the Life of that Ancient Servant of Jesus Christ: John Richardson. . . .* Philadelphia, [1774] 1783.

Ritter, Jacob. *Memoirs of Jacob Ritter. . . .* Philadelphia, 1844.

Rosencrantz, Herman. *The Life and Confession of Herman Rosencrantz. . . .* Philadelphia, 1770.

Ruether, Rosemary R., and Rosemary S. Keller, eds. *Women and Religion in America.* Vol. 2, *The Colonial and Revolutionary Periods: A Documentary History.* San Francisco, 1981.

Rush, Benjamin. *An Address to the Inhabitants of the British Settlements in America, upon Slavekeeping.* Philadelphia, 1773. Reprint, *An address to the Inhabitants of the British Settlements on the Slavery of Negroes in America.* New York, 1969.

———. *[The] Autobiography of Benjamin Rush: His "Travels Through Life," Together with His Commonplace Book for 1789–1813."* Ed. G. W. Corner. Princeton, N.J. 1948.

———. *Essays: Literary, Moral and Philosophical.* Ed. Michael Meranze. Schectady, N.Y., 1988.

———. *Lectures on the Mind.* Ed. Eric T, Carlson et al. Philadelphia, 1981.

———. *Letters of Benjamin Rush.* Ed. L. H. Butterfield. 2 vols. Princeton, N.J 1951.

———. *Medical Inquiries and Observations upon the Diseases of the Mind.* Philadelphia, 1812.

———. *My Dearest Julia: The Love Letters of Dr. Benjamin Rush to Julia Stockton.* New York, 1979.

———. "On Slave-keeping." In *The Selected Writings of Benjamin Rush,* ed. Dagobert D. Runes, 3–18. New York, 1947.

———. "[The] Influence of Physical Causes Upon the Moral Faculty" (1786). Reprinted in *The Selected Writings of Benjamin Rush.* ed. Dagobert D. Runes, 181–211. New York, 1947.

———. "Paradise of Negro Slaves." *Columbian Magazine* 1 (1788): 235–238. Reprinted in *Essays: Literary, Moral, and Philosophical,* ed. Michael Meranze, 187–190. Schenectady, N.Y., 1988.

Russell, Chloe. *The Complete Fortune Teller and Dream Book.* Boston, 1800.

Ryland, Robert. "Reminiscences of the First African Church, Richmond, Virginia, by the Pastor." *American Baptist Memorial* 14 (September-December, 1955): 211, 262–265, 323–325, 356.

Saffin, John. *A Brief and Candid Answer to a Late Printed Sheet, Entitled, The Selling of Joseph. . . .* Boston, 1701.

Sampson, Abel. *The Wonderful Adventure of Abel Sampson, related by himself: written by Edmund Hale Kendall.* Lawrence City, 1847.

Sampson, Meynard. *The Experiences of Meynard Sampson, Local Preacher of Methodist Episcopal Church. . . .* New York, 1828.

Sandiford, Ralph. *The Mystery of Iniquity, in a Brief Examination of the Practice of the Times.* 1729. Reprinted in *Am I Not a Man and a Brother: The Antislavery Crusade of Revolutionary America,* ed. Roger Bruns, 31–38. New York, 1977.

Sanger, Abner. *"Very Poor and Of a Lo Make": The Journal of Abner Sanger.* Ed. Lois K. Stabler. Portsmouth, N.H., 1987.

Sawyer, Lemuel. *Auto-biography of Lemuel Sawyer, Formerly Member of Congress from North Carolina, Author of the Biography of John Randolph.* New York, 1844.

Seaver, James E. *A Narrative of the Life of Mrs. Mary Jemison.* Ed. June Namias. Norman, Okla., [1824] 1992.

Sedgwick [or Sedgewick], Catherine Maria. *Married or Single?* 2 vols. New York, 1857.

———. *A New England Tale; or, Sketches of New-England Character and Manners.* Ed. Victoria Clements. New York, [1822] 1995.

———. *The Power of Her Sympathy: The Autobiography and Journal of Catherine Maria Sedgwick.* Ed. Mary Kelley. Boston, 1993.

———. "Slavery in New England." *Bentley's Miscellany* 34 (1853): 417–424.

Semple, Robert B. *A History of the Rise and Progress of the Baptists in Virginia.* Richmond, 1810.

Sewall, Samuel. *The Diary of Samuel Sewall.* 2 vols. New York, 1973.

Shaw, John Robert. *A Narrative of the Life and Travels of John Robert Shaw, the Well Digger. . . .* Lexington, Ky., 1807.

Shepard, Thomas. *Parable of the Ten Virgins.* London, 1660.

Sherman, Eleazar. *A Lecture on the Last Personal Coming of our Lord To Raise The Dead and Change the Living.* Taunton, Mass., 1843.

———. *The Narrative of Eleazar Sherman, Giving an Account of his Life, Experience, Call to the Ministry of the Gospel, and Travels as Such to the Present Time.* 3 vols. in 1. Providence, R.I., [1829] 1832.

———. *The Narrative of Eleazer Sherman. . . .* Vol. 4. Providence, R.I., 1835.

———. *Reply of Elder Eleazer Sherman, to Certain Charges Against his Moral Character. . . .* N.p., nd.

Siddons, Leonora. *The Female Warrior. . . .* New York, 1843.

Smellie, William. *The Philosophy of Natural History.* 2 vols. Edinburgh, 1799.

Smith, Margaret Bayard. *American Mother; or The Seymour Family.* Washington, D.C., 1823.

———. *The Diversions of Sydney.* Washington, D.C., 1805.

Smith, Richard. *The Trials of Richard Smith as Principal, and Ann Carson, alias Ann Smith, as Accessory, for the Murder of Captain John Carson on the 20th Day of January, 1816. . . .* Philadelphia, 1816.

Smith, Thomas. *Experience and Ministerial Labors of Rev Thomas Smith . . . , Compiled Chiefly from his Journal by Rev David Dailey. . . .* Ed. George Peck. New York, 1848.

Smith, Venture. *A Narrative of the Life and Adventures of Venture. . . .* Middletown, Conn., [1798] 1897.

Society of Friends. *Early Quaker Writings from the Library of the Society of Friends, London, 1660–1750.* London, 1977–1979.

Sperry, Rachel [pseudonym]. *A Brief Reply to the Late Writings of Louisa Baker . . . .* Boston, 1816.

Stanton, Daniel. *A Journal. . . .* Philadelphia, 1772.

Stephens, Ellen. *The Cabin Boy Wife. . . .* New York, 1840.

Stewart, Maria. *Religion And The Pure Principles of Morality, The Sure Foundation On Which We Must Build.* 1831. Reprint, *Maria W. Stewart. America's First Black Woman Political Writer,* ed. Marilyn Richardson, 28–42. Bloomington, Ind., 1987.

Stiles, Ezra. *Literary Diary of Ezra Stiles.* Ed. Franklin Dexter. 3 vols. New York, 1901.

Still, James. *Early Recollections and Life of Dr. James Still, 1812–1885.* New Brunswick, N.J., [1877] 1973.

Still, Peter. *The Kidnapped and the Ransomed; The Narrative of Peter and Vina Still After Forty Years of Slavery.* Related to Kate Pickard. Syracuse, N.Y., 1856.

Stinchfield, Ephraim. *Some Memoirs of the Life, Experience and Travels of Elder Ephraim Stinchfield. . . .* Portland, Me., 1819.

Stowe, Harriet Beecher. "Sojourner Truth, the Libyan Sibyl." *Atlantic Monthly,* April 1863, 473–481.

Swan, Frederic W. *Remarkable Visionary Dreams, of a Mulatto Boy, in Northfield, Mass. By the Name of Frederic W. Swan. Aged Thirteen Years. Together with A Sketch of his Life, Sickness, Conversion, and Triumphant Death. Taken from the mouth of his mother, his father being dead.* Chesterfield, N.H., 1822.

Swann, Jabez. *The Evangelist or Life and Labors of the Reverend Jabez Swann.* Waterford, Conn., 1873.

T.T. "A Dream." *The Liberator,* April 2, 1831.

———. "Another Dream." *The Liberator,* April 30, 1831.

Talmud Bavli: Berakhot. Ed. A. Zvi Ehrman. Vol. 4. Jerusalem, 1982.

Tanner, John. *A Narrative of the Captivity and Adventures of John Tanner During Thirty Years Residence Among the Indians.* New York, 1830.

Taylor, John. *A History of Ten Baptist Churches . . . in which will be seen something of a journal of the author's life. . . .* Frankfort, Ky., 1823.

Thomas, Ebenezer S. *Reminiscences. . . .* Hartford, Conn., 1840.

Thomas, Joseph. *The Life of the Pilgrim Joseph Thomas, Containing an Accurate Account of his Trials, Travails, and Gospel Labours Up To the Present Date.* Winchester, Va., 1817.

Tocqueville, Alexis de. *Democracy in America.* 2 vols. New York, [1835] 1945.

Traherne, Thomas. *The Poetical Works of Thomas Traherne.* Ed. Gladys I. Wade. New York, [1903] 1965.

Travis, Joseph. *Autobiography of the Rev. Joseph Travis. . . .* Nashville, Tenn., 1856.

Truth, Sojourner. *Narrative of Sojourner Truth.* Ed. Margaret Washington. New York, 1993.

———. *Narrative of Sojourner Truth, a Northern Slave. . . .* Ed. Olive Gilbert. Boston, 1850.

Tryon, Thomas. *Pythagoras.* London, 1691.

Tubbee, Okah. *A Sketch of the Life of Okah Tubee, alias William Chubbee, son of the head chief, Mosholeh Tubbee, of the Choctaw nation of Indians*, recorded by Laah Ceil Manatoi Elaah Tubbee. Springfield, Mass., 1848. Reprint, *The Life of Okah Tubbee.* Ed. Daniel Littlefield. Ann Arbor, Mich., 1988.

Turner, Nat. *The Confessions of Nat Turner.* Transcribed Thomas R. Grey. Baltimore, 1831.

[The] Universal Dream-Dictionary. . . . Philadelphia, 1797. [This is the same as part 2 of The Universal Interpreter of Dreams and Visions. Baltimore, 1795.]

[The] Universal Interpreter of Dreams and Visions. 2 parts. Part 2: *The Universal Dream-Dictionary. . . .* Baltimore, 1795.

Vandeleuer, John [pseudonym]. *A History of the Voyages and Adventures of John Van Delure. . .1796.* Montpelier, Vt. [ok?] 1812.

Vaux, Robert S. *Memoirs of the Lives of Benjamin Lay and Ralph Sandiford; Two of the Earliest Public Advocates for the Emancipation of the Enslaved Africans.* Philadelphia, 1815.

Walcot, James. *The New Pilgrim's Progress; or The Pious Indian Convert.* London, 1748.

Walker, David. *Walker's Appeal in Four Articles Together With A Preamble. . . .* 2nd ed. Boston, [1829] 1830. Reprinted in *"One Continual Cry": David Walker's Appeal to the Colored Citizens of the World, 1829–1830, Its Setting and Its Meaning*, by Herbert Aptheker, 62–148. New York, 1965.

Ware, Henry. *The Recollections of Jotham Anderson. . .* [pseudonym]. Boston, 1824.

Waterman, Zuriel. Dream. In Memorandum Book for the Sloop Retaliation. May 1780. In the Zuriel Waterman Papers. History of Medicine Division. National Library of Medicine, Bethesda, Md.

Watson, A. P., and Clifton H. Johnson, eds. *God Struck Me Dead: Religious Conversion Experiences and Autobiographies of Ex-Slaves.* Philadelphia, 1969.

Watson, Henry. *Narrative of Henry Watson, a Fugitive Slave.* Boston, 1848.

326

Watters, William. *A Short Account of the Christian Experience, and Ministereal Labours of William Watters*. Alexandria, Va., 1806?

Webb, Eliza Bowen [pseudonym; also Lucy Brewer, Louisa Baker, or Mrs. Lucy West]. *The Female Marine*. . . . 4th ed. N.p., 1818.

Wells, William Charles. *Two Essays . . . With a Memoir of his Life*. London, 1818.

Wesley, John. *The Works of John Wesley*. 3d ed. 14 vols. Grand Rapids, Mich., 1984.

Whitcomb, William W. Whitcomb-Jefferson Interview. May 31, 1824. Manuscripts Department. University of Virginia Library, Charlottesville, Va.

White, George. *A Brief Account of the Life, Experience, Travels and Gospel Labours of George White, An African; Written by Himself and Revised by A Friend*. New York, 1810.

White, K. *A Narrative*. . . . Schenectady, N.Y. 1809.

Wilkinson, Jemima. Jemima Wikinson Papers, 1771–1849. Cornell University Library, Ithaca, N.Y.

Willett, Edward. *The Matrimonial Life of Edward Willett; With a Variable Style*. New York, 1812.

Willey, Chloe. *A Short Account of the Life and Remarkable Views of Mrs. Chloe Willey*. . . . Amherst, Mass., 1807.

Wilmer, James Jones. *Memoirs*. Baltimore, 1792.

Wilson, Harriet E. *Our Nig*. New York, [1859] 1983.

Woolman, John. Book of Executorship. Historical Society of Philadelphia, Philadelphia.

———. *Considerations on Keeping Negroes: Recommended to the Professors of Christianity of Every Denomination. Part Second*. Philadelphia, 1762.

———. Journal. Pennsylvania Historical Society, Philadelphia.

———. *The Journal and Essays of John Woolman*. Ed. Amelia Mott Gummere. New York, 1922.

———. *[The] Journal and Major Essays of John Woolman*. Ed. Phillips P. Moulton. New York, 1971.

———. *[The] Journal of the Life, Gospel Labours, and Christian Experience of the Faithful Minister of Jesus Christ, John Woolman, Late of Mount-Holly, in the Province of New-Jersey*. In *The Works of John Woolman*. Part 1. Philadelphia, 1774.

———. *Some Considerations on the Keeping of Negroes: Recommended to the Professors of Christianity of every Denomination*. Philadelphia, 1754.

———. *The Works of John Woolman*. Two parts. Philadelphia, 1774.

Yonge, James. *The Journal of James Yonge*. . . . Hamden, Conn., 1963.

York, Brantly. *The Autobiography of Brantly York*. Durham, N.C., 1910.

Young, Benjamin Seth. *Testimony of Christ's Second Appearing*. Lebanon, Ohio, 1801.

Young, Jacob. *Autobiography of a Pioneer: or The Nativity, Experience, Travels and Ministerial Labors of Reverend Jacob Young; with Incidents, Observations and Reflections*. Cincinnati, 1860.

SECONDARY SOURCES

Abzug, Robert H. *Cosmos Crumbling: American Reform and the Religious Imagination*. New York, 1994.
———. *Passionate Liberator: Theodore Dwight Weld and the Dilemma of Reform*. New York, 1980.
Adams, Monni. "Fon Appliquéd Cloths." *African Arts* 13 (1979–80): 28–41.
Adams, William H. *Jefferson's Monticello*. New York, 1983.
Adorno, Theodore W., et al. *The Authoritarian Personality*. New York, 1950.
Alexander, Franz, and Thomas Morton French. *Psychoanalytic Therapy: Principles and Application*. New York, 1946.
Alford, C. Fred. *The Self in Social Theory: A Psychoanalytic Account of its Construction in Plato, Hobbes, Locke, Rawls and Rousseau*. New Haven, Conn., 1991.
Almeida, Bira. *Capoeira: A Brazilian Art Form*. Richmond, Calif., 1986.
Alpers, Edward A. "The Story of Swema: Female Vulnerability in Nineteenth-Century East Africa." In *Women and Slavery in Africa*, ed. Claire C. Robertson and Martin A. Klein, 185–199. Madison, Wis., 1983.
Ammerman, David. *In the Common Cause: American Response to the Coersive Acts of 1774*. Charlottesville, Va., 1974.
Appiah, Kwame Anthony. *In My Father's House: Africa in the Philosophy of Culture*. New York, 1992.
Appiah, Peggy. "Akan Symbolism." *African Arts* 13 (1979/80): 64–67.
Aptheker, Herbert. *American Negro Slave Revolts*. New York, 1943.
———. *Anti-Racism in U.S. History: The First Two Hundred Years*. New York, 1992.
———. *"One Continual Cry": David Walker's Appeal to the Colored Citizens of the World, 1829–1830, Its Setting and Its Meaning*. New York, 1965.
———. "The Quakers and Negro Slavery." *Journal of Negro History* 25 (1940): 331–362.
Aries, Philippe. *Western Attitudes Toward Death: From the Middle Ages to the Present*. Baltimore, 1974.
——— Aries, Philippe, and David E. Stannard, eds. *Death in America*. Philadelphia, 1975.
Armstrong, Nancy, and Leonard Tennenhouse. "The Interior Difference: A Brief Genealogy of Dreams, 1650–1717." *Eighteenth-Century Studies* 23 (1990): 458–478.
Ashworth, William B., Jr., "Natural History and the Emblematic World View." In *Reappraisals of the Scientific Revolution*, ed. David C. Lindberg and Robert S. Westman, 303–332. Cambridge, England, 1990.
Atwood, George E., and Robert D. Stolorow. *Structures of Subjectivity: Explorations in Psychoanalytic Phenomenology*. Hillsdale, N.J., 1984.
Augé, Marc. *Non-Places: Introduction to an Anthropology of Supermodernity*. London, 1995.
Auster, Paul. *The Red Notebook and Other Writings*. London, 1995.

Axtell, James. *The Invasion Within: The Contest of Cultures in Colonial North America*. New York, 1985.

Bakan, David. *Sigmund Freud and the Jewish Mystical Tradition*. Boston, 1958.

Baker, Frank. *From Wesley to Asbury: Studies in Early American Methodism*. Durham, N.C., 1976.

Barker-Benfield, G. J. *The Culture of Sensibility: Sex and Society in Eighteenth-Century Britain*. Chicago, 1992.

———. *The Horrors of the Half-Known Life: Male Attitudes Toward Women and Sexuality in Nineteenth-Century America*. New York, 1976.

Bastide, Roger. "Dreams and Culture." In *Dream Dynamics*, ed. Jules H. Masserman, 38–45. New York, 1971.

———. "The Sociology of the Dream." In *The Dream and Human Societies*, ed. Gustave E. Von Grunebaum and Roger Callois, 199–211. Berkeley, Calif., 1966.

Bateson, Gregory. "The Cybernetics of 'Self': A Theory of Alcoholism." In *Steps to an Ecology of Mind: Collected Essays in Anthropology, Psychiatry, Evolution, and Epistemology*, ed. Gregory Bateson, 309–313. San Francisco, 1972.

Bath, Michael. *Speaking Pictures: English Emblem Books and Renaissance Culture*. London, 1994.

Bauman, Richard. *Let Your Words Be Few: Symbolism of Speaking and Silence Among Seventeenth-Century Quakers*. Cambridge, England, 1983.

Bayley, Harold. *The Lost Language of Symbolism: An Inquiry Into the Origins of Certain Letters, Words, Names, Fairy Tales, Folklore and Mythologies*. 2 vols. London, 1912.

Baym, Nina. *Woman's Fiction: A Guide to Novels by and about Women in America, 1820–1870*. Ithaca, N.Y., 1978.

Beattie, John. "Representations of the Self in Traditional Africa." *Africa* 50 (1980): 313–320.

Beauvoir, Simone de. *The Second Sex*. 1st American ed. New York, 1953.

Bedini, Silvio A. "The Survey of the Federal Territory: Andrew Ellicott and Benjamin Banneker." *Washington History* 3 (1991): 76–95, 137–128.

———. *The Life of Benjamin Banneker*. New York, 1972.

Benstock, Shari. *The Private Self: Theory and Practice of Women's Autobiographical Writings*. London, 1988.

Beradt, Charlotte. *The Third Reich of Dreams*. Wellingborough, England, [1966] 1985.

Bercovitch, Sacvan. *The Puritan Origins of the American Self*. New Haven, Conn., 1975.

Berglund, Axel-Ivar. *Zulu Thought-Patterns and Symbolism*. Bloomington, Ind., 1976.

Berlin, Ira. *Many Thousands Gone: The First Two Centuries of Slavery in North America*. Cambridge, Mass., 1998.

———. "Time, Space and the Evolution of Afro-American Society on British Mainland North America." *American Historical Review* 85 (1980): 44–78.

Berlin, Ira, and Ronald Hoffman, eds. *Slavery and Freedom in the Age of the American Revolution*. Charlottesville, Va., 1983.

Bettelheim, Bruno, and Morris Janowitz. *Social Change and Prejudice*. New York, 1964.

Bierlich, Bernard. "The Head and the Heart: Luck, Divination and Lotto Playing in Northern Ghana." Manuscript, 1996.

Bilu, Yoram. "Sigmund Freud and Rabbi Yehuda Halevy: On a Jewish Mystical Tradition of 'Psychoanalytic' Dream Interpretation." *Journal of Psychological Anthropology* 2 (1979): 443–463.

Binger, Carl A. L. "The Dreams of Benjamin Rush." *American Journal of Psychiatry* 125 (1969): 1653–1659.

Bitel, Lisa M. "*In Visu Noctis*: Dreams in European Hagiography and Histories, 450–900." *History of Religions* 31 (1991): 39–59.

Bloch, Ruth H. "The Construction of Gender in a Republican World." In *The Blackwell Encyclopedia of the American Revolution*, ed. Jack P. Greene and J. R. Pole, 601–606. Cambridge, Mass., 1991.

———. "The Gendered Meanings of Virtue in Revolutionary America." *Signs* 13 (1987): 37–58.

Blumin, Stuart M. *The Emergence of the Middle Class: Social Experience in the American City, 1760–1900*. Cambridge, England, 1989.

Boles, John B. *Masters and Slaves in the House of the Lord: Race and Religion in the American South, 1740–1870*. Lexington, Ky., 1988.

Bollas, Christopher. *Being a Character: Psychoanalysis and Self Experience*. New York, 1982.

———. *Forces of Destiny: Psychoanalysis and Human Idiom*. Northvale, N.J., 1989.

———. *The Shadow of the Object: Psychoanalysis of the Unthought Known*. New York, 1987.

Bonime, Walter. "A Culturalist View: The Dream as Human Experience." In *Dream Psychology and the New Biology of Dreaming*, ed. Milton Kramer et al., 79–99. Springfield, Ill., 1969.

Bordin, Ruth O. "The Sect to Denomination Process in America: The Freewill Baptist Experience." *Church History* 34 (1964): 77–94.

Boydston, Jeanne. *Home and Work: Housework, Wages, and the Ideology of Labor in the Early Republic*. New York, 1990.

Branson, Susan. "Women and the Family Economy in the Early Republic: The Case of Elizabeth Meridith." *Journal of the Early Republic* 16 (1996): 47–71.

Braxton, Joanne M. *Black Women Writing Autobiography: A Tradition within a Tradition*. Philadelphia, 1989.

Breen, T. H. "Making History: The Force of Public Opinion and the Last Years of Slavery in Revolutionary Massachusetts." In *Through A Glass Darkly: Reflections on Personal Identity in Early America*, ed. Ronald Hoffman, Mechal Sobel, and Fredrika J. Teute, 67–95. Chapel Hill, N.C., 1997.

Brekus, Catherine A. *Strangers and Pilgrims: Female Preaching in America, 1740–1845*. Chapel Hill, N.C., 1998.

Brodie, Fawn M. *Thomas Jefferson: An Intimate History.* New York, 1974.

Brooke, John L. *The Refiner's Fire: The Making of Mormon Cosmology, 1644–1844.* Cambridge, England, 1994.

Brown, Earl Kent. *Women of Mr. Wesley's Methodism.* New York, 1983.

Brown, Kathleen M. *Good Wives, Nasty Wenches, and Anxious Patriarchs: Gender, Race and Power in Colonial Virginia.* Chapel Hill, N.C., 1996.

Brown, Richard D. "Modernization and the Modern Personality in Early America: A Sketch of a Synthesis." *Journal of Interdisciplinary History* 2 (1972): 201–228.

———. *Modernization: The Transformation of American Life, 1600–1865.* New York, 1976.

Brumble H. David, III. *American Indian Autobiography.* Berkeley, Calif., 1988.

Bruner, Jerome. *Acts of Meaning.* Cambridge, Mass.,1990.

———. "Life as Narrative." *Social Research* 54 (1987): 11–32.

Burke, Peter. *Popular Culture in Early Modern Europe.* New York, 1978.

Burrows, Edwin G., and Michael Wallace. "The American Revolution: The Ideology and Psychology of National Liberation." *Perspectives in American History* 6 (1972): 266–303.

Burton, Arthur, ed. *What Makes Behavior Change Possible?* New York, 1976.

Butler, Jon. *Awash in a Sea of Faith: Christianizing the American People.* Cambridge, Mass., 1990.

Butterfield, L. H. "The Dream of Benjamin Rush: The Reconciliation of John Adams and Thomas Jefferson." *The Yale Review* 40 (1950–1951): 297–319.

Byrne, Donald E.. Jr., *No Foot of Land: Folklore of American Methodist Itinerants.* Metuchen, N.J., 1975.

Calhoon, Robert H. "Loyalism and Neutrality." In *The Blackwell Encyclopedia of the American Revolution*, ed. Jack P. Greene and J. R. Pole, 247–259. Cambridge, Mass., 1994.

Calvert, Karen. *Children in the House: The Material Culture of Early Childhood, 1600–1900.* Boston, 1992.

Campbell, James. *Recovering Ben Franklin: An Exploration of a Life of Science and Service.* Chicago, 1999.

Carnes, Mark C. *Secret Ritual and Manhood in Victorian America.* New Haven, Conn., 1989.

Cashin, Joan E. *A Family Venture: Men and Women on the Southern Frontier.* Baltimore, 1994.

———. "Introduction." In *Our Common Affairs: Texts From Women in The Old South*, ed. Joan E. Cashin, 1–42. Baltimore, 1996.

Chambers-Schiller, Lee. *Liberty, A Better Husband: Single Women in America: The Generations of 1780–1840.* New Haven, Conn., 1984.

Chantiles, Vilma Liacouras. *The Food of Greece.* New York, [1975]1992.

Chilcote, Paul W. *She Offered Them Christ: The Legacy of Women Preachers in Early Methodism.* Nashville, Tenn., 1993.

Christaller, J. G., comp. *Three Thousand Six Hundred Ghanian Proverbs. . . .* Lewiston, Me., 1990.

Clouston, William Alexander. *Hieroglyphic Bibles, Their Origin and History*. New York, 1894.

Cogan, Frances B. *All-American Girl: The Ideal of Real Womanhood in Mid-Nineteenth-Century America*. Athens, Ga., 1989.

Cohen, Patricia Cline. *A Calculating People: The Spread of Numeracy in Early America*. Chicago, 1982.

Conrad, Earl. *Harriet Tubman: Negro Soldier and Abolitionist*. New York, 1942.

Conroy, David W. "Development of a Revolutionary Organization." In *The Blackwell Encyclopedia of the American Revolution*, ed. Jack P. Greene and J. R. Pole, 223–230. Cambridge, Mass., 1994.

Cooley, Steven D. "Manna and the Manual: Sacramental and Instrumental Constructions of the Victorian Methodist Camp Meeting During the Mid-Nineteenth Century." *Religion and American Culture* 6 (1996): 131–159.

Cooper, J. C. *An Illustrated Encyclopedia of Traditional Symbols*. London, 1978.

Coser, Lewis. "Greedy Organizations." *Archives Européennes de Sociologie/European Journal of Sociology* 8, no. 2 (1967): 196–215.

Cott, Nancy F. "Passionlessness: An Interpretation of Victorian Sexual Ideology, 1790–1850." *Signs* 4 (1978): 210–236.

Covitz, Joel. *Visions of the Night: A Study of Jewish Dream Interpretation*. Boston, 1990.

Cox, Stephen D. *"The Stranger Within Thee": Concepts of the Self in Late-Eighteenth-Century Literature*. Pittsburgh, 1980.

Craven, Avery. *Rachel of Old Louisiana*. Baton Rouge, La., 1975.

Creel, Margaret Washington. *"A Peculiar People": Slave Religion and Community-Culture Among the Gullahs*. New York, 1988.

Curley, Richard T. "Dreams of Power: Social Process in a West African Religious Movement." *Africa* 53, no. 3 (1983): 20–37.

Curry, Leonard P. *The Free Black in Urban America, 1800–1850: The Shadow of the Dream*. Chicago, 1981.

Curti, Merle. "The American Exploration of Dreams and Dreamers." *Journal of the History of Ideas* 27 (1966): 341–391.

Dabney, Virginius. *The Jefferson Scandals: A Rebuttal*. New York, 1981.

D'Andrade, Roy G. "Anthropological Studies of Dreams." In *Psychological Anthropology: Approaches to Culture and Personality*, ed. Francis L. K. Hsu, 296–332. Homewood, Ill., 1961.

Davie, Sharon. " 'Reader, my story ends with freedom': Harriet Jacobs's *Incidents in the Life of a Slave Girl*." In *Famous Last Words: Changes in Gender and Narrative Closure*, ed. Alison Booth, 86–109. Charlottesville, Va., 1993.

Davis, David Brion. *The Problem of Slavery in Western Culture*. Ithaca, N.Y., 1966.

Davis, Lance, and Stanley Engerman. "The Economy of British North America: Miles Traveled, Miles Still to Go." *William and Mary Quarterly* 56 (1999): 9–22.

Dayton, Cornelia Hughes. *Women Before the Bar: Gender, Law, and Society in Connecticut, 1639–1789*. Chapel Hill, N.C., 1995.

Dekker, Rudolf M., and Lotte C. van de Pol. *The Tradition of Female Transvestism in Early Modern Europe*. New York, 1989.

D'Elia, Donald J. "Benjamin Rush: Philosopher of the American Revolution." *Transactions of the American Philosophical Society* 64, pt.5, (1974): 1–113.

D'Emilio, John, and Estelle B. Freedman. *Intimate Matters: A History of Sexuality in America*. New York, 1988.

Demos, John. "Historical Treatment of the Age Group." In *Major Transitions in the Human Life Cycle*, ed. Alvin C. Eurich, 69–90. Lexington, Mass., 1981.

De Pauw, Linda Grant. "Women in Combat: The Revolutionary War Experience." *Armed Forces and Society* 7 (1981): 209–226.

Desrochers Robert E., Jr., " 'Not Fade Away': The Narrative of Venture Smith, an African American in the Early Republic." *The Journal of American History* 84 (1997–98): 40–66.

Devereux, George. *Reality and Dream: Psychotherapy of a Plains Indian*. New York, 1969.

Dillenberger, John. *The Visual Arts and Christianity in America: The Colonial Period through the Nineteenth Century*. Chico, Calif., 1984.

Dodds, E. R. *The Greeks and the Irrational*. Berkeley, Calif.,1964.

Douglas, Jack C. "The Emergence, Security and Growth of the Sense of Self." In *The Existential Self in Society*, ed. Joseph A. Kotarba and Andrea Fontana, 69–99. Chicago, 1984.

Douglas, Mary. *Natural Symbols: Explorations in Cosmology*. London, 1970.

Drake, St. Clair. *Black Folk Here and There: An Essay in History and Anthropology*. 2 vols. Los Angeles, 1987.

Drake, Thomas E. *Quakers and Slavery in America*. Gloucester, Mass., [1950] 1965.

Dutton, Paul Edward. *Politics of Dreaming in the Carolingian Empire*. Lincoln, Neb., 1994.

Earle, Alice M. *Child Life in Colonial Days*. New York, 1889.

Edel, Leon. *Stuff of Sleep and Dreams; Experiments in Literary Psychology*. New York, 1982.

Edelman, Gerald. *The Remembered Present: A Biological Theory of Consciousness*. New York, 1989.

Eggan, Dorothy. "The Significance of Dreams for Anthropological Research." *American Anthropologist* 51 (1949): 171–198.

Egnal, Marc, and Joseph A. Ernst. "An Economic Interpretation of the American Revolution." *William and Mary Quarterly* 29 (1972): 3–32.

Elbaz, Robert. *The Changing Nature of the Self: A Critical Study of the Autobiographic Discourse*. London, 1988.

Elias, Norbert. *The Society of Individuals*. Oxford, 1991.

Ellis, Joseph J. *American Sphinx: The Character of Thomas Jefferson*. New York, 1997.

Ellison, Ralph. "Flying Home." In *Black Identity: A Thematic Reader*, ed. Francis E. Kearns, 277–299. New York, 1970.

Erikson, Erik H. *Childhood and Society*. 2d ed. New York, 1963.

———. *Dimensions of a New Identity*. New York, 1974.

Fabian, Ann. *Card Sharps, Dream Books, and Bucket Shops: Gambling in Nineteenth-Century America*. Ithaca, N.Y., 1990.

Fausto-Sterling, Anne. "The Five Sexes: Why Male and Female are Not Enough." *The Sciences* 33 (March/April 1993): 20–24.

Ferguson, Harvie. *The Lure of Dreams: Sigmund Freud and the Construction of Modernity*. New York, 1996.

Fernandez, James W. *Persuasions and Performances: The Play of Tropes in Culture*. Bloomington, Ind., 1986.

Ferris, William. "Vision in Afro-American Folk Art: The Sculpture of James Thomas." *Journal of American Folklore* 88 (1975): 115–131.

Field, Margaret J. *Search for Security: An Ethno-psychiatric Study of Rural Ghana*. Evanston, Ill., 1962.

Fields, Barbara J. *Slavery and Freedom on the Middle Ground: Maryland During the Nineteenth Century*. New Haven, Conn., 1985.

Finke, Roger, and Rodney Stark. *The Churching of America, 1776–1990: Winners and Losers in Our Religious Economy*. New Brunswick, N.J., 1992.

Fischer, Steven R. *The Complete Medieval Dreambook: A Multilingual, Alphabetical Somnia Danielis Collation*. Bern, 1982.

———. "Dreambooks and the Interpretation of Medieval Literary Dreams." *Archiv Fr Kulturgeschichte* 65 (1991): 1–20.

———. *The Dream in the Middle High German Epic*. Bern, Switzerland, 1987.

Fisher, Humphrey J. "Dreams and Conversion in Black Africa." In *Conversion to Islam*, ed. Nehemia Levtzion, 217–235. New York, 1979.

Fisher, Mark Miles. "Lott Carey." American Baptist Historical Society, Rochester, N.Y.

Fiss, Harry. "An Empirical Foundation for a Self Psychology of Dreaming." *The Journal of Mind and Behavior* 7 (1986): 161–192.

———. "The 'Royal Road to the Unconscious.' " In *The Functions of Dreaming*, ed. Alan Moffitt, Milton Kramer, and Robert Hoffman, 381–418. Albany, N.Y., 1993.

Flax, Jane. *Disputed Subjects: Essays on Psychoanalysis, Politics and Philosophy*. New York, 1993.

———. *Thinking Fragments: Psychoanalysis, Feminism, and Postmodernism in the Contemporary West*. Berkeley, Calif., 1990.

Fliegelman, Jay. *Declaring Independence: Jefferson, Natural Language, and the Culture of Performance*. Stanford, Calif., 1993.

———. *Prodigals and Pilgrims: The American Revolution against Patriarchal Authority, 1750–1800*. Cambridge, England, 1982.

Fortes, Meyer. *Religion, Morality and the Person: Essays on Tallensi Religion*. Ed. Jack Goody. Cambridge, England, 1987.

Fosshage, James L. "Dream Interpretation Revisited." In *Frontiers in Self Psychology*, ed. Arnold Goldberg, 161–175. Hillsdale, N.J., 1988.

———. "The Psychological Function of Dreams." In *Psychoanalysis and Contemporary Thought* 6 (1983): 641–669.

Foster, Eugene A., et al. "Jefferson Fathered Slave's Last Child." *Nature* 396 (November 5, 1998): 27–28.

Foucault, Michel. *The Care of the Self*. New York, [1984] 1988.

———. "Dream, Imagination, and Existence." In *Dream and Existence: A Special Issue of the Review of Existential Psychology and Psychiatry* 19, no. 1 (1986): 29–78.

———. *Technologies of the Self: A Seminar with Michel Foucault*, ed. Luther H Martin, Huck Gutman, and Patrick H. Hutton. London, 1988.

Fox, Christopher. *Locke and the Scriblerians: Identity and Consciousness in Early-Eighteenth-Century Britain*. Berkeley, Calif., 1988.

———. "Locke and the Scriblerians: The Discussion of Identity in Early Eighteenth Century England." *Eighteenth-Century Studies* 16 (1982–83), 1–25.

Fox-Genovese, Elizabeth. *Within the Plantation Household: Black and White Women of the Old South*. Chapel Hill, N.C., 1988.

Franklin, Phyllis. *Show Thyself a Man: A Comparison of Benjamin Franklin and Cotton Mather*. The Hague, 1969.

Freeman, Lucy, and Alma Bond. *America's First Woman Warrior: The Courage of Deborah Sampson*. New York, 1992.

Freud, Sigmund. *The Interpretation of Dreams*. Trans. James Trachey. London, 1954.

Frey, Sylvia R. *Water from the Rock: Black Resistance in a Revolutionary Age*. Princeton, N.J.,1991.

Frieden, Ken. *Freud's Dream of Interpretation*. Albany, N.Y., 1990.

———. "Talmudic Dream Interpretation, Freudian Ambivalence, Deconstruction." In *The Dream and the Text: Essays on Literature and Language*, ed. Carol Schreir Rupprecht, 103–111. Albany, N.Y., 1993.

Fries, Adelaid L. *The Road to Salem*. Chapel Hill, N.C., 1944.

Gabel, Stewart. "Monitoring the State of the Self in Dreams: Historical Perspectives and Theoretical Implications." *Psychoanalysis and Contemporary Thought* 14 (1991): 425–451.

Gadlin, Howard. "Private Lives and Public Order: A Critical View of the History of Intimate Relations in the United States." In *Close Relationships: Perspectives on the Meaning of Intimacy*, ed. George Levinger and Harold L. Raush, 33–72. Amherst, 1977.

Garber, Marjorie. *Vested Interests: Cross-Dressing and Cultural Anxiety*. New York, 1992.

Gardner, Howard. *Frames of Mind: The Theory of Multiple Intelligences*. New York, 1983.

Geerts, Clifford. " 'From the Native's Point of View': On the Nature of Anthropological Understanding." In *Culture Theory: Essays on Mind, Self, and Emotion*, ed. Richard A. Shweder and Robert A. LeVine, 123–136. Cambridge, England, 1984.

Genovese, Eugene D. *From Rebellion to Revolution: Afro-American Slave Revolts in the Making of the Modern World*. Baton Rouge, La., 1979.

Georgia Writers' Project, Works Project Administration. *Drums and Shadows: Survival Studies Among the Georgia Coastal Negroes*. Athens, [1940] 1986.

Gilbar, Sandra M. "Soldier's Heart: Literary Men, Literary Women, and the Great War." *Signs* 8 (1983): 422–450.

Gilje, Paul A. *The Road to Mobocracy: Popular Disorder in New York City, 1763–1834*. Chapel Hill, N.C., 1987.

Gillespie, Joanna Bowen. " 'The Clear Leadings of Providence': Pious Memoirs and the Problems of Self-Realization for Women in the Early Nineteenth Century." *Journal of the Early Republic* 5 (1985): 197–221.

Gillis, John R. "From Ritual to Romance: Toward an Alternative History of Love" In *Emotion and Social Change: Toward a New Psychohistory*, ed. Carol Z. Stearns and Peter N. Stearns, 87–121. New York, 1988.

Glass, James M. *Shattered Selves: Multiple Personality in a Postmodern World*. Ithaca, N.Y., 1993.

Godbeer, Richard. " 'The Cry of Sodom': Discourse, Intercourse, and Desire in Colonial New England." *William and Mary Quarterly* 52 (1995): 259–286.

Godwin, Robert. "On the Function of Enemies: The Articulation and Containment of the Unthought Self." *The Journal of Psychohistory* 22 (1994): 79–102.

Goffman, Erving. *Relations in Public: Microstudies of the Public Order*. New York, 1972.

Gomez, Michael A. *Exchanging Our Country Marks: The Transformation of African Identities in the Colonial and Antebellum South*. Chapel Hill, N.C., 1998.

Goodell, Abner C., Jr. "John Saffin and His Slave Adam." *Colonial Society of Massachusetts Publications. Transactions, 1892–1894* 1 (1895): 85–113.

Gordon-Reed, Annette. *Thomas Jefferson and Sally: An American Controversy*. Charlottesville, Va., 1998.

Graff, Harvey J. *Conflicting Paths: Growing Up in America*. Cambridge, Mass., 1995.

Gravely, Will B. "The Rise of African Churches in America (1786–1822): Reexamining the Contexts." *Journal of Religious Thought* 41 (1984): 58–73.

Greenberg, David F. *The Construction of Homosexuality*. Chicago, 1988.

Greenberg, Kenneth S. "The Nose, the Lie, and the Duel in the Antebellum South." *American Historical Review* 95 (1990): 57–74.

Greenberg, Ramon. "Self-Psychology and Dreams: The Merging of Different Perspectives," *Psychiatric Journal of the University of Ottawa* 12 (1987): 98–102.

Greenberg, Ramon, Howard Katz, Wynn Schwartz, and Chester Pearlman. "A Research-Based Reconsideration of the Psychoanalytic Theory of Dreaming." *Journal of the American Psychoanalytic Association* 40 (1992): 531–550.

336

Greenberg, Ramon, and Chester Pearlman. "A Psychoanalytic-Dream Continuum: The Source and Function of Dreams." *International Review of Psycho-Analysis* 2 (1975): 441–448.

Greenblatt, Stephen Jay. *Renaissance Self-Fashioning: From More to Shakespeare*. Chicago, 1980.

Greene, Thomas M. *The Light in Troy: Imitation and Discovery in Renaissance Poetry*. New Haven, Conn., 1982.

Gregg, Gary S. *Self-Representation: Life Narrative Studies in Identity and Ideology*. New York, 1991.

Greven, Philip. *The Protestant Temperament: Patterns of Child-Rearing, Religious Experience, and the Self in Early America*. New York, 1977.

Grimsted David A. "Anglo-American Racism and Phillis Wheatley's 'Sable Veil,' 'Length'ned Chain,' and 'Knitted Heart.' " In *Women in the Age of the American Revolution*, ed. Ronald Hoffman and Peter J. Albert, 379–381. Charlottesville, Va., 1989.

Grimsted, David. *American Mobbing, 1828–1861: Toward Civil War*. New York, 1998.

Grossi, Elizabeth. " 'It is Worth That Makes the Man': The First Generation of African-American Leaders in New York City." M.A. thesis, Hunter College, City University of New York, 1993.

Guiley, Rosemary E. *The Encyclopedia of Witches and Witchcraft*. New York, 1989.

Gundaker, Grey. "Tradition and Innovation in African-American Yards." *African Arts* 26 (April 1993): 58–96.

Guralnick, Margot. "The All-Seeing Eye: Masonic Images Once Infiltrated All of America." *Arts and Antiques* [volume available?](1988): 62–67.

Habermas, Jurgen. *The Structural Transformation of the Public Sphere: An Inquiry into a Category of Bourgeois Society*. Cambridge, Mass., 1989.

Halevi, Sharon. "The Path Not Taken: Gender and Race in the South Carolina Backcountry, 1750–1800." Ph.D. dissertation, University of Iowa, 1995.

Hall, Calvin S., " 'A Ubiquitous Sex Difference in Dreams' Revisited." *Journal of Personality and Social Psychology* 46 (1984): 1109–1117.

Hall, Calvin S., G. W. Domhoff, K. A. Blick, and K. E. Weesner. "The Dreams of College Men and Women in 1950 and 1980: A Comparison of Dream Content and Sex Differences." *Sleep* 5 (1982): 188–194.

Hall, David D. "The Uses of Literacy in New England, 1600–1850." In *Printing and Society in Early America*, ed. William L. Joyce et al., 1–47. Worcester, Mass,. 1983.

———. "The World of Print and Collective Mentality in Seventeenth-Century New England." In *New Directions in American Intellectual History*, ed. J. Higham and P. Conkin. Baltimore, 1979.

———. *Worlds of Wonder, Days of Judgment: Popular Religious Beliefs in Early New England*. New York,1989.

Halttunen, Karen. "Humanitarianism and the Pornography of Pain in Anglo-American Culture." *American Historical Review* 100 (1995): 303–334.

Hambrick-Stowe, Charles E. "The Spiritual Pilgrimage of Sarah Osborn (1714–1796)." *Church History* 61 (1992): 408–421.

Handler, Mimi. "Masonic Symbols: Decorating Our History." *Early American Life* 24 (August 1993): 45–55.

Hanley, F. William. "Erickson's Contribution to Change in Psychotherapy." In *Ericksonian Approaches to Hypnosis and Psychotherapy*, ed. Jeffrey Zeig, 29–36. New York, 1982.

Hartmann, Ernest. *Dreams and Nightmares: The New Theory on the Origin and Meaning of Dreams*. New York, 1998.

Haskell, Robert E. "Giambattista Vico and the Discovery of Metaphoric Cognition." In *Cognition and Symbolic Structures: The Psychology of Metaphoric Transformation*, ed. Robert E. Haskell, 67–82. Norwood, N.J., 1987.

Hatch, Nathan O. *The Democratization of American Christianity*. New Haven, Conn., 1989.

Havens, Leston L. *A Safe Place: Laying The Groundwork of Psychotherapy*. Cambridge, Mass., 1996.

Hawke, David Freeman. *Benjamin Rush: Revolutionary Gadfly*. Indianapolis, 1971.

Hazlip, Sirlee Taylor. *The Sweeter the Juice: A Family Memoir in Black and White*. New York, 1955.

Hegel, George W. F. *The Phenomenology of Mind*. Trans. J. B. Baillie. London, 1910.

Heideking, Jürgen. "The Image of an English Enemy During the American Revolution." In *Enemy Images in American History*, ed. Ragnhild Fiebig-von Hase and Ursalu Lehmkuhl, 91–108. Providence R.I., 1997.

Heilbrun, Carolyn G. *Writing a Woman's Life*. New York, 1988.

Hempton, David. *The Religion of the People: Methodism and Popular Religion c.1750–1900*. London, 1996.

Heyrman, Christine Leigh. *Southern Cross: The Beginnings of the Bible Belt*. Chapel Hill, N.C., 1997.

Hilmer, Mary Adams. "The Other Diary of Samuel Sewall." *New England Quarterly* 55 (1982): 354–367.

Hodes, Martha. *White Women, Black Men: Illicit Sex in the Nineteenth-Century South*. New Haven, Conn., 1997.

Hoffman, Ronald. "The 'Disaffected' in the Revolutionary South." In *The American Revolution: Explorations in the History of American Radicalism*, ed. Alfred F. Young, 273–316. DeKalb, Ill., 1976.

Hoffman, Ronald, and Peter J. Albert, eds. *Religion in a Revolutionary Age*. Charlottesville, Va., 1994.

Holt, Thomas C, "Marking: Race, Race-Making, and the Writing of History." *American Historical Review* 100 (1995): 1–20.

Humez, Jean M. "In Search of Harriet Tubman's Spiritual Autobiography." *National Women's Studies Association Journal* 5 (1993): 162–182.

———. " 'My Spirit Eye': Some Functions of Spiritual and Visionary Experience in the Lives of Five Black Women Preachers, 1810–1880." In *Women and The Structure of Society*, ed. Barbara J. Harris and JoAnn K. McNamara, 129–143. Durham, N.C., 1984.

———. "Reading *The Narrative of Sojourner Truth* as a Collaborative Text." *Frontiers* 16 (1996): 29–52.

Huntley, Frank L. "*The Garden of Cyrus* As Prophecy." In *Approaches to Sir Thomas Browne*, ed. C. A. Patrides, 132–142. Columbia, Mo., 1982.

Hurry, Robert J. "An Archeological and Historical Perspective on Benjamin Banneker." *Maryland Historical Magazine* 84 (1989): 361–369.

Hyatt, Harry Middleton. *Hoodoo–Conjuration–Witchcraft–Rootwork; Beliefs Accepted by Many Negroes and White Persons. . . .* 5 vols. Cambridge, Md., 1970–1978.

Imhof, Arthur E. "Life-Course Patterns of Women and Their Husbands: 16th to 20th Century." In *Human Development and the Life Course: Multidisciplinary Perspectives*, ed. Aage B. Sørensen, Franz E. Weinert, and Lonnie R. Sherrod, 247–270. Hillsdale, N.J., 1986.

Irwin, Lee. "Contesting World Views: Dreams Among the Huron and Jesuits." *Religion* 22 (1992): 259–269.

Isaac, Glynn. "The Food-Sharing Behavior of Protohuman Hominids." *Scientific American* 238, no.4 (1978): 90–108.

Isaac, Rhys. "Evangelical Revolt: The Nature of the Baptist's Challenge to the Traditional Order in Virginia, 1765–1775." *William and Mary Quarterly* 31 (1974): 345–368.

Jackson, Luther P. "Religious Development of the Negroes in Virginia from 1770 to 1860." *Journal of Negro History* 16 (1931): 68–239.

Jackson, Margaret Y. *The Struggle For Freedom: Phase I as Revealed in Slave Narrative of the Pre-Civil War Period (1840–1860)*. Chicago, 1976.

James, William. *The Principles of Psychology*. 2 vols. New York, 1893.

Jedrej, M. C., and Rosalind Shaw. *Dreaming, Religion and Society in Africa*. Leiden, 1992.

Jelinek, Estelle C. "Disguise Autobiographies: Women Masquerading As Men." *Women's Studies International Forum* 10 (1987): 53–62.

Johnson, Paul E., and Sean Wilentz. *The Kingdom of Matthais: A Story of Sex and Salvation in Nineteenth Century America*. New York, 1994.

Johnston, James Hugo. *Race Relations in Virginia and Miscegenation in the South, 1776–1860*. Amherst, Mass., 1970.

Jones, Major J. *The Color of God: The Concept of God in Afro-American Thought*. Macon, Ga., 1988.

Jordan, Judith V. "A Relational Perspective for Understanding Women's Development." In *Women's Growth in Diversity: More Writings from the Stone Center*, ed. Judith V. Jordan, 9–24. New York, 1997.

Jordan, Winthrop D. *White over Black: American Attitudes toward the Negro, 1550–1812*. Chapel Hill, N.C., 1968.

Joyner, Charles. " 'Believer I Know": The Emergence of African American Christianity." In *African American Christianity: Essays in History*, ed. Paul E. Johnson, 18–46. Berkeley, Calif., 1994.

———. *Down By The Riverside: A South Carolina Slave Community*. Urbana, Ill., 1984.

Jung, Carl G. *Collected Works of C. G. Jung*. Trans. R. F. C. Hull. 21 vols. London, 1953–1973.

———. *Dreams*. Trans. R. F. C. Hull. Princeton, N.J., 1974.

———. *Symbols of Transformation*. 2d ed. Princeton, N.J., 1967.

Juster, Susan M. *Disorderly Women: Sexual Politics & Evangelicalism in Revolutionary New England*. Ithaca, N.Y., 1994.

———. "Patriarchy Reborn: The Gendering of Authority in the Evangelical Church in Revolutionary New England." *Gender and History* 6 (1994): 58–81.

———. "To Slay the Beast: Visionary Women in the Early Republic." In *A Mighty Baptism: Race, Gender, and the Creation of American Protestantism*, ed. Susan M. Juster and Lisa MacFarlane, 19–37. Ithaca, N.Y., 1996.

Juster, Susan M., and Lisa MacFarlane, eds. *A Mighty Baptism: Race, Gender, and the Creation of American Protestantism*. Ithaca, N.Y., 1996.

Kafer, Peter. "Charles Brockden Brown and Revolutionary Philadelphia: An Imagination in Context." *The Pennsylvania Magazine of History & Biography* 116 (1992): 467–498.

Kamen, Michael. "Changing Perceptions of the Life Cycle in American Thought and Culture." In *Selvages and Biases: The Fabric of History in American Culture*. Ithaca, N.Y., 1987.

Kaplan, Louis. *A Bibliography of American Autobiographies*. Madison, Wis., 1962.

Kaplan, Sidney. *The Black Presence in the Era of the American Revolution, 1770–1800*. Greenwich, Conn., 1973.

Katz, Jonathan. *Gay American History: Lesbians and Gay Men in the U.S.A.* New York, 1976.

Kelly, Joan. *Women, History and Theory: The Essays of Joan Kelly*. Chicago, 1984.

Kerber, Linda K. "Can a Woman Be an Individual? The Discourse of Self-Reliance." In *Toward an Intellectual History of Women: Essays*. Chapel Hill, N.C., 1997.

———."Separate Spheres, Female Worlds, Woman's Place: The Rhetoric of Women's History." *Journal of American History* 75 (1988): 9–39.

———. *Women of the Republic: Intellect and Ideology in Revolutionary America*. New York, 1986.

Kessler-Harris, Alice. *Out to Work: A History of Wage-Earning Women in the United States*. New York, 1982.

Kett, Joseph F. *Rites of Passage: Adolescence in America, 1790 to the Present*. New York, 1977.

———. "The Stages of Life." In *The American Family in Social-Historical Perspective*, ed. Michael Gordon, 166–191. 2d. ed. New York, 1978.

Kimmel, Michael. *Manhood in America: A Cultural History*. New York, 1996.

Kindermann, Wolff. *Man Unknown to Himself: Kritische Reflexion der Amerikanischen Aufklärung: Crèvecoeur, Benjamin Rush, Charles Brockden Brown*. Tübingen, 1993.

Kitch, Sally L. *Chaste Liberation: Celibacy, and Female Cultural Status.* Urbana, Ill., 1989.

Klinghoffer, Judith Apter, and Lois Elkis. " 'The Petticoat Electors': Women's Suffrage in New Jersey, 1776–1807." *Journal of the Early Republic* 12 (1992): 159–193.

Kloos, John M. *A Sense of Deity: The Republican Spirituality of Dr. Benjamin Rush.* Brooklyn, N.Y., 1991.

Kluckhohn, Clyde, and William Morgan. "Some Notes on Navaho Dreams." In *Psychoanalysis and Culture: Essays in Honor of Géza Róheim,* ed. George B. Wilbur and Werner Muensterberger, 120–131. New York, 1965.

Kohli, Martin. "The World We Forgot: A Historical Review of the Life Course." In *Later Life: The Social Psychology of Aging,* ed. Victor W. Marshall, 271–303. Beverly Hills, Calif., 1986.

Kohut, Heinz. *The Restoration of the Self.* New York, 1977.

———. *The Search for the Self; Selected Writing of Heinz Kohut.* Ed. Paul H. Ornstein. 4 vols. Madison, Conn., 1978–1991.

Kreissman, Bernard. *Pamela-Shamela: A Study of the criticisms, Burlesques, Parodies, and Adaptations of Richardson's "Pamela".* Lincoln, Neb., 1960.

Kruger, Steven F. *Dreaming in the Middle Ages.* Cambridge, England, 1992.

Kujawa, Sheryl Anne. "Religion, Education and Gender in Eighteenth Century Rhode Island: Sarah Hagar Wheaton Osborn, 1714–1796." Ed.D. dissertation, Teachers College of Columbia University, 1993.

Kulikoff, Allan. "The American Revolution, Capitalism, and the Formation of the Yeoman Classes." In *Beyond the American Revolution: Explorations in the History of American Radicalism,* ed. Alfred F. Young, 80–119. DeKalb, Ill., 1993.

Kulikoff, Allan. "Was the American Revolution a Bourgeois Revolution?" In *The Transforming Hand of Revolution: Reconsidering the American Revolution as a Social Movement,* ed. Ronald Hoffman and Peter J. Albert, 58–89. Charlottesville, Va., 1996.

Lacey, Barbara E. "The Bonds of Friendship: Sarah Osborn of Newport and the Reverend Joseph Fish of North Stonington, 1743–1779." *Rhode Island History* 4 (1986): 127–136.

———. "The World of Hannah Heaton: The Autobiography of an Eighteenth-Century Connecticut Farm Women." *William and Mary Quarterly* 45 (1988): 280–304.

Laden, Marie-Paule. *Self-Imitation in the Eighteenth-Century Novel.* Princeton, N.J., 1987.

Laing, R. D. *The Divided Self: An Existential Study in Sanity and Madness.* London, 1969.

Lander, Eric S., and Joseph J. Ellis. "Founding Father." *Nature* 396 (November 5, 1998): 13–14.

Laughlin, Charles D. Jr., John McManus, Robert A. Rubinstein, and Jon Shearer. "The Ritual Transformation of Experience." *Studies in Symbolic Interaction* 7: (1986): 107–136.

Laurie, Bruce. *Artisans into Workers: Labor in Nineteenth-Century America.* New York, 1991.

————. *Working People of Philadelphia, 1800–1850.* Philadelphia, 1980.

Lawton, Samuel Miller. "The Religious Life of South Carolina Coastal and Sea Island Negroes." Ph.D. dissertation, George Peabody College for Teachers, 1939.

Lebsock, Suzanne. *The Free Women of Petersburg: Status and Culture in a Southern Town, 1784–1860.* New York, 1984.

Lee, S. G. "Social Influences in Zulu Dreaming." *Journal of Social Psychology* 47, (1958): 265–283.

LeGoff, Jacques. *Time, Work and Culture in the Middle Ages.* Chicago, 1980.

Lemisch, Jesse. "Listening to the Inarticulate: William Widger's Dream and the Loyalties of American Revolutionary Seamen in British Prisons." *Journal of Social History* 3 (1969): 1–29.

Levenduski, Cristine M. *Peculiar Power: A Quaker Woman Preacher in Eighteenth-Century America.* Washington, D.C., 1996.

————. " 'Remarkable Experiences in the Life of Elizabeth Ashbridge': Portraying the Public Woman in Spiritual Autobiography." *Women's Studies* 19 (1991): 271–281.

Leverenz, David. *The Language of Puritan Feeling: An Exploration in Literature, Psychology, and Social History.* New Brunswick, N.J., 1980.

LeVine, Robert A. *Dreams and Deeds: Achievement Motivation in Nigeria.* Chicago, 1969.

————. "The Self and Its Development in an African Society: A Preliminary Analysis." In *Psychosocial Theories of the Self,* ed. Benjamin Lee, 43–65. New York, 1982.

————. "The Self in an African Culture." In *Psychoanalytic Anthropology After Freud: Essays Marking the Fiftieth Anniversary of Freud's Death,* ed. David H. Spain, 37–47. New York, 1992.

Lewin, Bertram D. *The Image and the Past.* New York, 1968.

Lewis, Jan. "Happiness." In *The Blackwell Encyclopedia of the American Revolution,* ed. Jack P. Greene and J. R. Pole, 641–647. Cambridge, Mass., 1991.

Lhamon, W. T., Jr. *Raising Cain: Blackface Performance from Jim Crow to Hip Hop.* Cambridge, Mass., 1998.

Lienhardt, Godfrey. "Self: Public, Private. Some African Representations." In *The Category of the Person: Anthropology, Philosophy, History,* ed. Michael Carrithers, Steven Collins, and Steven Lukes, 141–155. Cambridge, England, 1985.

Lifshin, Lyn, ed. *Ariadne's Thread: A Collection of Contemporary Women's Journals.* New York, 1982.

Lincoln, Jackson Steward. *The Dream in Primitive Cultures.* London, 1935.

Lloyd, Geoffrey E. R. *Polarity and Analogy: Two Types of Argumentation in Early Greek Thought.* Cambridge, England, 1966.

————. "Right and Left in Greek Philosophy." In *Right & Left: Essays on Dual Symbolic Classification,* ed. Rodney Needham, 167–186. Chicago, 1973.

Lobody, Diane Helen. " 'A Wren Just Bursting Its Shell': Catherine Livingston Garrettson's Ministry of Public Domesticity." In *Spirituality and Social Responsibility: Vocational Vision of Women in The United Methodist Tradition*, ed. Rosemary Skinner Keller, 19–40. Nashville, Tenn., 1993.

———. "Lost in the Ocean of Love: The Mystical Writings of Catherine Livingston Garrettson." Ph.D. dissertation, Drew University, 1990.

" 'That language might be given me': Women's Experience in Early Methodism." In *Perspectives on American Methodism: Interpretive Essays*, ed. Russell E. Richey et al. Nashville, Tenn., 1993.

———." 'That language might be given me': Women's Experience in Early Methodism." In *Perspectives on American Methodism: Interpretive Essays*, ed. Russell E. Richey et al. Nashville, Tenn., 1993.

Lockridge, Kenneth. *On the Sources of Patriarchal Rage: The Commonplace Books of William Byrd II and Thomas Jefferson, and the Gendering of Power in the Eighteenth Century*. New York, 1992.

Loehrich, Rolf. *Thought Operations with Dreams and Reconstructions of Symbolic Systems*. Vol. 3 of *Exercitium Cogitandi*. Oxford, England, 1978.

Loewenberg, Bert James, and Ruth Bogen, eds. *Black Women in Nineteenth-Century American Life*. University Park, Pa., 1976.

Lomax, Alan. *Folk Songs of North America, in the English Language*. New York, 1960.

Lott, Eric. *Love and Theft: Blackface Minstrelsy and the American Working Class*. New York, 1993.

Lovejoy, David S. *Religious Enthusiasm in the New World: Heresy to Revolution*. Cambridge, Mass., 1985.

———. "Samuel Hopkins: Religion, Slavery and the Revolution." *New England Quarterly* 40 (1967): 227–243.

———. "Shun Thy Father and All That: The Enthusiasts Threat to the Family." *New England Quarterly* 60 (1987): 71–85.

Lowenthal, David. *The Past Is a Foreign Country*. Cambridge, England, 1985.

Lyons, Claire. "Sex Among the Rabble: Gender Transitions in an Age of Revolution, Philadelphia, 1750–1830." Ph.D. dissertation, Yale University, 1996.

Lyons, John O. *The Invention of the Self: The Hinge of Consciousness in the Eighteenth Century*. Carbondale, Ill., 1978.

Mabee, Carleton. *Sojourner Truth: Slave, Prophet, Legend*. New York, 1995.

MacDonald, Robert H. "The Frightful Consequences of Onanism: Notes on the History of a Delusion." *Journal of the History of Ideas* 28 (1967): 423–431.

Mack, Phyllis. "Gender and Spirituality in Early English Quakerism, 1650–1665." In *Witnesses for Change: Quaker Women Over Three Centuries*, ed. Elizabeth Brown and Susan Stuard, 31–63. New Brunswick, N.J., 1989.

Madden, Etta. "Reading, Writing, and the Race of Mother Figures: Shakers Rebecca Cox Jackson and Alonzo Giles Hollister." In *A Mighty Baptism: Race, Gender and the Creation of American Protestantism*, ed. Susan Juster and Lisa MacFarlane, 210–234. Ithaca, N.Y., 1996.

Malone, Dumas, and Steven H. Hochman. "A Note on Evidence: The Personal History of Madison Hemings." *Journal of Southern History* 41 (1975): 523–528.

Manuel, Frank. "Toward a Psychological History of Utopias." *Daedalus* 94 (1965): 293–322.

Maresca, Frank, and Roger Ricco. *Bill Traylor: His Art, His Life.* New York, 1991.

Marienstras, Elise. "Liberty." In *The Blackwell Encyclopedia of the American Revolution,* ed. Jack P. Greene and J. R. Pole, 609–615. Cambridge, England, 1991.

Marietta, Jack D. *The Reformation of American Quakerism, 1748–1783.* Philadelphia, 1984.

Matthews, Jean V. "Consciousness of Self and Consciousness of Sex in Antebellum Feminism." *Journal of Women's History* 5 (1993): 61–78.

Mbiti, John S. *African Religions and Philosophy.* London, 1969.

McCusker, John J., and Russell R. Menard. *The Economy of British America, 1607–1789.* Chapel Hill, N.C., 1985.

McElroy, Guy. C. *Facing History: The Black Image in American Art, 1710–1940.* San Francisco, 1990.

McGowan, William H. "The Dream of Ezra Stiles: Bishop Berkeley's Haunting of New England." *Studies in Eighteenth-Century Culture* 11 (1981): 181–198.

McKenzie, Peter. "Dreams and Visions from Nineteenth Century Yoruba Religion." In *Dreaming, Religion and Society in Africa,* ed. M. C. Jedrej and Rosalind Shaw, 126–134. Leiden, 1992.

Medlicott, Alexander, Jr. "The Legend of Lucy Brewer: An Early American Novel." *New England Quarterly* 39 (1966): 461–473.

Meier, Pauline. *From Resistance to Revolution: Colonial Radicals and the Development of American Opposition to Britain, 1765–1776.* London, 1973.

Meranze, Michael. "Introduction." In *Benjamin Rush, Essays, Literary, Moral and Philosophica,* ed. M. Meranze. Schenectady, N.Y., 1988.

Merritt, Jane T. "Dreaming of the Savior's Blood: Moravians and the Indian Great Awakening in Pennsylvania." *William and Mary Quarterly* 54 (1997): 723–746.

Miller, Patricia Cox. *Dreams in Late Antiquity: Studies in the Imagination of a Culture.* Princeton, N.J., 1994.

Miller, Peggy J. "Narrative Practices: Their Role in Socialization and Self-construction." In *The Remembering Self: Construction and Accuracy in the Self-Narrative,* ed. Ulric Neisser and Robyn Fivush, 158–179. Cambridge, England, 1994.

Minkema, Kenneth P. "Jonathan Edwards on Slavery and the Slave Trade." *William and Mary Quarterly* 54 (1997): 823–834.

Mintz, Steven, and Susan Kellogg. *Domestic Revolutions: A Social History of American Family Life.* New York, 1988.

Misch, Georg. *A History of Autobiography in Antiquity.* 2 vols. Westport, Conn., 1973.

Mitchell, Trent A. "The Politics of Experiment in the Eighteenth Century: The Pursuit of Audience and the Manipulation of Consensus in the Debate Over Lightning Rods." *Eighteenth Century Studies* 31 (1998): 307–332.

Modell, Arnold H. *The Private Self.* Cambridge, Mass., 1993.

Moffitt, Alan, Milton Kramer, and Robert Hoffman, eds. *The Functions of Dreaming.* Albany, N.Y., 1993.

Moore, Thomas. *Care of the Soul: A Guide for Cultivating Depth and Sacredness in Everyday Life.* New York, 1992.

Molino, Anthony. "Christopher Bollas." In *Elaborate Selves, Reflections and Reveries of Christopher Bollas, Michael Eigen, Polly-Yopung-Eisendrath, Samuel and Evelyn Laeuchil and Marie Coleman Nelson,* ed. Anthony Molino, 11–60. New York, 1996. [*The Psychotherapy Patient,* 10, (1996).]

Morgan, Philip D. *Slave Counterpoint: Black Culture in the Eighteenth-Century Chesapeake & Lowcountry.* Chapel Hill, N.C., 1998.

Morris, Brian. *Anthropology of the Self: The Individual in Cultural Perspective.* London. 1993.

Mpier, Mubuy Mubuy. "Dreams Among the Yansi." In *Dreaming, Religion and Society in Africa* ed. M. C. Jedrej and Rosalind Shaw, 100–110. Leiden, 1992.

Mutwa, Vusamazulu Credo. *Song of the Stars: The Lore of a Zulu Shaman.* Ed. Stephen Larsen. Barrytown, N.Y., 1996.

Nash, Gary B. *Forging Freedom: The Formation of Philadelphia's Black Community.* Cambridge, Mass., 1988.

———. *Race and Revolution.* Madison, Wis., 1990.

———. *Social Change, Political Consciousness, and the Origins of the American Revolution.* Cambridge, Mass., 1979.

———. *The Urban Crucible; Social Change, Political Consciousness, and the Origins of the American Revolution.* Cambridge, Mass., 1981.

Nash, Gary B., et al., eds. *The American People: Creating a Nation and a Society.* New York, 1996.

Needham, R. "The Left Hand of the Mugwe." *Africa* 30 (1960): 20–33.

Newfield, Christopher J. "Loving Bondage: Emerson's Ideal Relationship." *American Transcendental Quarterly* 5 (1991): 183–193.

Nichols, Lee C. "Variations of the Prophetic Dream in Modern Russian Literature." In *The Dream and the Text: Essays on Literature and Language,* ed. Carol Schreier Rupprecht, 284–305. Albany, N.Y., 1993.

Nissenbaum, Stephen. *Sex, Diet and Debility in Jacksonian America: Sylvester Graham and Health Reform.* Chicago, 1988.

Norton, Mary Beth. *Liberty's Daughters: The Revolutionary Experience of American Women, 1750–1800.* Glenview, Ill., 1980.

———. " 'My Resting, Reaping Times': Sarah Osborn's Defense of Her 'Unfeminine' Activities, 1767." *Signs* 2 (1976): 515–529.

Nussbaum, Felicity A. *The Autobiographical Subject: Gender and Ideology in Eighteenth-Century England.* Baltimore: 1989.

Ofari, Earl. *"Let Your Motto Be Resistance": The Life and Thought of Henry Highland Garnet*. Boston, 1972.

O'Flaherty, Wendy Doniger. *Dreams, Illusion, and Other Realities*. Chicago, 1984.

O'Keefe, Richard. " 'Demonology': Emerson's Dreams." *American Transcendental Quarterly* 8 (1994): 5–16.

Olderr, Steven. *Symbolism: A Comprehensive Dictionary*. Jefferson, N.C., 1986.

Omoyajowo, J. A. *Your Dreams: An Introductory Study*. Ibadan, Nigeria, 1965.

O'Nell, Carl. *Dreams, Culture and the Individual*. San Francisco, 1976.

Ornstein, Paul H. "On Self-State Dreams in the Psychoanalytic Treatment Process." In *The Interpretations of Dreams in Clinical Work*, ed. Arnold Rothstein, 87–104. Madison, Conn., 1987.

Ottenberg, Simon. *Boyhood Rituals in an African Society: An Interpretation*. Seattle, 1989.

Painter, Nell Irvin. "Representing Truth: Sojourner Truth's Knowing and Becoming Known." *The Journal of American History* 81 (1994): 461–492.

———. *Sojourner Truth: A Life, A Symbol*. New York, 1996.

———. "Soul Murder and Slavery: Toward A Fully Loaded Cost Accounting." In *U.S. History as Women's History: New Feminist Essays*, ed. Linda K. Kerber, Alice Kessler-Harris, and Kathryn Kish Sklar, 125–146. Chapel Hill, N.C., 1995.

Palmer, Barbara D. "The Inhabitants of Hell: Devils." In *The Iconography of Hell*, ed. Clifford Davidson and Thomas H. Seiler, 20–41. Kalamazoo, Mich., 1992.

Parrinder, Geoffrey. *West African Psychology; A Comparative Study of Psychological and Religious Thought*. London, 1951.

Payne, Daniel. *History of the African Methodist Episcopal Church*. Nashville, Tenn., 1891.

Payne, Rodger M. "Metaphors of the Self and the Sacred: The Spiritual Autobiography of the Rev. Freeborn Garrettson." *Early American Literature* 27 (1992): 31–47.

———. *The Self and the Sacred: Conversion and Autobiography in Early American Protestantism*. Knoxville, Tenn., 1998.

Pease, Jane H., and William H. Pease. "Black Power—the Debate in 1840." *Phylon* 29 (1968): 19–26.

———. *Black Utopia: Negro Communal Experiments in America*. Madison, Wis., 1972.

———. *Ladies, Women and Wenches: Choice and Constraint in Antebellum Charleston and Boston*. Chapel Hill, N.C., 1990.

———. *They Who Would Be Free: Blacks' Search for Freedom, 1830–1861*, New York, 1974.

Peckham, Howard H., ed. *The Toll of Independence: Engagements and Battle Casualties of the American Revolution*. Chicago, 1974.

Petry, Ann. *Harriet Tubman: Conductor on the Underground Railroad*. New York, 1955.

Peyer, Bernd. "Samson Occom: Mohegan Missionary and Writer of the 18th Century." *American Indian Quarterly* 6 (1982), 208–217. 1997.

Poe, William A. "Lott Carey: Man of Purchased Freedom." *Church History* 39 (1970): 49–61.

Pollock, John. *John Wesley.* London, 1989.

Preston, Dickson J. *Young Frederick Douglass: The Maryland Years.* Baltimore, 1980.

Price, Jacob M. "Reflections on the Economy of Revolutionary America." In *The Economy of Early America: The Revolutionary Period, 1763–1790,* ed. Ronald Hoffman et al., 303–324. Charlottesville, Va., 1988.

Puckett, Newbell Niles. *Folk Beliefs of the Southern Negro.* New York, [1926] 1968.

Purcell, Sheila, Alan Moffitt, and Robert Hoffman. "Waking, Dreaming, and Self-Regulation." In *The Functions of Dreaming,* ed. Alan Moffitt, Milton Kramer, and Robert Hoffmann, 197–260. Albany, N.Y., 1993.

Quarles, Benjamin. " 'Freedom Fettered': Blacks in the Constitutional Era in Maryland, 1776–1810, An Introduction." *Maryland Historical Magazine* 84 (1989): 299–304.

———. "Harriet Tubman's Unlikely Leadership." In *Black Leaders of the Nineteenth Century,* ed. Leon F. Litwack and August Meier, 43–57. Urbana, Ill., 1988.

———. "The Revolutionary War as a Black Declaration of Independence." In *Slavery and Freedom in the Age of the American Revolution,* ed. Ira Berlin and Ronald Hoffman, 283–384. Charlottesville, Va., 1983.

Quinn, D. Michael. *Early Mormonism and the Magic World View.* Salt Lake City, 1987.

Rattray, R. S. *Religion and Art in Ashanti.* Oxford, 1927.

Ravenel, Harriott Horry. *Eliza Pinckney.* New York, 1896.

Ray, Keith. "Dreams of Grandeur: The Call to the Office in Northcentral Igbo Religious Leadership." In *Dreaming, Religion and Society in Africa* ed. M. C. Jedrej and Rosalind Shaw, 55–70. Leiden, 1992.

Reilly, Carroll. *A Dictionary of Colonial American Printers' Ornaments and Illustrations.* Worcester, Mass., 1975.

Reynolds, Pamela. "Dreams and the Constitution of Self among the ZeZuru." In *Dreaming, Religion and Society in Africa,* ed. M. C. Jedrej and Rosalind Shaw, 21–36. Leiden, 1992.

Richey, Russell E. *Early American Methodism.* Bloomington, Ind., 1991.

Richling, Barnet. " 'Very Serious Reflections': Inuit Dreams About Salvation and Loss in Eighteenth-Century Labrador." *Ethnohistory* 36 (1989): 148–169.

Ricoeur, Paul. *Time and Narrative.* Chicago, 1983.

Riordan, Liam. "Identity and Revolution: Everyday Life and Crises in Three Delaware River Towns." In *Pennsylvania History* 64 (1997): 56–101.

Roediger, David R. *The Wages of Whiteness: Race and the Making of the American Working Class.* London, 1992.

———. *Towards the Abolition of Whiteness: Essays on Race, Politics, and Working Class History.* London, 1994.

Roland, Alan. *In Search of Self in India and Japan: Toward a Cross-Cultural Psychology.* Princeton, N.J., 1988.

Rorabaugh, W. J. " 'I Thought I Should Liberate Myself from the Thraldom of Others': Apprentices, Masters, and the Revolution." In *Beyond the American Revolution: Explorations in the History of American Radicalism,* ed. Alfred F. Young, 185–220. DeKalb, Ill., 1993.

Rossi, Ernest Lawrence. *Dreams and the Growth of Personality: Expanding Awareness in Psychotherapy.* New York, 1972.

———. *The Psychobiology of Mind-Body Healing: New Concepts of Therapeutic Hypnosis.* New York, 1986.

Rotundo, E. Anthony. *American Manhood: Transformations in Masculinity from the Revolution to the Modern Era.* New York, 1993.

Royster, Charles. *A Revolutionary People at War: The Continental Army and American Character, 1775–1783.* New York, 1981.

Rubin, Julius H. *Religious Melancholy And Protestant Experience in America.* New York, 1994.

Runcie, John. " 'Hunting the Nigs' in Philadelphia: The Race Riot of August 1834." *Pennsylvania History* 39 (1972): 187–218.

Rupprecht, Carol Schreier, ed. *The Dream and the Text: Essays on Literature and Language.* Albany, N.Y., 1993.

Ryan, Mary P. "A Women's Awakening: Evangelical Religion and the Families of Utica, New York, 1800–1840." In *Women in American Religion,* ed. Janet Wilson James, 89–110. Philadelphia, 1980.

Sabean, David. *Power in the Blood*: *Popular Culture and Village Discourse in Early Modern Germany.* Cambridge, England, 1984.

Sand, Shara, and Ross Levin. "Music and Its Relationship to Dreams and the Self." *Psychoanalysis and Contemporary Thought* 15 (1992): 161–197.

Sandburg, Carl. *Abraham Lincoln: The War Years.* 4 vols. New York 1939.

Schafer, Roy. *Retelling a Life: Narration and Dialogue in Psychoanalysis.* New York, 1992.

Scharff, Jill Savage. *Projective and Introjective Identification and the Use of the Therapist's Self.* Northvale, N.J., 1992.

Schmidt, Leigh Eric. *Holy Fairs: Scottish Communions and American Revivals in the Early Modern Period.* Princeton, N.J., 1989.

Schneider, A. Gregory. *The Way of the Cross Leads Home: The Dosmestication of American Methodism.* Bloomington, Ind., 1993.

Schneider, Mabel. "John Bunyan's *The Pilgrim's Progress* in the Tradition of the Medieval Dream Visions." Ph.D. dissertation, University of Nebraska, 1969.

Schultz, Ronald. "God and Workingmen: Popular Religion in the Formation of Philadelphia's Working Class, 1790–1830." In *Religion in a Revolutionary Age,* ed. Ronald Hoffman and Peter J. Albert, 125–155. Charlottesville, Va., 1994.

Schwartz, Delmore. In Dreams Begin Responsibilities. Norfolk, Conn., 1938.

Schwarz, Philip J. "Clark T. Moorman, Quaker Emancipator." *Quaker History* 69 (1980): 27–35.

Scott, Anne Firor. "Self-Portraits: Three Women." In *Uprooted Americans: Essays to Honor Oscar Handlin*, ed. Richard L. Bushman, 43–76. Boston, 1979.

Scott, Joan. "Gender: A Useful Category of Historical Analysis." *American Historical Review* 91 (1986): 1053–1075.

Seavey, Ormond. *Becoming Benjamin Franklin*. University Park, Pa., 1988.

Sedgwick, Eve K. *Between Men: English Literature and Male Homosocial Desire*. New York, 1985.

Seeman, Erik R. "'Justise Must Take Plase': Three African Americans Speak of Religion in Eighteenth-Century New England." *William and Mary Quarterly* 56 (1999): 393–414.

Seligman, C. G. "Appendix to Chapter XXI." In *Religion and Art in Ashanti*, by R. S. Rattray, 197–204. Oxford, 1927.

Sensbach, Jon F. *A Separate Canaan: The Making of an Afro-Moravian World in North Carolina, 1763–1840*. Chapel Hill, N.C., 1998.

Shafton, Anthony. *Dream Reader: Contemporary Approaches to the Understanding of Dreams*. Albany, N.Y., 1995.

Shaw, Rosalind. "Dreaming as Accomplishment: Power, The Individual and Temne Divination." In *Dreaming, Religion and Society in Africa*, ed. M. C. Jedrej and Rosalind Shaw, 36–54. Leiden, 1992.

Shea, Daniel B. "Elizabeth Ashbridge and the Voice Within." In *Journeys in New Worlds: Early American Women's Narratives*, ed. Daniel B. Shea, 119–146. Madison, Wis., 1990.

———. "The *Journal* of John Woolman." In *Spiritual Autobiography in Early America*, 45–86. Princeton, N.J., 1968.

Shepard, Thomas. *Parable of the Ten Virgins*. London, 1660.

Shorter, Aylward. *Jesus and the Witchdoctor: An Approach to Healing and Wholeness*. London, 1985.

Shortt, S. E. D. "Conflict and Identity in Massachusettes: The Louisbourg Expedition of 1745." *Histoire Sociale-Social History* 5 (1972): 166–185.

Shweder, Richard A., and Edmund J. Bourne. "Does the Concept of the Person Vary Cross-culturally?" In *Culture Theory: Essays on Mind, Self and Emotion*, ed. Richard A. Shweder and Robert A. LeVine, 158–199. Cambridge, England, 1984.

Silverman, Kenneth. *Edgar A. Poe: Mournful and Never-Ending Rememberance*. London, 1992.

Slap, Joseph W., and Eugene E. Trunnell. "Reflections on the Self State Dream." *Psychoanalytic Quarterly* 56 (1987): 251–262.

Sleeper-Smith, Susan. "The Dream as a Tool for Historical Research: Reexamining Life in Eighteenth-Century Virginia through the Dreams of a Gentleman: William Byrd, II, 1674–1744." *Dreaming* 3 (1993): 49–69.

Slotkin, Richard. *Regeneration through Violence: The Mythology of the American Frontier, 1600–1860*. Middletown, Conn., 1973.

Smith, Billy G. *The 'Lower Sort': Philadelphia's Laboring People, 1750–1800*. Ithaca, N.Y., 1990.

———. "The Material Lives of Laboring Philadelphians, 1750–1800." *William and Mary Quarterly* 38, (1981): 163–202.

Smith, Billy G. "Poverty and Economic Marginality in Eighteenth-Century America." *Proceedings of the American Philosophical Society* 132 (1988): 85–118.

Smith, Daniel Scott. "The Long Cycle in American Illegitimacy and Prenuptual Pregnancy." In *Bastardy and Its Comparative History: Studies in the History of Illegitimacy and Marital Nonconformity in Britain, France, Germany, Sweden, North America, Jamaica, and Japan*, ed. Peter Laslett, 362–378. London, 1980.

Smith, Edward D. *Climbing Jacob's Ladder: The Rise of Black Churches in Eastern American Cities, 1740–1877*. Washington, D.C., 1988.

Smith-Rosenberg, Carroll. *Disorderly Conduct: Visions of Gender in Victorian America*. New York, 1985.

———. "Domesticating 'Virtue': Coquettes and Revolutionaries in Young America." In *Literature and the Body: Essays on Populations and Persons*, ed. Elaine Scarry, 160–184. Baltimore, 1988.

———. "The Female World of Love and Ritual: Relations Between Women in Nineteenth-Century America." *Signs* 1 (1975): 1–30.

Snell, Bruno. *The Discovery of the Mind: The Greek Origins of European Thought*. New York, 1960.

Sobel, Mechal. "The Revolution in Selves: Black and White Inner Aliens." In *Through A Glass Darkly: Reflections on Personal Identity in Early America*, ed. Ronald Hoffman, Mechal Sobel, and Fredrika Teute, 163–205. Chapel Hill, N.C., 1997.

———. *Trabelin' On: The Slave Journey to an Afro-Baptist Faith*. Westport, Conn., 1979.

———. *The World They Made Together: Black and White Values in Eighteenth-Century Virginia*, Princeton, N.J., 1987.

Soderlund, Jean R. *Quakers and Slavery: A Divided Spirit*. Princeton, N.J., 1985.

Spacks, Patricia Meyer. *Imagining a Self: Autobiography and Novel in Eighteenth-Century England*. Cambridge, Mass., 1976.

Spufford, Margaret. *Small Books and Pleasant Histories: Popular Fiction and Its Readership in Seventeenth Century England*. Athens, Ga., 1982.

St. Pierre, Mark, and Tilda Long Soldier. *Walking in the Sacred Manner: Healers, Dreamers, and Pipe Carriers—Medicine Women of the Plains Indians*. New York, 1995.

Stampp, Kenneth M. *The Peculiar Institution: Slavery in the Ante-Bellum South*. New York, 1969.

Stansell, Christine. *City of Women: Sex and Class in New York, 1789–1860*. New York, 1986.

Stanton, Lucia. " 'Those Who Labor for My Happiness': Thomas Jefferson and His Slaves." In *Jeffersonian Legacies*, ed. Peter S. Onuf, 147–180. Charlottesville, Va., 1993.

Starling, Marion Wilson. *The Slave Narrative: Its Place in American History*. Washington, D.C., 1988.

Starobinski, Jean. *The Invention of Liberty, 1700–1789*. Trans. Bernard Swift. Geneva, 1964.

Starr, Rebecca K. "Political Mobilization, 1765–1776." In *The Blackwell Encyclopedia of the American Revolution*, ed. Jack P. Greene and J. R. Pole, 231–239. Cambridge, Mass., 1994.

States, Burt O. *Dreaming and Storytelling*. Ithaca, N.Y., 1993.

Stearns, Carol Z. " 'Lord, Help Me Walk Humbly': Anger and Sadness in England and America, 1570–1750." In *Emotion and Social Change: Toward a New Psychohistory*, ed. Carol Z. Stearns and Peter N. Stearns, 39–68. New York, 1988.

Stearns, Peter N. *Be a Man: Males in Modern Society*. 2d ed. New York, 1990.

Stearns, Peter N., and Jan Lewis. *An Emotional History of the United States*. New York, 1998.

Stearns, Peter N., and Carol Z Stearns. *Anger: The Struggle for Emotional Control in America's History*. Chicago, 1986.

———, eds. *Emotion and Social Change: Toward a New Psychohistory*. New York, 1988.

Stevens, Abel. *The Women of Methodism: Its Three Foundresses, Susana Wesley, the Countess of Huntingdon, and Barbara Heck. . . .* New York, [1866] 1987.

Stewart, James Brewer. "The Emergence of Racial Modernity and the Rise of the White North, 1790–1840." *Journal of the Early Republic* 18 (1988): 181–222.

Stewart, Margaret E. "John Woolman's 'Kindness Beyond Expression': Collective Identity *vs.* Individualism and White Supremacy." *Early American Literature* 26 (1991): 251–275.

Stockholder, Kay. "World in Dream and Drama: A Psaychoanalytic Theory of Literary Representation." *Dalhousie Review* 62 (1982): 374–396.

Sweet, Leonard I. "Samuel Hopkins, Father of African Colonization." In *Black Images of America, 1784–1870*, by Leonard I. Sweet, 23–34. New York, 1976.

Tadman, Michael. *Speculators and Slaves: Masters, Traders and Slaves in the Old South*. Madison, Wis., 1989.

Taylor, Alan. "The Early Republic's Supernatural Economy: Treasure Seeking in the American Northeast, 1780–1830." *American Quarterly* 38 (1986): 6–34.

———. "Rediscovering the Context of Joseph Smith's Treasure Seeking." *Dialogue* 19 (1986): 18–28.

Taylor, Charles. *Sources of the Self: The Making of the Modern Identity*. Cambridge, Mass., 1989.

Tedlock, Barbara, ed. *Dreaming: Anthropological and Psychological Interpretations*. Cambridge, England, 1987.

Teute, Fredrika J. "In 'the gloom of evening': Margaret Bayard Smith's View in Black and White of Early Washington Society." In *The Proceedings of the American Antiquarian Society* 106, part I (1996): 37–58.

———. " 'A Wild, Desolate Place': Life on the Margins in Early Washington." In *Southern City, National Ambition: The Growth of Early Washington D.C., 1800–1860*, ed. Howard Gillette, Jr., 47–68. Washington, D.C., 1995.

Thomas, Keith. *Religion and the Decline of Magic: Studies in Popular Beliefs in Sixteenth and Seventeenth Century England.* London, 1971.

Thompson, Robert Farris. *Flash of the Spirit: African and Afro-American Art and Philosophy.* New York, 1983.

Thorndike, Lynn. "Ancient and Medieval Dream Books." In *A History of Magic and Experimental Science,* 2:290–302. New York, 1959.

Thorp, Daniel B. "Chattel with a Soul: The Autobiography of a Moravian Slave." *Pennsylvania Magazine of History & Biography* 112 (1988): 433–451.

Tobin, Jacqueline L., and Raymond G. Dobard. *Hidden in Plain View: A Secret Story of Quilts and the Underground Railroad.* New York, 1999.

Tolpin, Paul. "Self Psychology and the Interpretation of Dreams." In *The Future of Psychoanalysis: Essays in Honor of Heinz Kohut,* ed. Arnold Goldberg, 257–271. New York, 1983.

Towner, Lawrence W. "The Sewall-Saffin Dialogue on Slavery." *The William and Mary Quarterly* 21 (1964): 40–52.

Ullman, Montague. *Appreciating Dreams: A Group Approach.* Thousand Oaks, Mich., 1996.

———. "Dreams and Society." In *The Variety of Dream Experience,* ed. Montague Ullman and Claire Limmer, 279–294. New York, 1987.

———. "Social Roots of the Dream." *American Journal of Psychoanalysis* 20 (1960): 180–196.

———. "Societal Factors in Dreaming." *Contemporary Psychoanalysis* 9 (1973): 282–293.

Ullman, Montague, and Nan Zimmerman. *Working with Dreams.* New York, 1979.

Ulrich, Laurel Thatcher. " 'Daughters of Liberty': Religious Women in Revolutionary New England." In *Women in the Age of the American Revolution,* ed. Ronald Hoffman and Peter J. Albert, 211–243. Charlottesville, Va., 1989.

———. "Housewife and Gadder: Themes of Self-sufficiency and Community in Eighteenth-Century New England." In *"To Toil the Livelong Day": America's Women at Work, 1780–1980,* ed. Carol Groneman and Mary Beth Norton, 21–34. Ithaca, N.Y., 1987.

Vande Kemp, Hendrika. "The Dream in Periodical Literature: 1860–1910." *Journal of the History of the Behavioral Sciences* 17 (1981): 88–113.

Vlach, John Michael. *The Afro-American Tradition in Decorative Arts.* Cleveland, 1978.

Volkan, Vamik D. "The Need to Have Enemies and Allies: A Developmental Approach." *Political Psychology* 6 (1985): 219–247.

———. *The Need to Have Enemies and Allies: From Clinical Practice to International Relationships.* Northvale, N.J.: 1994.

Von Grunebaum, G. E., and Roger Callois, eds. *The Dream and Human Societies.* Berkeley, Calif., 1966.

Von Mehren, Joan. *Minerva and the Muse: A Life of Margaret Fuller.* Amherst, Mass., 1994.

Waldstreicher, David. *In The Midst of Perpetual Fetes: The Making of American Nationalism, 1776–1820*. Chapel Hill, N.C., 1997.

Walker, Barbara G. *The Woman's Dictionary of Symbols and Sacred Objects*. London, 1988.

Wallace, Anthony F. C. *The Death and Rebirth of the Seneca*. New York, 1970.

———. "Dreams and Wishes of the Soul: A Type of Psychoanalytic Theory Among the Seventeenth-Century Iroquois." *American Anthropologist* 60 (1958): 234–248.

Walters, Wendy W. " 'One of dese mornings, bright and fair,/take my wings and cleave de air,': The legend of the flying Africans and diasporic consciousness." *Melus* 22 (1997): 3–30.

Warren, Joyce W. *The American Narcissus: Individualism and Women in Nineteenth-Century American Fiction*. New Brunswick, N.J., 1984.

Washington, Margaret. " 'Where the Spirit of the Lord Is, There is Liberty': The Spiritual Provenance of Sojourner Truth." Paper delivered at conference, "More Than Cool Reason," Haifa, Israel, January 20, 1998.

Watzlawick, Paul. *The Language of Change: Elements of Therapeutic Communication*. New York, 1978.

Watzlawick, Paul, John H. Weakland, and Richard F. Fisch. *Change: Principles of Problem Formation and Problem Resolution*. New York, 1974.

Weinstein, Arnold. *Fictions of the Self: 1550–1800*. Princeton, N.J., 1981.

Weinstein, Fred, and Gerald M. Platt. *The Wish to Be Free: Society, Psyche, and Value Change*. Berkeley, Calif., 1969.

Weintraub, Karl Joachim. *The Value of the Individual, Self and Circumstance in Autobiography*. Chicago, 1978.

Weiss, Harry B. "Oneirocritica Americana: The Story of American Dream Books." *Bulletin of the New York Public Library* (June-July 1944).

———. *Oneirocritica Americana: The Story of American Dream Books*. New York, 1944.

Wells, Robert V. *Revolutions in Americans' Lives: A Demographic Perspective on the History of Americans, Their Families, and Their Society*. Westport, Conn., 1982.

———. *Uncle Sam's Family: Issues in and Perspectives on American Demographic History*. Albany, N.Y., 1985.

Welter, Barbara. "She Hath Done What She Could: Protestant Women's Missionary Careers in Nineteenth-Century America." In *Women in American Religion*, ed. Janet Wilson James, 111–126. Philadelphia, 1980.

Werner, John M. *"Reaping the Bloody Harvest": Race Riots in the United States During the Age of Jackson, 1824–1849*. New York, 1986.

Wheelwright, Julie. *Amazons and Military Maids: Women Who Dressed as Men in the Pursuit of Life, Liberty and Happiness*. London, 1989.

White, Michael. "Family Therapy, Training, and Supervision in a World of Experience and Narrative." In *Experience, Contradiction, Narrative and Imagination: Selected Papers of David Epston and Michael White, 1889–1991*, ed. David Epston, 75–96. Adelaide, Australia, 1992.

White, Shane. *Somewhat More Independent: The End of Slavery in New York City, 1770–1810.* Athens, Ga., 1991.

Whitty, J. H. *Poe and the Southern Literary Messenger.* New York, 1970.

Wigger, John H. "Taking Heaven by Storm: Enthusiasm and Early American Methodism, 1770–1820." *Journal of the Early Republic* 14 (1994): 167–194.

Wilentz, Sean. *Chants Democratic: New York City and the Rise of the American Working Class, 1788–1850.* New York, 1984.

Williams, Delores S. "Visions, Inner Voices, Apparitions, and Defiance in Nineteenth-Century Black Women's Narratives." *Women's Studies Quarterly* 21 (1993): 81–89.

Williams, William Henry. *The Garden of American Methodism: The Delmarva Peninsula, 1769–1820.* Wilmington, Del., 1984.

Williamson, Joel. *New People; Miscegenation and Mulattoes in the United States.* New York, 1980.

Wittlinger, Carlton O. *Quest for Piety and Obedience: The Story of the Brethren in Christ.* Nappanee, Ind., 1978.

Wohlberg, Laurie. "Quaker Women and the American Revolution." M.A. thesis, University of Haifa, 1988.

———. "Women and the Making of American History." Ph.D dissertation, University of Haifa. 1995.

Wood, Peter H. " 'Liberty Is Sweet': African-American Freedom Struggles in the Years before White Independence." In *Beyond the American Revolution: Explorations in the History of American Radicalism,* ed. Alfred F. Young, 149–184. DeKalb, Ill., 1993.

Woods, John. "The Correspondence of Rush and Sharp." *Journal of American Studies* 1 (1967):1–38.

Woodson, Carter G. "The Beginnings of Miscegenation." *Journal of Negro History* 3 (1918): 335–353.

Wright, Donald R. *African Americans in the Colonial Era: From African Origins Through the American Revolution.* Arlington Heights, Ill., 1990.

———. *African Americans in the Early Republic, 1789–1831.* Arlington Heights, Ill., 1993.

Yee, Shirley J. *Black Women Abolitionists: A Study in Activism, 1828–1860.* Knoxville, Tenn., 1992.

Young, Alfred F. "Afterward: How Radical Was the American Revolution?" In *Beyond the American Revolution: Explorations in the History of American Radicalism.* Ed. A. F. Young, 317–364. DeKalb, Ill., 1993.

———. "American Historians Confront 'The Transforming Hand of Revolution.' " In *The Transforming Hand of Revolution: Reconsideridng the American Revolution as a Social Movement,* ed. Ronald Hoffman and Peter J. Albert, 346–492. Charlottesville, Va., 1996.

———. "George Robert Twelves Hewes (1742–1840): A Boston Shoemaker and the Memory of the American Revolution." *William and Mary Quarterly* 38 (1981): 561–623.

————. *Masquerade: The Life and Times of Deborah Sampson Gannett, Continental Soldier*. New York, forthcoming.

Zilversmit, Arthur. "Quok Walker, Mumber, and the Abolition of Slavery in Massachusetts." *William and Mary Quarterly* 25 (1968): 614–624.

Zwarg, Christina. *Feminist Conversations: Fuller, Emerson and the Play of Reading*. Ithaca, N.Y., 1995.

355

Index

Abbot, Benjamin, 13, 221
abolitionists, 65, 107, 299n.23. *See also*
  Anderson, William J.; Asher, Jeremiah; Brown, William Wells; Churchman, John; Clarke, Lewis; Clarke, Milton; Douglass, Clay; Garnet, Henry
  Highland; Garrettson, Freeborn;
  Grandy, Moses; Grimes, William; Hen-
  son, Josiah; Hopper, Issac T.; Hopkins,
  Samuel; Jacobs, Harriet; Lane, Luns-
  ford; Lay, Benjamin; Lee, Jarena; Le-
  land, John; Malvin, John; Mifflin, War-
  ner; Offley, G. W.; Prince, Nancy;
  Pyle, Robert; Rush, Benjamin; Sandi-
  ford, Ralph; Smith, Venture; Stewart,
  Maria W.; Truth, Sojourner; Tubman,
  Harriet; Walker, David; White,
  George; Woolman, John
Abrams, Joseph, 240
abuse, 49. *See also* rape; violence
Adam [Saffin], 140
Adams, Abigail, 165–66
Adams, Hannah, 289n.2
Adams, John, 35, 165–66
affection, 175
Africa, 206, 226, 230, 260nn. 95 and 97,
  261n.101, 264n.131, 271n.57, 278n.10,
  282n.65; Rushæs attitude toward, 85
African Methodist Episcopal Church,
  114, 184
Africans, dreams of, 42
Afro-Christianity, 109
aggression, 5, 6, 262n.114, 287n.44. *See
  also* anger; rage; violence
Agrippa [Sedgwick], 308n.103
Alby, Ann Eliza Dow, 293n.66
Alfred, C. Fred, 247n.33
alien others, 3, 14, 26, 27. *See also* al-
  terity; anti-me; enemies
alienation, 242
Allen, Elizabeth, 289n.2
Allen, Richard, 114, 184–85
alligator, symbolism of, 275n.119
All-seeing Eye, 39

alterity, 5, 6, 14, 27, 48, 56, 61, 126, 144,
  182, 187, 188, 227, 242. *See also* alien
  others; anti-me; enemies
Anderson, William J., 218; childhood of,
  118–19; drawing of, 120; as a free
  man, 124; self-emancipation of, 121–
  22
Andrew [Ofodobenda Wooma], 282n.65
androgynous, 145, 311n.124
anger, 115, 139, 142, 172, 190, 221,
  311n.124; of women, 166
Anglican Church, 147
animals, symbolism of, 257n.75
annointment, 194. *See also* Elizabeth;
  Garrettson, Catherine Livingston;
  Lee, Jarena; Lincoln, Salome; Newell,
  Fanny; Samson, Deborah
Anthony, Susanna, 29, 177, 178, 221,
  248n.41, 254n.54, 298n.134, 299n.18;
  attitude of towards death, 211
anti-me, 26. *See also* alien others; alterity; enemies
apple, symbolism of, 240
Aquilla [Shinns], 66, 268n.40, 269n.43
Arew, Dorothy, 303n.63
Aristotle, 258n.76
Arms, Mary L. Day, 58, 265n.12
army, symbolism of, 270n.49
Artemidorus, 37, 38, 70, 257n.70; on can-
  nibalism, 73; on sex, 41
Asbury, 275n.124
Asbury, Frances, 53, 89, 147, 150; god-
  children of, 287n.56; on slavery, 94;
  will of, 287n.56
Ashanti, 43
Ashbridge, Elizabeth Sampson Sullivan,
  171–75, 213
Asher, Jeremiah, 215, 218, 278n.8
assertiveness, 286n.22
atrocities, 22. *See also* rape; violence
auditory dreams. *See* dreams
Augustine, 251n.12
Auster, Paul, 3
autobiographies, archives of 252n.31.
  See also narratives